Contents

Introduction vi

Bloodstone 1

Blue Magic 7

Chairmen of the
Board 16

The Chi-Lites 22

The Delfonics 33

The Dells 44

The Dramatics 57

The Emotions 68

First Choice 76

The Friends of
Distinction 82

Al Green 89

Isaac Hayes 104

The Intruders 118

Millie Jackson 124

Gladys Knight
and the Pips 132

Jean Knight 147

The Main Ingredient .. 152

The Manhattans 161

Harold Melvin and
the Blue Notes 171

The Moments
(Ray, Goodman
and Brown) 183

New Birth 194

The Ohio Players 201

The O'Jays 213

Billy Paul 231

Freda Payne 236

The Spinners 243

The Staple Singers 255

The Stylistics 263

The Temprees 273

The Three Degrees 277

War 287

The Whispers 296

Barry White 305

Bobby Womack 319

Betty Wright 332

Bibliography 339

Index 345

Acknowledgments

First and foremost, I give thanks to God for instilling in me the idea to write this book, for providing me with the gifts and blessings necessary to complete this project, and for allowing my life to be touched by everyone who was helpful throughout this process.

I thank my mother, Jacqueline Taylor Anderson, for all of her traits she instilled in me, for her love and her sacrifice, for reminding me how hard I worked at this project, and for her patience and understanding that this is what I wanted to do.

I thank my father, Donald Taylor, for all of his traits he instilled in me, for his love and his guidance, for being my best friend as well as my father, for driving me all across the Tri-State area to conduct interviews, for the use of his massive record collection, and for telling me "whenever something in life knocks you down, get right back up."

Thank you to the following people who granted me interviews. I am eternally grateful for your time and consideration, and for the impact your music had on me during my childhood years: Gerald Alston, Ron Banks, Chuck Barksdale, Keith Beaton, Leroy "Sugarfoot" Bonner, Billy Brown, Randy Cain, Nicholas Caldwell, Valerie Holiday Christie, Eugene "Bird" Daughtry, Leaveil Degree, Willis Draffen, Harry Elston, Rochelle Fleming, Cuba Gooding, Al Goodman, Jean "Knight" Harris, Major Harris, Wilbert Hart, William Hart, Millie Jackson, General Norman Johnson, Lonnie Jordan, Robert "Squirrel" Lester, Charles Love, Winfred "Blue" Lovett, Harold Melvin, Glenn Montgomery, Herb Murrell, Billy Paul, Freda Payne, Jasper "Jabbo" Phillips, Harry Ray, Vernon Sawyer, Wendell Sawyer, Howard Scott, Wallace Scott, Walter Scott, Tony Silvester, Mavis Staples, Roebuck "Pops" Staples, Marshall Thompson, Wanda Hutchinson Vaughan, Harry Williams, Jimmy "Diamond" Williams, Walter Williams, Melvin Wilson, Bobby Womack, Betty Wright.

Thank you to the following people for setting up interviews, for sharing your knowledge of music or of the book publishing

A TOUCH OF
CLASSIC
SOUL

Soul Singers of the Early 1970s

MARC TAYLOR

Aloiv Publishing Co. ✦ Jamaica, New York

A Touch of Classic Soul © 1996 by Marc Taylor

All rights reserved. No part of this book may be reproduced in whole or in part, except for the quotation of brief passages in review, without prior permission from Aloiv Publishing Co., P.O. Box 34-0484, Jamaica, New York, 11434-0484

Book design by Sara Patton, Maui, Hawaii
Printed and bound in the United States

industry, and for directly or indirectly enhancing the quality of this project: John Abbey, Jack Bart, Black Women in Publishing, the staff at BMI, David Booth, Fred Bronson, Billie Bullock, Bill Carpenter, Wanda Croudy, Willie D., Betty Davis, Joseph Davis, Jr., Doug Dixon, Esq., Deborah Ewings, Jimmy Ferrell, Connie Finch, Mary Flowers, Michael Gardner, Emma Garrett, Phillip Gay, Jerry Goodman, Harry Gordon, Terri Hinte, Roy S. Johnson, Kim Jones, Susan Kendrick, Bob Killbourn, Lisa Kreda, Glen Larusso, Becky Lehner, Paul Martin, Esq., Ovelia Melvin, MLB, Donna Moore, Carol Parker-Lewis, Sara Patton, Kofi Pendergrass, Dan Poynter, Publishers Marketing Association, Gwendolyn Quinn, Walt Reeder, Jonathan Rudnick, Robin Ryland, Winston Sanders, Rochelle Schlosser, Julia Shaw, Yvonne Simpkins, Nina Smith, the staff at Sweetwaters, Marshall Sylver, Gregory Thomas, Jimmy Thomas, Mark Townsend, the staff at Universal Attractions, Inc., Steve Van Ness, Adam White, Eric Willis.

Thank you to Ray, Goodman and Brown — Al Goodman, Billy Brown, and the late Harry Ray — who gave me my first-ever interview when I was just "a kid out here with a pen and a sheet of paper."

Thanks to Dr. Teresa Williams, whose *New York Trend* monthly newspaper provided a forum for my "oldies but goodies" column long before "Classic Soul" came back into fashion.

Thank you to Ann Brown for making me a better writer.

Many thanks to Lee Hildebrand and Robert Pruter for their editing.

Special thanks to Rob Bowman for his diligent editing and fact checking, and for taking me literally when I said "be tough, I can take it."

In addition to those previously mentioned, thank you to the following people who either directly or indirectly pushed me to strive for excellence: Jim Freeman, Michael (The King of Pop) Jackson, Douglas Taylor.

An extra special thanks to George Anderson, Richard Wilkins, Connie Sledge, and Viola Marie Smith Taylor & Family.

Introduction

The history of modern African-American music is usually interpreted as black music of the 1960s. To some extent this is understandable, since artists such as James Brown, Aretha Franklin, and the long list of stars on Motown's roster were the ones who broke down the barriers that had previously kept black music separate from the pop mainstream.

Several of their counterparts in the early 1970s built on these breakthroughs. At the start of the new decade, Isaac Hayes transcended the boundaries of soul music with his *Hot Buttered Soul* album, making him the genre's first superstar in the 1970s. After the success of Hayes' soundtrack for *Shaft* in 1971, the stage was set for Curtis Mayfield to reach his commercial and creative peak the following year with the score to *Superfly*. Mayfield had further success with other film scores, including *Claudine*, *Let's Do It Again*, and *Sparkle*. Motown's legendary writing and producing team of Brian Holland, Lamont Dozier, and Eddie Holland set up their own Hot Wax and Invictus labels, which spawned several hits in the early 1970s, primarily by Chairmen of the Board, Honey Cone, and Freda Payne. Producers Kenny Gamble and Leon Huff formed Philadelphia International Records, creating smashes for the O'Jays, Harold Melvin and the Blue Notes, Billy Paul, the Intruders, and the Three Degrees, which would dominate R&B music through the mid-'70s. Gamble and Huff's occasional partner and occasional rival Thom Bell produced a series of soft-soul hits for the Delfonics, the Stylistics, and the Spinners. This soft-soul sound in black music was further popularized by the Moments, the Chi-Lites, and Blue Magic, groups that emphasized high-tenor leads. The early 1970s also saw former gospel artists the Staple Singers, Al Green, and the Emotions make a successful transition into the R&B/pop mainstream.

Unfortunately, the soul artists of that era have not been regarded with the same reverence as the artists of the 1960s. The music of the early 1970s has lived on, as evident by pop stars Simply Red, New Kids on the Block, and Paul Young having success with their respective covers of "If You Don't Know Me By Now," "Didn't I (Blow Your Mind This Time)," and "Oh Girl." However, the artists who originated these songs — Harold Melvin and the Blue Notes, the Delfonics, and the Chi-Lites — along with many of their contemporaries have been relatively forgotten.

Chronicled in *A Touch of Classic Soul: Soul Singers of the Early 1970s* are the careers of 35 of the top soul music artists of the early to mid-1970s. In the interviews I conducted with several of these artists, they described how their singing careers began, how they got their first professional break, how some of their biggest hits were created, the experience of reaching the height of their success, how they were affected by the rise of disco in the mid-'70s, and what inner forces push them to keep performing today.

I was flexible in deciding who to include in the book. While most of the artists featured are obvious choices, some inclusions need explaining. The Dells and the Intruders had their biggest hits in the mid- to late-1960s. However, they are included here because of their consistent chart presence in the early 1970s — particularly the Dells, who scored ten top 20 R&B hits between 1970 and 1975. I also included the Manhattans and the Whispers, groups whose commercial peak came in the late 1970s and early 1980s, respectively. Yet these groups were consistently on the charts in the early '70s and often perform today in tandem with their soul contemporaries whose greatest success came in the first half of the 1970s.

There have been numerous excellent books written by and about nearly every major artist who appeared on the Motown roster. Therefore, I did not include Motown here except for the Spinners and Gladys Knight and the Pips, groups who enjoyed their greatest success after leaving Motown. I also did not include groups such as Earth, Wind and Fire; Rufus; or the Isley Brothers; who were primarily funk groups who hit their commercial prime in the late '70s. Perhaps that is another book.

The interviews for this book were conducted under various circumstances. Some of the more memorable included: catching up with Blue Magic at 2:00 A.M. after a performance; Chuck Barksdale of the Dells and Freda Payne each giving me an hour of their time at their respective hotels on the day of their concerts; Millie Jackson in-between gigs at the Apollo Theater; Ron Banks of the Dramatics and Walter Williams of the O'Jays each giving me an hour of their time over the phone; and Bobby Womack expressing so much concern about my telephone bill during our 90-minute cross-country interview that he called me back so he could pick up half of the tab.

For various reasons, some artists were unable to spare the time to talk. Yet, I *had* to include Al Green, Isaac Hayes, Gladys Knight and the Pips, the Spinners, and Barry White. Therefore, I wrote lengthy profiles on each one.

Everyone interviewed for the book was gracious, and nearly everyone expressed appreciation that someone who was a child during their commercial prime wanted to write at length about their careers. Perhaps these artists are also aware that their music has been too long underrated. As General Johnson of Chairmen of the Board told me, "What [blacks] do, we forget about it and nobody writes about the history of it. That's why I'm doing this interview."

Times do seem to be changing for the better. Several of the country's top urban radio stations have switched to a "classic soul" format as R&B fans have developed a newfound appreciation for the soul music of the 1960s, 1970s, and 1980s. This new appreciation is further evident by the soundtrack to the 1995 film *Dead Presidents*, a collection of 12 soul classics, which topped the R&B album charts. Like *Shaft* and *Superfly* nearly 25 years ago, it can be argued that the soundtrack to *Dead Presidents* was largely responsible for the success of the film.

If you are someone who fondly remembers the soul music from "back in the day," it is my hope that you will enjoy this book. Consider *A Touch of Classic Soul: Soul Singers of the Early 1970s* to be your companion to the great soul music from the first half of the '70s and the artists who created it.

– MARC TAYLOR
JUNE 1996

Bloodstone

A five-man vocal and instrumental group from Kansas City, Bloodstone found success in the early 1970s with a sound that shifted from smooth pop/soul ballads like "Outside Woman" and "Give Me Your Heart" to guitar-dominated funk, such as "Do You Wanna Do a Thing." Best remembered for their 1973 hit "Natural High," Bloodstone was able to diversify its sound by alternating the talents of its two lead singers, Charles McCormick and Harry Williams.

The group originally formed in 1962 out of two competing high-school bands in Kansas City, Missouri. Both groups dropped the non-rehearsing members and organized as one band called the Sinceres. The five-member group consisted of Charles McCormick, Charles Love, Roger Durham, Willis Draffen, Jr., and Harry Williams. Willis Draffen, Jr. recalls, "We all grew up together in the same neighborhood and went to Central High School in Kansas City, Missouri. In high school we went to concert choir class and got together that way. Harry [Williams] had a singing group and I had a three-piece band. We had problems with people coming to rehearsals, and later on we decided to pull the two together, the band along with the vocal group."

The group performed *a capella* in Kansas City and quickly gained a reputation as one of the area's top acts. In 1968, the Sinceres, as they were then known, moved to Los Angeles, dropped their instruments in favor of a backup band, and concentrated on their vocals. They had trouble finding work, however, being told they needed to play their own instruments.

Heading back to Kansas City, they spent the next three months woodshedding, changed their name to Bloodstone to reflect their newfound harder sound, and soon returned to Los Angeles.

Their return to Los Angeles was a triumphant one. The group garnered enough of a reputation to play in some of the area's top clubs, including the Coconut Grove, the Apartment, and the International Hotel. Shortly afterwards they signed a contract to be managed by two relative newcomers, George Braunstein and Ronald Hamady. Feeling they had little left to conquer in Los Angeles, Bloodstone went to England in 1971 on the advice of their managers. In England, the group was introduced to producer Mike Vernon, with whom they began a long association.

"We had done a lot of nightclub work in Los Angeles and we had just about covered the area," says Draffen. "We had been seen on many local shows there and we ran into some producers and managers who wanted to take us to Europe. We thought we would have a better chance of becoming successful [in Europe].

"We were in London and the opportunity came about to do a show with Al Green, who was very hot then. We took that opportunity to do the show, actually for no money. They allowed us to go on before Al Green and we got over a 20-minute standing ovation. After that, Al had a hard time going on. There were record company executives there who wanted to talk to us. Later on our managers met with them and we ended up signing a contract with Decca Records. Decca's subsidiary company here in the States was London Records."

Bloodstone returned to Los Angeles for their first recording, "Natural High." Written by Charles McCormick, whose falsetto carried the lead, "Natural High" was marked by its 1950s-style harmonies, graceful guitar break, and jazzed-up ending. This dreamy ballad was Bloodstone's biggest hit, reaching the top 10 on the R&B and pop charts in the summer of 1973 and selling over a million copies to give the group a gold record.

Charles Love remembers, "We laid the rhythm track and

put vocals on 'Natural High' and we had a string session where they had violins on top of that. I think after we did the whole thing, we realized that we had something going.

"[The success] was indescribable. We were celebrating all over the place. Champagne was pouring everywhere. We actually cried; we shed tears of joy to know that all the work we had done over the years was now beginning to pay off. It was a very special moment to know that we were going to be successful."

At the height of their success, tragedy struck the group when Roger Durham died in October 1973. Harry Williams recalls, "Roger was a guy who was a great, great, great guy and it was a real miss when he passed away because it was he and myself who started the group. We pretty much put everyone together, and it really was a tragic thing. For awhile we went with someone else, Ron Bell, who replaced him for awhile, but Roger was irreplaceable."

Bloodstone followed "Natural High" with two top 10 R&B hits, the mid-tempo "Never Let You Go" (number seven) and the ballad "Outside Woman," the latter being a plea for a mistress to be patient, which reached number two in the spring of 1974. Both of these songs featured the baritone of Harry Williams instead of McCormick's falsetto. At a time when most ballads released by male vocal groups were dominated by a tenor voice (such as in Bloodstone's biggest hit, "Natural High"), the group was careful not to get pigeonholed into the tenor-dominated sound.

Charles Love explains, "We came along admiring groups like the Temptations, the Four Tops, and the Impressions, but basically it was the Temptations who we, more or less, envied. The Temptations had a lot of talented guys and multiple voices. We noticed that we had two outstanding talents at that time with Charles McCormick who sang lead on 'Natural High,' and Harry Williams who sang 'Outside Woman,' 'Never Let You Go,' and later 'We Go a Long Way Back' and 'Go on and Cry.' Therefore, we figured that we should bounce around and not get pigeonholed with that one style."

Bloodstone rounded out 1974 with "That's Not How It Goes," a blues-flavored, mid-tempo track about a man finding out through improper channels about his impending fatherhood. The group made a return to the top 10 in the spring of 1975 with Charles McCormick returning to lead vocals on "My Little Lady." Two more singles, the McCormick-led ballad "Give Me Your Heart" and the funky "Do You Wanna Do a Thing," made the R&B top 20 in 1975 and 1976.

By this time the disco sound was beginning to dominate the airwaves, eliminating many of the stand-up ballad groups, and Bloodstone was no exception. With most of the group's music sliding between ballads and guitar-dominated funk, disco was a musical genre completely foreign to them. Previously, the closest Bloodstone came to disco was "My Little Lady." Throughout the disco period, the group recorded little.

"[The disco era] was tough because we never had a chance to perform the disco," contends Love. "We stuck to our guns. We still sang the lovely, beautiful ballads and slow songs of romance, things like that. We missed the disco dancing period altogether. As a matter of fact, we put out hardly any music during this time."

In 1975 the group wrote the music for, financed, and starred in the motion picture musical comedy *Train Ride to Hollywood*. "We had always wanted to be one of the first groups to be involved in a full-length motion picture," says Draffen. "We pioneered that. I'd like to think there was only one other group that was doing that, and that was Earth, Wind and Fire [*That's the Way of the World*]. It kinda just happened. We ran into a scriptwriter by the name of Dan Gordon who wrote *Train Ride to Hollywood* especially for Bloodstone. It was a lot of fun acting, and just going through the mechanics of acting was fun. Show business is great."

Bloodstone was relatively inactive for the remainder of the decade. They did record the *Don't Stop* album on Motown Records in 1979, which met with little fanfare. However, despite their limited success, the group has fond memories of their experience with Motown. "After years of admiring the

Motown groups, it was exciting to be a part of the Motown family," says Williams. "Mr. Gordy, whom I have a lot of respect for, is a great person, great personality; the whole Gordy family is. It was very nice to be a part of it."

In 1981, charter member Charles McCormick left Bloodstone and was replaced by Ron Wilson. Also in 1981, Bloodstone came to the attention of the Isley Brothers, and after a six-year absence, returned to the R&B charts in the spring of 1982 when the doo-wop-flavored "We Go a Long Way Back" on the Isley's T-Neck label reached number five.

"After a few years of being dormant, especially during the disco era, we just weren't doing much of anything at that particular time," says Draffen. "We met a lady by the name of Kitty Sears, who had known the Isley Brothers quite well. She asked us if we would like for her to submit something to the Isley Brothers, and of course we said that we would. She did, and they liked what they heard. The song was 'We Go a Long Way Back.' They signed us and we cut the single 'We Go a Long Way Back.' The single took off and they came back at us right away asking for an album. We were prepared, so we cut an album with them."

The group followed with "Go on and Cry" that summer, which made the R&B top 20. Three further releases on the T-Neck label charted: "My Love Grows Stronger" (1982), "Instant Love," and "Bloodstone's Party" (1984).

In 1984, Ernie Isley, Marvin Isley, and Chris Jasper left the Isley Brothers and secured a recording contract with CBS as Isley Jasper Isley. A year later the remaining Isleys closed down T-Neck Records and signed with Warner Brothers. With no record label to call home, Bloodstone stopped recording and performing although no official breakup was announced.

The legacy of Bloodstone's music provided a boost to the group in 1993 when the male R&B trio After 7 used the chorus of "Natural High" in a medley of their remake of the Originals' 1969 hit, "Baby I'm for Real." This gave impetus to Bloodstone's decision to begin performing again after a nine-year layoff. By 1994, the lineup included Draffen, Love, Williams, and Wilson.

"We were still together during this time," says Draffen. "We weren't doing any live performances but we were still around. We had not broken up or anything like that. We felt that the time was right to get back out here. After hearing other groups come back we decided to do the same thing. And the fact that some of the younger groups are using our music, for instance After 7 and their using 'Natural High,' made us want to get out here even more. We started putting the pieces together and so far it's working out just fine."

While continuing to perform, in 1994 Bloodstone made plans to record and distribute their own live album. Draffen notes, "This is the first time Bloodstone has had the chance to produce their own music. We're just happy about that. The fact of the matter is, distribution is done not so much by the larger companies, but by the independents. We have the opportunity now as black entrepreneurs to excel in that area and we're going to take advantage of it.

"It's great being alive but it's even greater doing what we like to do and that's entertaining people, and especially when we're well received. There's no feeling like that. We want to keep doing that, so we're ready to roll."

Blue Magic

The last of the great love ballad vocal groups of the early 1970s, Blue Magic infused the rock and roll sound of the 1950s with their own Philadelphia sound to create a string of dreamy love songs. However, the impact of Blue Magic cannot be measured by the group's chart success, which includes one gold single ("Sideshow") and album (*Blue Magic*). Led by the distinctive high tenor of Ted Mills, this Philadelphia quintet has garnered a loyal and dedicated following who respond to the quality and wholesome message of their songs.

The members of Blue Magic were all raised in the North Philadelphia area. The group consisted of Ted "Wizard" Mills (lead tenor), Keith Beaton (second tenor), Richard Pratt (bass), Vernon Sawyer (second tenor, baritone), and Vernon's brother Wendell (baritone). "We all grew up together," says Beaton. "We came from the same neighborhood and went to the same school. Basically, Wendell, Vernon, and myself went to the same elementary school and part of junior high together. Their mother, I call my mother. I lost my mother at a very early age and [their mother] took care of me."

Beaton, Pratt, and the Sawyer brothers sang in a group called the Shades of Love, while Mills, a singer and songwriter, was part of a group called the Topics. In 1973, Delfonics member Randy Cain brought Mills in to do some writing with producers Al Rubens, Steve Bernstein, and Bruce Gable, collectively known as WMOT (We Men of Talent). A short time later the Shades of Love came in for an audition. Although the group performed admirably, they lacked a standout lead singer. WMOT executives decided to put Mills with the Shades of Love, and renamed the group Blue Magic.

The first song they recorded, Mills' haunting ballad "Spell," was produced by Norman Harris, one of the top producers in Philadelphia. This launched the beginning of a long collaboration between the producer and the group. In addition to Harris, Blue Magic had access to some of the finest writing, producing, and arranging talent in Philadelphia, including Bobby Eli, Vinnie Barrett (Gwen Wolfolk), and Vince Montana.

Through WMOT Productions, Blue Magic was signed to Atlantic/Atco Records and began touring to promote the single, which would become a top 30 R&B hit in the spring of 1973. Vernon Sawyer remembers, "We toured all over. We put 'Spell' out as our first record and 'Guess Who' on the flip side. We just went out and started working the cities, the small towns, and small venues until the record really caught on. Everybody took to the record immediately. The jocks and everybody were so supportive at that time and it was just a phenomenal situation for us."

During a tour overseas, the quintet had a conflict with the Ike and Tina Turner Revue. Beaton recalls, "We had a problem in Germany with Ike and Tina. It really wasn't Tina, it was Ike. We were the opening act and we were getting more applause than him; not Tina because when she came on, she got an equal amount of applause. What they did was cut our show shorter and shorter each night, and then they fired us off the tour. They were expecting Blue Magic to be folk singers or a country and western band; [Ike] really didn't know. When we got over there, our records were hotter than theirs were. We played Copenhagen and Germany with them. Our album was number one in London and he fired us just before we got there. The tour was supposed to be for eight weeks but they fired us in the third week. That helped our career somewhat because of the publicity we got off of that. We were the opening act and we were becoming the main attraction without trying. We were just out there trying to learn."

Upon returning to the States, Blue Magic's third single, the ethereal "Stop to Start," was becoming their biggest hit to date, peaking at number 14 on the R&B charts early in 1974 and paving the way for what would be the group's biggest seller. Released in the spring of 1974, the melancholy "Sideshow" topped the R&B charts for one week, was a top 10 pop hit, and was certified gold. With this Philly soul classic serving as an impetus, Blue Magic's self-titled debut album was certified gold. "To come out the first time around with a gold record, that's very unusual for acts to do that," says Vernon, "but the chemistry was right and the timing was right."

The *Blue Magic* album was not a typical compilation of eight filler tracks put together to capitalize on the success of one smash single. Virtually every song from the album would have its own identity and remain a classic for Blue Magic fans some 20 years later. The album included the Mills-penned "Tear It Down" and "What's Come Over Me," the up-tempo "Welcome to the Club," and the seven-minute "Just Don't Want to Be Lonely," a million-seller that same year for the Main Ingredient. Although the songs fell short of achieving chart success, these tracks, particularly the pleading "What's Come Over Me," would remain an integral part of Blue Magic's stage performance. Wendell Sawyer explains, "There are studio songs and there are stage songs. We took a studio song ['What's Come Over Me'] and changed it to a stage song. It's similar to the song that's on the record but we give it more feeling when we do it on stage. The record is good but to see someone's expression, that this is something that really happened . . . 'what's come over me,' everyone has gone through some phase of their life that something has happened, and we portray an image and a picture. It's like reading a quick book so they can really understand the song."

A Blue Magic live performance was a dazzling spectacle, including lead singer Ted Mills holding a note until he got at least three standing ovations. The group was fitted for identical sky-blue suits and white shoes, reflecting the styles of the 1950s. Each member also wore a homburg. Vernon, who was responsible for the stage wardrobe, recalls, "That was our signal, one of our calling cards. The magic man comes out with his hat and cane and his cape and all of his magic tricks, so we thought the hats would signify the magic part of [our act]. We'd come out and razzle and dazzle. We had a production of bombs exploding, the clown outfits, and balloons when we did 'Sideshow.' We had a whole production around the hats and it really worked well for us."

Of equal importance to Blue Magic's stage performance was their choreography. One song may have required 20 to 25 steps before Mills sang the first note, and each set of moves would culminate in a pirouette. Keith Beaton, better known as "Faststepping," was responsible for the group's split-second choreography. He says, "Wendell, Vernon, and I would go to the Uptown [Theater in Philadelphia] together and watch the Delfonics, the Temptations, and Gladys Knight and the Pips. What I did was take their steps and just use my mind to do it our way. I used some of their movements but just changed it to our style. But a little bit of it came from everybody."

Vernon adds, "We worked hard on that. One of our main issues was the choreography. We wanted to have a fast-paced show where each song had a different routine to it. We rehearsed very hard for that and it paid off. It was very instrumental in our act."

The combination of a gold debut album and a mesmerizing stage performance took Blue Magic to the top of the R&B music world in less than two years. However, Vernon Sawyer downplayed the group's superstar status. "We never really considered ourselves superstars," he says. "We felt blessed just to have the talent to get into the business because it's so hard for acts to break into this business. Maybe people saw us as superstars but we never really felt we were superstars. They may have put us on that pedestal, but it didn't mean anything to us. We're very humble and down-to-earth people. We met and greeted people and treated them as equals. The superstar status never really crossed our minds."

Blue Magic followed their successful debut with *The Magic*

of the Blue, from which the single "Three Ring Circus" became their second top 10 R&B hit (number five). The seemingly overnight success of the group did have its pitfalls, as the music industry saw Blue Magic as getting too big too fast. Wendell explains, "We could've been bigger than we were but there was an element that came in because of ourselves and the people who were handling us. It's called ego. This ego made somebody think that because you had a million-seller off of the first one, the world was yours; you pushed people around; you said things about people you shouldn't have said. Not coming from us directly but from our management. With us it came about that we didn't pay dues.

"A lot of people didn't like us. In less than a year we shot up, had a gold record, and were named the number one group of the year. A lot of people thought that we were supposed to suffer and go through the bad times. Whereas today it's okay, during that period of time all of the groups like the O'Jays had to go through the sweating and the tears for several years before they got their first hit. When we came through, it was a lot easier.

"A lot of disk jockeys out there didn't like us and a lot of people in the industry didn't like us just on the fact that we didn't pay dues. They said, 'There are people who've been in the business 15 years to get where you're at right now. You didn't pay dues. I'm not playing your records.' These people will try to hurt you or hinder your career and try to slow you down. Through the negative field that was surrounding us with that attitude, in a way, it hindered a lot of our music.

"We had good albums, very good albums, but they didn't get the play that the first one got. They put [*Blue Magic*] out and it started attracting attention. That was the cheapest album we ever recorded. The next one cost almost three times as much, that's how much we put into it, and . . . nothing. And the next one . . . nothing. On those next two or three albums, that's when they made us pay our dues. So we've paid our dues now."

Another element that hindered the success of Blue Magic was the rise of disco, which picked up steam during the run of

The Magic of the Blue. Beaton recalls, "I felt as though [disco] hurt us in a way; it slowed us down. On our first album we had a couple of disco songs so we were able to survive, but our second album wasn't disco at all."

The Magic of the Blue did contain two extended dance-track songs, "Never Get Over You" and "Let Me Be the One." However, the emphasis of the album was on its ballads, and neither of these up-tempo songs could measure up to "Welcome to the Club" and "Look Me Up" from its predecessor.

"We called [disco] the plague," says Wendell. "During that period of time people started going over to disco and the stand-up acts were pushed aside a little bit. There were a lot of good groups out there that couldn't make it anymore; they couldn't hang together. It was hard staying together but we did it anyway. We felt strong that we had a purpose. Fortunately we had a lot of true followers who were still into our music, so it kept us alive throughout that period."

For the remainder of the decade, Blue Magic had success with "Chasing Rainbows" (1975), a joyous track despite its theme of a man's grief for a deceased lover, "Grateful" (1976), and "Summer Snow" (1977). In 1978 Michael Buchanan and Walter Smith replaced the Sawyers on the *Message from the Magic* album. However, the brothers soon returned. After leaving Atco, Blue Magic recorded for Capitol Records and Mirage but with little success. Wendell explains, "At that point in time, the producers and radio people were keyed towards one source of music and our music was not in anymore. It was difficult for us but we just had to keep going."

In 1985 charter member Richard Pratt left the group. "Sometimes when things seem like they're not going to turn over, you want to do something else," says Wendell. "We decided to stick it out and he moved on to something else. We wish him well. He's doing all right in North Carolina. He has his wife and his children and he's happy. We see him now and then. It just wasn't his thing anymore."

While the group shopped for a record deal, they continued to tour. "For about five or six years we kind of stagnated, trying to figure out which way to go," says Vernon. "The disco and rap kind of flushed out the stand-up acts and it was a problem for awhile trying to get a record company to get interested in us."

Wendell adds, "A lot of people didn't know we were still around. If they don't hear you on the air, they think you're gone."

In 1988 Blue Magic signed with rap mogul Russell Simmons' Def Jam label, a move that created curiosity as to why a rap-oriented person would have interest in a stand-up vocal group from the 1970s. Wendell explains, "Russell was a fan of ours for years. He used to stay backstage and listen to us. At the time when we were hitting the top of the charts, Russell was not in the business but he was looking forward to getting into the business. We had a chance to work with him through Vincent Bell, who was a friend of his, and Alvin Moody. These are young guys who grew up and entered the music business and said, 'There's Blue Magic. I can get a chance to work with them.' A lot of people still think there is a place in this business for Blue Magic. All we have to do is find the right chemistry. We did it once, we can do it again. We just have to find the right format and the right timing. I think that's what [Russell] was shooting for.

"The good thing about it is that by coming from a different era altogether and hooking up with the components in the music that's happening now, it placed us on the map."

Released in the spring of 1989, *From Out of the Blue* yielded two top 20 R&B hits with "It's Like Magic" and the up-tempo "Romeo and Juliet." There was speculation as to whether producers Vincent Bell and Alvin Moody could combine the trademark Blue Magic sound with a '90s edge. "The song 'It's Like Magic' . . . I had that song for 10 years," says Vernon. "We never recorded the song until Vincent Bell heard the song and said, 'This is vintage Blue Magic.' It turned out to be the most played song on the album."

Wendell adds, "Vinny Bell was into our music a long time ago so he knew that he couldn't put out the sound that we had then. He had to update it but keep the same feel. It takes the right chemistry and he used the right chemistry."

"It's Like Magic" was one of very few songs on the *From Out of the Blue* album that was reminiscent of Blue Magic's earlier hits. The album had an ample supply of mid-tempo and up-tempo tracks, particularly the finale, "Dancin' to the Flag," which added some diversity to the group's sound rather than keeping it locked into Mills' tenor. Wendell Sawyer was the primary beneficiary of this change.

He says, "If you notice, there's not too much tenor sound on the air. So how can you take the tenor and make it into a hit if it's not hitting already? You have to either go with the grain or take enough power to change the grain, and with power comes money. You could do it, but would you want to invest that kind of money? I feel as though natural lead baritone, along with tenor, is the right combination. We have to maintain our sound. Without the tenor sound it's not Blue Magic. Ballads are good but they don't get that much airplay during the daylight hours. We needed something that's up-tempo, still had that Blue Magic sound, and had some tenor in it. It's not easy. We were going against a lot of stuff but we've maintained ourselves. One thing Russell did do was give us some airplay during that period of time. I don't think too much emphasis was placed on us, whereas they thought [*From Out of the Blue*] would do good itself instead of getting behind it and pushing it a little more."

"*From Out of the Blue* did very well for us," adds Vernon. "Def Jam is more associated with rap than anything. Their whole forte is rap. The R&B thing was something new to them so they really didn't know how to market it as well as they thought they did. There was some lack of . . . knowledge.

"Def Jam did a helluva job considering the situation they were under. They just didn't have the staff to really target R&B. It takes time to work up to a situation like Blue Magic. It has to be worked into certain areas and markets."

Beginning in 1991, lead singer Ted Mills left Blue Magic for a solo career. His spot in the lineup was taken over by Rod Wayne. Blue Magic continues to perform before enthusiastic audiences throughout the world. In 1994 they released the single

"That's the Kind of Love I Need," backed by the Wayne-penned "We Had a Fight Last Night" on Big East Entertainment/Spectrum Records.

"I think the wholesome music and the strings and the pretty stuff is now starting to surface again," says Vernon. "Hopefully we'll be a part of that realm."

Chairmen of the Board

A four-man vocal group formed by ex-Motown writers Holland-Dozier-Holland, Chairmen of the Board was the first group signed to the trio's Invictus Records. The quartet spearheaded the early success of the label with a string of hits between 1970 and 1972, most notably "Give Me Just a Little More Time" and "Pay to the Piper." Primary lead singer General Johnson enjoyed further success as a songwriter.

The legendary writing and producing team of Eddie Holland, Brian Holland, and Lamont Dozier left Motown Records in 1968 citing non-payment of royalties, and formed their own Invictus and Hot Wax labels. While at Motown, the trio either individually or collectively generated hits for virtually every major artist on the roster. Having had monumental success with the Four Tops, the Holland brothers and Dozier were interested in forming a male quartet to record for Invictus. The first person they recruited was General Norman Johnson.

Johnson, originally from Norfolk, Virginia, started singing in church with his father at age six. By age 12, he had formed his first group, the Humdingers. However, Johnson did not have any success until his senior year of high school, when he became a member of the Showmen. A two-day recording session at Minit Records in New Orleans produced eight songs, including the peppy rock-and-roll classic "It Will Stand." That song, which would become a national anthem for beach music lovers, and a lesser hit, "39-21-46," were the only notable hits by the group during their seven-year tenure.

Johnson initially caught the attention of Brian Holland when a reissue of "It Will Stand" became a hit in Detroit in 1964. However, Johnson was never brought to Motown because his voice was too similar to Levi Stubbs, lead singer of the Four Tops. When Holland-Dozier-Holland formed Invictus four years later, they were able to sign Johnson to a contract with the help of Jeffrey Bowen, a one-time Motown producer, now working at Invictus/Hot Wax. Chairmen of the Board was formed with Johnson; Danny Woods, an Atlanta native, who was in a local band, the Tears, before performing as a solo artist in Detroit; Eddie Custis, formerly of Lee Andrews and the Hearts and Huey Smith and the Clowns; and Harrison Kennedy, formerly of the Stoned Soul Children.

General Johnson remembers, "[Holland-Dozier-Holland] were interested in me. Jeffrey Bowen called me to come to Detroit to be in this situation, Invictus, after they had left Motown. That's how I met Brian, Lamont, and Eddie. They knew what they wanted but didn't know if I was the right person that was doing the song 'It Will Stand.' We met in a little room and they said, 'Let me hear it,' and I sang 'It Will Stand.' From that point on, I was in.

"They got different artists from all over different places. I, at the time, was from Norfolk, Virginia. Danny Woods was from Atlanta, although he was staying in Detroit. Harrison Kennedy was from Canada, and Eddie Custis was from Philadelphia. [Holland-Dozier-Holland] just went around different places looking for other members."

Their first record, the Motown-flavored "Give Me Just a Little More Time," released at the beginning of 1970, would be the group's most successful. The song, which introduced Johnson's distinctive "B-r-r-r" hiccuping vocal delivery to the music audience, became a top 10 hit on both the pop and R&B charts and was certified gold. Johnson, who wanted to use Chairmen of the Board primarily as a showcase for his writing talent, curiously had mixed feelings about the success of "Give Me Just a Little More Time" because the song enhanced his reputation as a singer.

He explains, "I didn't want 'Give Me Just a Little More Time.' When I went to Invictus Records my main purpose was to learn to write songs. I had been with them for about a year or so, working at my craft. That's what I wanted to do. I didn't want to sing at that point. After I started working with the writing and production, I just wanted to write songs for different artists. When the record came out I was rooting for it, but then again, I was rooting against it until all of a sudden I just said, 'I don't want a failure record.'"

With the success of a hit record, touring followed and with it came the inevitable problems caused by Chairmen of the Board being an ensemble of four veteran lead singers with different musical backgrounds. "We used to hate each other," says Johnson. "It's funny now. We didn't get along at all off the stage but on the stage it was fine because we were doing different kinds of music. However, because each of us was doing a different type of music, it made some of the guys feel uneasy because of some of the places we were playing. If we were playing a get-down type of place and a guy was singing 'My Way,' then you've got a problem, or if we were at a get-down type of place and a guy is singing rock-and-roll, it caused a problem. There were four egos because you had four lead singers, not a lead singer and a background."

He adds, "The very first record we did was a hit and our very first job was the Apollo Theater. We were doing the choreography and kept bumping into each other. It turned out to be a blessing in disguise because [the choreography] took something away from us, especially since we were all lead singers. With us it was an individual thing, so . . . no more choreography."

Two more singles released that year, the edgy "(You've Got Me) Dangling on a String" and the bouncy and carefree "Everything's Tuesday," both made the R&B top 20. The B-side of "Everything's Tuesday," "Patches," a song written by General Johnson about a boy's forced passage into manhood as a result of his father dying, became an international hit for Clarence Carter.

Danny Woods, who sang in a higher yet harder tone than

Johnson, took over the lead vocals on the Chairmen's next single, "Pay to the Piper," released in the fall of 1970. The theme of the song, a man expecting a "nightcap" from his date as a repayment for his time and money spent, is one that would surely draw the ire of feminist groups were it released today. Johnson, who co-wrote the song, notes, "Back then there were no feminist groups. We probably would receive some flak for it now but it's the truth. It would probably still be a hit today. It's the truth, and what's wrong with the truth?"

Perhaps the most baffling part of the song was the coda, "Ask your mama." "That was the selling part of the song," says Johnson. "It was just an ad-lib. Eddie Holland was the one who actually said that. We were in the studio dubbing parts of the song and he just came up with 'ask your mama.'"

The group's eponymous track, "Chairman of the Board," whose instrumental breaks blended blues and rock with soul, gave the group their fifth top 20 R&B hit in little more than a year, peaking at number 10.

In 1971 General Johnson began to fulfill his dream of writing for other acts on Holland-Dozier-Holland's Invictus and Hot Wax labels. Often working in tandem with Greg Perry, he wrote "Somebody's Been Sleeping (In My Bed)" for 100 Proof Aged In Soul; "Bring the Boys Home" for Freda Payne; and Honey Cone's three biggest hits, "Want Ads," "Stick Up," and "One Monkey Don't Stop No Show." In recognition of his success, BMI (Broadcasting Music, Inc.) honored him with the 1972 R&B Songwriter of the Year award.

Chairmen of the Board had three minor hits in 1971 with the funky "Hanging on to a Memory," "Try on My Love for Size," and the anti-war "Men Are Getting Scarce." The cohesiveness of the group began to unravel in 1972. Solo albums by Johnson (*Generally Speaking*), Kennedy (*Hypnotic Music*), and Woods (*Aries*) slowed the momentum of the group. Also in 1972, legal problems with Invictus Records resulted in Chairmen of the Board leaving the label.

Johnson points out, "We would still be together today, but business is business. With Chairmen of the Board it wasn't a fact that our popularity declined or my creative juices had gone under. It was a thing of business. I didn't want to fall into the same trap that most black artists fell into; you get a bad contract but because of the fame you want to stay right there. I said, 'Forget the fame. I want cash.' That's what I did. I left them even though I did live quite comfortably then.

"I had so much success in that short period of time it gave me the opportunity to weigh success against failure, capital gain against zero. I wanted to renegotiate. They were stubborn, told me that I could not do it. So, I just stopped."

By this time, Eddie Custis left the group, followed by Harrison Kennedy, who was replaced by saxophonist Ken Knox. "Eddie Custis left because of personal problems," recalls Johnson. "Harrison stayed with us until the lawsuit, then he went to Canada. This left just me and Danny. We got along well. After the lawsuit we decided to go to England and start working. We had a seven-piece band and one of the guys [Knox] who played in the band was brought up front."

Invictus Records continued to release old material by Chairmen of the Board until 1976. They had their final top 10 R&B hit with "Finders Keepers," peaking at number seven in the spring of 1973. The Chairmen spent the next three years touring from six to eight months a year in Europe before finally disbanding in 1976.

Johnson embarked on a solo career, releasing an unsuccessful self-titled album on Arista Records in 1978. He describes his time with Arista as "not that great of an experience because it made my music sterile."

In the late 1970s, General Johnson started Surfside Records in Charlotte, North Carolina. He reformed Chairmen of the Board with Woods and Knox to capitalize on the popularity of the music of the Showmen and Chairmen of the Board with beach music fans. He says, "I put together this little label in the Southeast and said, 'If I do it this time, I'm doing it for myself.'"

While having the freedom to write and record in his own style of music, Johnson performs with the Chairmen in the Southeast an average of 250 dates a year, a situation he finds to be sadly ironic. "[The southeast region] is infested with colleges and clubs," he says. "When you hear Carolina beach music you're talking about black soul music. This is strange. This is how things change. I'm singing soulful music but I haven't sung for a black audience in 12 years. That tells you something. It's like everything else. What [blacks] do, we forget about it and nobody writes about the history of it, and as time goes by, it becomes other people's music. That's the problem with our youth today. They don't know where they came from. If it's not written so they can read it, they really would think that Elvis [Presley] was the first rock-and-roll singer. I'm not just confining it to music, it's . . . whatever. There's not enough history of what we do. I hate it because we have so many great artists whom nobody remembers; great, *great* artists."

The Chi-Lites

With a string of hits sharply contrasting forlorn half-sung, half-spoken ballads, such as "Have You Seen Her" and "A Letter to Myself," and militant, up-tempo funk, most notably "Give More Power to the People" and "We Are Neighbors," the Chi-Lites were one of the top falsetto-lead vocal groups in the 1970s. Led by the songwriting and production talents of lead singer Eugene Record, this Chicago quartet was a pivotal force in soul music between 1970 and 1974, creating a body of work that has proven to be not only innovative, but timeless.

The Chi-Lites' roots are deep in the South Side of Chicago, where two doo-wop outfits, the Chantours and the Desideros, sang. The Chantours formed in 1958, and consisted of Eugene Record (lead), Robert "Squirrel" Lester (second tenor), Clarence Johnson (baritone), Burt Bowen (baritone), and Eddie Reed (bass). They recorded on Leo Austell's Renee label, and also Vee Jay and Mercury, with limited success. The Desideros, who formed in 1959, consisted of Marshall Thompson (baritone), Creadel "Red" Jones (bass), Del Brown (tenor), and Eddie Sullivan (tenor). They hooked up with Austel to record "I Pledge My Love" on his Renee label in 1960, which flopped. The groups became familiar with each other in the late 1950s by performing in talent shows in Chicago. Soon a friendly rivalry developed. The remnants of each group — Record, Lester, Johnson, Thompson, and Jones — joined together in 1960 and created the Hi-Lites.

Marshall Thompson remembers, "We all knew each other from high school and talent shows. We would work talent shows against the Chantours and we would always win. We would get up there and dance, dance, dance. All they could do was sing. When it came to dancing they had two left feet. Soon after, we felt we could add something to each other's group and we joined together. We just felt that it would click."

The group landed a recording contract with Mercury Records and released the single "Pots and Pans" in 1961, which flopped. After being dropped from the Mercury label they had to change their name due to another group with the name Hi-Lites. They affixed a C to their name, which also identified them as being from Chicago. Known as Marshall and the Chi-Lites, the newly named group made a few recordings for Daran, a regional record company owned by Thompson's cousin James Shelton. In 1964, after one single, Johnson left and the group continued as a quartet. They came back with a follow-up single, "I'm So Jealous," which achieved local success, and Mercury leased it from Daran and put it out on its Blue Rock label. By now the group called itself only the Chi-Lites. During this time Record continued to drive a cab. Thompson, son of noted jazz drummer Marshall Thompson, Sr., was a house drummer at the Regal Theater, where he backed such soul notables as Major Lance, the Dells, and the Flamingos.

Two more Blue Rock releases went nowhere despite the group developing a local following. A big break finally came when the group met Carl Davis, producer and A&R man for Brunswick Records. Brunswick, an independent label based in New York, had offices in Chicago run by Davis. "I met Otis Leavill on the bus and he told me to come down and see Carl Davis," recalls Thompson. "So we went down to this company and went into this little office for our audition and Otis Leavill told Carl, 'Hey, man, you better come down and check these guys out.' Everyone was impressed with what we had and we ended up signing with Brunswick."

Once at Brunswick, lead singer Record began perfecting his craft as a songwriter and later as a producer. He was often paired with fellow Brunswick artist Barbara Acklin, who initially came to the company as a secretary/receptionist. Among their early collaborations were Acklin's biggest hits, "Love Makes a Woman" and "Am I the Same Girl," and Young-Holt Unlimited's "Soulful Strut" (actually the instrumental backing of Acklin's "Am I the Same Girl").

The Chi-Lites got their first hit early in 1969 with "Give It Away," written by Record with Carl Davis. This light, mid-tempo track, which introduced Record's falsetto to the soul audience while the remaining members mainly chanted the title phrase in support, made the R&B top 10.

"That was a great feeling, to finally get a hit," says Robert Lester. "We had been together for 10 years without much success or records that got radio play outside of Chicago, so for this one to finally make some noise for us was a great feeling."

Thompson adds, "After 'Give It Away' became a hit we started going to the Apollo Theater to perform. It was good to be at the Apollo but we never got any money from it. We only made $2 a show. That's what we had to live on. We didn't even have enough money to stay in the hotel across the street. We had to put all of our money together and bunk up in one place."

The Chi-Lites maintained their strong position with the soul audience with "Let Me Be the Man My Daddy Was," a soft and somewhat down-home, earthy ballad, co-written by Record and Acklin. In 1970, the group changed the pace for their follow-up releases, "24 Hours of Sadness," "I Like Your Lovin' (Do You Like Mine)," and "Are You My Woman (Tell Me So)." For this last release, the Chi-Lites borrowed heavily from the Norman Whitfield-produced Temptations' sound of the late '60s and early '70s, when the Motown group was going through its "psychedelic period" and having enormous success with their message songs such as "Cloud Nine," "Runaway Child, Running Wild," and "Ball of Confusion." A primary beneficiary of this new sound was "Red" Jones, whose bass was brought out further from the background harmonies of Lester and Thompson, like Melvin Franklin of the Temptations. The new sound worked for the Chi-Lites as "Are You My Woman (Tell Me So)" returned them to the R&B top 10.

In 1971, the Chi-Lites had their breakthrough year and established themselves in the pop market. Continuing with an up-tempo funk, the group branched out into militancy with "(For God's Sake) Give More Power to the People," another Record-penned and produced track, which gave all four members a chance at singing lead, while the song was anchored by Jones' bass. The song was appropriate for the mood of the times and became the Chi-Lites' biggest hit at that time, reaching number four on the R&B charts and surprisingly becoming their first top 30 pop hit.

"At that time there was a lot going on in the world, particularly with the Vietnam War and other unrest and injustice," says Lester. "As artists, we wanted to sing about the situations in the world, and it would also give us a chance to broaden our sound.

"We were heavily influenced by the Temptations and we wanted to carry that sound further. In the '60s, before the Temptations, you had the Impressions who were singing the message songs and were having great success with them. Then the Temptations followed with the message songs during their psychedelic period, and had crossover success with them. So we tried to be an extension of what they were doing even though we were a bit surprised when 'Give More Power to the People' did cross over."

The Chi-Lites followed with the similar "We Are Neighbors" in the summer of 1971, which became a top 20 R&B hit. However, "Neighbors" did not fare as well as its predecessor on the pop charts, perhaps due to the song's theme of open housing being a bit too specific, as opposed to the general militancy of "Give More Power to the People."

Before the year was over the Chi-Lites had their first certified smash with "Have You Seen Her." The release of "Have You Seen Her" marked a turning point in the musical direction of the Chi-Lites. Previously known for their pretty ballads and militant brand of funk, this song featured lead singer Record, heartbroken and vulnerable as he half-talks and half-sings throughout the ballad. Adding to the song's appeal was the now superior harmonized backing of the group, particularly on the song's opening, an indication of how far the Chi-Lites had grown since "Give It Away" three years earlier. Record, who along with Barbara Acklin wrote "Have You Seen Her" five years prior to its release, was initially apprehensive about releasing it, due to the song's length of more than five minutes at a time when a three-minute song was standard for receiving radio airplay. "Have You Seen Her" ended up being the last single placed on the *(For God's Sake) Give More Power to the People* album. At the time of its release, Brunswick Records was pushing another single, "I Want to Pay You Back (For Loving Me)." Radio deejays began playing "Have You Seen Her" from the album, prompting a surprised Brunswick to release it as a single. "Have You Seen Her" topped the R&B charts for two weeks and became their first major crossover success (rising to number three on the pop charts) and their first gold record.

" 'Have You Seen Her' wasn't intended to be released as a single; it was originally a B-side," contends Thompson. "We had no idea that song would be a hit and even as it was climbing the charts we had no idea how well it was doing. We did a show in St. Louis during that time, and after we sang all of our songs we left the stage, and the crowd kept calling us back to do 'Have You Seen Her.' We didn't know what was going on and we had no idea it was such a big hit. It wasn't a part of our show and we barely remembered the words to it. When the audience called us back out there, all we knew was 'have you seen her,' 'have you seen her.' We were more surprised than anyone when that song became the hit that it did, but when it did, it was truly a great feeling."

With the surprise release and later success of "Have You Seen Her" coming near the same time as the release of "I Want to Pay You Back (For Loving Me)," the latter enjoyed only modest success, peaking at number 35 on the R&B charts. It was an undeserved showing for this beautiful ballad, which easily could have been a hit had it not been relegated to afterthought status. The same can be said for "Yes I'm Ready (If I Don't Get to Go)," an unsung ballad from *Give More Power to the People*, which epitomized the group's superior harmonies tied around the lead of Record. All five standouts plus the up-tempo "What Do I Wish For" helped the *Give More Power to the People* album achieve million-selling status and arguably rank as the group's finest output.

The Chi-Lites carried this momentum to the height of their success the following year with the release of "Oh Girl." Beginning with the forlorn sound of a harmonica played by Cy Touff, and Record sounding helpless throughout the song, this ballad, mixed with a country-western flavor, topped both the pop and R&B charts in the spring of 1972 and was another million-seller. Record kept the same formula with the follow-up, "The Coldest Days of My Life," later that summer. On this track the despondent voice of Record was surrounded by the chirping of birds and a lightly blowing windstorm that increased in intensity over the course of eight minutes, giving the song its dramatic, tearful effect. The addition of the sound effects worked as "The Coldest Days of My Life" made the R&B top 10 (number eight).

Later that summer the Chi-Lites released "A Lonely Man" almost as an afterthought, perhaps because of its close similarity to "Have You Seen Her." Employing the same "girl that got away" theme as its previous four releases, "A Lonely Man" was similar to "Have You Seen Her," with the superior harmonized backing of the group on its opening, Record again mixing talk and song throughout, and its six-minute length. Despite its potential, "A Lonely Man" achieved modest chart success, peaking at number 25. However, the song would increase in popularity over time and has become something of a classic for Chi-Lites fans some 20-plus years later.

"We always make sure to do 'A Lonely Man' when we perform," says Lester. "Sometimes the audience gives us a big ovation at the beginning of the song because it sounds a lot like 'Have You Seen Her' until they realize, 'Okay, it's not that one yet.' But once we finish, ['A Lonely Man'] gets a strong ovation on its own merit."

All three standout ballads, plus the bouncy, mid-tempo "Living in the Footsteps of Another Man," were included on the album *A Lonely Man* and pushed the disc to gold status. Led by a string of hits and back-to-back gold albums in the 1971-72 period, the Chi-Lites became international superstars.

"Everything was happening so fast at that time we almost didn't realize what was going on," says Thompson. "When all of [the success] happened, we were traveling all over the world . . . Singapore . . . Japan, you name it. Being on stage singing songs like 'Oh Girl' and 'Have You Seen Her' and knowing that these songs have sold in the millions . . . the feeling was almost indescribable. It's something that you would actually have to go through and experience."

Lester adds, "Brunswick Records was really behind us at that time and they were responsible for keeping us out there. We were their top priority and everyone concentrated on seeing to it that everything was done for us. That was something we appreciated because with Brunswick being an independent, it was a relatively small company. Most of the top black music coming out at that time was from Motown or one of the major labels. Brunswick didn't have all of the resources available to the other companies but they used everything they did have to keep us out there and allow us to compete with the other groups."

In addition to Eugene Record's creative talents as a songwriter and producer, the Chi-Lites utilized the services of some of Chicago's best R&B technicians, including arrangers Tom (Tom Tom) Washington, Willie Henderson, and Sonny Sanders; engineer Bruce Swedien; and drummer Quinton Joseph.

The Chi-Lites ended their most successful year with the release of "We Need Order" in the fall of 1972. For this track Record returned to his psychedelic period but with a softer brand of funk and a little less militancy. The Chi-Lites were back to their spoken/sung ballads with "A Letter to Myself," released at the beginning of 1973, and reaching number three on the R&B charts.

During 1973, personal problems caused bass Creadel Jones to leave the group. The Chi-Lites released their self-titled second album of that year, which contained three outstanding hits. The album's first single was "Stoned Out of My Mind." Perhaps not wanting to be pigeonholed as strictly a composer of pathos-filled ballads and militant up-tempo funk, Record arranged the song for his lead falsetto and the background vocals to be carried several ranges higher, giving the song a joyous flavor. The change worked as "Stoned Out of My Mind," again co-written with Acklin, reached number two on the R&B charts and cracked the pop top 30. The Chi-Lites returned to funk with "I Found Sunshine," released later that fall. Employing the dominance of a guitar instead of the horn-laden arrangements exhibited on their previous funk tracks, "I Found Sunshine" made the R&B top 20. The group followed with one of their more outstanding tracks, the country-western-flavored "Homely Girl," about a plain girl who grows into a beautiful woman. The song reached number three on the R&B charts in early 1974 and was the strongest collaboration between Record and Stan McKinney, a country music deejay from Kentucky. Record and McKinney paired on three other cuts from the album, "Go Away Dream," "I Never Had It So Good (And Felt So Bad)," and "I Forgot to Say I Love You Till I'm Gone."

The Chi-Lites added a heavier, more orchestral production to their 1974 *Toby* album and produced three solid hits. Record kept his tenor higher than usual on the first single, "There Will Never Be Any Peace (Until God Is Seated at the Conference Table)," a beautiful ballad that reached number eight on the R&B charts that spring. After following up with "You Got to Be the One," which peaked at number 15 that summer, the Chi-Lites released "Toby," an underrated classic from the catalog of songs co-written by Record and Acklin. This sad ballad about mourning the loss of a childhood friend was another big hit for the group; it peaked at number seven on the R&B charts and would be their final top 10 hit on Brunswick.

The group's next effort, *Half of Love* in 1975, was perhaps their weakest. It generated only one minor hit, with "It's Time for Love"/"Here I Am" peaking at number 27. It was the Chi-Lites' first album not to generate any top 10 hits. The group was still trying to fill the position of bass singer vacated when

Creadel Jones left two years earlier. They first tried T.C. Anderson on the *Toby* album. For *Half of Love* they used Anderson on some tracks and Willie Kersey on others. They finally settled on David (Doc) Roberson, who was a member of a local Chicago group, the Five Wagers.

The year 1976 proved to be the undoing of the Chi-Lites. In a nationwide federal investigation of the record industry the previous year, seven of Brunswick's New York-based officials were tried and convicted of a variety of charges, including payola, mail fraud, and income tax evasion. These assessments brought the investigation down on the artists as well. In January 1976 the Chi-Lites were found guilty of tax evasion and later fined and sentenced to a year's probation. With this disarray, coupled with the country's change in musical taste to disco, the Chi-Lites' sales suffered.

"When Brunswick had their problems, that hurt us a lot," says Lester. "With all of the problems they were having, they weren't able to promote us like they did earlier, and our records suffered. Whatever negative feelings or bitterness we may have had at that time about what happened to us as a result of Brunswick's problems, we've put them aside. Instead, we focus on how Brunswick put the records out there and promoted the songs, which has allowed us to still be around here today as a result of songs like 'Have You Seen Her' and 'Oh Girl.'"

One other major casualty of 1976 occurred when Eugene Record left the Chi-Lites for a solo career with Warner Brothers. Record's tenure at Warner produced the highly acclaimed yet uncommercial *The Eugene Record* (1977) and *Trying to Get You* (1978).

Marshall Thompson reformed the Chi-Lites, adding tenors David Scott and Danny Johnson, and moved the group to Mercury Records. During their tenure at Mercury, the Chi-Lites released two albums, *Happy Being Lonely* (1976) and *The Fantastic Chi-Lites* (1977). Despite the fine quality of the material, neither album sold well, nor did any of the singles released during this period. Their best showing at Mercury was the title cut from *Happy Being Lonely*, which reached the R&B top 30.

"When we signed with Mercury it was at a time when they still had the Ohio Players on their roster," says Lester. "They were the hottest group out there at that time, so all of Mercury's attention was geared towards them. We weren't prepared for that. We were used to being in a situation like the one we had at Brunswick, where we were the focal point of the company. We would walk into a meeting and there would be all of these record company executives sitting around talking about seven or eight different acts on the label and we may have heard our names mentioned once."

With neither Record nor the Chi-Lites having any substantial hits during the latter part of the decade, the group reunited in 1980 with all four original members. Thompson recalls, "We had a big hit in Chicago with 'My First Mistake.' That song was really big in Chicago. I called Gene and told him how big this hit was, 'My First Mistake.' And the more we talked about it, he said, 'I want to come back but only if it's just the four original Chi-Lites.' So, that's what we did. We reformed with only the original four of us. We even found Red [Jones]. I had to put out an APB on him and we were able to find him. To get back to the way it originally was, we even went back with Carl Davis."

The Chi-Lites signed with Davis' Chi-Sound Records in 1980 but had no success until 1982, first with the disco-flavored "Hot on a Thing (Called Love)," and the following year with "Bottom's Up" reaching the top 10. These were the group's two biggest hits since "Toby" in 1975. The following year Jones again retired and the Chi-Lites continued as a trio. Later in the decade Record also left for good. His spot was taken over by Anthony Watson.

The group received a huge boost in 1990 when rap/pop superstar M.C. Hammer had a top 10 pop hit with a remake of "Have You Seen Her" and British pop star Paul Young had a top 10 hit with his cover version of "Oh Girl." "That was great for us," says Thompson. "We got a lot of recognition from that. When those two records came out it gave us the opportunity to make more money when we performed. I handle the bookings for us and when those songs were out, I was able to go to the promoters and say, 'These two songs here ['Have You Seen Her' and 'Oh Girl'], you know, we're the ones who made them first.'"

The Chi-Lites today perform as a trio consisting of Thompson, Lester, and Watson, although they allow room for the return of Eugene Record and Creadel Jones. "We'll always hold Gene's spot and Red's spot," says Thompson. Despite not having a record deal, the Chi-Lites remain popular on the club circuit and perform an average of three to four times a month.

"Today when we sing songs like 'Oh Girl' and 'Have You Seen Her,' the response we get from the audience is as if we just recorded them," says Lester. "As long as that happens, we'll stay out here. We have no plans for stopping. We'll keep doing this even when they have to roll us out there in wheelchairs."

The Delfonics

The Delfonics pioneered the soft-soul sound of the late 1960s and early 1970s with a string of hits written by lead singer William Hart and producer Thom Bell. With the combination of Hart's clear, high tenor and the introduction of Bell's string-filled orchestral productions on songs such as "La-La Means I Love You" and "Didn't I (Blow Your Mind This Time)," this Philadelphia trio enjoyed tremendous success between 1968 and 1971 and paved the way for the influx of tenor-dominated ballad groups of the early 1970s.

The origin of the Delfonics begins in Philadelphia with William Hart who, inspired by Frankie Lymon and the Teenagers, organized his first group, the Veltones, when he was 14.

He recalls, "Frankie Lymon had a lot of influence on me. When I was younger I sang all of his songs. Then I learned how to pronounce my words clearly on a record. I thought it was very important that the diction be clear. As the lead singer, I patterned myself after Frankie Lymon, not with the little-boy flavor, but with that particular type of pronunciation. Then I heard Little Anthony. He had more of an adult feel with his pronunciation. I also added Dionne Warwick, and then my own natural ability because I sang in that high register. I took those tones and I used my own creative movement to create my sound out of those tones because they were, to me, the clearest and the cleanest singers that I had ever heard, and I thought that would be a great example.

"As a young boy I was clearly thinking about the direction I wanted to go because everyone would tell me, 'Wow, you sing better than Frankie Lymon. If you ever got a chance, you'd be great.' I heard this around 12, 13, 14 years old. Then when I got around 15, 16, 17 I started hearing Anthony and the Imperials, and I began to create my style from them."

The Veltones consisted of Hart, Randy Cain, Stan Lathan, Donald Cannon, and Ricky Johnson. The group began their career performing at local dances and in small clubs in and around the Philadelphia area. When Johnson left to become a minister, the group became the Four Guys. Upon high school graduation, Randy Cain went to college at Lincoln University in Oxford, Pennsylvania, and Hart reformed the group, naming them the Orphonics.

"When I went off to college I didn't want to go," remembers Cain. "I had to go to my father's alma mater, which was Lincoln, and I protested. It was all dudes then. After two years I came back and rejoined the group. I told William that I was back. From there we started working again."

In 1966, the group came to the attention of manager Stan Watson, who brought them to Cameo Records and introduced them to Thom Bell, a writer/arranger and session pianist for the Cameo label. By this time Orphonics member Richie Daniels was drafted into the armed forces and the group was down to a trio, renamed the Delfonics. The group now consisted of William Hart (tenor lead), his younger brother Wilbert (baritone lead), and Randy Cain (second tenor). Hart says, "When we formed the Orphonics, we were a powerful harmonizing street-corner group but we didn't have any idea which direction to go. It all fell into place when Stan Watson came into the barbershop to get his hair cut. Stan heard me singing in the barbershop and he hooked me up with Thom Bell."

Wilbert Hart adds, "Stan was a hustler. He'd get some money and he knew what to do with it. Stan wasn't musically inclined in any way but he knew a record company in Philadelphia called Cameo Parkway, and he knew Thom Bell who used to work on the staff. Stan hooked us up with Tommy and took us down to Cameo Parkway. This was Thom's first time working with the group."

In the summer of 1966, Bell produced the William Hart-penned "He Don't Really Love You." Cameo passed on this effort, so Watson sold it to the Moon Shot label. The song achieved regional success and Cameo opted to release the group's next single, a William Hart-Bell ballad called "You've Been Untrue." However, the company soon folded. The regional success of these two songs gave Watson the impetus to form Philly Groove Records for the group. Their first recording for the new label was "La-La Means I Love You," based on the sounds William Hart's son used to repeat. Like most of the Delfonics' future recordings, the song was co-written by William Hart and Bell. "La-La Means I Love You" introduced the string-filled arrangement that would become a production trademark of Thom Bell. The ballad was a top five hit on both the pop and R&B charts in 1968 and transformed the Delfonics from a local attraction into international superstars.

William Hart recalls, "We were getting demands all over the country for jobs and we weren't quite prepared for that because we didn't have a band. But we eventually got that together and then we started rolling."

Wilbert adds, "When 'La-La' became a success it was like hitting the lottery. When 'La-La' came out I was about 19 or 20. At that age you don't realize where you're at because you're concentrating on maybe the wrong things, and at that time we didn't have proper management or guidance. We were like kids in a candy shop. We didn't know how to count the money. It was coming so quick and we were traveling every day. We had these guys up in New York counting our money and sending our money back. Then when we'd get home — we made maybe $300,000 for the month on the road — and then when you got home there was $150,000 and these people are talking about, 'Oh, we made phone calls, we did this, we did that, etc. . . .' It was crazy. The money was so plentiful we didn't even count it; and you never thought it was going to end."

The Delfonics followed "La-La Means I Love You" with a string of hit singles in 1968 and 1969. With each single, Bell backed the high tenor of William Hart's lead with a heavy orchestration of strings and woodwinds. "Thom Bell came up with something unique with our sound," says Wilbert Hart. "He came up with the kettledrums and the strings and the French horn, that kind of thing, real classy. The arrangements were strong. As far as the movements and the structures and the strings and how he did things like that, it was very important. It was us and him, him and us. It was a good mixture. Tommy was a great part of what happened. I don't think what happened would've happened if he wasn't there."

Led by William Hart's tenor and Bell's production, the Delfonics were pioneers of the tenor-dominated "soft soul" sound of the late 1960s and early 1970s. This was a sound introduced at the height of the psychedelic era, which was dominated by Sly and the Family Stone, the Woodstock festival, and "message" songs. Despite the group's deviation from this musical trend, the popularity of their sound grew with each release and paved the way for the tenor-dominated love ballad groups of the 1970s such as the Chi-Lites, the Moments, the Stylistics, and Blue Magic.

"I just decided to do what I do best," says William Hart. "I was going to sing pretty ballads and eventually I figured that everybody likes something pretty. I had a little strategy built within me somehow that I wanted to not compete, but where I had my own little sound where there wouldn't be any type of competition. So, when we came onto the scene we exploded because it was something different and it was up to date. Then you had the Moments, then you had the Stylistics. We were one of the most imitated professional groups by other professional groups I think there ever was. However, it kept the Delfonics' name in people's minds because everybody said, 'There goes somebody else sounding like the Delfonics.' So, when we didn't have a record going, that kept our name out there for us and it made it good for us because we're still able to work across the country today."

Wilbert Hart adds, "There was no one out there doing what we were doing. We were the first. We were right on time.

When something like that happens and people recognize you and they don't put you with another act, they say, 'Oh, you guys are unique.'

"We always had our segment of people. There were always those people who would gravitate to that type of music. Groups like Sly and the Family Stone and War crossed over into that pop thing. We crossed over some with 'La-La' and later with 'Didn't I [Blow Your Mind This Time]' and that got us into that segment. I figured that [the soft-soul sound] would keep on. The records were doing pretty decent. Every record that came from Philadelphia with the production of Thom Bell and Kenny Gamble did well. That was a lock. As long as we used musicians and arrangements from Philly, we basically were locked in there."

The Delfonics followed "La-La Means I Love You" with two pleading ballads in 1968, "I'm Sorry" and "Break Your Promise," both of which became top 15 R&B hits. Of his writing style, William Hart says, "My whole ideology of writing songs is nothing but clean songs. Nothing to do with sex, just a broken-hearted young man whose girlfriend left him, and songs that were very warm, touching, and sad, per se. I've always been afraid to write a song that had anything to do with sex, violence, filth, anything that had to do with that, yet they always referred to the Delfonics' music as the sounds of sexy soul. I never understood how they could give us that title. After we got going, [Philly Groove] began to name the albums on their own and we had nothing to do with it. We were cutting records and the next thing I knew it was 'the sounds of sexy soul' and I'm wondering how they could do this. There's not a lyric in any of my records where you could say, 'Well, this could mean that.' I was very careful with that because I believe that God gives you the talent and I don't think that you have to sing filthy music. I think it's alright with God if you sing songs that are pretty and beautiful and wonderful; songs your mother and daughter can listen to. That's just been my attitude with regard to writing those songs, yet they put 'the sounds of sexy soul.'"

Bell slightly changed the tempo for the group's next release. Opening with a dramatic, almost frantic feeling and featuring bassoons, the straightforward "Ready or Not Here I Come," backed by the popular ballad "Somebody Loves You," became the group's fourth and fifth straight hits in less than a year. The year 1969 saw the Delfonics score with "You Got Yours and I'll Get Mine." This single started a new trend for the group by opening with the baritone of Wilbert Hart and leading into William's tenor rather than featuring William's lead all the way through.

The group's next single would be their biggest seller. Released at the beginning of 1970, the ethereal "Didn't I (Blow Your Mind This Time)" opened with a French horn, and again featured the baritone of Wilbert Hart for much of the song. Despite the song's dreamy melody, the lyrics pointed to breaking away from an unfaithful lover. The conflict worked as "Didn't I" became a top 10 pop hit, reaching number three on the R&B charts and selling over a million copies. The following year "Didn't I" netted the Delfonics a Grammy Award for best R&B vocal performance by a group.

Beginning with the release of "La-La Means I Love You" at the start of 1968, the Delfonics had become mainstays near the top of the R&B charts, while peaking somewhere in the middle of the pack on the pop charts. Despite sticking with the same tenor-dominated love ballad formula exhibited on their previous releases, "Didn't I" was the group's only single after "La-La" to achieve pop success.

Wilbert Hart explains, "A lot of times the record company won't give you the proper accounting. They know how you're coming into the deal; you're not coming into the deal real strong. They know what they can tell you and what they don't have to tell you. We had something like 14 records in a row to hit the charts and we weren't getting the proper accounting for them. 'Ready or Not Here I Come' crossed over . . . big time. We didn't get the proper accounting for it. That one may have been a million-seller. They didn't want to tell us it was a million-seller because they didn't want to pay us on a million.

I believe, although I don't have any concrete proof, that it did [sell a million copies]."

The group's success continued with the release of "Trying to Make a Fool of Me" in the spring of 1970. This slightly mid-tempo track, featuring trade-off leads by the Hart brothers, was the group's third straight top 10 R&B hit, peaking at number eight. The Delfonics rounded out the year with the highly successful "When You Get Right Down to It."

Inner turmoil that had been brewing within the group reached its head at the beginning of 1971. As a result, Randy Cain left and was replaced by Major Harris. Cain recalls, "February of 1971 was when I first left the group. I just got tired of the fighting. When I got fed up, I left. Major was my friend. Earlier I told the fellas that if ever we added a fourth guy, it would be [Harris]. He sang with Nat Turner's Rebellion and they would open for us. I was standing in the wings watching. Then I ran and got the fellas and said [Harris] would make a fourth Delfonic. When I left, Major stepped in my place as an employee."

Harris, a native of Richmond, Virginia, first recorded a song in 1959 called "Just a Bad Thing" with a group, the Charmers. As a teenager, he worked with the Teenagers and the Jarmels, the latter with whom he had a few hits, including "A Little Bit of Soap." In 1965, Harris signed with Okeh Records and cut five little-noticed records. After working with the Impacts, he moved to Philadelphia in 1969 and became the featured vocalist in a group called the Nat Turner Rebellion, also signed to the Philly Groove label, before joining the Delfonics.

Also in 1971, the successful musical collaboration between the Delfonics and Thom Bell ended when Bell left to shift his production attention to the Stylistics. Fortunately, at the time of Bell's departure the Delfonics had fully established their reputation for "soft-soul" music.

William Hart notes, "[Bell's departure] did affect the group in the '70s but we had already established hit records and I was writing them anyway. When Bell left I wrote the record '[For the Love] I Give to You' and that was a big record all over the country. So we had established the groove and I had established the fact that all I had to do was get somebody to put the music under my songs the way I'd like it and it should carry on. My voice was already established as the lead singer of the Delfonics and the outcry was basically for that sound."

"It did have a big effect on us," adds Wilbert Hart. "It didn't stop us because after he left that's when 'I Give to You' and 'Hey Love' came out. It had a lot of influence on us; it hurt. All of the songs that the Stylistics had, we would've had . . . Oh! . . . We would've been bigger than the Beatles!"

When Thom Bell broke his ties with the Delfonics, William Hart became the creative force behind the group's music. The Delfonics got off to an auspicious start in the post-Bell era with the release of the haunting ballad "Hey Love," which became a number nine R&B hit in the spring of 1971. However, Hart could not completely recapture the magic of previous years and the group's recording success was short-lived. The trio was only able to achieve two top 15 R&B hits with "Walk Right Up to the Sun" (fall of 1971), and the haunting "Tell Me This Is a Dream" (spring of 1972). After minor hits in 1973 and 1974 with "I Don't Want to Make You Wait," and "I Told You So," the Delfonics had their final chart entry with "Lying to Myself" in the spring of 1974. The group later recorded for Curtis Mayfield's Curtom label but with limited success.

By this time, Major Harris left the Delfonics for a solo career with Atlantic Records, where his steamy 1975 ballad "Love Won't Let Me Wait," featuring the moans of Philadelphia background singer Barbara Ingram, sold over a million copies and netted him a Grammy nomination for best male R&B vocal. However, Harris' solo success was short-lived as he fell victim to the disco phenomenon. He explains, "Disco hurt a lot. People were only dancing to the music. There wasn't much singing anymore. Everything was about the track. It got away from the real songs. It was only the older people who started liking the good stuff."

When Major Harris left the Delfonics, Randy Cain rejoined, and the group remained popular on the nightclub circuit for the remainder of the decade and into the early 1980s despite the lack of a current single. For a period in the '80s there were two groups of competing Delfonics. In 1991 the three original members (William, Wilbert, and Randy) plus Major Harris reunited to form one group. "Major left and I came back in '75," remembers Cain. "The group broke up for real in '79. I came down with pneumonia. We were working so much that I had walking pneumonia and didn't know it. In 1982 [William and Wilbert] split up. William and I started communicating again in '85 but it took us until '87 to really sit down and start talking. We talked until '89, then we started walking together to get through all of the stuff that we went through that wasn't good and we got back to the 13-year-old guys sitting on my steps talking about how we wanted to make it big someday. In 1990 we all got back together."

The legacy of the Delfonics' music provided a boost to the group in the early '90s. In 1989, teen sensation New Kids on the Block had a top 10 pop hit with a remake of "Didn't I (Blow Your Mind This Time)." "That was great," says Wilbert Hart. "That was a blessing from God because when that happens, a whole new audience gets a chance to hear your music. What really made me feel good about it was that they didn't change anything. Everything was exactly the same as when we did it. It was actually the same record. We have some crossover action but our audience is actually 35 to 40 and up. Now we have 17- and 18-year-olds hearing the same thing that we did, so it was great. It helped."

He further adds, "We've been blessed by God. At the time we came out you had Woodstock and the whole hippie life. We've been lucky that people remember us. That music was something that you could remember. The music of the '70s had structure and stories. People of our age right now have money and they're in a position to do things. That allows us to play in good clubs and travel around the world because they remember us."

In 1991, "La-La Means I Love You" and "Didn't I (Blow Your Mind This Time)" were featured in Robert Townsend's film *The Five Heartbeats*, perhaps as a consolation for the group not appearing in the movie. Wilbert Hart explains, "Robert was traveling around with us and the Dells, and it was between us and the Dells as to who would be doing the soundtrack. They won out over us. The Dells are a great group. He had a choice between the Delfonics and the Dells, and he chose the Dells. He made the right choice. I wasn't mad or anything because the thing I like about what he did, and it helped us out, was that he used our music. That was a great help."

The following year, due to some apparent bad blood between the Hart brothers, the quartet split again. By 1994 Wilbert Hart and Major Harris were performing as Wil Hart and the Delphonics, adding Frank Washington, formerly of the 1970s soul group the Futures ("You Got It"). William Hart and Randy Cain remained as the Delfonics and added Samuel Thompkins (no relation to Stylistics' lead singer Russell Thompkins, Jr.) to round out the trio.

While both groups are currently seeking record deals, they continue to perform in nightclubs throughout the U.S. and abroad for the legion of fans they have attained over the past 25 years.

William Hart points out, "My brother decided to leave me and Randy and go out and use my name, the Delfonics, which I have a trademark on. It's against the law to do that. They even spell it different. That's what you call an obvious infringement to deceive the public. Had it been anybody else, I probably would've had him in court.

"It's sad but it's the truth. If there was anything wrong with what we were doing, Randy would've left. If [Wilbert] would come back, people would enjoy seeing the original Delfonics as they were. It's a sad story. I'm not bad-mouthing him or anything. I'm just telling the truth and I like for the truth to be known to the people because people want to know what the hell is going on. The majority of the Delfonics are right here, Randy Cain, William Hart, and Samuel Thompkins, and we just carry on.

"The older crowds who have young kids, they come out in droves because they want to see the 'oldies but goodies' show. It's just great to see the people and how they're starving for clean, upright music again. We just go around singing 'Didn't I [Blow Your Mind This Time],' 'La-La Means I Love You,' '[For the Love] I Give to You,' 'Somebody Loves You,' 'Ready or Not Here I Come,' and those types of songs, all of the songs that have meaning to them. That's where we're coming from today."

The Dells

Led by Marvin Junior's gruff baritone and Johnny Carter's answering lead falsetto, the Dells were one of the more impressive soul groups of the 1960s and early 1970s. Primarily a ballad group, the quintet's remarkable vocal blend allowed them to combine contemporary R&B with their doo-wop origin to rise to success in the late 1960s with such classics as their remakes of "Stay in My Corner" and "Oh What a Nite." The Dells were able to prop up the Chess label in the early part of the 1970s by maintaining their consistent presence on the charts, particularly with "The Love We Had (Stays on My Mind)" and "Give Your Baby a Standing Ovation." Having performed together for more than 40 years with only one personnel change, the pride of Harvey, Illinois remains arguably the most respected vocal group among its R&B contemporaries.

Originally known as the El Rays, the group began singing together in the early 1950s when they were attending Thornton Township High School in Harvey, Illinois. The original members were Johnny Funches (tenor, lead), Verne Allison (second tenor), Mickey McGill (baritone), Chuck Barksdale (bass), Marvin Junior (baritone, lead) and Mickey's brother Lucius.

After honing their skills on street corners and at a local ice cream parlor, the sextet went to Chicago to audition for Leonard Chess, owner of Chess Records. Chess signed the group to his Checker subsidiary in 1953 and released their *a capella* "Darling I Know," backed with "Christine." The record sold mildly in Chicago but had no impact elsewhere. Shortly afterwards, Lucius McGill quit the group. The remaining quintet soon came under the guidance of Harvey Fuqua and the Moonglows, who taught them to sing five-part harmony. In 1955, the group, now known as the Dells, signed with Vee-Jay Records. Their first effort, "Tell the World," sold mildly, as did their next release, "Dreams of Contentment." The Dells had their breakthrough with their third Vee-Jay release. Penned by Funches and Junior, the classic doo-wop ballad "Oh What a Nite" became a top five R&B hit and sold a million copies.

Chuck Barksdale recalls, " 'Oh What a Nite' was released in late '55. I had left the group because we weren't doing that much as a group. Otis Williams and the Charms had a record out that was moving along well. I had met with Otis Williams at some point in Detroit. Because his bass singer for one reason or another had left the group, he asked me what the Dells were doing. I told him the Dells weren't doing that much as a group, so he asked me to come with them for five to six months until this guy got his head together. So I went to Cincinnati and we hooked up. We rehearsed and went out on the road. I was not there on the original version of 'Oh What a Nite.' Calvin Carter, who was an A&R director for Vee-Jay at that time, had to sing bass in my absence.

"I happened to be back in Cincinnati about early '56 and I hear this record on WCIN, 'Oh What a Nite,' and the disk jockey is making such a big deal about 'Oh What a Nite.' I called Mickey [McGill] and said, 'Man, that's a smash record. Everybody in Cincinnati loves it . . . I'll be home.'

"When I got home the record was beginning to take some huge leaps and bounds. There were only two other records that were bigger than 'Oh What A Nite' at that time period. 'Blueberry Hill' was number two and 'Don't Be Cruel' by Elvis Presley was number one. At that time critics called our music race music. Alan Freed would not play our record. In fact, he said it on the radio one time, 'The number 24 record on the list is considered a race record, so we'll go to record number 25.' So, there it is again. The racism that exists today existed back then. They just don't say it now but they blatantly said it then.

"We went to the Apollo for the first time, got to New York and it scared us half to death. The first big band arrangement we got was written by a brother who was a junkie. He wrote the song in the wrong key. Here it is we get to the world-famous Apollo Theater and we got an arrangement written in the wrong key. The person who saved us, Sammy Lowe, took the song and transposed it overnight and gave us our first real serious big band arrangement."

The Dells followed with several singles in 1957 and 1958, particularly "Why Do You Have to Go" and "Pain in My Heart," but none of their releases had the widespread appeal of "Oh What a Nite."

In 1958 a car accident on the Ohio Turnpike hospitalized most of the group and they disbanded for two years. When the Dells reunited in 1960, Johnny Funches did not return. His lead tenor spot was taken over by Johnny Carter, a former member of the Flamingos. The Dells soon developed a pattern using Junior's harsh baritone as the principal lead with Carter's piercing falsetto coming in as an answer lead.

In an effort to improve their sound, the Dells aligned themselves with Curt Stewart, the music director for Sarah Vaughan and Della Reese. "Curt Stewart was a great influence on the Dells," says Barksdale. "He moved us out of the doo-wop realm and into a jazz vocal format. Curt Stewart was a musical genius. One of his main fortes was that he was a great vocal teacher. He took the Dells, five guys who came off the street, who really had no formal musical training, and took us into training by sitting us down at the piano and giving us jazz-type chords that would end up being jazz standards.

"Curt took the time and had the patience to give us the tutelage because he heard something that we didn't even know was there. He said, 'Wow, here are five young black men who have something here that is very unique. They come from off the corner. They can sing if given the proper input by someone who knows how to teach them to sing.' So he took us into his hands and physically sat us down on a day-to-day basis and worked with us hours on top of hours at no charge. It was like a personal achievement to him to hear his musical compositions come out in form from our voices from what he heard that our voice textures did have."

Stewart arranged for the Dells to become background singers for Dinah Washington on the latter's tour, and they cut four songs with her on her 1959 *Tears and Laughter* album. After this album, Carter and Barksdale remained with Washington, while the other Dells went back to Vee-Jay, with Dallas Taylor of the Danderliers singing lead on 1961's "Swingin' Tears."

The Dells got back together in 1962 and cut four singles for Argo Records (another division of Chess) and had a moderate local hit later that year with "Bossa Nova Bird." While at Argo, they gained a reputation as more of a jazz ensemble than an R&B group. "We never left R&B," notes Barksdale. "I think it was a case of our broadening our scope in terms that we were stereotyped as being just a doo-wop group."

In 1964, with their jazz reputation still intact, the Dells returned to Vee-Jay Records. Barksdale says, "In 1964 we recorded an album called *It's Not Unusual*. This was a jazz album produced by Calvin Carter that we did on the Vee-Jay label. The title came from the song recorded by Tom Jones. His version was just about to be released in the United States and Calvin Carter wanted us to cover the record. On that album we recorded a number of jazz-type songs, 'Little Darling,' 'My Baby Just Cares for Me,' and some other great standards which kind of took us away from the doo-wop type sound."

When the Dells returned to Vee-Jay, the company was in economic difficulty and close to being shut down. The group's only commercial success was "Stay in My Corner," which made it to number 23 on the R&B charts in 1965.

In the summer of 1966, the Dells returned to Chess Records. Barksdale remembers, "Prior to coming to Chess, Vee-Jay had folded because the IRS had closed them down with big tax problems and some other problems. We ended up going back to Leonard Chess and he gave us another contract. The Dells were on Chess for the second or third time in our career. We started off at Chess as the El Rays, went across the street to Vee-

Jay and changed our name to the Dells. We stayed there until 1957 or '58 and went back to Chess and cut some records there, so it was a ping-pong type of thing for a number of years."

The turning point in the Dells' career came in 1967 when Chess teamed the group with producer Bobby Miller and arranger Charles Stepney. "In terms of being on the totem pole, we were at the very bottom of the totem pole of the Chess roster when we met Bobby Miller," says Barksdale. "Prior to that, we were doing some nightclubs throughout Chicago, singing jazz. One of the jazz trios we worked for was fronted by Charles Stepney. We built a beautiful relationship with Charles Stepney while working in the nightclubs. We then met Bobby Miller and found out he was a songwriter. We went to Leonard Chess and said, 'We have the songwriter, we have the arranger. Give us a shot.' We went in and, unbeknownst to us, a string of fantastic hits followed this, with most of the writing being done by Bobby Miller. Bobby Miller had, at that time, one of the greatest talents for songwriting, especially the ballads. From Bobby Miller we had huge records."

The pairing of the Dells with Miller and Stepney produced immediate rewards, starting with the *There Is* album in 1968. The album, which produced six hits, transformed the Dells from a moderately successful R&B group into pop superstars. The run of the *There Is* album began with the sweet, doo-wop-flavored ballad, "O-o, I Love You," backed with the title song, which, ironically, the group initially did not like.

Barksdale explains, "Bobby Miller had a strange rhythmic pattern. 'There Is' is more like cut-cut-cut-cut and that's what threw me when I first heard it. When we first heard it we said, 'Man, what the hell is this?' But Charles Stepney heard something in 'There Is' and he found out where Bobby was coming from and was able to put it into a musical rhythmic pattern that would probably work.

"When we recorded it we also recorded the ballad, 'O-o, I Love You' and it was doing quite well. We ran into Harvey Fuqua, who was now working at Motown, and we were playing the latest releases. We played 'O-o, I Love You' and then the flip side, 'There Is.' When he heard 'There Is' he said, 'That's the hit.' The rest is history. ['There Is'] turned out to be one of our biggest hits."

While "O-o, I Love You" was moderately successful, peaking at number 22 on the R&B charts in the spring of 1968, "There Is" became the group's first top 20 pop hit. Other uptempo highlights from the album included "Wear It on Our Face"; "Show Me," a bouncy, tambourine-thumping, gospel-flavored track; and the Motown-flavored "Run for Cover."

The highlight of the ballads was a remake of their 1965 Vee-Jay song "Stay in My Corner." This soulful classic featured Marvin Junior holding a note for an astounding 16 seconds. It spent three weeks at the Number One spot on the R&B charts in the summer of 1968 and was the group's first top 10 pop hit. Barksdale explains how the remake of "Stay in My Corner" came about.

"We recorded 'Stay in My Corner' in 1964 prior to Vee-Jay going under. The original version of 'Stay in My Corner' is one that I did not like but it was one that was climbing the R&B charts during the destruction of Vee-Jay Records. When Vee-Jay closed down, 'Stay in My Corner' became a part of our show. Everywhere we went we sang 'Stay in My Corner' and it became a *main* part of our show. We were at Chess finishing up the album and we recorded it in order to fill in the rest of the album.

"I literally had to go out into the studio and show Stepney where the section is where Marvin Junior holds this note for a long period of time, which was virtually unheard of at that point. It ended up being a six-minute, ten-second record. This was going to be the first long-playing single in history. We didn't know this. We were just extending it and this was due to the fact that Marvin could hold this note for such a long period of time.

"What they did was put out the three-minute, five-second version. The general public and the disk jockeys wanted the long version. The disk jockeys said they could have their lunch, call their ladies up, go home and check on the kids, and come back and it would still be playing.

"We were in Germany and when we came back, the reporters met us at the airport and wanted to know how did we feel having the success of the record that shot up the charts out of nowhere. We asked them, 'What are you talking about?' and they said, ' "Stay in My Corner," it's huge.' "

Commenting on the phenomenal success of the *There Is* album, Barksdale says, "We were overwhelmed by the success of the album. Very thankful and appreciative. I didn't really understand the magnitude that the album was going to have on the country and in parts of the world. It amazed us inasmuch that, to be well received and to have a record company at that point in time that was giving us very good support, and to be able to sell a record in the numbers that we were able to do was very uplifting."

The Dells' follow-up album, *Always Together*, produced a number three R&B hit late in 1968 with the ballad title song. Other songs from the album to chart in 1969 were "Does Anybody Know I'm Here" and "I Can't Do Enough."

That same year the Dells released *Love Is Blue*, which produced three solid hits. The first, an "I Can Sing a Rainbow/Love Is Blue" medley, peaked at number five on the R&B charts in the spring of 1969. Next was a remake of their 1956 hit, "Oh What a Nite." Beginning with an opening monologue by Barksdale and featuring trade-off leads by Junior and Carter, "Oh, What a Night" (with a new spelling and punctuation) topped the R&B charts in the fall of 1969 and was the group's second top 10 pop hit.

Barksdale says, "Leonard Chess had a great record mind, plus he owned the publishing rights to 'Oh What a Nite.' In 1969 he said, "Oh What a Nite' was such a huge hit in 1956. I think it's time to re-record that song.' At first we were a little reluctant but we re-recorded it and it ended up being bigger the second time than it was the first time."

"On the Dock of the Bay," an up-tempo version of the Otis Redding hit, followed and climbed the R&B charts to number 13 late in 1969.

In the fall of 1969, the Dells were dealt a huge blow when Leonard Chess died of a heart attack. Barksdale recalls, "Leonard Chess had a great impact on the group because he kept giving us chance after chance after chance. Fortunately, or unfortunately, I was with Leonard the day he died. I was not with him *when* he died but how that happened was, we were supposed to rehearse at the studio on that particular day. Leonard either didn't have his car at the studio or didn't feel like driving. I took him to WVON, which was one of the biggest R&B stations in the country. I'm sitting in the car listening to probably another station when one of the disk jockeys came out and told me, 'Leonard said that he's gonna be here a little longer than he anticipated so you can go ahead and leave.' So, I went to the studio. When I got to the studio I think the guys had gotten kind of discouraged because I hadn't been there for the rehearsal. Everyone decided to go their own separate ways.

"A short while later I'm driving in my car and I turn on the radio and I keep hearing 'And Leonard Chess was . . .' I said, 'Wait a second. This is all past tense.' And finally the announcer mentioned that Leonard Chess died. We immediately went over to Chess and walking into that building was like walking into a tomb. We were in shock. I had just left the man! He had told me in the car, 'I'm getting ready to make you bigger than the Four Tops.' I said, 'Okay, that's fine. Right now I'm still in awe of the success that we're having now. If you want to make us bigger, fine. I'm happy with what we're doing now. I'm not totally satisfied but if you want to make us bigger, go for it.' But . . . it was not meant to be."

Leonard Chess' death created a great deal of instability at the record label. Leonard's son Marshall was named president of Chess Records but was soon replaced by record industry veteran Len Levy, who moved the record company to New York. In 1971, Marvin Schlacter, president of Janus Records, was named president of Chess. Throughout this confusion, the Dells were the one group that carried Chess in the '70s.

Towards the end of 1969, the Dells released one of their finest albums, *Like It Is, Like It Was.* The first two singles, "Oh, What a Day" and "Open Up My Heart," became top 10 hits in the spring of 1970. The group then charted throughout the year with a series of remakes: the Coronets' "Nadine," Lee Andrews and the Hearts' "Long Lonely Nights," and the Five Keys' "The Glory of Love."

"We sustained Chess but we didn't realize it at that time," says Barksdale. "We were kind of caught up in the moment, not really realizing who we were. We didn't have the understanding nor the respect of who we were at that point. People were loving the Dells' records but people didn't know the Dells. The Dells didn't know themselves. In retrospect, we didn't know we were carrying the record company but we *knew* we were carrying the record company. Had we been more business-minded we may have put ourselves in a better financial position with them rather than for them to position us. That's very much what happened. They positioned the Dells into a position where they were in control."

One other personnel change directly impacting the Dells occurred in 1970 when Bobby Miller left Chess to go to Motown. Charles Stepney took over the production of the group, who began this new phase of their career with the release of *Freedom Means* in 1971. The album gave the Dells a hit with "The Love We Had (Stays on My Mind)," a beautiful ballad that reached number eight on the R&B charts that summer.

Barksdale explains, "Stan Hoffman and Marv Schlacter took over Chess after Leonard Chess died. Prior to that, Bobby Miller was shafted. Marshall Chess and Bobby Miller had a dispute and Bobby Miller thought that the grass was greener over at Motown where he did cut a couple of albums. In the meantime, Charles Stepney had pretty much taken over as producer of the Dells. *Freedom Means* was the album that I helped co-produce with Charles Stepney.

" 'The Love We Had [Stays on My Mind],' . . . that's a special song. That one gets me even today some 20 years later. The melody and the lyric content are so together. Plus I had a few experiences that kinda related to the lyrics.

"Stepney was the producer for the most part. The brother

was so heavy. He was a very black-minded man, a very well-informed man; someone who I wish brothers and sisters today could've known. This is another part of us not knowing who we were. Had we really known who we were, we would've never let the unit be divided. Bobby Miller, Charles Stepney and the Dells . . . we were the nucleus of the power and we didn't understand it."

Two subsequent 1972 albums, *The Dells Sing Dionne Warwicke's Greatest Hits* and *Sweet As Funk Can Be,* went nowhere and in 1973, the Dells switched over to Detroit-based producer Don Davis. Davis gave the Dells an updated sound and took them away from the heavy arrangements exhibited on their previous albums. He immediately rejuvenated the group, starting with the title track from the *Give Your Baby a Standing Ovation* album. This tribute to women, which reached number three on the R&B charts in the spring of 1973, was the Dells' only "certified" gold record.

Barksdale explains, "Leonard Chess was not a part of the RIAA, the people who certify gold records. He had his own version of a gold record. We might have sold three million before Leonard Chess would give you a Leonard Chess version of a gold record. We have a wall full of those. The first RIAA-certified gold record we got was for 'Give Your Baby a Standing Ovation' but we know better. 'Stay in My Corner' sold three million and still counting. We weren't paid on three million but these numbers we found out later, years after we started delving more into the business aspect of the industry."

The Dells followed with two more top 10 R&B hits in 1973, "My Pretending Days Are Over" (number 10) and the haunting "I Miss You" (number eight). Further notable songs produced by Davis in 1974 included "I Wish It Was Me You Loved," the funky "Learning to Love You Was Easy (It's So Hard Trying to Get Over You)," and "Bring Back the Love of Yesterday," a smooth, mid-tempo track with Chuck Barksdale on lead.

When Chess folded in 1975, the Dells signed with Mercury Records, where they released *We Got to Get Our Thing Together* (1975) and *No Way Back* (1976). The group's three years on

Mercury proved to be uneventful as the rise of disco in the late '70s brought about the demise of most vocal groups.

"I don't think disco, per se, hurt the Dells," says Barksdale. "Once again, by us not understanding who we were as a mainstay in the business we allowed ourselves to be chewed up by various producers who were trying to get into the disco sound. They wanted us to do a couple of disco songs but that wasn't our forte. You don't do that. You don't mix apples and oranges. It was in bad taste. It was a period of adjustment that we had to go through."

The Dells later recorded for ABC (1978), 20th Century (1981), Private I (1984), Veteran (1988), and Urgent (1989) but with limited commercial success. Despite a less than glorious recording career at this time, the group remained fairly strong on the club circuit.

The Dells received a huge boost in the late '80s when filmmaker Robert Townsend sought out the group to be technical consultants for his new film, *The Five Heartbeats*, originally a comedy about a black vocal group. Barksdale recalls, "We were working at the Wiltern Theater in Los Angeles doing a little mini-tour with the Delfonics. A young lady, Kitty Sears, brought Robert backstage to meet us. After the introductions, he ran it down as to why he really wanted to meet us. He wanted to put together a comedy about black stand-up vocal groups. Well . . . that kinda hit the main vein. Ain't nothing funny about being a black stand-up vocal group, as Marvin [Junior] ran it down to him. It's a very serious situation with black brothers struggling out there on the highway, getting stopped by the police, the racism, not being able to eat where we wanted to eat, staying in the flophouses . . . After Marvin ran it down to him, he said, 'Wait a minute. This isn't what I was going to write about but I like this idea better than the idea about a comedy.'

"Originally he just wanted to use 'Stay in My Corner' and 'Oh, What a Night' as two of the songs that were going to be in the movie. After hearing this from Marvin and the rest of the Dells about the seriousness of the black struggle, the brother wanted to know if it would be alright if he and one or two of his partners followed us around the country.

"People said, 'Man, why would y'all give this guy freedom to do all of this without getting some money?' If we had been the Temptations or the [Four] Tops, the Whispers or brothers that really had their business together and had a manager, then . . . We have no manager. God manages the Dells. I don't know why, but we've encountered many guys who always talked about wanting to manage the Dells. Somehow, something always happened where it just fell through.

"Robert followed us around for about six weeks on this mini-tour, getting information from us on a day-to-day basis, watching the reaction of the crowd to the various songs we sang, watching our dress, watching our mannerisms, taking a little more advice. As far as being technical advisors, about 85 percent of [*The Five Heartbeats*] was about the Dells' life story. The Dells had a cameo part that was supposed to be in the movie. Either 'Stay in My Corner,' which we did in the cameo, didn't fit or they didn't like what they shot. I'd rather think that it just didn't fit rather than us failing our acting debut. Either way, our part wound up on the editing floor."

The Dells' "Stay in My Corner" appeared on the film's 1991 soundtrack along with an original recording, "A Heart Is a House for Love," which was the group's first top 20 R&B hit in well over a decade. "I think to compensate for not appearing in the movie, and it definitely did as far as we were concerned, we were given 'A Heart Is a House for Love' to record," says Barksdale. "We hadn't had a hit record in 18 years. 'A Heart Is a House for Love' was the first hit record that the Dells had in 18 *long* years. So . . . we were quite happy with that."

The success of "A Heart Is a House for Love" also opened the Dells up to a younger audience who were not aware of the rich history of music the group made with their hits from the '60s and early '70s. Barksdale notes, "The young kids today come to concerts now and they're singing the song and they want to meet the Dells, a bunch of old men who've been together for 40 years. Grandmothers are bringing their daughters who are bringing their children. I think this is one of the things we've been blessed to do; to be around to see generations and generations and generations of people still following the Dells. It's just a beautiful feeling."

In 1992 the Dells fulfilled their 20-year dream by working with legendary producers Kenny Gamble and Leon Huff for their *I Salute You* album. "Working with Gamble and Huff was like a dream come true," Barksdale says. "Our album *I Salute You* was truly a labor of love. This was an album that we thought we were going to record with Gamble and Huff in 1972 but ended up recording it in 1992. It was wonderful. The camaraderie was instantaneous."

The *I Salute You* album was released in tandem with the Dells celebrating their 40th anniversary. "God put this group together. There are a lot of groups that have had to endure worse things than we've had to endure. But out of the many, there are only a few. And we've been blessed to be one of the few that are still around today. We're very, *very* thankful. We take nothing for granted. We take it as a blessing. I want to meet these young brothers and sisters out here. I want to be able to let them know that we are very appreciative of what has happened to us over the 40 years."

The Dramatics

A five-man vocal group from Detroit, the Dramatics recorded some of the finest soul music of the early 1970s. Known primarily for their smoldering ballads, such as "In the Rain" and "Hey You! Get Off My Mountain," this quintet displayed their versatility and were equally successful with up-tempo tracks, notably "Whatcha See Is Whatcha Get" and "Get Up and Get Down." With stunning choreography and stage presence, and featuring a lineup that included three singers who could assume the lead, the Dramatics, unlike many stand-up vocal groups of the era, were able to attain their popularity during the disco period and become one of the biggest soul groups of the decade.

The Dramatics, originally known as the Dynamics, formed at Pershing High School in Detroit in 1964. The original members were Ron Banks (lead and first tenor), Larry Reed (second tenor), Elbert Wilkins (first and second tenor), Larry "Squirrel" Demps (baritone), Robert "Duke" Ellington (bass), and Roderick Davis (bass). All attended Pershing High School with the exception of Banks, who was attending Cleveland Junior High. The teenagers, heavily influenced by their idols, the Temptations, began their career performing in local halls and clubs.

Lead singer Ron Banks recalls, "We met at a talent show out on the tennis courts of Pershing High School. At the time everybody was in a different group. We ended up getting together, bringing in a couple of cats out of each group, and we just became a group of our own. I was 12 at the time.

"We were definitely influenced by the Temptations as well as the other groups that came under the Motown stable. We were impressed by how polished they used to be, how determined they were to be successful, and then by the total outcome of the proper ingredients put together by Berry Gordy and his whole staff that he had over there. Eddie [Kendricks] was one of the people I studied when I was coming up. Eddie had the best melody going. Eddie could make a melody out of a song. I studied Curtis Mayfield for pronunciation and the way he could dictate a song, and then Nancy Wilson, probably for performance."

Ellington soon dropped out of the group to continue his studies. In 1965, while the quintet was performing at a local talent show called Mr. Kelly's, they met the niece of Ed Wingate, who owned Wingate Records. Wingate's niece set up an audition for the group on a Sunday and Wingate signed them the following day. They recorded three songs for the Wingate label, most notably "Inky Dinky Wang Dan Doo," but the songs were met with little fanfare. The label folded in the latter part of 1966. In 1967, the quintet signed with Sport Records and had a moderate hit with "All Because of You" (number 43, R&B). By now they were known as the Dramatics, a name chosen by Demps. The move to Sport Records came a year after the Dramatics passed up a possible opportunity to sign with Motown for fear of being lost in the shuffle.

"That was one of the things we were concerned about even at that young age," notes Banks. "We had an opportunity to go to Motown in '66 when Berry Gordy purchased Golden World Records from Ed Wingate. We had the opportunity to possibly sign but at that time they had 70 acts signed to the roster already. They probably weren't doing anything with them except maybe eight, and five of them would get a song maybe once every three or four years. So we said we'll take our chances another way because there had to be somebody else who was looking for another group that was trying as hard as we were trying, and the Lord blessed us with some great guidance with many people throughout our career."

In 1969, the Dramatics were signed to Memphis-based Stax Records through Don Davis, a one-time session guitar player for the Golden World label, who was now one of Detroit's most successful non-Motown producers. The revised lineup now included Banks, Wilkins, Demps, William "Wee Gee" Howard (baritone), and Willie Ford (bass). Their first single, the Temptations-flavored "Your Love Was Strange," featured Howard on lead, and the record flopped. The following year Stax dropped the group.

"We hooked up with Stax through Don Davis who was recording Johnnie Taylor at the time," recounts Banks. "We had an in line with him from when he was at Golden World with Ed Wingate while we were there. He knew of us."

The Dramatics maintained their relationship with Davis and spent 1970 working with former Motown talent developer Dick Scott. In 1971 Davis put the quintet in touch with his songwriter-producer associate, Tony Hester. This proved to be the turning point in the group's career. Hester wrote and produced a series of songs that got the Dramatics re-signed to the Stax/Volt label, and ended up being the material for their first album.

Banks remembers, "We got with Tony Hester and he showed us the songs off of [what would be] our first album, which included 'Whatcha See Is Whatcha Get,' 'In the Rain,' 'Fall in Love Lady Love,' and 'Thankful for Your Love,' and we went back to the studio and recorded those songs. Don Davis took them back and presented them to Stax and they were just truly elated about it, and it just helped us believe in what we were trying to do. At that time we might have been at a young age, but eight years is a long time to try to be successful. We were finally getting ready to get our first national million-seller when that happened and we were just elated and extremely blessed. Then we knew it was really time to go to work."

The album, titled *Whatcha See Is Whatcha Get,* produced three solid hits. The first release was the mid-tempo, Latin-flavored title track. Featuring the baritone of Howard for 90 percent of the song, "Whatcha See Is Whatcha Get" was a top

10 pop and R&B hit in the summer of 1971, and the group's first million-seller. The song was released at a time when comic Flip Wilson popularized the phrase "Whatcha see is whatcha get" on his variety television show, then the number-two-rated program in the country.

"I definitely think that Tony did [the phrase] from *The Flip Wilson Show*," says Banks, "but he had a clever way that he put it. He put 'Whatcha See Is Whatcha Get' through a love situation, and I thought that was deep."

The Dramatics followed with "Get Up and Get Down," a Temptations-styled funk track calling everyone to the dance floor, which became a top 20 R&B hit late in 1971. The group's next single would be their biggest seller. Released in early 1972, the ballad "In the Rain" featured the tenor of Banks on lead vocal, and was highlighted by the use of a thunderstorm for sound effects. This moody soul classic topped the R&B charts for four weeks and was the group's second top 10 pop hit and million-seller. The *Whatcha See Is Whatcha Get* album was further enhanced by the ballads, the appreciative "Thankful for Your Love" and "Fall in Love Lady Love."

"We felt like any young kid would feel to see a dream come true," says Banks on the group's initial success. "We were living the dream come true but because of our upbringing we knew it was time for us to establish ourselves beyond just one-hit artists from 'Whatcha See Is Whatcha Get.' And then we also knew one thing, that our work was cut out for us because people were now listening to us. Now we had to make certain that every cut, every song we sang, we sang it like it was going to be a million-seller. With that type of determination, and definitely through the blessings of Jesus Christ, we had belief that we could do it."

The group added to its newfound success by seizing the opportunity to be the opening act on an eight-month tour with James Brown. "We actually toured with James Brown for three years," says Banks. "It started out as a weekend tryout and we, along with the Stylistics, ended up with him for three years. That's when the Stylistics and the Dramatics got so close.

James was historically known for picking up the new artists with the new hit records. He messed around there and he had us, and then the Stylistics hit up. He looked around and every record that each of us put out was a top hit record, so he didn't have to look any further.

"We had a built-in show and it was truly a blessing in dis guise for us because we had the opportunity with James to perform, where we may have been singing on shows that might have been a sellout, maybe a lot of clubs, we ended up performing in front of nothing but coliseum crowds where every performance you were doing anywhere from 10 to 15 thousand a night. Consequently, that many people got a chance to see you perform and in time, as records got bigger and better for those three years between '71 and '74, the world was really just getting to know us. But . . . being able to perform in front of that many people, you're talking about four to five times a night, all kinds of cities and places, it was definitely a step in the right direction."

In the spring of 1973, the Dramatics released the ballad "Hey You! Get Off My Mountain," which was their third top five R&B hit. The group then followed with the melodic, midtempo "Fell for You." Both songs were featured on the album *A Dramatic Experience.* However, the album was more noted for the three Hester-penned songs that condemned drug abuse: "The Devil Is Dope," "Beware of the Man (With the Candy in His Hand)," and "Jim, What's Wrong with Him."

Banks explains, "[These songs] were anti-drug songs which actually were much before their acceptance as far as radio play. We almost ended up going underground with that album. We were lucky to have record smashes and radio play with 'Hey You! Get Off My Mountain,' and then 'Fell for You' but the message songs were underground and that's why they were buying [the album] so much. All of the cats who were into getting high and the ones who didn't want to get high were buying them, and playing them, and singing them to each other, and then we looked up and damn near had a cult following. A lot of people who didn't know us from our records, or *Soul Train,* or the James Brown shows, that didn't have the money to do that, got a chance to start hearing us when ordinarily they wouldn't have. We got real close to a lot of the cats in the streets because they understood where we were coming from. We knew overall that the dope was not good for our people so we weren't knocking what they were doing but at the same time, we were. We were saying, hopefully you're not using it but if you are, just remember this while you're doing it. Maybe you'll stop quicker so you don't get hooked. That was the message through all that stuff."

By this time William Howard and Elbert Wilkins had left the group. After leaving the Dramatics, Wilkins registered the group name for himself, and along with Howard, added Dupree Sims and Isaac Reed to form a second set of Dramatics. This group signed to Mainstream Records, but only got the chance to release one single, "No Rebate on Love," which peaked at number 26 on the R&B charts in the fall of 1975.

Wilkins and Howard were replaced in the original group by Lenny Mayes and L. J. Reynolds. Prior to joining the Dramatics, Mayes sang with a local Detroit group called Sunrise Movement. Reynolds, a native of Saginaw, Michigan, had been a member of Chocolate Syrup, famed for the song "Let One Hurt Do." At the urging of Don Davis and Stax Records, the original unit changed its billing to "Ron Banks and the Dramatics." These two sets of Dramatics toured the concert circuit for four years before Banks' group won a court battle, giving them full access to the name.

Don Davis and Jimmy Roach took over production for the *Dramatically Yours* album, released in 1974. The ballad, "Toast to the Fool," actually released two years earlier, was the album's most successful single and was a top 20 R&B hit. The popular "And I Panicked" was released almost as an afterthought and resulted in the group's poorest chart showing, peaking at number 49. However, at this time Stax Records was beset with financial problems that would soon lead to the label's collapse.

The Dramatics left Stax in 1974 for a short stay at Cadet, a subsidiary of Chess Records. Their one album recorded on

Cadet was a collaboration with the Dells entitled *The Dells vs. The Dramatics*. The Dramatics sang four of the album's nine songs and paired with the Dells on an additional two, most notably the ballad "Love Is Missing from Our Lives," which achieved modest chart success in the summer of 1975 (number 46, R&B).

"We wanted to test the waters at Chess," explains Banks. "We really weren't that overwhelmed with what they were doing with some of their artists but we had an opportunity to sign and do a one-album deal with them called *The Dells vs. The Dramatics*. In all reality this was a young group with an experienced group that took us under their wing and was willing to help us get a little further in our career. We had the opportunity to work with a more established group and at that time we weren't 'smelling our pee' because we knew we had so much further that we wanted to travel. Us being united with the almighty Dells . . . hey, let's do it. We did it and it became a great success for us because it gave us an older audience. This was added to the younger audience that we had, plus the ones that were already buying records, not just buying records but would come to your show. Now we got a chance to create a club atmosphere crowd so we could do the concerts and when the concert season was damn near over, we could go back through all those major markets and even some secondary markets, plus some third markets and major clubs and play the club market.

"That was the key to our whole success because our strong suit has always been our live performance. Now we had a chance to work them from the clubs so when it came to the concerts, we already had a built-in audience that knew about us. All we had to do was serve 'em up right at the concerts. It's easier said than done. It's just a challenge that we accepted because we believe that if they spend the money and time to come see you, then you need to go to work and kill 'em."

Also of significance with the album was the finale of the group's musical relationship with the late Tony Hester. From the album, Hester produced three singles that charted: "Choosing Up on You," backed with the eerie "Door to Your Heart" in the summer of 1974, and "Don't Make Me No Promises" later that fall. Recalling the group's collaboration with Hester, Banks says, "Man . . . the world misses a Tony Hester. He was a genius with a pen and he had his own route of getting what he wanted to get out of you. You had to sing his melodies. You could do your own thing but you had to sing his melodies, maybe 70 percent of the song; and his melodies and his approach were just one of a kind."

The following year the Dramatics moved to ABC. The group's move to ABC came at the beginning of the disco phenomenon. Unlike their vocal contemporaries who were known strictly for their tenor-dominated ballads, the Dramatics varied the tempo with their biggest hits and featured the baritone of William Howard and later L.J. Reynolds as much, if not more than the tenor of Banks. As a result the Dramatics were able to establish their own identity and did not suffer a decline in popularity during the run of disco.

Banks explains, "[Motown producer] Norman Whitfield taught us something when we were very young, even before we had our first songs out, 'Your Love Is Strange' and 'Whatcha See Is Whatcha Get,' to create our own identity. Because we came up in an umbrella of five singers out of Detroit, people would always look at us initially and say, 'They sing damn near as good as the Temptations.' You can't run behind the Temptations. The Temptations are an institution. We had to create some diversity and a sound that was Dramatics' way. Fortunately we were able to do that with the different vocal styles we had. We had a lot of the same arsenal that the Temptations had but we had to do it our way 'cause there ain't but one Temptations."

The Dramatics began 1975 with the release of "Me and Mrs. Jones," a cover of the 1972 Billy Paul classic. The remake brought the Dramatics back to the top 10 as their version peaked at number four on the R&B charts. " 'Me and Mrs. Jones' was a song that we did in our live show for many years and it was very popular with our club crowd," says Banks. "We had turned in an album at ABC and Otis Smith, who was the president of black music there, asked us if we had another song that we could put on the album. We went back home and recut 'Me and Mrs. Jones' and we submitted it. The next thing we knew that was the lead song. They wouldn't even take it off the album for a long time because they wanted to make [the public] buy the album. It was just a great song from the beginning when Gamble and Huff did it on Billy Paul. It was a great performance by Billy Paul and we wanted to do it how a group would do it, the Dramatics' way."

The Dramatics followed with "(I'm Going By) The Stars in Your Eyes" in the summer of 1975 and "You're Fooling You" later that year. Beginning late in 1976, the quintet had three straight top 10 hits, starting with "Be My Girl," a beautiful ballad which peaked at number three. They followed with "I Can't Get Over You" and "Shake It Well." The latter was a funk track completely out of character for the group, which surprisingly became one of their biggest hits, peaking at number four in the summer of 1977.

Banks notes, "We had tremendous support at ABC. Otis Smith made certain that we got a lot of visibility. The team of Otis Smith, ABC's machinery, our management, our determination, and the people that we had around us who were rooting for us all contributed to our success. All of the cats at the radio stations were really behind us. They gave us an opportunity and that's when it really happened; when we were at ABC. Cats that even promoted the records, their staff was A-number one with us. So many people helped us independently it was just a massive onslaught to make certain things happened for us to keep us competitive because there were so many artists that were hitting behind us like Rufus and Chaka Khan, Earth, Wind and Fire, Maze, the Emotions. There were a bunch of them out there. If you wanted to create some identity, you had to get your own thing, so we brought our fire."

In 1978, the core of the group began to unravel. Banks began to turn his attention to the Brides of Funkenstein, an offshoot of George Clinton's Parliament/Funkadelic band. He also became involved with outside production work. In 1979 he wrote and produced "Why Leave Us Alone," a top 10 hit for the group Five Special, of which his brother Bryan was a member.

"I wrote ['Why Leave Us Alone'] for us, which as it turned out would've been a monster smash on the Dramatics," says Banks. "The guy we had been with, Don Davis, wanted all of my publishing on the tune. By this time we had gotten somewhat wise, executively. I wasn't about to write this tune and give him all of the publishing, so I decided to cut this on my brother and his group. I knew they had a group that had a lot of talented cats in it. [Davis] had no idea that record would be that big. There's no way in the world he would've let that record get away from the Dramatics, but he did."

In 1980, Demps and Reynolds left — Reynolds for a solo career. Craig Jones was added and the Dramatics continued as a quartet. The group completed its stay at MCA (which had previously acquired ABC) and signed with Capitol Records. Banks handled production and co-wrote six of the eight songs that appeared on their first Capitol album, *New Dimensions*, including two singles which charted in 1982: "Live It Up" and "Treat Me Right." The following year the group disbanded for five years.

Banks explains, "We just felt that we had become too stagnated and everybody was individually thinking about trying to do other things; producing other acts and solo albums. I think, with the frustration of the business and all of our time and effort, we needed a break. It might've been the best thing that ever happened to us, the fact that we went on a hiatus between '82 and '87 because when we got back together we realized the audience that we had, maybe we took some of that for granted during our later years in the 1970s and early 1980s. Maybe that's why we had become so frustrated. We had forgotten what was really happening. We had already had an audience. But when we got back together we realized the audience that we still did have, and it was just something to realize that the Dramatics will always be the trump card. We don't care whatever else we do individually, whether it be solo albums or producing other artists. That's great but when we know that we can tour and sing in front of hundreds of thousands of people every year *without* a current record, then we know we're getting ready to serve them right up."

In 1987, Banks, Reynolds, Howard, Mayes, and Ford reunited to record *A Dramatic Reunion* on Fantasy Records. Two years later they released *Positive State of Mind*. In 1991 the group consisted of Banks, Reynolds, Mayes, and Ford. The legacy of the Dramatics provided a boost in 1993 when new gangsta rap sensation Snoop Doggy Dogg sought out the group to sing vocals on "Doggy Dogg World," the third single released from his multi-platinum *Doggy-Style* album.

"It's amazing how that happened," says Banks. "We were just going in there to sing some stuff behind a cat who was supposed to be a new rapper. We didn't know this cat was getting ready to sell five million albums in 17 days. This cat is *huge*. He said he wanted some real singers. He didn't want samples, so he picked us. He said that his mom and dad used to play us all the time in his house, so this brother was down with the Dramatics. It was really a dream come true and a blessing in disguise."

The Dramatics today remain a popular nightclub attraction here and abroad and perform an average of two to three times a month, usually in tandem with the Stylistics and the Chi-Lites. "We locked up with the Stylistics and the Chi-Lites and between the three there's a lot of history and hit records. You can see that everybody takes a lot of pride in what we're doing and we do it as a cohesive unit. It's not a situation where 'let me do better than you.' Our situation is 'let us all do great.' It's the same way when we work with others like Ray, Goodman and Brown or the Manhattans. We've gotten to the point where we realize that, collectively, we're an equal success; individually, you're standing alone. But the power is being united together and you have to find the right chemistry for what works for you at that particular time. I also think it's important for whichever one of us might break out and have a hit record to watch out for the other acts. You try to help them along until they run up on a smash. Today might be my day but tomorrow might be yours. That's my philosophy."

The Emotions

A family trio of sisters, the Emotions made a switch from gospel to secular music in the late 1960s and became arguably the most successful black female group of the 1970s. Recording for the Stax label early in the decade, the Hutchinson siblings cut a series of soulful songs enriched by their sweet, gospel-tinged harmonies, particularly on "So I Can Love You" and "Show Me How." However, the group had their biggest success in the latter part of the decade, with hits like "Best of My Love" and "Don't Ask My Neighbors," under the guidance of Earth, Wind and Fire's Maurice White.

Sheila, Wanda, and Jeanette Hutchinson, who hail from Chicago, began performing at ages three, four, and five, respectively, under the guidance of their father Joe, Sr. Originally called the Heavenly Sunbeams, and later the Hutchinson Sunbeams, the trio performed with their father as a gospel unit from 1956 until 1968. During this time they toured with the likes of Mahalia Jackson, the Soul Stirrers, and the Mighty Clouds of Joy.

Wanda remembers, "We were born in 1950 [Jeanette], '51 [Wanda], and '53 [Sheila]. The first 13 or 14 years of our lives we were going around with my father's group out of Terre Haute, Indiana that his mother had started, and they were called the Hutchinson Terre Haute Sunbeams. That's where we later got our gospel name, the Hutchinson Sunbeams.

"My father had a group called the Wings of Heaven and we would go to all of their church programs where they would sing. Because we were in all of the rehearsals, we would sing the songs and people would turn around and watch us sing instead of his group. It really didn't dawn on him to have us singing as a group, not at that age. We started singing the songs and he would give us parts. That was his thing in the group; he gave people parts. We started singing at the landlord's church; that's how we actually started singing.

"The first show we ever did was *The Jerry Van Dyke Show* in Terre Haute. It was a talent show and the first song we sang was 'Tell Him What You Want.' It was a gospel song that Albertina Walker made famous."

Beginning in 1962, the group became Three Ribbons and a Bow (Joe, Sr. was the beau), and recorded an unsuccessful series of singles for such Chicago labels as One-der-ful, Vee-Jay, and Twin Stacks. Only their 1967 Twin Stacks single "Bush Fire" created enough noise in their hometown that it was picked up for national distribution by Bell Records.

In 1968 the trio won a talent contest at the Regal Theater in Chicago. The first prize was a recording contract with Memphis-based Stax/Volt Records. Other reports differ, stating that while on tour, they met the Staple Singers, who helped them get a recording contract with Stax. Actually, it was a combination of both.

Wanda explains, "In '68 and '69 when we went to Chicago we would go to the Staple Singers' church and my father met Pervis and Pops Staples and all of them. At that time both of us were still gospel groups. We started singing there just about every Sunday and we would go around to different churches.

"On Wednesday night it was talent show night at the Regal Theater. On the particular night that we sang, the Five Stairsteps auditioned. We won, and the first prize was a record contract with Stax Records. Pervis talked to my father that night and asked to manage us, and he convinced my father that we should do rhythm and blues instead of gospel."

Changing their name to the Emotions, the trio made the transition from gospel to secular music without any difficulty. Never a hard-run, gut-wrenching gospel act to being with, the girls placed their emphasis on the harmony. In their songs they often had the lead parts harmonized as opposed to featuring one singer up front. "The way my father constructed our harmonies was to have us sing in a manner that the harmony itself was the lead," says Wanda. "Whatever the arrangement was, one girl would sing a line, another girl would sing another line, and then each one would always have a verse."

Upon their arrival at Stax, the Emotions were assigned to hit-making writing and producing duo Isaac Hayes and David Porter. The group's first single was "So I Can Love You," written by Sheila Hutchinson. With the production of Hayes and Porter adding a warm and soulful touch to the sisters' gospel-tinged harmonies, "So I Can Love You" rose to number three on the R&B charts and cracked the pop top 40 in the spring of 1969. "It felt good, having your friends at school tell you, 'I heard you on the radio' and to hear yourself and know that you helped write the song," says Wanda. "It felt cool. I remember us studying on the road and getting a lot of homework done while we were on the road. The teachers gave us more work to do because they felt we would miss out on something, but it was very cool."

Over the next two years Hayes and Porter wrote and produced a series of songs for the Emotions which fared well on the R&B charts and made them an important act on the Stax label. With each single, Hayes and Porter created a heartfelt and passionate atmosphere tied around the superior harmonies of the group. Among them were "The Best Part of a Love Affair"; "Stealing Love," a perky mid-tempo track backed by the touching ballad "When Tomorrow Comes"; and perhaps the group's finest output on the Stax label, "Show Me How," a sensuous ballad that became a top 15 hit in the fall of 1971.

"It was fabulous working with Isaac Hayes," says Wanda. "We always thought he really cared about what we thought about the music. That was unusual. We found out later how unusual that was. It was very good."

However, by 1971, Isaac Hayes had achieved superstar status as a solo performer, leaving the Emotions to be shuffled between various in-house producers. Also at this time, Jeanette

Hutchinson left the group to get married, and was replaced for four years by Theresa Davis. For the remainder of their tenure on the Stax label, the Emotions had minor success in 1972 with "My Honey and Me," and "I Could Never Be Happy," a song very similar in style to the Diana Ross version of "Ain't No Mountain High Enough."

After Stax Records folded in 1975, the Emotions spent time writing songs and touring sporadically. By now Jeanette was back in the group. The following year they came in contact with Maurice White, who played in a Chicago music revue with the girls in the '60s when they were still known as the Hutchinson Sunbeams. White was now leader of the group Earth, Wind and Fire. Introducing a blend of jazz, funk and soul, by 1975 Earth, Wind and Fire had attained astounding success and was in the process of becoming one of the decade's top acts.

Wanda recalls, "A friend of ours, Ron Ellison, knew Charles Stepney and he told my father, 'You know, Charles Stepney's over here. He's done Minnie Riperton, he's working with Ramsey [Lewis] and Maurice [White]. You should bring the girls over.' We went over to Charles Stepney's house and Charles asked us if we had any songs. Since the time we wrote 'So I Can Love You' we wrote *a lot* of songs. He had some songs but he put them aside when he heard ours. I was playing the piano and the first songs that I played for him were 'I Don't Wanna Lose Your Love,' 'How Can You Stop Loving Someone,' and 'No Plans for Tomorrow,' the songs that ended up being on the *Flowers* album."

It was through Stepney that the Emotions connected with White, who signed them to his Kalimba Productions and brought the trio to Columbia Records. An association with White was significant because the Emotions were able not only to survive the disco era, but also thrive during this period. While most female R&B vocal groups who found success during the early 1970s faded away during the height of the disco period, the Emotions found a new level of commercial success. Wanda points out, "Because of Maurice being with Earth,

Wind and Fire, and them having that groove that was happening at that time, it helped us. He put that groove with our vocal harmony and it went through the disco period. Because [Earth, Wind and Fire] was an instrumental group, I always felt like we were the vocal part of his horn arrangements."

In 1976 White and Stepney produced the Emotions' first Columbia album, *Flowers,* on which the sisters wrote five of the nine songs. White and Stepney updated the sisters' gospel-flavored harmonies, yet they showed enough appreciation for the group's sound to not allow their vocals to be flooded out by heavy arrangements. The first entry was the smooth, mid-tempo "Flowers," backed by the dance track "I Don't Wanna Lose Your Love"; both became top 20 R&B hits. Wanda initially wrote "I Don't Wanna Lose Your Love" as a ballad, but White decided to speed it up. Further enhanced by Wanda's beautiful ballad, "How Can You Stop Loving Someone," the *Flowers* album was certified gold.

"When we recorded *Flowers* we did it in Chicago and, because most of the songs were songs we already knew, it took us exactly one week to record it with all of the vocals on the album. That's why I don't understand the extremely high budgets right now. We did the *Rejoice* album [in California] and the budget for that one was five times the amount."

After the *Flowers* album Jeanette left again to stay home with her family and was replaced by younger sister Pamela. The group's next album, *Rejoice,* recorded in 1977, contained what would become the Emotions' biggest hit, "Best of My Love." For this song Wanda had to sing her vocals an octave higher than usual. The change worked, adding an exuberance to the dance track that earned the sisters a gold record for selling over a million copies. "Best of My Love" topped the R&B charts for four weeks and the pop charts for five weeks in the summer of 1977, and later won the group a Grammy for best R&B vocal performance by a duo, group or chorus.

"Working with Maurice was exciting but it could also be a challenge," says Wanda. "I used to always sing low-key and he got me to sing a lot higher than I thought I could, like on 'Best of My Love.' He established the lead singer by the tempo of the song. I did the up-tempo songs and the gospel stuff, Sheila would sing all of the ballads, and Jeanette, the in-between stuff.

"I remember Maurice saying there was another song at that time called 'Best of My Love' [by the Eagles], and he seemed to think the fact that it was out nearly the same time helped our song go pop."

There were several more outstanding tracks from the *Rejoice* album that became popular. The follow-up to "Best of My Love" was the Skip Scarborough-penned ballad "Don't Ask My Neighbors," which became the group's second straight R&B top 10 hit. White was more comfortable working with the Emotions on the second album and added the trademark Earth, Wind and Fire ingredients, particularly horns, to the group's vocals. The production on tracks such as "Key to My Heart," "Blessed," and "How'd I Know That Love Would Slip Away" solidified Wanda's claim of the group being the vocal part of White's horn arrangements. *Rejoice* topped the R&B charts for seven weeks, made the pop top 10, and was certified platinum.

"When we were doing *The Jerry Van Dyke Show* and in-between the first recording contract, we were for three or four years on a gospel radio show called Jubilee's Showcase and my father would always tell them, 'One day, you're gonna see my girls; they'll be bigger than bubble gum.' He would always end the program with that. When 'Best of My Love' was out and we were backstage somewhere in Philadelphia, the manager came back and told us we just won the Grammy nomination, and that was the first thing I thought of, 'Oh, this is what Dad was talking about. I guess we're bigger than bubble gum now.'

"It was so much excitement then, and being nervous all the time before you went on stage. I think I took it a little harder than the rest. When we went to New York and this fan club thing started up, that was something we really weren't used to. They had some type of initiation where these 50 girls came and stayed in our room in New York and they asked you all these questions. They started sending out all this information to these teen magazines and we started getting people to write in. We were wondering what made people do this. I was never a fan of anyone. But it was fun. We're still in touch with the girl who was president of the fan club and she became like a sister to us."

In the summer of 1978, *Sunbeam*, the group's third album produced by White, was released. The single "Smile" reached number six on the R&B charts. Further singles from the album to chart were "Whole Lot of Shakin'" and "Walking the Line." By this time Jeanette rejoined the group, replacing Pamela, who resumed her studies. The following summer the Emotions collaborated with Earth, Wind and Fire on the energetic "Boogie Wonderland," which became a top 10 hit on both the pop and R&B charts.

When Maurice White started his own ARC label (distributed by Columbia), the Emotions followed. Their first release on the new label was *Come into Our World*. In addition to containing "Boogie Wonderland," the singles "What's the Name of Your Love" and "Where Is Your Love" charted. The following year Wanda, along with her husband Wayne Vaughan, co-wrote Earth, Wind and Fire's 1981 smash hit "Let's Groove." The Emotions later recorded the highly acclaimed *Sincerely* on Chicago-based Red Label Records in 1984 but met with limited success. At this time Jeanette was replaced by Adrienne Harris. After switching to Motown for *If Only I Knew* the following year, the sisters stopped recording.

"We agreed to sit down and have families," explains Wanda. "I have five kids. We didn't want to be traveling up and down the road during those years. Since we were out here in California we got hooked into the unions where you do commercial work. I did a lot of consulting with different record companies to help them with their groups and arrangements. I kinda like that. I was doing exactly what I wanted to do and not having to run up and down the road and still could be pregnant and work. Jeanette has gotten into so many choirs that she's in. We were all still involved in music. Sheila did go into hairdressing for awhile in Chicago and she did all of the Johnson Afro Sheen commercials, so she stayed home with my mother in Chicago."

Although the sisters are no longer in the mainstream of popular music, their sound has not been forgotten. "Don't Ask My Neighbors" has become something of a classic, gaining more recognition as time passed than it did in 1977, as the follow-up to "Best of My Love." Legendary singer Nancy Wilson covered the song on her 1990 *A Lady with a Song* album and featured the Emotions in the video. "I know Nancy and her dear friend Dionne Warwick, whom we keep in touch with," explains Wanda. "Through Dionne we were able to hook up with Nancy. She was playing at the Strand [in California] and she asked us to come through. She called us on stage and we all sang it that night and we went in and cut the video with Philip Bailey. Sheila was in the hospital at the time so Philip did the video with us."

In 1991 it was widely speculated that new pop sensation Mariah Carey heavily sampled the rhythm track and "whoa-whoa" hook from "Best of My Love" for her hit song "Emotions." Two years later there was a heavy influence of "So I Can Love You" in Carey's hit song "Dreamlover." "That's really something because if we could prove it we'd be in the money," says Wanda. "But the attention from when she came out in '91 with that 'Emotions' tune . . . We were in Chicago doing a performance at the Regal Theater because it was homecoming week. People who knew us were outraged that we let her do that and saying that they went to the store thinking it was us. You just didn't know people felt like that and we kinda felt great about it. It was as if they were honoring us."

In 1994 the sisters returned to the recording studio to begin work on a gospel album which they plan to have released independently.

First Choice

With the combination of a Philadelphia-MFSB dance beat and lyrics about a flamboyant black urban lifestyle on songs such as "Armed and Extremely Dangerous" and "The Player," First Choice was very popular with black audiences in the early 1970s. Being primarily associated with dance music, this female trio from Philadelphia, led by Rochelle Fleming, was one of very few R&B stand-up vocal groups to retain its popularity in the disco era.

First Choice, originally a quintet led by Rochelle Fleming and Annette Guest, formed in 1971 while each member still attended Overbrook High School in Philadelphia. After performing at local talent shows and informal gatherings, the group decided they could sing as well as some of the entertainers they heard on the radio and went to radio station WDAS to see Georgie Woods, the city's top disk jockey.

Lead singer Rochelle Fleming remembers, "I formed the group in the ninth grade. I always wanted to sing and I started to get serious about it around the ninth and tenth grade. In the beginning there were five of us. Annette Guest and myself were the originals. We couldn't even come up with a name. We rehearsed in her mother's house and started appearing in talent shows.

"We finally got up enough nerve to go see Georgie Woods, who was a big disk jockey at WDAS in Philly. We went to his office, very boldly, and told him that we could sing and we wanted to sing for him. He came with us to Annette's mother's house because it was close to the radio station. I was the lead singer so I did most of the singing. We brought him a lot of Aretha [Franklin] and he was totally amazed at us. He was just totally shocked. He just couldn't believe we had that kind of talent."

Through Woods, the girls met producer/songwriter Norman Harris, and Stan Watson, who previously managed the Delfonics. "Georgie called Norman Harris on the phone and told him about us," recalls Fleming. "Norman said, 'Are you sure this isn't a hoax?' And Georgie Woods said, 'No, I'm telling you, these girls can *sing.*' Soon afterwards, Norman Harris heard us and he loved us. Norman, at the time, didn't want to manage so he introduced us to Stan Watson whom we liked right away."

By this time the group was down to a quartet consisting of Fleming, Guest, Wardell Piper, and Mulaney Star. Norman Harris and Allan Felder wrote the group's first song, the frantic "This Is the House Where Love Died." The song was leased to New York's Wand/Sceptor label in 1972 and flopped. Soon afterwards, Mulaney Star left to settle into domestic life.

The following year First Choice signed with the Philly Groove label in their hometown for their second single, "Armed and Extremely Dangerous." This campy single, a warning about the potential of being jilted by a lover, combined with an infectious MFSB Philly dance beat, became a top 30 pop hit, peaking at number 11 on the R&B charts and selling nearly a million copies.

"We were surprised when 'Armed and Extremely Dangerous' became a hit," says Fleming, "especially after the first [song]. We were 18 years old, graduating from high school and marching down the aisle and kids at the ceremony were looking at us and saying, 'Those are the girls with the song on the radio.' It was just a great feeling."

After First Choice recorded "Armed and Extremely Dangerous," Wardell Piper left the group. She later became a disco singer and had a top 20 hit in 1979 with "Super Sweet." Her spot was taken over by Joyce Jones. The success of "Dangerous" led to an appearance at New York's prestigious Copacabana with the Stylistics, a startling leap for a new group singing primarily black music. "The Stylistics were friends of ours from back in the day," notes Fleming. "I knew Russell [Thompkins] very well. It was a very exciting time for us to be playing the Copa with them. Stevie Wonder was in the audience. He came onstage to sing 'Armed and Extremely Dangerous' with us and he knew every lyric. Afterwards he took pictures with us and told us that we were extremely talented and would go very far. That was the highlight of the experience."

First Choice followed "Armed and Extremely Dangerous" with the popular "Smarty Pants" in the fall of 1973, and "Newsy Neighbors" early the following year. All three songs and a popular remake of Al Green's "Love and Happiness" appeared on the group's first album, *First Choice — Armed and Extremely Dangerous.* In recognition of their early success, *Cash Box* and *Record World* named them 1973's best new rhythm and blues female vocal group.

The trio was unable to retain its success on the pop charts because their future singles were aimed exclusively at the black audience. This was epitomized by their next single, "The Player," released in the summer of 1974. On the surface, "The Player" was similar to "Armed and Extremely Dangerous" in terms of its Philly dance beat and warning about the potential of being heartbroken. However, while "Dangerous" was clean and somewhat gimmicky, the theme of "The Player" centered on an inner-city hustler. This was done primarily to capitalize on the popularity of the leading characters of several "blaxploitation" films of that period, such as *Shaft, Superfly,* and *The Mack.* The black audience bought it up as "The Player" became First Choice's only top 10 R&B hit, peaking at number seven.

"We weren't concerned with crossover back then,' says Fleming. "Whereas today crossover is totally important, back then we felt that it was more important to play for a black audience."

After "Guilty" became a top 20 hit in 1975, First Choice left Philly Groove for Warner Bros. Records. Also at this time Joyce Jones left the group and was replaced by Ursula Herring.

Despite high expectations, including an appearance at the label's massive four-day series of concerts called California Soul, First Choice's career at Warner was short-lived. Their 1976 album *So Let Us Entertain You* produced only a minor hit in "Gotta Get Away (From You)." The following year they signed with Salsoul Records.

"When we left Warner for Salsoul we couldn't believe it," says Fleming. "When we signed with Warner we thought we would be with them for awhile. It was hyped, the press was really into the group and then two months later we signed with Salsoul. We never even heard of them. We were *very* upset and we voiced our opinions about it. We just couldn't understand why we were leaving a big record label."

The move to Salsoul Records turned out to be a blessing in disguise for First Choice. The disco phenomenon was in full bloom by then and Salsoul Records, led by the Salsoul Orchestra ("You're Just the Right Size," "Nice and Nasty") and Double Exposure ("Ten Percent," "My Love Is Free"), was a front-runner among record labels cashing in on disco. Although the rise of disco severely hindered most R&B stand-up vocal groups, First Choice did not suffer a decline in popularity. Fortunately for them, their two biggest hits, "Armed and Extremely Dangerous" and "The Player," were dance records and established a foundation for the group to be associated with dance music. First Choice also benefited from the racism in the music industry, which for a time labeled all black dance music as disco. Although the group's sound never did actually change, First Choice was quickly classified as a disco group. This classification also made it appear as if First Choice was singing disco as far back as 1973's "Armed and Extremely Dangerous."

Fleming points out, "Making a transition to disco was no problem at all for us. From the beginning we were used to dance music and songs that had extended tracks; that's how Norman [Harris] wrote for us. When we performed, the clubs would pump up the extended track on songs that were long enough to do so, so making a transition to disco was no trouble at all."

The trio's first album on Salsoul, *Delusions*, was one of their finest, and produced three solid hits. The first release, "Doctor Love," issued in the summer of 1977, was a massive disco hit that, according to Fleming, "brought our morale back up after leaving Warner." This was followed by a cover of Stevie Wonder's "Love Having You Around," and the popular "Let No Man Put Asunder," which would become more widely recognized by its repeated phrase, "it's not over."

First Choice followed *Delusions* with the equally impressive *Hold Your Horses* album in 1979. For this disc another personnel change occurred, with Debbie Martin replacing Ursula Herring. The first-release title track gave the group a minor hit, as did "Great Expectations." However, the follow-up, "Double Cross," and the funky "Love Thang" were more popular with the disco audience. Fleming says, "I always felt 'Love Thang' should have been the first single. That was the first funky tune we did. When we sang it onstage we felt really good, dancing and wiggling all over the place."

With disco still at its peak and First Choice at the height of their success, fate stepped in and the group split up after legal entanglements with Salsoul Records. The last album released by First Choice was *Breakaway* in 1980. Fleming recalls, "There was a transition of management and there were a lot of legal hassles, including the name, which we thought of collectively. We didn't want to be with Salsoul anymore. They offered to sell us the name but we weren't about to buy a name that we came up with in the first place. We left the company after weeks of legal mess and dealings with attorneys. We stayed together for the rest of that year but after that, we broke up. I still had the fight in me. I was willing to go down with the ship but the morale was gone and everyone decided to call it quits. We toasted our goodbyes and parted as friends. Annette and I are still very close. After that, I stayed away from the industry for two years."

In the wake of the disco era, First Choice emerged as disco icons as their music continues to be played in nightclubs today. "Let No Man Put Asunder" and "Love Thang," neither of which was originally released as a single, were later revived and have since become nightclub anthems. Both songs, along with "Double Cross," have been heavily sampled by house music producers. Fleming, who still performs today and signed a recording contract with Cutting Records in 1994, says, "It feels good that ['Love Thang'] is still being played; same with 'Asunder.' I still perform at some of the clubs that we used to do and I still sing 'Doctor Love,' 'It's Not Over' ['Let No Man Put Asunder'], 'Double Cross,' and 'Love Thang.' No matter how many songs I may do as a solo artist, I'll always do those four songs. You can't really get rid of that type of sound; it will always be there. Club music is disco and house music is still disco. There's a little more bass and it's a little more pumped up but it's definitely the same thing."

She further adds, "Those who've been sampling my vocals, it's time for them to stop. When I come back out this time I'm coming back out to stay. It's gonna work this time."

The Friends of Distinction

A Los Angeles-based soul/MOR (middle-of-the-road) group, the Friends of Distinction enjoyed great popularity between 1969 and 1971 with their smooth and sophisticated vocal delivery on hits such as "Grazing in the Grass" and "Going in Circles." Led by Harry Elston and Floyd Butler, this four-member vocal group often drew comparison to the Fifth Dimension.

The founding members of the group, Harry Elston and Floyd Butler, spent their early years in Southern California. Elston, who was born in Dallas, Texas, moved to the West Coast as a youngster. The erstwhile duo sang regularly while in high school and later at San Diego City College, which they attended for several years before spending two years in the armed forces.

Upon receiving their discharges, both moved to Los Angeles to continue college and also to try to break into the music field. In the early 1960s Elston and Butler got together with two other Los Angeles friends, Lamonte McLemore and Marilyn McCoo, to form the Hi-Fi's. At the time, McLemore was a photographer at the Los Angeles-based magazine *Elegant* where Elston worked as an advertising salesman. The Hi-Fi's, also known as the Vocals, sang in local clubs and, in 1964, came to the attention of Ray Charles. Charles took the quartet on tour with him for six months in 1965 and produced one single for them, the jazz-flavored "Lonesome Mood," which drew some local attention.

Harry Elston remembers, "Floyd and I met when we were youngsters, about five or six years old. We met in the San Diego projects. Through the church, my family and his family became good friends. Later when I was in L.A. he moved there and we became roommates. We made our professional debut in a group called the Hi-Fi's.

"It was definitely an experience to be youngsters and traveling with the great Ray Charles. We called him Mr. C. At the time he had the original Raelettes. We were actually in awe of him in the very beginning. He had a plane which we called 'the buzzard' and that got us from gig to gig to gig. Once we became acclimated to the tour, we had fun."

Creative differences caused a break in the Hi-Fi's, and McLemore and McCoo went on to become charter members of the Fifth Dimension. After the group broke up, things slowed down for Butler and Elston. They worked regular jobs while looking for an opportunity to get back into the music industry. In early 1968, they decided to form a new group and brought in Jessica Cleaves and Barbara Jean Love. Both Cleaves and Love started singing in their church choirs at an early age. Cleaves honed her talent at Valley Junior College and the California Institute of the Arts. Love, the daughter of Los Angeles disk jockey Reuben Brown, first thought of singing professionally during her years at Los Angeles City College.

Elston recalls, "Floyd was working for the Urban League and I was with Continental Airlines. I made a decision that I wanted to get back into music; I still wanted to sing. We spent some time doing promotion. One promotion we did was to book the Fifth Dimension. I worked the graveyard shift so that I could have the daytime hours free. I spent that time listening to all types of music being played on the radio. After awhile [Floyd and I] started talking about getting back into it.

"Where he worked he would interview ladies coming in looking for jobs. One day Jessica came in. She was only 17 years old and she had these thick glasses. Floyd heard of her talent and invited her in. I knew of Barbara from the past but I didn't know she could sing; I just knew she was very pretty. She heard about the auditions that were going on and after she auditioned, she came in."

With the quartet complete, they practiced diligently before deciding on their next move. At the time, Jim Brown, former football star turned actor, was supporting the Black Economic Union and dropped in on one of the group's practices. He was impressed enough to sign the Friends to a contract with the BBC, an organization founded to help artists break into the entertainment industry. Elston remembers, "At the time, Booker Griffin, an associate of ours, was heavily into politics and he came into contact with Jim Brown. We were rehearsing at a place called the Maverick Flat and Jim came in one day to hear us. He asked me if I was serious about [a music career] and wanted to know what I needed for us to get over the top. I told him I needed rehearsal money for our keyboard player, Clarence McDonald. Jim gave me $50 a week. I had to hound his ass for it but he gave it to me."

After several more rehearsals, the group was showcased for a private gathering of music executives at an exclusive nightclub called the Daisy. After an impressive showing, the Friends of Distinction received several offers and decided to sign with RCA.

"After many, many rehearsals and finally getting our performance down, we showcased at a place called the Daisy in Beverly Hills," says Elston. "This place was *it.* Jim was in the mix at the time and we were spoiled because of our association with him. We became part of the BBC management and Paul Block, who was a giant in the industry, became our manager. We were very successful at the Daisy, and the next day *six* record companies came to me and said, 'Harry, we gotta talk.' I was young and didn't know the ropes. I didn't realize the situation that I was in. Usually it's the other way around. It was really a trip. I got a good vibe from John Florez, who was one of the staff producers at RCA. We were new, he was new, and it was fresh. He had in mind Ray Cork [Jr.], an arranger. We had never met him or heard his music but he turned out to be a helluva arranger."

In early 1969 the Friends of Distinction released "Grazing in the Grass," a vocal version of the Number One pop hit less than a year earlier for South African trumpeter Hugh Masekela. Elston, who wrote the lyrics, explains, "We would be on the road traveling 300 to 400 miles to a gig and we would go past these fields of cows. I would say to Floyd, 'Man, these cows sure have got it made. All they have to do is eat and shit all day long.' I wrote a song and called it 'Flaking in the Grass.' I took it to RCA and they said I couldn't do this. I changed 'flaking' to 'grazing' and after they heard it, we got clearance." The Friends' peppy vocal version of "Grazing in the Grass," with its catchy "can you dig it?" phrase, was a top five hit on the pop and R&B charts and sold over a million copies.

For the follow-up single, in an apparent attempt to pull the Friends away from the MOR classification and promote them as more of an R&B group, RCA released "Going in Circles" instead of "I Really Hope You Do." "RCA dictated the songs that got released as singles," says Elston. "At the time we thought 'I Really Hope You Do' was strong enough to stand by itself as a release but RCA put it on the other side of 'Grazing.' 'Circles' just happened. The people made 'Circles.' We didn't think about the black thing but we knew ['Going in Circles'] was a black record. It really pisses me off that back then, because you were a black group, you had to start off in the black market. That wasn't true for everybody. Fortunately for us, it wasn't. It came down to politics with the record company. You had the black division pulling against the pop division, which was promoting us as an R&B group."

Released in the summer of 1969, the hypnotic "Going in Circles," with Butler on lead, was a top 20 pop hit, reached number three on the R&B charts, and was the Friends' second million-seller. Despite high promise, "I Really Hope You Do," a beautiful pop ballad featuring Jessica Cleaves on lead vocals, was never released as an A-side. All three songs appeared on the Friends' debut album, *Grazin'*, which also included a cover of the Hi-Fi's single "Lonesome Mood."

The success of debut back-to-back million-sellers took the Friends of Distinction from obscurity to the top of the music world in less than a year. The group toured almost 40 weeks a year, headlining such prestigious clubs as Caesars Palace and the Flamingo Hotel in Las Vegas and the Copacabana in New York. Prior experience with the Hi-Fi's helped the founding members cope with this newfound success. Elston explains, "[Floyd and I] were exposed to the women and the spotlight at a young age from when we were in the Hi-Fi's. Lamonte McLemore was, and still is, a fantastic photographer, so we were always surrounded by all these women. By the time the success with the Friends came along, we had the women thing in order. When everything came it happened so fast that it was a whirlwind experience but Jim [Brown] was there to anchor us and we were all very supportive of each other."

With similarities in vocal harmonies and in name, the Friends of Distinction were often compared to the Fifth Dimension. As 1969 was the year that the Friends came into the national spotlight, and also the peak year for the Fifth Dimension, who placed two songs ("Aquarius/Let the Sunshine In" and "Wedding Bell Blues") at the top of the pop charts, this comparison became increasingly common.

Elston points out, "[The comparison] may have been a help because it did open some doors. The first time I heard the comparison was when we were appearing at a club in Bloomfield, Indiana. The Fifth Dimension appeared there the week before and one of the newspapers did a comparison between the two. We were considered the naughty boys and girls whereas the Fifth Dimension were considered to be the clean-cut colored kids from California. We were always considered to be the more black of the groups. We took it in stride. We were happy just to be out there."

After the *Highly Distinct* album in the fall of 1969, Jessica Cleaves left and was replaced by Charlene Gibson. Gibson sang lead on the Friends' next hit, the warm, mid-tempo "Love or Let Me Be Lonely" in early 1970. "Lonely" was a top 15 R&B hit and did even better on the pop charts, peaking at number six, selling nearly a million copies.

Two other releases that made the R&B charts were the energetic "Time Waits for No One" in 1970 and the funky "I Need

You" in 1971. However, both of these songs were actually pop records which crossed over to R&B. The Friends of Distinction were caught in the bind of being promoted as an R&B group without having a pure soul sound. The group never did release a follow-up single in the same vein as "Going in Circles" to firmly establish a black base. Another problem that hindered the group was the inability of RCA to cater to the black audience properly.

"RCA could either make you or break you," says Elston. "We called RCA act killers. They had Sam Cooke, Harry Belafonte, and Jesse Belvin, who was supposed to be RCA's Nat King Cole. When we came along, RCA was not ready for a black group. With our association with Jim Brown, and being from California, we were an easier group to package. We were able to perform with people like Laura Nyro, John Denver, and Cannonball Adderly. RCA deserves credit because they hung for awhile, they did put us out there, but there were a lot of internal politics at RCA."

In the early '70s, constant personnel changes began to plague the cohesiveness of the group. Barbara Love left the group and was replaced by a series of other vocalists. Then Charlene Gibson left and Love returned. By early 1971, Jessica Cleaves returned to the group but Love again decided to leave. The Friends were now down to a threesome. "It was rough," admits Elston. "Charlene Gibson came to us while we were in Milwaukee, which was like a godsend, so things were smooth for a minute. But then the women kept coming in and out. It was rough because we weren't hot like we were before, but Floyd and I kept on stepping."

The Friends continued to perform until they officially disbanded in 1975. On Sunday, April 29, 1990, Floyd Butler passed away at age 48 after suffering a massive heart attack. It is sadly ironic that earlier in the day Butler and Elston discussed plans of reviving the Friends of Distinction after more than a decade of inactivity. Harry Elston did revive the Friends two years later, adding Ghee Brown, Petsye Powell, and Patti Brooks, who previously had a disco hit with "After Dark." "Floyd and I decided that we would be the ones to put the group back together, so now I'm doing it for myself and for Floyd," says Elston. "I rationalized that there is still a market out there for the Friends. I have longevity and experience. I planted a lot of seeds and things are now starting to come around."

Al Green

With an amazing run of chart success that included hits such as "Let's Stay Together," "I'm Still in Love with You," and "Call Me (Come Back Home)," singer-songwriter Al Green was arguably soul music's leading vocalist and sex symbol in the early to mid-1970s. An integral part of Green's success was the production of Willie Mitchell, who also co-wrote most of Green's hits. Green's gospel-trained voice, floating anywhere from an ethereal whisper to a deep groan, was combined with Mitchell's orchestration of the Hi Records house band to create a successful formula that would sell a reported 30 million records by 1976. At the height of his popularity, Green abandoned secular music to become a successful gospel artist. However, a mid-1990s revival of Green's songs from his secular glory days demonstrated that his early hits were not only innovative and soothing, but timeless as well.

One of nine children, Al Greene was born in Forrest City, Arkansas in 1946. He initially became interested in singing by listening to Sam Cooke and Swan Silvertones lead singer Claude Jeter. At age seven he wanted to join his family gospel group, the Greene Brothers, consisting of his brothers Walter, William, and Robert. Told he was too young and his voice too weak, Al remained undaunted, and by age nine, had become an integral part of the group. The quartet, along with their father, garnered attention on the gospel circuit in the South and later throughout the Midwest after the family moved to Grand Rapids, Michigan in 1959. A few years later, 16-year-old Al was fired from the group when his father heard him listening to a Jackie Wilson record.

Once Al developed a taste for the music of Wilson, Sam Cooke, Otis Redding, and James Brown, he became consumed with secular music. In 1964 he formed a soul group, the Creations, with his high-school friends Palmer James, Curtis Rogers, and Gene Mason. The Creations enjoyed some local success on Zodiac Records and built a small following by playing in clubs on the "chitlin' circuit" of the South and Midwest. To increase their share of the profits, James, Rogers, and Mason started a record label called Hot Line Music Journal. James and Rogers then formed the Soul Mates, also comprising Al's brother Robert and friend Lee Virgins. In 1967 they persuaded Al to cut one of their songs, called "Back Up Train." The recording, a gentle and soft performance, was picked up for national distribution by Bell Records. Early in 1968, "Back Up Train" reached number five on the R&B charts and sold half a million copies for Al Greene and the Soul Mates; a surprising success considering that soul music during this time was dominated by the hard-core, gritty sounds coming out of Stax and Atlantic.

The Soul Mates were unable to come up with an adequate follow-up to "Back Up Train." Later releases "Don't Hurt Me No More" and "Lover's Hideaway" sold well locally but did not draw any national interest. The failure of the group to maintain their initial impact, coupled with the Hot Line Music Journal label getting deep into financial difficulty, caused the Soul Mates to disband. Al Green went solo, dropping the last letter of his surname, and continued singing in small clubs, often without pay. While performing at a club in Midland, Texas in 1969, he met Willie Mitchell, the vice-president and chief producer at Hi Records in Memphis.

Mitchell, a native of Ashland, Tennessee, studied trumpet in high school and formed his first band in 1954. He did session work for Sun Records and Capitol, and recorded an album with B. B. King for RPM Records. By the end of the 1950s, his group had become the house band for Reuben Cherry's Home of the Blues label. In 1963 Mitchell joined Hi Records, a label formed six years earlier by Joe Cuoghi, one of the largest record retailers in Memphis; Quinton Claunch, who in 1964 became a co-owner of Goldwax Records; and Ray Harris, a former Sun Records session musician. During the 1960s Mitchell recorded a series of R&B instrumental hits, including "Buster Browne" (1965), "Bad Eye" (1966), "Soul Serenade" (1968), "Prayer Meetin'" (1968), "30-60-90" (1969), and "My Babe" (1969). His band also backed most of the other R&B artists on Hi. In the spring of 1970 Mitchell became vice-president of the company. After Cuoghi died of a heart attack later that summer, Mitchell took over the reins and abandoned his own recording career.

When Green and Mitchell crossed paths that night in Midland, Texas, Green was not carrying his own musicians. The club owner arranged for Mitchell's band to work with Green after playing their own set. Mitchell assessed Green's talent and potential and asked the young singer to come to Memphis to record some songs for the Hi label. Initially reluctant to move to Memphis, Green nevertheless decided to give it a try. Mitchell then set a timetable of 18 months to make Green a star.

At Hi, Green was paired with the label's house band, the Hi Rhythm Section, which featured Leroy Hodges (bass), Mabon "Teenie" Hodges (guitar), Charles Hodges (organ), Wayne Jackson (trumpet), James Mitchell (baritone sax), Andrew Love (tenor sax), Ed Logan (tenor sax), Jack Hale (trombone), and Howard Grimes (percussion). However, Al Jackson, the drummer for Booker T. and the MGs, played on most of the sessions. Green, Mitchell, and Jackson initially struggled to come up with an appropriate sound for the singer, as is evident from Green's first single, a failed cover of the Beatles' "I Want to Hold Your Hand." Green followed with the deep soul "One Woman," which also did nothing.

In the spring and summer of 1970, Green was still singing deep soul but managed a minor hit in the funky, call-and-response "You Say It" (number 28 R&B) and the psychedelic-flavored "Right Now, Right Now" (number 23 R&B). While driving through Memphis one rainy night, Green heard the

Temptations' "I Can't Get Next to You," a psychedelic funk track that had topped the charts in the fall of 1969. He reworked the arrangement, adding a slow, bluesy flavor. With emphasis on Hi's horn section and a gritty guitar break, Green was able to improvise and vamp, and interpret the song as if it were his own. The cover version gave him his first significant Hi hit, peaking at number 11 on the R&B charts late in 1970. Green stayed in blues territory with a revival of Roosevelt Sykes' "Driving Wheel" in the spring of 1971, but it did not achieve the same results, only reaching number 46.

Mitchell's goal to make Green a star in 18 months came true on the latter's next single, "Tired of Being Alone." Written by Green, the song became his first solo top 10 hit, peaking at number 7 on the R&B charts in the summer of 1971. It also reached number 11 on the pop charts and gave him his first gold record. Like Green's previous releases, "Tired of Being Alone" was anchored by Hi's horn section. However, it was evident that Mitchell and Green were close to getting the sound they wanted. Mitchell toned down Green's voice slightly but the singer was still able to vamp and ad-lib as his voice traveled from a near growl to a light falsetto.

All five chart entries were included on Green's highly acclaimed *Al Green Gets Next to You* album. The album also included impressive remakes of Freddie Scott's "Are You Lonely for Me" and the Doors' "Light My Fire."

Green's next effort would make him the number one soul artist in the country. Released late in 1971, "Let's Stay Together" achieved a level of success matched by few soul songs recorded before or since. The single topped the R&B charts for nine weeks, which tied a record set by the Four Tops' "I Can't Help Myself" in 1965. It also reached the summit of the pop charts for a week early in 1972 and sold 2.8 million copies. Green, who wrote the song along with Mitchell and Al Jackson, reportedly did not like the final version because his voice sounded too thin. However, it was the softness of his voice that gave the song its magic. Mitchell finally had the sound he wanted. Gone was the gut-wrenching deep soul exhibited on the singer's earlier Hi singles. While the Hi horn section introduced the song, as it would continue to do on virtually all of Green's hits, the rhythm section was softened to allow his tenor and the background vocals of Charles Chalmers and Donna and Sandra Rhodes to float effortlessly across the backing of the band. In "Let's Stay Together" Green assumed the role of a man seeking reconciliation after a recent breakup. This theme would set the foundation for Green, who came to be regarded as the soul music love man of the early 1970s. Led by the title song, the *Let's Stay Together* album topped the R&B charts for 10 weeks and sold nearly two million copies. Like Isaac Hayes and Marvin Gaye before him, and Stevie Wonder and Barry White soon to come, Green helped break the myth that black artists could not sell albums. That *Let's Stay Together* achieved monumental success is a testament to the popularity of the title song. None of the album's remaining eight songs were released as singles. The only other legitimate highlight was a remake of the Bee Gees' recent Number One pop hit, "How Can You Mend a Broken Heart." Over the course of six minutes, Green's voice fluctuated from a soft whisper to the pleading growl of a Baptist preacher, while continuing to sprinkle "la-la's" throughout the song. Integral to the strength of the song were the backing vocals of Rhodes, Chalmers, and Rhodes. Although Green's version of "Broken Heart" was never released as a single, the song has enjoyed tremendous durability alongside his numerous hits, and for a period of time in the 1980s it was the only secular song he performed live.

Green's 1972 album *I'm Still in Love with You* was perhaps his finest. The disc solidified his status as a superstar and a sex symbol, and gave him the consistent crossover success achieved by an earlier gospel-trained vocalist turned pop star, Sam Cooke. The album's first release, "Look What You Done for Me," was his third straight gold record; it spent four weeks at the number two spot on the R&B charts in the spring of 1972 and peaked at number four on the pop charts. Again written by Green, Mitchell, and Jackson, "Look What You Done for Me" employed the same production formula exhibited on Green's two previous million-sellers: the horn section intro; the softening of the arrangement and of Green's voice; and the prominent backing vocals of Rhodes, Chalmers, and Rhodes.

Green's next single, "I'm Still in Love with You," would be the zenith of this soft sound. Again cushioned by the laid-back production of Mitchell, Green sings in a falsetto, his voice barely above a whisper, any semblance of the gutsy vocals on his early releases now a fleeting memory. The song's laid-back flavor helped Green maintain his presence on the pop charts as "I'm Still in Love with You" went to number three. The song also topped the R&B charts for two weeks in the summer of 1972 and became his fourth million-selling single.

One of the most enduring songs from the *I'm Still in Love with You* album was the "Teenie" Hodges and Green-penned "Love and Happiness." On this track, the Hi house band was allowed to cut loose, as Green returned to his gospel roots and gritty vocals as exhibited on his earlier Hi singles. With its somewhat funky production being a complete departure from the formula employed on Green's previous million-sellers, Hi chose not to issue the song as a single until 1977, after Green's career had cooled. However, "Love and Happiness" has become a much-covered soul classic and remains the song with which Green is most identified.

All three songs, plus a popular remake of Kris Kristofferson's "For the Good Times," propelled the *I'm Still in Love with You* album to million-seller status.

With Mitchell's hit-making formula intact, Green ended his most successful year with "You Ought to Be with Me" late in 1972. Produced in the same vein as his four previous million-sellers, this track topped the R&B charts for a week, hit number three on the pop charts, and was another million-seller. However, by now Green and Mitchell were being accused of putting out records that sounded too similar.

Al Green dominated a year (1972) as no other performer had ever done. He wrote and recorded four million-selling singles, released two million-selling albums, and had total record sales of over 10 million. At the end of the year, awards and accolades came in droves. *Rolling Stone* magazine named him the top rock and roll/pop star of 1972, and in an unprecedented sweep, the three leading American trade publications, *Record World*, *Cashbox*, and *Billboard*, all chose him as the year's top male vocalist.

Fueled by his success on vinyl, Al Green became one of the hottest concert attractions in the country. At the height of his superstar reign, he toured nearly 40 weeks a year, consistently selling out arenas such as the Forum in Los Angeles and the Spectrum in Philadelphia. With a string of hits about the positive side of love relationships, Green's appeal was near universal. However, nearly 70 percent of his live audience consisted of African-American women.

When Green was not on tour or writing and recording new material, he could often be found spending anywhere from 12 to 16 hours a day at his Memphis office, running Al Green Enterprises. He was his own manager, handled his own bookings, ran his own publishing company (Al Green Music), and employed a staff of nearly 40 people.

Despite criticism of "making the same record," Green began 1973 with his third gold album, as *Call Me* was a million-seller on initial orders alone. The title song was another million-seller, spending two weeks at the number two spot on the R&B charts early in 1973, and becoming a top 10 pop hit. "Call Me (Come Back Home)" had added significance because it was the last song to feature drummer Al Jackson as a co-writer. Although Jackson was prominent in establishing the Hi sound, he never did cut his ties with the crosstown Stax label, and he was often unavailable. Guitarist "Teenie" Hodges stepped in as a co-writer with Green on the singer's next single, "Here I Am (Come and Take Me)." On the surface, Green's audience hardly noticed the difference; the song spent three weeks at the number two spot on the R&B charts in the summer of 1973, and was a top 10 pop hit and his seventh straight million-seller. However, with the absence of Jackson's sophisticated, jazz-influenced sound, "Here I Am" marked a return to the rougher, deep-soul sound exhibited on Green's early Hi singles.

Green began 1974 with *Livin' for You* becoming his fourth straight gold album. The first single release, the album's title track, topped the R&B charts for a week early in the year. However, "Livin' for You" was his first single since "Tired of Being Alone" to miss the pop top 10, and it broke his string of seven million-sellers. Although the lyrical content of "Livin' for You" was somewhat bland in comparison to his previous efforts, it was ironic that this ballad marked the beginning of Green losing his crossover audience. Unlike the previous single, "Here I Am (Come and Take Me)," "Livin' for You" utilized the smooth sound that was integral to the widespread appeal of his 1972 and 1973 smashes.

Green's return to a growling, tougher, deep soul sound was evident on his next single, "Let's Get Married," an up-tempo track that was a complete departure from the string of hits that made him a household name. The black audience bought it up as "Let's Get Married" reached number three on the R&B charts in the spring of 1974. However, this new sound did not fully capture the pop audience. The song failed to crack the pop top 30, Green's poorest showing on the pop charts in three years.

Part of the reason for the drop in sales can be traced to the absence of Jackson. However, during this time, Green was in the process of negotiating a new contract with London Records (which distributed Hi). As a result, neither he nor Mitchell took part in the process of selecting the songs to be released as singles. Green also had no decision-making part in the cover of the *Livin' for You* album, which depicted him as a giant cartoon, ignoring an offered rose.

Shortly after midnight on October 18, 1974, Green returned to his plush Memphis home with Mary Woodson, whom he'd known for about a year, and another friend, Corlotta Williams. After Ms. Williams went to another part of the house, Ms. Woodson, the mother of three children in Madison, New Jersey, proposed marriage to Green, but he declined. Green then went upstairs to take a bath. As he was getting out of the bathtub, Ms. Woodson burst through the bathroom door and scalded him with a pot of boiling Cream of Wheat cereal mixture (although it was widely reported to have been grits). After Ms. Williams came to Green's aid, Woodson fatally shot herself with a .38 caliber pistol. The 29-year-old Woodson had reportedly been under psychiatric care due to a previous suicide attempt. Green suffered second-degree burns on his back, arms, and stomach, and was hospitalized for 11 days.

Rumors persisted that the incident prompted Green to become a born-again Christian, but the singer reportedly claimed that his spiritual rebirth occurred in 1973. However, his Christianity did become more noticeable from this point. When performing live, he added more religious songs to his established crowd-pleasing love songs. Green's live act also took on a more sophisticated look. A white business suit now replaced the white leather pants, high boots, and silk shirts unbuttoned to the waist. His band was also more conservatively dressed in suits instead of wearing hats and big boots.

The burn incident did not adversely affect record sales. Green "rebounded" late in 1974 with *Al Green Explores Your Mind*, which achieved platinum sales only two days after its release. The album's success was fueled by "Sha La La (Make Me Happy)," a tune Green wrote for Woodson. Free from the contract negotiations that limited his creative output on his previous effort, "Sha La La" was a refreshing mid-tempo track that had Green singing in his laid-back falsetto for the majority of the song but still tossing in laughs and groans whenever he pleased. The song reached number two on the R&B charts for two weeks, returned Green to the pop top 10, and was his eighth and final million-selling single. The first evidence of Green's music turning towards Christianity was on "God Bless Our Love" and the blues-flavored "Take Me to the River." Although "Take Me to the River" was never released as a single, it remained a popular song in Green's repertoire and a cover version later became the Talking Heads' first hit.

The first hit by Green that had a strong gospel influence was "L-O-V-E (Love)," which topped the R&B charts for two weeks in the spring of 1975. On this mid-tempo track, he sang about salvation, glory, and the heavens.

Later that fall, Green, like several veteran soul artists, jumped aboard the disco bandwagon with the title track from his *Full of Fire* album. Despite the song being a total transformation from his previous material, and an obvious display of how he and Mitchell were following new trends, "Full of Fire" topped the R&B charts for a week late in 1975. This was Green's sixth and final chart-topper.

Although Green moved away from the sound that gave him his biggest hits, 1975 was still a stellar year for him. At year's end he received a Grammy nomination for "L-O-V-E (Love)"; was named number one R&B vocalist by *Cash Box*; was named number one male best-selling R&B vocalist by *Record World*; and was honored for number one best-selling male vocalist and number one R&B LP by *Billboard*.

In April 1976 Green bought a church building in Memphis and became its minister, having been ordained a pastor of the Full Gospel Tabernacle church. Green still continued to tour, but whenever logistically possible, he would fly back to Memphis to preach at his church.

Later that fall "Keep Me Cryin'" reached number four on the R&B charts and was his final collaboration with Mitchell. When Green turned to gospel the following year, he parted company with Mitchell, who had little knowledge of or interest in gospel music. Green began recording at his own American Music Recording Studio with a new band consisting of Reuben Fairfax (bass), James Bass (guitar), Johnny Toney (drums), Buddy Jarrett (alto sax), Fred Jordan (trumpet), and Ron Echols (tenor and alto sax).

Green's production debut was *The Belle Album*, released in 1977. The title track was a semi-autobiographical tale about a preacher's conflict between a sexual life and a more spiritual one. Unlike Green's work with Mitchell, where the production was almost as prominent as his voice, "Belle" was sparely produced, allowing his vocals to shine through. The song was his final secular hit of the decade, peaking at number nine on the R&B charts in the fall of 1977. The album's only other moderate hit was "I Feel Good," giving Green further support with the dance crowd.

He retained his new band for *Truth 'n' Time*, released in 1978. The album gave Green a two-sided chart entry with "To Sir with Love" backed by the dance track "Wait Here," but they resulted in the lowest chart showing of his career.

During a concert performance in Cincinnati in 1979, Green fell 12 feet from a stage and hit a steel instrument case, barely escaping serious injury. He spent a total of 15 days in the hospital, and took the accident as a signal to make a full commitment to gospel music.

In 1980, following a successful concert in London where he performed many of his old hits, Green surprised his fans with the release of *The Lord Will Make a Way*. Released on Myrrh, a Christian label in Waco, Texas, it was his first pure gospel album.

Two years later Green joined forces with Patti Labelle for the Broadway production of Vinette Carroll's gospel-based musical, *Your Arm's Too Short to Box with God*, which enjoyed a successful run.

Green continued to churn out gospel albums at a rate of one per year, and he drew large audiences to concerts in the States and abroad to hear his gospel-only performances. Although Green never won a Grammy award for his secular hits of the 1970s, he was a consistent winner in the 1980s for his gospel albums. He won the 1981 award for best soul gospel performance, traditional for *The Lord Will Make a Way*; the same award in 1982 for *Precious Lord*, plus best soul gospel performance, contemporary for *Higher Plane*; in 1983, best soul gospel performance, male for *I'll Rise Again*; and in 1984, best soul gospel performance by a duo or group for his duet with Shirley Caesar, "Sailin' on the Sea of Your Love" from her LP *Sailin.'*

In 1986 Green reunited with Willie Mitchell for *He Is the Light*, his first album on A&M Records. To familiarize themselves with past greatness, they recorded the album at Mitchell's Royal Recording Studio in Memphis, where Green recorded most of his hits in the 1970s, and they used many of the musicians from the previous decade, including bassist Leroy Hodges, guitarist Teenie Hodges, and sax player Andrew Love.

Green returned to the R&B charts in the spring of 1987, with "Everything's Gonna Be Alright" reaching number 22. The song also won him a Grammy for best soul gospel performance, male. The following year he had a number nine pop hit with "Put a Little Love in Your Heart," a duet with rock singer Annie Lennox.

While Green continued to release gospel albums, his previous success in the soul/pop field got him elected into the Rock and Roll Hall of Fame in 1994. His performance of "Take Me to the River" at the 1995 award ceremony was the highlight of the evening. The election came at a time when there was a resurgence of interest in the music of Al Green. Fueling this resurgence was the fact that the vocalist was once again mixing some of his old hits into his gospel performances. A successful greatest hits package was released in 1995 and "Tired of Being Alone" was among the 12 R&B classics chosen for the highly successful soundtrack to the 1995 film *Dead Presidents.* Later in 1995 Green signed with MCA Records and released *Your Heart's in Good Hands,* which gave him a moderate hit with the title track.

With the revival of interest in the soul music of the 1970s, it is only fitting that Al Green's name is once again alive in the industry. Whether it is the 1970s or 1990s, whether he is singing gospel or secular music, whenever Al Green spreads his message of love and happiness, he remains one of the most remarkable and exciting vocalists around.

Above: BLUE MAGIC.
(L-R) Wendell Sawyer,
Keith Beaton, Vernon Sawyer,
Richard Pratt, Ted Mills
(Courtesy *Blues and Soul* magazine)

Right: AL GREEN.
(Courtesy *Blues and Soul* magazine)

Below: THE DRAMATICS.
(Courtesy of Fantasy Records)

Above: THE DELLS. (L-R) Chuck Barksdale, Johnny Carter, Marvin Junior, Mickey McGill, Verne Allison (Courtesy *Blues and Soul* magazine)

Below: THE EMOTIONS. (Courtesy of Showtime Archives [Toronto])

Top: FIRST CHOICE. (L-R) Rochelle Fleming, Annette Guest, Ursula Herring (Courtesy *Blues and Soul* magazine)

Center: THE CHI-LITES. (L-R) Robert "Squirrel" Lester, Creadel "Red" Jones, Marshall Thompson, Eugene Record (Courtesy of Showtime Archives [Toronto])

Right: THE DELFONICS. Randy Cain, William Hart, Wilbert Hart (Courtesy of Showtime Archives [Toronto])

Isaac Hayes

A multi-talented artist known as Black Moses at the height of his popularity, Isaac Hayes transcended the boundaries of soul music in the late 1960s and 1970s. With a craft for turning pop/MOR tunes such as "By the Time I Get to Phoenix" and "Walk on By" into elaborate, lushly orchestrated recordings introduced by lengthy monologues or "raps," Hayes garnered enormous success in the early 1970s. He first came to prominence in the 1960s as a writer and producer for Stax Records. Working with David Porter, Hayes generated nearly all of Sam and Dave's classic recordings, as well as hits for Carla Thomas, Mable John, Ruby Johnson, and Johnnie Taylor. As a performer, his groundbreaking 1969 album *Hot Buttered Soul* broke two myths of popular music: that black artists could not sell albums in large numbers, and that three minutes was the limit for a song to receive radio airplay. Two years later, his soundtrack for the film *Shaft* paved the way for several other soul artists to score motion pictures. With seven gold or platinum albums between 1969 and 1973, Hayes was soul music's first superstar in the 1970s, and he created a body of music whose influence is still felt more than two decades later.

Isaac Hayes was born in Covington, Tennessee in 1942. When he was a year and a half old, his mother died. His father soon left home, leaving Isaac and his sister to be raised by their sharecropping grandparents. In an effort to improve the family's poor conditions, Isaac's grandfather moved the family 30 miles to Memphis when Isaac was six. This attempt proved futile and Isaac was forced to alternate between going to school and working in the cotton fields. When Isaac was 11, his grandfather died. Isaac continued to take time off from school to pick cotton and perform other odd jobs, working as a stock boy and dishwasher.

Hayes developed an avid interest in music while in high school. He sang bass for a gospel group called the Morning Stars and also with an R&B group called the Teen Tones. By his late teens, Hayes was married and about to become a father. When he finally graduated from Manasas High School, his musical talent earned him seven scholarships. However, he was forced to turn them all down due to his family obligations. Hayes then took a job at a local meat-packing house. He accepted whatever musical jobs he could find and began to master the piano, guitar, and saxophone in the process.

In 1962, Hayes was given his first opportunity to make a record. The result was "Laura We're on Our Last Go Round" on Youngstown, which disappeared without a trace. After this disappointment, he went back to playing local gigs. While playing in a backup band at a club, Hayes got his big break when he was asked to step in as a pianist for the club's regular band. The bandleader was baritone saxophonist Floyd Newman, a charter member of the Stax Records house band, the Mar-Keys. Hayes had previously auditioned at Stax on three different occasions and was turned down each time. However, Newman was impressed with Hayes' talent and recruited him as an organist on his 1963 Stax record "Frog Stomp." Stax president Jim Stewart then hired Hayes for session work, particularly as a fill-in for Booker T. Jones when the latter was away at college. Hayes' first session at Stax was with Otis Redding for an LP entitled *The Great Otis Redding Sings Soul Ballads.* He would continue to work regularly with Redding until the singer died in a 1967 plane crash.

While at Stax, Hayes reacquainted himself with David Porter, a friend and rival singer from his high school days. Porter, a Memphis native born in 1941, initially started singing in a gospel group at age six. At night, going by the name of Little David, he performed in various Memphis clubs. In 1961 Porter made his recording debut with "Chivalry"/ "Farewell" for the local Eagle label, but the song went nowhere. Later that year he joined Stax Records as a staff writer. When Hayes came to Stax, it was Porter who convinced him that they should team up. They worked out an arrangement where Porter would write the lyrics and Hayes would set the music.

The duo was unsuccessful at first and Hayes briefly returned to recording. In 1965 he cut an unsuccessful instrumental single, "Blue Groove," under the name Sir Isaac and the Doo-Dads. Hayes and Porter caught their big break later in 1965, when Atlantic Records head Jerry Wexler sent the recording duo Sam and Dave to Memphis to record at the Stax studios. Stax was distributed by Atlantic at the time. All of the writers and producers at Stax submitted material to Sam and Dave, but nothing clicked until they collaborated with Hayes and Porter. Their first effort together, "I Take What I Want," failed to chart. Hayes and Porter then came up with "You Don't Know Like I Know," which became a top 10 R&B hit for Sam and Dave in 1966. The duo followed up with the energetic "Hold On! I'm a Coming," which topped the R&B charts for a week that spring and became a soul standard. After four more R&B hits — "Said I Wasn't Gonna Tell Nobody," "You Got Me Hummin'," "When Something Is Wrong with My Baby," and "Soothe Me" — Sam and Dave reached the pinnacle of their success with the Hayes and Porter-penned and produced "Soul Man." One of the most successful songs in the history of soul music, this much-covered classic topped the R&B charts for seven weeks in the fall of 1967. Sam and Dave had top 10 success early the following year with "I Thank You." However, Stax ended its distribution deal with Atlantic in May 1968 and the duo's records began appearing on Atlantic. They enjoyed moderate success on the R&B charts with four songs remaining from their Stax sessions, most notably "Can't You Find Another Way (Of Doing It)" (1968) and "Soul Sister, Brown Sugar" (1969), but their fortunes soon declined.

Fortunately for Hayes and Porter, the break between Stax and Atlantic did not have an adverse effect on their status as one of the hottest writing and production teams in soul music. In addition to Sam and Dave, they created hits for such artists as Carla Thomas ("Let Me Be Good to You" and "B-A-B-Y"), Johnnie Taylor ("I Had a Dream" and "I Got to Love Somebody's Baby"), and the Emotions ("Show Me How").

Hayes' earlier ambition to become a singer resurfaced at this time. During a staff birthday party in 1967, he, along with Stax vice-president Al Bell, returned to the studio for an informal session following an overindulgence in champagne. With Bell at the controls, Hayes sang and played the organ. The only other musicians featured were drummer Al Jackson and bassist Donald "Duck" Dunn. The results of this informal and un-rehearsed affair was an album entitled *Presenting Isaac Hayes,* released on Atlantic Records in February 1968. Hayes, who re-portedly did not expect the album to be released, was unhappy with the final results. Sales of the album were low and Hayes returned to arranging in the studio.

In May 1968, Gulf & Western took over Stax Records. In an effort to reach the growing segment of affluent African-Americans who were now buying albums instead of singles, Stax set a quota of 27 albums to be released for an upcoming sales meeting the following May. This was part of a publicity campaign to put all of its artists in front of the public. Hayes and Porter spent the next few months recording all the big names at Stax. After realizing that they were still an album short, vice-president Bell approached Hayes and told him he needed one out from him also. Little was expected of Hayes in com-parison to the big-name artists on Stax; as a result, he faced little pressure. Given the freedom to do as he pleased, he took the Bar-Kays rhythm section into the Ardent Recording Studio, backed them with female background singers, and arranged a loose, unconventional workout.

The result was *Hot Buttered Soul,* which would revolutionize soul music. The music was different from anything that had ever been tried before. Hayes took familiar pop/MOR tunes and changed the length, the tempo, and the overall arrange-ment so that only the title, the chord progression, and the lyrics remained from the original. The music emphasized lavish orchestrations and wah-wah guitar, similar to the psychedelic sound created by Motown producer Norman Whitfield, but with more of an easy-listening flavor. More important, Hayes bucked the three-minute time barrier necessary for most songs to receive radio airplay. *Hot Buttered Soul* contained only four songs, ranging in length from five to nearly 19 minutes. The album received significant airplay on R&B, pop, easy-listening, and jazz stations. And in his husky baritone, Hayes introduced narrative monologues or "raps" that would soon be copied by numerous other artists for years to come.

By industry standards, the album should have been a commercial failure, and Stax initially treated it as such. *Hot Buttered Soul* was issued on the company's Enterprise subsidiary in the summer of 1969 and received little promotion. Within three months of its release, however, the album outsold the company's entire catalog. Two of the album's songs, "By the Time I Get to Phoenix" and "Walk on By," were significantly edited from their full-length versions and combined as a two-sided single release, both making the pop top 40. The former was perhaps the most overt display of how Hayes brought a number of innovations to R&B music. Penned by Jim Webb, "By the Time I Get to Phoenix" was originally a million-seller in 1967 for pop/country star Glen Campbell. When Hayes rearranged the song he added an introductory monologue about a man who is heartbroken because of a woman and finally decides to leave her. At the end of the story, Hayes sang the lyrics in a laid-back, deep baritone. Spoken over the backdrop of an organ chord and a steady, almost hypnotic beat of a cymbal, this rap lasted a good nine minutes. Miraculously recorded in one take, the song ran 18 minutes and 40 seconds.

Equally important to the success of the album was Hayes' sensuous 12-minute reworking of Hal David and Burt Bacharach's "Walk on By." The extravagant horns and strings of the orchestral musicians introduced a version that was highlighted by the contrast of Hayes' deep baritone and the prominent harmonies of female background singers, both sung to the backdrop of a soft, steady drumbeat. Hayes was able to arrange the entire package and transform this pop/MOR standard into something that was entirely his own. Although Hayes would have greater chart success with future singles, "Walk on By" remains the song with which he is most frequently identified by African-Americans.

Rounding out the album were "One Woman," where Hayes portrayed a man torn between his wife and his mistress, and the ultra-funky "Hyperbolicsyllabicsesquedalymistic." When all was done, *Hot Buttered Soul* topped the R&B and jazz charts, reached the pop top 10, and became the first Stax album to go platinum, selling 3.5 million copies.

With just one album, Isaac Hayes was transformed from a successful writer and producer into a bona fide superstar. Shortly after the album's success, there was the inevitable demand for personal appearances. Whereas in the past a little-known Hayes performed in small clubs in Memphis, he was now asked to appear before thousands throughout the country. Initially apprehensive about performing before such large audiences, Hayes' concerts soon took on the same extravagance as his recordings. In a typical performance, he was accompanied by a large orchestra, a rhythm section, and three female backup singers — "Miss Hot," "Miss Buttered," and "Miss Soul." Hayes came onstage dressed in a flamboyant cape and floppy hat. A bald dancing girl dressed in a bodystocking came forward to remove his cape and hat, revealing Hayes' imposing visual image: tall, muscular, bearded, and bald. His body was covered to the waist with tights, and he wore fur cuffs around his ankles. His stage gear was topped with a chain vest over his bare chest, and he often wore sunglasses. Sitting behind an elevated organ, and occasionally moving to play other instruments, Hayes performed for two or more hours without intermission. With the inclusion of his raps, he usually performed no more than six songs during this time. When he finished, he left the stage and did not give encores.

Hayes followed the mammoth success of *Hot Buttered Soul* with *The Isaac Hayes Movement* in the spring of 1970. In the same mold as its predecessor, Hayes took four well-known songs, extended their length, and gave them lavish orchestrations. *The Isaac Hayes Movement* was a concept album centered around problems in male-female relationships. In his 12-minute cover of the Beatles' "Something," Hayes had second thoughts about walking away from a relationship. He again borrowed from the catalogue of Burt Bacharach and Hal David, turning their "I Just Don't Know What to Do with Myself" into a seven-minute tale of trying to cope with a recent breakup. In the melancholy "One Big Unhappy Family," Hayes sang about the importance of being discreet about his domestic problems. The highlight of the album was his nearly 12-minute remake of Jerry Butler's 1964 hit, "I Stand Accused." Hayes again introduced the song with a street-corner rap, this time confessing his love for another man's lady. Spoken over a piano backup, this rap became something of a black national anthem. An edited version of "I Stand Accused" was released as a single and peaked at number 23 in the fall of 1970. Fueled by this song, *The Isaac Hayes Movement* was another huge success, reaching number eight on the album charts and earning gold status.

On his fourth album, *To Be Continued*, released in the fall of 1970, Hayes started receiving criticism from some who thought his music was becoming stagnant. His albums were beginning to be geared more towards the middle-of-the-road listener as he began playing to increasingly white audiences. Hayes still knew how to flesh out a song by backing it with a lush orchestral arrangement, as evident from an 11-minute remake of "The Look of Love." The song was largely ignored by the black audience when released as a single, and failed to crack the R&B charts. It did not fare much better on the pop charts either, reaching number 79 in the spring of 1971. Despite its minimal success on the charts, Hayes' remake of "The Look of Love" has grown in stature over the years. R&B diva Anita Baker covered the song on her 1994 *Rhythm of Love* album, reportedly due to inspiration she received from Hayes' remake. His version was also one of 12 soul classics chosen for the highly successful soundtrack to the 1995 film *Dead Presidents*.

"Ike's Mood" failed to chart when released as a single, but like "The Look of Love," it has proven to have a legacy; the piano break was heavily sampled by rap music artists during that genre's infancy in the early 1980s. Led by "The Look of Love," "Ike's Mood," and a remake of Ruby and the Romantics' "Our Day Will Come," the *To Be Continued* album achieved gold status.

Hayes' career reached new heights when he was approached by film director Gordon Parks and producer Joel Freeman to write the music for *Shaft*, a 1971 film starring Richard Roundtree, about a black New York City detective. The film and its double-album soundtrack were released in the fall of 1971, and both were highly successful. The soundtrack topped the R&B, pop, and jazz charts and became the fastest-selling album in Stax history. The success of the album was triggered by its relentless, mostly instrumental title track, which spent two weeks atop the pop charts. A second hit from the soundtrack was "Do Your Thing," a 19-minute workout of jazz and funk. An edited version was released as a single early in 1972; it reached number three on the R&B charts. Although no further tracks from *Shaft* were released as singles, the album included several underrated standouts: the perky "Cafe Regio's," the moody and laid-back "Bumpy's Lament," the graceful "Ellie's Love Theme," and the somber "Soulsville," Hayes' dark view of the ghetto. The latter song, prominently featuring female backing vocals, served as the background for one of the film's most vivid scenes, in which Roundtree's John Shaft searched through Harlem for an assistant.

It can be argued that the soundtrack was responsible for the success of the film, or vice versa. Either way, Hollywood knew a good thing when they saw it. Film companies scrambled to make movies centered around black superheroes. Of equal importance was finding a soul artist to handle the soundtrack. As something of an unspoken rule, most of these soundtracks were dominated by the wah-wah guitar that was so prevalent in "Theme from *Shaft*." Many of these motion pictures, later to be called "black exploitation" or "blaxploitation" films, were forgettable, as were their soundtracks. However, the genre did produce its musical gems, most notably Curtis Mayfield's *Superfly* (1972), *Claudine* (1974), and *Sparkle* (1976); Willie Hutch's *The Mack* (1973); and Norman Whitfield's *Car Wash* (1976) and *Which Way Is Up* (1978).

Awards for Hayes came in bunches. The *Shaft* soundtrack won a Grammy for best original score for a motion picture or television special, and "Theme from *Shaft*" won for best instrumental arrangement and for best engineered recording. The theme song also won an Oscar for best song, and a similar honor at the Golden Globe Awards. At the Academy Awards ceremony on April 10, 1972, Hayes gave an elaborate stage presentation of "Theme from *Shaft*," complete with dancers, flashing lights, smoke, and steam; it was a total contrast to the theretofore ultra-conservatism of the event.

At the time of the 1972 Academy Awards, Hayes had a minor hit with a cover of Al Green's recent Number One single, "Let's Stay Together." Hayes' version was primarily a sax-playing instrumental, save for the female background singers who repeated the chorus. Curiously, the song never made it onto a contemporary album.

Hayes' follow-up to *Shaft* was the *Black Moses* double-album, released at the beginning of 1972. Featured on the album was a slow remake of the Jackson Five's "Never Can Say Goodbye," which was issued as a single a year earlier and peaked at number five on the R&B charts. Hoping to have lightning strike twice in the same place, Hayes returned to the catalogue of Burt Bacharach and Hal David for remakes of "(They Long to Be) Close to You" and "I'll Never Fall in Love Again." He also covered Jerry Butler's "Never Gonna Give You Up" and "A Brand New Me" in search of another "I Stand Accused." Unfortunately, the results were halfhearted and the album yielded no further hits. Nevertheless, *Black Moses* still reached the top 10 and earned Hayes another gold disc, mostly on the strength of his larger than life reputation after the success of *Shaft*.

The album was more noteworthy for Hayes' visual image. In 1970, an assistant to Hayes gave him the moniker "Black Moses" in reference to his position as the black leader of the music world. Stax then took the handle and marketed it as the title to Hayes' album. Although Hayes did not originate Black Moses, he played up to it. The album was packaged in a sleeve which folded out to form a large cross and was illustrated with a biblically-attired Hayes by a riverbank with his eyes (covered with sunglasses) looking skyward.

Hayes' fans also saw him as something of a messiah. His enormous success gave hope to the black community who saw him rise from harrowing poverty to the top of the music world. Adding to this image was the visibility of Hayes' affluent lifestyle. He owned three homes, nine luxury cars, and six motorcycles, and maintained a staff of 80 (mostly padded with hometown friends).

Black Moses marked the beginning of the end for Hayes as the prominent superstar of black music. In the spring of 1972 he reunited with David Porter for a duet, "Ain't That Loving You (For More Reasons Than One)." Produced and performed in the same deep soul mold as the material they generated for Sam and Dave the previous decade, the song barely cracked the R&B top 40. Later that fall, Hayes wrote the theme song for *The Men*, an ABC-TV spy and police anthology series. Done in the same vein as *Shaft*, the frantic, all-instrumental "Theme from *The Men*" became a top 40 hit.

Hayes' recording career was relatively quiet in 1973. That summer he released a live double LP, *Live at the Sahara Tahoe*, which earned another gold disk. The album was also noteworthy in that Hayes became the only R&B or rock artist ever to release three consecutive double albums. His name remained in the spotlight that year due to the emergence of Barry White. White, assisted by arranger Gene Page, also favored lavish arrangements and lengthy songs, as evident from his debut album, *I've Got So Much to Give*, which contained only five songs. With White's deep bass and pillow-talk raps on display throughout most of his lushly orchestrated songs, the initial comparison to Hayes was inevitable, though neither artist would publicly admit to it. Although both artists favored lengthy, heavily orchestrated songs featuring introductory raps, White was not merely a carbon copy of Hayes. Whereas Hayes' creativity lay in producing an elaborate remakes of others' tunes, White wrote most of his songs. Hayes also rapped from a street-wise perspective about the variables of male-female relationships; White's raps led you straight to the bedroom (as he claims his music has done for half of the world). Nevertheless, with White bursting onto the scene in 1973 with "I'm Gonna Love You Just a Little More Baby" at a time when Hayes' star was beginning to fade, many observed it as a passing of the torch.

Towards the end of 1973, Hayes released *Joy*. The album contained only five songs, all written by Hayes, and displayed a better mix of the ingredients that gave him his earlier success: the lush orchestrations, the lengthy raps, and the prominent female vocal background of Hot Buttered Soul. The 16-minute title track, with its hypnotic bassline, was edited and released as a single that became a top 10 R&B hit. The remaining songs were ballads: the defiant "I'm Gonna Make It (Without You)"; "A Man Will Be a Man," where Hayes is apologetic after cheating on his lady; and the erotic "The Feeling Keeps on Coming" and "I Love You That's All," the latter perhaps the zenith of his sensuality. Like its predecessors, *Joy* earned gold status.

Like several other record companies, Stax tried to capitalize on the legacy of *Shaft*. Hayes scored both *Three Tough Guys* and *Truck Turner* in 1974. He made his acting debut in the former, and starred in the latter as a bounty hunter. However, both movies and their soundtracks were unsuccessful in comparison to *Shaft*.

During this time, Hayes' relationship with Stax was deteriorating. He did not feel the company was adequately promoting his records, and he later hit Stax with a $5.3 million lawsuit for allegedly not paying him money from his royalties. Hayes and Stax subsequently settled out of court, but when the financially-riddled Stax folded in the fall of 1975 and had its assets sold at auction, Hayes reportedly claimed that he still had not received millions of dollars due him.

After breaking his ties with Stax, Hayes formed his own Hot

Buttered Soul label and got a distribution deal with ABC Records. On this new label, Hayes produced his backup singers, Hot Buttered Soul Unlimited; a female vocalist named Gentry; a vocal group called the Masqueraders; and his own backup musicians, the Isaac Hayes Movement. However, most of these projects were never released.

Hayes' debut album on his new label was *Chocolate Chip*, released in the summer of 1975. The title song, a thunderous, hard-driving track, was aimed at those who emulated "the players" from that era's "blaxploitation" films. Perhaps the album's strongest song was the ballad "Come Live with Me." Led by these two singles, both top 20 R&B hits, the *Chocolate Chip* album was something of a comeback for Hayes, earning gold status. In 1976 he released *Groove-A-Thon* and *Juicy Fruit*. Geared towards the disco market, the albums were a display of how Hayes was now following trends instead of setting them. Neither of these albums were big sellers.

Hayes had big plans for Hot Buttered Soul Records. He set up a business that included a studio, 16 offices, and numerous employees. It was designed to handle publishing, touring and business administration for Hayes and the other artists on the label. However, with recent poor record sales, funds were dwindling, and this affected Hayes' creative freedom. Once the master of covering someone else's song and interpreting it into something entirely his own, Hayes was now pressured to write his own material in order to reap greater royalties. He also set unrealistic time frames to complete his albums. *Groove-A-Thon* was completed in seven days, from original concept to final mix.

Hayes' problems in 1976 were not restricted to recording. Unfortunately, for most of his show business career he had paid more attention to the show instead of the business. Due to financial mismanagement, poor financial advice, and his own personal extravagance, he found himself $6 million in debt and was forced to declare bankruptcy late that year.

In the spring of 1977, Hayes joined Dionne Warwick for a world tour billed as "A Man and a Woman." They later released a double live album of the same name. This was the final release on Hot Buttered Soul and the end of Hayes' association with ABC Records.

Hayes joined Polydor Records in June 1977 and released *New Horizon* early the following year. Although the album was not a huge success, two of its songs charted: the funky "Out of the Ghetto" and an edited version of the disco-flavored "Moonlight Lovin' (Menage a Trois)." The ballads "It's Heaven to Me" and the exotic "Don't Take Your Love Away" marked the beginning of Hayes returning to the style of music from earlier in his career. Later in 1978 he released *For the Sake of Love*. From this album, "Zeke the Freak" was a top 20 R&B hit and was an even bigger success with the disco audience.

Hayes' earlier association with Dionne Warwick paid off handsomely for both artists in 1979. When Warwick went to Hayes looking for new material, she wanted to use "Deja Vu," a tune Hayes wrote for himself two years earlier. He reluctantly gave it up; the song was highly instrumental in reviving her career, which had been dormant for the previous five years.

Towards the end of 1979, Hayes released his third Polydor LP, *Don't Let Go*, which went gold. The success of the album was spurred by the title track, an updated disco-styled remake of a 1961 hit for Roy Hamilton, which became a top 20 pop and R&B hit. Almost as an afterthought, a second single, "A Few More Kisses to Go," was released in the spring of 1980. Somewhat unfashionable in the age of disco, this smoldering ballad was not a chart success at the time of its release, but has grown in stature to rank alongside Hayes' other classic recordings.

Hayes also found time in 1979 to record a duet album with Millie Jackson, entitled *Royal Rappin's*. From the album, two singles charted: "Do You Wanna Make Love" and "You Never Cross My Mind."

After the 1980 release of *And Once Again*, Hayes abandoned his own recording career. For the early part of the 1980s, he went into a period of semi-retirement, only appearing to do sporadic production work for Dionne Warwick, Linda Clifford, and Donald Byrd.

In 1986 Hayes resurfaced on Columbia Records with *U-Turn*. The album's lead single was "Hey Girl," a cover of Freddie Scott's 1963 hit. Hayes incorporated this remake into an anti-crack rap, which included a romantic touch. Released as a single, "Ike's Rap"/ "Hey Girl" became a top 10 R&B hit late in 1986; the song perhaps appeared as a novelty to the younger record-buying public not accustomed to Hayes' trademark rap from the early 1970s. Other standouts from the album included the ballad "I Can't Take My Eyes off You" and the smooth, mid-tempo "Thing for You," the latter charting in early 1987.

Two years later Hayes released *Love Attack*, but to only modest response. He did not appear on the charts again until he performed a duet with Barry White, "Dark and Lovely," which peaked at number 29 early in 1992 and appeared on White's album *Put Me in Your Mix*.

In 1995 Hayes returned to his Memphis roots for the release of two albums, *Branded* and the instrumental *Raw and Refined*, on Point Blank Records. The two albums served as something of a retrospective of his career. Hayes reunited with David Porter for "Thanks to the Fool," actually a continuation of "I Stand Accused." He also produced remakes of "Soulsville" and "Hyperbolicsyllabicsesquedalymistic." Although the albums were well received by music critics, they were not commercially successful.

As of 1996, the music audience has not embraced the legacy of Isaac Hayes with the same appreciation reserved for Barry White, Al Green, and Marvin Gaye. However, with the importance of the body of music created by Hayes, particularly between 1969 and 1971 with *Hot Buttered Soul* and *Shaft*, it is just a matter of time before this multi-talented singer-composer-arranger-producer-trendsetter is given his just due as a musical genius.

The Intruders

Led by the distinctive straining vocals of Samuel "Little Sonny" Brown and the arrangements of Kenny Gamble and Leon Huff, the Intruders were one of the more consistent and successful soul groups of the late 1960s and early 1970s and were the foundation of the Gamble and Huff music empire of the 1970s. With their string of hits in the mid- and late 1960s, particularly "Cowboys to Girls" and "(Love Is Like a) Baseball Game," this Philadelphia quartet consistently kept the early version of the Philly sound before the public. Once this sound coalesced in the 1970s, the Intruders' success culminated with the perennial Mother's Day favorite, "I'll Always Love My Mama."

Originally composed of five members, the Intruders began in Philadelphia in the mid-1950s as a street-corner doo-wop group. When the initial group broke up, the Intruders reformed in 1960 as a quartet consisting of Samuel "Little Sonny" Brown (lead), Robert "Big Sonny" Edwards, Eugene "Bird" Daughtry, and Phil Terry.

Bird Daughtry remembers, "We started in 1952 at Big Jimmy's Barber Shop. We were doing hair and one night we went out singing, drinking that wine . . . just being young boys. We crashed a party and they said, 'Oh, the intruders.' That's how we got the name of the Intruders. When we were young, we were bucks. We came a long way. We were gang-warring and all that, but we found a new life in singing. When we started singing we cut all the bad boys and the bad girls loose. We did house parties, singing doo-wop and *a capella*. Before that we were gospel singers. From 14 to 21 we didn't know any difference. All we knew was that we were having a good time."

Their first recording, "I'm Sold on You" backed by "Come Home Soon," released on the small Gowen label in 1961, quickly disappeared. In 1964 the group met local musicians Kenny Gamble and Leon Huff. Huff played piano on the group's second single, "All the Time," released on Musicor Records. Both Gamble and Huff had considerable experience as session players. Gamble fronted a band called the Romeos. It included Thom Bell (piano), who would become a leading architect of the Philly soul sound in the 1970s, and Roland Chambers (guitar), later a mainstay of MFSB. Huff, a native of Camden, New Jersey, worked as a session musician and writer for Mercury Records in New York and produced a hit for Camden group Patti and the Emblems called "Mixed Up, Shook Up Girl." The duo met in 1964 at a Cameo Records session where Huff played piano on "The 81," a Gamble-penned minor hit for Candy and the Kisses. Huff soon replaced Bell in the Romeos. When the group disbanded, Gamble and Huff produced sessions on a freelance basis. With a $700 loan from local clothing manufacturer Ben Krass, the two formed Excel Records in 1965 and gave the Intruders a sizable regional hit with the haunting "Gonna Be Strong."

"We met [Gamble and Huff] on a rainy night at a place in New Jersey," recalls Bird. "They played behind us. All we had on were mixed clothes like regular clothes. We got up there and sang and as soon as we got off, we went straight to Leon's house in the projects in Camden [New Jersey], and that's when we started to get our stuff together.

"Working with them was tremendous. All six of us stayed at the Schubert Theater on Broad and South for months getting the tunes together. They were the writers and producers and I really loved that. They taught us a lot of things and we taught them a lot of things."

In 1966 the Excel label name was changed to Gamble Records and the Intruders had their first hit with "(We'll Be) United." With Little Sonny's distinctive, nasal voice; the intricate harmonies of Big Sonny, Terry, and Bird; plus the big orchestral arrangements of Gamble and Huff being introduced to a widespread audience, this ballad reached number 14 on the R&B charts. After the mild success of the follow-up, "Devil with Angel's Smile," the group reached the top 10 for the first time in 1967 with "Together." Success continued that year with "Baby I'm Lonely," backed by the popular "A Love That's Real." A third 1967 release, "Check Yourself," an up-tempo, almost frantic track completely out of character for the group, failed to chart.

The Intruders began 1968 with their biggest seller. Again written by Gamble and Huff but this time aided by a Bobby Martin arrangement, "Cowboys to Girls" employed the novel theme of progressing from childhood to adolescence. The song topped the R&B charts for a week, was a top 10 pop hit, and sold over a million copies.

"At that particular time I didn't like 'Cowboys to Girls,'" contends Bird, "but I *love* it now. We were going to the Howard Theater in DC and it was on the radio that we sold a million. I told the driver of our mobile home to pull over, and we all got out and kissed the ground. It felt good. Queen Booking Agency was helping us then and we were working steady. We would come home a day and go back out again. We just kept going, and going, and going. When we would do a show, checks were always coming and we always had pockets full of money. We didn't know we were supposed to get excess gross or whatever. We didn't worry about that. The thing is, God helped us."

The Intruders followed with "(Love Is Like a) Baseball Game" later that year, which rose to number four on the R&B charts, and the catchy "Slow Drag," which peaked at number 12. As Gamble and Huff continued to feel around, trying to develop their own sound, the Intruders remained consistent in 1969 and 1970 with "Me Tarzan, You Jane," "Lollipop (I Like You)," the highly popular "Sad Girl," "Old Love," "Tender (Was the Love We Knew)," and "When We Get Married," the latter a remake of the Dreamlovers' 1961 hit.

In 1971, Little Sonny briefly left the group to get married. He was replaced by Bobby Starr on the single "I'm Girl Scouting" before returning to sing lead on "Pray for Me," "I Bet He Don't Love You (Like I Do)" and "(Win, Place or Show) She's a Winner."

By 1973, Kenny Gamble and Leon Huff had established their sound, a combination of an updated big-band arrangement and a disco beat perfected by their house band, MFSB. Having recently formed their own Philadelphia International label, the duo had blockbuster success with Harold Melvin and the Blue Notes, the O'Jays, and Billy Paul, and were on the verge of becoming the decade's leading figures in soul music.

The Intruders received a shot in the arm that year with the release of "I'll Always Love My Mama" and "I Wanna Know Your Name," both of which became top 10 R&B hits. Gamble and Huff gave the group an updated sound, complete with the lush orchestral backing of the MFSB band, despite the vocalists maintaining their now outdated doo-wop style. "I Wanna Know Your Name" contained a rap at the end of the song, a trend being popularized at that time by Isaac Hayes, Barry White, and Harold Melvin and the Blue Notes (on their 1972 hit "I Miss You").

"That was a present from God," says Bird. "When 'I Wanna Know Your Name' came out it was just for love people to get themselves together. You want to know what the lady is about and what the man is about."

Adding to the appeal of "I'll Always Love My Mama" was the second half of the song, featuring the foursome reminiscing about their childhoods while backed by an infectious MFSB-Philly dance beat. "I started that," says Bird. "We did the first side but we still had the second part. Something just hit me and it came through. I just started talking and I'd point to the next fella and motion for him to say something, then the next fella . . . say something, then the next fella . . . say something. That's how it came through and it came out right. It was just off the top of the head."

Both songs were pulled from the *Save the Children* album, a concept album promoting family unity. "The purpose of *Save the Children* was to let the people know that you have to save the kids that are coming up today," says Bird. "If you don't save the kids that are coming up today, they'll be worse than they are now. In our day there was gang-warring but there was no shooting and killing. There'd be a little fighting and stuff, then you'd shake hands and go on about your business. Nowadays, if we don't wake our kids up now, we'll never make it."

The Intruders reached the charts late in 1974 with "A Nice Girl Like You" and in the spring of 1975 with a cover of the Carpenters' 1971 hit "Rainy Days and Mondays." Later in 1975 the group broke up as three of its members walked away from the entertainment industry. Bird explains, "When we came back from England [in 1975], Big Sonny and Phil became Jehovah's Witnesses, and Little Sonny went to work for the government. I continued doing what I'm doing now. You don't knock someone when they want to do something. They didn't want to sing anymore and retired. They had enough of the bright lights and wanted to go into something else."

Although the Intruders disbanded, the group's music remained alive in the early 1980s, particularly in 1981 when Tierra had a huge hit with "Together" interwoven with the "shoot 'em up" hook from "Cowboys to Girls." Two years later Bird reformed the Intruders, incorporating a completely new lineup under the guidance of Glenn Montgomery and lead singer Harry Moon, whose voice bears a striking resemblance to the distinctive lead of Little Sonny.

"After the group broke up I moved to New Orleans," says Bird. "I came back [to Philadelphia] in 1983. I decided to go on and do this one last time, for my last time. I sang for awhile, then I got sick so I turned it over to my 'baby brother' [Montgomery] and my cousins. I kept them in the cellar for two years and groomed them so they could be who they are today.

"We pray every night before we hit the stage. We thank God for us being here, we thank God for getting us home, thank God for letting us live, thank God that our voices are still in shape. I can still sing. I get up there and mess around a little bit. I only do about two or three minutes; then I'm outta there.

"I prefer just handling the business, traveling, relaxing, and meeting different people as I go along in life. We all share together. We have a meeting every week. We rehearse every week and we continue on until we get what God wants us to have."

The new lineup of the Intruders consists of Montgomery, Moon, Philip Gaye, James Murphy, and Edward Barnes. Bird continued to manage the group until failing health sidelined him in 1994. With Montgomery taking the helm, the group currently performs an average of four to five times a month.

"It hasn't been easy to step into the shoes of Bird, Little Sonny, Big Sonny, and Phil," says Montgomery. "They did a great job building a foundation for that sound. We're trying to hold up the name and keep it going. I hope all the fans of the Intruders will come and give us a listen. We come direct from them and with their blessings. We're just carrying the flag for them and we hope we can do them as proud as they have done us."

Millie Jackson

illie Jackson became known as the X-rated rap queen in the 1970s for her raunchy yet humorous live performances and equally outrageous albums, such as *Feelin' Bitchy* and *Get It Out 'Cha System*. However, before Jackson shot to international stardom with her 1975 concept album, *Caught Up*, she had long established herself as a prominent soul singer. With early hits such as "Ask Me What You Want" and "Hurts So Good," Jackson was one of the leading artists on Spring Records and was instrumental in the label's early success in the 1970s.

Millie Jackson was born in Thompson, Georgia, a small town near Augusta, in 1944. She lived there until age 15, before moving to Newark, New Jersey to live with a relative. Two years later Jackson began a modeling career, mainly for confession magazines such as *Bronze Thrills* and *Jive*. Her singing career actually began on a dare. In 1964, on a wager, she jumped onstage at the Palms Cafe in Harlem and started singing.

"I've had nerve like that all my life," she says. "Somebody was there, saw me and hired me to do the Crystal Ballroom. Upstairs there used to be a ballroom that had live music every night. From there I went to Club Zanzibar [in New Jersey]."

After performances at Club Zanzibar and at Brooklyn's 521 Club, Jackson spent a year and a half on the road as a background vocalist for L.C. Cooke (Sam's brother). She briefly performed with the Charlie Lucas band, but when they headed to California, Jackson left and returned to New York, where she took a job as an assistant supervisor at Kimberly Knitwear.

In 1969, through songwriter Billy Nichols, Jackson signed with MGM Records and recorded the single "A Little Bit of Something," which met with little success.

She recalls, "Billy Nichols was the bandleader at the Crystal Ballroom. He had so much faith in me. He was doing a lot of stuff with Suron Productions, and every time somebody in the record business needed a singer, he would call me. I went down and auditioned with [Suron] and they recorded me and put me out on MGM."

After the failure of "A Little Bit of Something," Jackson got out of her contract with MGM and remained relatively inactive for two years. In 1971 she signed with recently formed Spring Records, which was distributed by Polydor. Her first Spring single was "A Child of God (It's Hard to Believe)," a ballad penned by her and Don French. The record was a moderate hit, peaking at number 22 on the R&B charts late in 1971.

Jackson had a banner year in 1972. Working with writer/ producer Raeford Gerald, she began the year with "Ask Me What You Want," a mid-tempo combination of Southern soul and Motown, which peaked at number four on the R&B charts that spring and cracked the pop top 30. Jackson's follow-up, "My Man, A Sweet Man," a bouncy, almost speeded-up version of Martha and the Vandellas' "Jimmy Mack," was nearly as successful, becoming a top 10 R&B hit that summer. "I Miss You Baby," a song similar in production to "Ask Me What You Want," was released late in 1972 and reached number 22. All three songs were included on Jackson's self-titled Spring debut album. In recognition of her success, she was named 1972 Most Promising Female Vocalist by NATRA.

"It was nice to have a record on the radio and to hear yourself but basically it was just something that I wanted to do," she says. "It was just extra money and having fun. I didn't consider myself a star, then or now. I didn't think it would last, that's why I took a leave of absence from my day gig . . . I'm still on leave!"

After the funky and gritty "Breakaway" became a top 20 R&B hit in the spring of 1973, Jackson released her biggest single, "Hurts So Good," which was included in the soundtrack of the "blaxploitation" film *Cleopatra Jones*. This smoldering, deep soul ballad peaked at number three on the R&B charts and reached number 24 on the pop charts. "Hurts So Good" also marked the beginning of Jackson's association with producer Brad Shapiro. On this track, Shapiro slowed down the tempo, allowing Jackson to sing in her natural voice. She explains, "Previously, I had a producer [Raeford Gerald] who was a Motown fan and he went strictly for that Motown sound. I was not being me. 'Hurts So Good' was the first song that came out with my natural voice. At that time, all the women that had hit records had very high voices and I had this man-sounding voice. They used to speed up my records after they were recorded to make my voice sound higher. If you listen to 'My Man, A Sweet Man' and 'Ask Me What You Want,' people think I was a kid back then. 'Hurts So Good' was the first one that had my actual voice."

In 1974 Jackson followed "Hurts So Good" with the haunting, mid-tempo "I Got to Try It One Time" (# 21 R&B), where she contemplates infidelity, and "How Do You Feel the Morning After" (# 11 R&B), where she plays the role of a jilted lover.

The following year, Jackson released the *Caught Up* album, which would catapult her to international stardom. Again working in tandem with Shapiro, *Caught Up* was a concept album and marked Jackson's debut as a producer. The album featured a remake of Luther Ingram's 1972 hit "(If Loving You Is Wrong) I Don't Want to Be Right," which included a rap developed over two years of live performances. In her rap, Jackson captured the advantages and disadvantages of being "the other woman" in a love triangle. The song served as the foundation for the entire first side.

She says, "I thought '[If Loving You Is Wrong] I Don't Want to Be Right' served a purpose with that 'caught up' situation with the three people in the web. It just seemed to be appropriate for the title *Caught Up*.

"I had been doing 'If Loving You Is Wrong' live for a couple of years. Every time I would repeat a club, people would ask for it and I just decided that this [could be] a hit to do it like

I'm doing it with the rap and everything. [Spring] wouldn't let me [produce myself] because I was a writer and a singer. Singers didn't produce back then so they were trying to find a producer to come and hear me and see if I had something. They thought of Don Davis out of Detroit and Brad Shapiro. [At the time] Don was producing Johnnie Taylor and Brad was doing Wilson Pickett. So, I said, 'Pick one. Either one should be able to produce me.' They came up with Brad. He flew out to where I was working and heard me do it but he didn't know how to get it on tape to make it work like I was doing it [live]. He came back and told them that I had to go down [to Muscle Shoals, Alabama] to record it. At the time you rarely had three-minute records; two-forty-five was tops. Three minutes was a long record. This record was six minutes and change. After we finished it, it was like, 'Okay, now where do we go? It seems strange to do a bunch of three-minute records after this.' I decided to keep the story line going. We decided to do a whole side with the story line. Then I felt that now you've heard the mistress' side, we need to hear what the wife has to say about it, so I did the other side . . . without permission."

At a time when concept albums of any kind were a rarity for female soul artists, Spring was initially reluctant to release *Caught Up*. Further fueling their trepidation, given the content of the lyrics there was a question of the album receiving sufficient airplay. Once released, many radio DJ's refused to play it, or bleeped out some of the words if they did. Fortunately for Jackson, one of her biggest supporters was Frankie Crocker, the top radio personality of WBLS, New York's number one black music station.

She explains, "When we brought the album back, [Spring] was afraid to release it. They kept it for about three months, afraid to release it, and they finally played it for Frankie Crocker. I guess you could say I owe a great chunk of my career to Frankie Crocker because [the success of *Caught Up*] was the beginning of Millie Jackson. Until then, I had 'My Man, A Sweet Man' and 'Ask Me What You Want' but they were just songs. [The public] didn't know who made them. They bought the records but the name Millie Jackson wasn't established; the songs were established rather than me. [When *Caught Up* came out] that's when Millie Jackson became known. I guess I owe my career to Spring and *Millie Jackson*, the name, to Frankie Crocker.

"I was looking forward to seeing the album read 'Produced by Brad Shapiro *and* Millie Jackson.' Instead the album read 'Produced by Brad Shapiro; album concept by Millie Jackson.' I went down there and raised holy hell. I was *irate*. They said, 'How many hats do you want to wear? You're singing, you're writing, you've got your own publishing company, and you manage yourself.' I answered, 'Every one that fits my f – – – head!' They said, 'We already printed 50,000 of them but the next ones to come out will have your name as producer.' That's the kind of company Spring was. We laughed about it and went to lunch."

After the gold success of *Caught Up*, Jackson released *Still Caught Up* in 1976, which continued the triangle theme. The album contained a two-sided hit with "Leftovers," where she portrays the mistress; and "Loving Arms," a heartfelt ballad where she is the despondent wife.

With her successful concept albums, the importance of the chart position of her singles was merely an afterthought for Jackson. Although her albums received limited airplay due to much of the material being laced with profanity, Jackson became something of a cult figure, attaining a loyal following of mostly working-class African-American adults. An added benefit of no longer being dependent on radio airplay was Jackson's ability to avoid being affected by the rise of disco music, which severely hindered several of her traditional soul contemporaries from the early part of the decade. Both *Feelin' Bitchy* (1977) and *Get It Out 'Cha System* (1978) went gold. The former, despite being a no-holds-barred recording similar to her raunchy live performances, produced a top 10 hit with "If You're Not Back in Love By Monday."

She points out, "*Feelin' Bitchy* was the biggest album I ever had and *Get It Out 'Cha System* was the second biggest album

I ever had. [Lack of airplay] didn't bother me. I wish I had a song now that they'd buy that didn't get any airplay."

During this time Jackson expanded her career by producing a vocal trio, the Facts of Life, who had a hit in 1976 with "Sometimes." Jackson also became an astute businesswoman. She managed and co-produced herself and administered her own music publishing company, Double Ak-Shun Music. Describing her business acumen, she says, "I'm just logical. I've always been a logically-minded person. It never made sense to me to give somebody 25 percent of my *gross* income and all they did was talk to your booking agent and say, 'She'll take the job.' When I first came along I worked for Kimberly Knitwear and I could buy very expensive uniforms dirt cheap. I already had a record company and I already had an agent, so why am I going to give someone 25 percent of my money? No one could ever explain to me why I needed them. I went to school, so I can count my money."

In 1979 Jackson teamed up with Isaac Hayes, often considered to be her male counterpart, for a series of duets on an album titled *Royal Rappin's*. Two songs from the album charted: "Do You Wanna Make Love" and "You Never Cross My Mind." She recalls, "I really enjoyed working with Ike. Ike and I got an album in at $25,000 under the budget. I had never sung with anyone before. I didn't know harmony at that time, I do now but then, I didn't. I just knew it would take forever to do the voices. We did the tracks and I sent him the tracks, with the words and all of that. We came into Atlanta and we did all of the vocals in two days. He just sang harmony to what I was singing and it was like, 'Wow, we're $25,000 under budget!' I just knew it would click. [The duet] was supposed to be done with Joe Simon but Joe didn't want to sing with me. I never did find out why . . . probably my reputation. I was wondering who else I could do this with. I looked down the roster and decided Isaac. We're both rappers . . . 'That's it!' It's just natural. I called him up and he agreed to do it."

In the early 1980s Jackson continued to release albums on Spring, including the double live LP *Live and Uncensored* (1980),

For Men Only (1980), *Live and Outrageous [Rated XXX]* (1982), and *E.S.P.* (1983).

After Spring went under in the early 1980s, Jackson re-emerged on Jive, the American subsidiary of the British label Zomba, for the release of *An Imitation of Love* in 1986. The album gave her two top 10 hits with the dance track "Hot! Wild! Unrestricted! Crazy Love," and "Love Is a Dangerous Game." Jackson's newfound success on the singles charts allowed a younger audience a chance to get a glimpse of the artist they had previously perceived as off-limits. She explains, "My audience is now younger because all of these kids who couldn't listen to me ten years ago because their parents said 'No' are grown now. When I worked with the Jacksons several years ago, I wondered why they would put me on the show with these kids. Then I realized they're not kids anymore; they're grown. I got over like a fat rat because the kids aren't kids anymore, which meant that the audience were no longer kids; they're grown people. My audience has become much younger because I'm that taboo that they were not supposed to be introduced to. Now that they're older, they want to see what they weren't supposed to see."

Jackson released three more albums on the Jive label: *The Tide Is Turning* (1988), *Back to the S@#t!* (1989), and *Young Man, Older Woman* (1991). The title song of the latter served as the basis for a full theatrical play of the same name, which she stars in.

In 1993 she signed with Ichiban Records to release *Young Man, Older Woman — The Cast Album.* She says, "At the time the play was out and I wanted the cast album out. I had known [Ichiban president] John Abbey for years and I gave him a call and he said, 'We want an album out on you.' So I said, 'Well, do the cast album and I'll give you one on me.' And he agreed. That was it. I like little companies where you can just go in and talk to the owner."

As of 1996 Millie Jackson continues to chalk up rave reviews for her performance in the musical comedy play *Young Man, Older Woman.* In addition to Jackson, the cast includes her daughter Keisha, actor/comedian Reynaldo Rey, Doug Smith, and later singer Al Goodman of Ray, Goodman and Brown. Her latest studio album was the 1995 release of *It's Over!?*

Still a top concert attraction with her cult-like following, before the play caught on Millie Jackson performed between 35 and 40 weeks a year. She says, "I'm doing less but still about 30-something weeks a year. I used to do 40-something a year but now I'm doing 30-something. I'll keep doing it as long as they send money. Just send money and I'll be there."

Gladys Knight
AND THE Pips

With a recording career that has spanned more than 30 years, Gladys Knight and the Pips are without a doubt one of the most durable and successful groups in the history of modern popular music. Led by Gladys' deep, gospel-infused alto and the intricate harmonies of the Pips, this Atlanta-based family group is always right at home, whether singing the soulful "If I Were Your Woman," an MOR ballad such as "Neither One of Us," or a dance track like 1987's "Love Overboard." In the early stages of their career a tightly-choreographed stage act made Gladys and the Pips a popular attraction despite an erratic recording career. The quartet's first consistent run of hits came in the mid-1960s on Motown's Soul label, led by the huge "I Heard It Through the Grapevine." Moving to Buddah in the early 1970s, the group reached the pinnacle of their success with a series of soul/MOR hits, such as "Midnight Train to Georgia" and "Best Thing That Ever Happened to Me." After a rocky period in the late 1970s, the group made a triumphant return in the 1980s with "Landlord" and "Save the Overtime (For Me)." With nearly 40 hit songs to their credit, Gladys Knight and the Pips have created a body of work ranking among the finest in contemporary R&B/pop music and have earned their place as one of the most respected vocal groups of all time.

Gladys Knight was born in Atlanta in 1944. At age four she joined the Mount Moriah Baptist Church choir and toured Georgia and Alabama with the Morris Brown gospel choir.

Two years later, a seven-year-old Gladys appeared on *Ted Mack's Amateur Hour* and won the $2,000 first prize for her rendition of Nat King Cole's "Too Young." In 1952 at her brother Merald "Bubba" Knight's birthday party, Gladys, Bubba, their sister Brenda, and cousins William and Eleanor Guest put on an impromptu concert. Impressed with their harmony, other family members encouraged them to continue as a singing group, and the Pips were formed. They chose their name in honor of another cousin, James "Pip" Woods, who became their first manager and arranged gigs for them at local clubs. While performing secular music as the Pips, the quintet sang gospel music as the Fountaineers.

In 1957 the Pips hooked up with Supersonic Productions and joined Sam Cooke and Jackie Wilson on the road. Wilson arranged for the group to record for his label, Brunswick Records. The result was "Whistle My Love," issued in early 1958, which went nowhere. The following year Eleanor and Brenda left the group to get married and go to college. They were replaced by their cousin Edward Patten and by Langston George.

In 1960 the Pips were appearing at the Builders Club in Atlanta. Club owner Clifford Hunter and his partner Tommy Brown recorded the group singing a version of the 1952 Johnny Otis-penned "Every Beat of My Heart" and released it on their newly formed Huntom label. The song took off in Atlanta and Hunter sold the rights to Vee-Jay Records in Chicago. Meanwhile, the record caught the attention of Bobby Robinson, owner of Fury Records in New York. Robinson signed the group to his label, renamed them Gladys Knight and the Pips, and had them re-record the song. In the spring of 1961, both versions hit the charts. The Pips' more soulful, yet primitive version on Vee-Jay topped the R&B charts while their newer, "supper club" version on Fury peaked at number 15. Both recordings, featuring a deep, rich alto on lead, sounded like they were sung by a woman much more mature than the then 16-year-old Gladys.

After their second single on Fury, a cover of Jesse Belvin's "Guess Who," failed to chart, the group rebounded early in

1962, with "Letter Full of Tears" rising to number three. In April 1962, Langston George quit and was never replaced. A short time later the group temporarily broke up when Gladys married and had a child. During this interim, the three Pips worked as background session singers. They also recorded two little-noticed singles on Fury, which was now on the verge of being shut down due to problems with the IRS. In June 1964, Gladys returned and the group was signed to Maxx Records. They had modest success that year with "Giving Up," a brooding ballad penned by Van McCoy. Gladys and the Pips released four more singles on Maxx: "Lovers Always Forgive" (1964), "Either Way I Lose," "Who Knows," and "If I Should Ever Fall in Love" (all 1965). However, all of these songs sold poorly and Maxx Records soon folded.

With the help of talent promoter Marguerite Mays and choreographer Cholly Atkins, Gladys and the Pips earned a reputation as a top-notch live act. Dressed in elegant suits, the three Pips were a dazzling display of spins and dips as they sang background behind Gladys' gospel-flavored soul lead in a tightly choreographed stage act.

In 1966 the group was booked as special guests on a Motown package tour. On the strength of audience reception, they were offered a recording contract by owner Berry Gordy. Gladys was reluctant to sign with Motown, feeling that the group would be lost in the shuffle of the label's Detroit-based artists who had already risen up in the ranks by 1966. However, the Pips were attracted to Motown's ability to get their artists booked into some of the country's more prestigious nightclubs. When the group took a democratic vote to decide on Motown, Gladys voted against, but the three Pips voted in favor of the move, so they signed.

The quartet debuted on Motown's Soul label in the summer of 1966 with the percussion-driven "Just Walk in My Shoes," produced by Johnny Bristol and Harvey Fuqua, but it failed to chart. Norman Whitfield took over production on their next single, "Take Me in Your Arms and Love Me," but it also did nothing. The group's third Soul single, "Everybody Needs

Love," a soft, doo-wop-flavored track whose production did not quite match Gladys' earthy vocals, managed to reach number three on the R&B charts in the summer of 1967.

Gladys and the Pips finally broke through in the fall of 1967 with the release of "I Heard It Through the Grapevine." Whitfield initially recorded the song with the Miracles, the Isley Brothers, and Marvin Gaye, but none of those versions were released. He found the perfect match for "Grapevine" with Gladys and the Pips. Out of deep respect for the group, Whitfield let them have considerable input in the song's arrangement. The result was a torrid, percussive, call-and-response track, which allowed Gladys free rein to spit fire with her furious, gospel-driven vocals over the course of three minutes. "Grapevine" immediately shot up the R&B charts, where it stayed at Number One for six weeks. The song also gave the group the crossover smash they were seeking, as it reached number two on the pop charts for three weeks, and sold over two million copies.

Despite the magnitude of "I Heard It Through the Grapevine," Gladys and the Pips were unable to establish their identity with the song because of Motown's penchant for having several of their artists record the same material. Whitfield, whose productions epitomized this custom, cut a completely different version of "Grapevine" with Marvin Gaye the following year. In most cases with Motown, if a song became a hit for one artist, a different version was merely added as a filler track for another artist's album. Unfortunately for Gladys and the Pips, Gaye's dark, haunting version of "Grapevine" topped the pop charts for seven weeks, was Motown's biggest selling single at that time, and became the song from the 1960s which Gaye was most identified with.

Gladys and the Pips followed "I Heard It Through the Grapevine" with "The End of Our Road" in early 1968, a song similar in production to its predecessor, that peaked at number five on the R&B charts. As with "Grapevine," Whitfield had Gaye cut a cover version of "The End of Our Road," which became a moderate hit for him in 1970.

In the summer of 1968 the group had their fourth top 10 Soul hit, with Gladys assuming the role of a jilted woman attending the wedding of her former lover in "It Should Have Been Me." A year went by before Gladys and the Pips had another significant hit: a psychedelic remake of Shirley Ellis' 1964 smash "The Nitty Gritty," which spent two weeks at the number two spot on the R&B charts in the summer of 1969. Later that year they hit paydirt again with "Friendship Train," a refreshing song in the context of the angry mood of the country during this time. Here Gladys delivered a plea for peace, harmony, justice, and freedom over Whitfield's ever-popular psychedelic production. "Friendship Train" brought the group its first Grammy nomination for best R&B vocal performance by a duo or group. Previously, "I Heard It Through the Grapevine" received a Grammy nomination for best R&B *solo* vocal performance, female. Gladys and the Pips' final collaboration with Whitfield, "You Need Love Like I Do (Don't You)," reached number three on the R&B charts in the spring of 1970.

Clay McMurray took over production of the group on "If I Were Your Woman," a song he co-wrote with Gloria Jones (who recorded the original version of Soft Cell's 1982 hit "Tainted Love") and Pam Sawyer. An elegant yet emotional ballad, "If I Were Your Woman" pulled Gladys and the Pips away from the up-tempo funk exhibited on their Whitfield-produced hits and brought them back to the style they were accustomed to before coming to Motown. The song topped the R&B charts for a week early in 1971 and brought them back to the pop top 10. It also received Grammy nominations for best R&B song and best R&B performance by a duo or group.

Gladys kept the emotion up full tilt on the follow-up single, "I Don't Want to Do Wrong," a song the group co-wrote with Johnny Bristol and former Marvelette Catherine Anderson Schaffner. On this track she sought the strength to remain faithful when her lover had been away too long. Gladys' gospel-fueled intensity, coupled with more prominent backing from the Pips, propelled this ballad to number two on the R&B charts for four weeks in the summer of 1971.

The group ran their top 10 streak to six at the end of 1971 with the passionate ballad "Make Me the Woman That You Go Home To," again written and produced by McMurray. The spring 1972 release of "Help Me Make It Through the Night," although credited to Gladys Knight and the Pips, was in reality a solo Gladys recording. The song, the group's first to crack the easy-listening charts, received a Grammy nomination for best R&B vocal performance by a duo, group, or chorus.

In March 1973 the group's contract with Motown expired. During their seven-year tenure with Motown, the record shows that both Gladys' fears and the Pips' expectations were met. Berry Gordy promised the group hits and he delivered. Twelve of their singles made the R&B top 10, 10 of them reaching the top three. This was a chart run the quartet did not achieve on any label before or after Motown. As the three Pips had predicted, the group gained wider exposure by being booked into better clubs and appearing more frequently on television specials, including Ed Sullivan's final show on June 6, 1971.

However, Gladys' 1966 suspicion also proved right. Despite the group's string of hits and their popularity with audiences, they were never a top priority at the label, as evidenced by their being shifted around to various producers during their tenure. Whereas Motown diligently presented its other superstar acts to the pop market, Gladys Knight and the Pips were regarded as strictly an R&B act. By the time the group's contract with Motown expired, only two of their singles—"I Heard It Through the Grapevine" and "If I Were Your Woman"—reached the pop top 10. Dissatisfied with their low position on Motown's totem pole, the group signed with Buddah Records.

At the time Gladys and the Pips signed with Buddah, Motown released "Neither One of Us (Wants to Be the First to Say Goodbye)," an elegant, middle-of-the-road ballad, which topped the R&B charts for four weeks in the spring of 1973 and reached number two on the pop charts. The song was the group's first collaboration with up-and-coming songwriter Jim Weatherly, an ex All-American quarterback at the University of Mississippi. Motown quickly packaged an album entitled

Neither One of Us, which became a million-seller (the group's first) and included another hit, "Daddy Could Swear (I Declare)," co-written by Gladys and Bubba.

Buddah Records president Art Kass promised Gladys and the Pips a lot and he immediately delivered. He allowed them to co-produce *Imagination*, their first album for the label, and paired them with producer Tony Camillo. The group's first Buddah release was Weatherly's "Where Peaceful Waters Flow," whose grace and elegance made it an appropriate follow-up to "Neither One of Us." Despite its middle-of-the-road overtones, "Where Peaceful Waters Flow" still became an R&B hit, reaching number six in the summer of 1973.

Gladys and the Pips next carried this momentum into what would be their signature song and the highlight of their recording career, "Midnight Train to Georgia." Again written by Weatherly, the song was originally called "Midnight Plane to Houston," under which title he recorded a version himself for Amos Records. The title was changed to "Midnight Train to Georgia" by Atlanta producer Sonny Limbo and was recorded by Cissy Houston (Whitney's mother and a former member of the Sweet Inspirations) for Janus Records in 1972, but this version failed to become a hit. The song was then forwarded by Weatherly's publisher to Gladys and the Pips. On the Pips' version of "Midnight Train to Georgia," Gladys was both laid-back and emotional as her Southern-soul vocal delivery marked a return to her church roots. The song was also earmarked by the Pips through the integration of their famous "ooh-ooh," representing a train whistle. This soulful classic, about Gladys joining her man on a journey home after he failed to achieve stardom in Los Angeles, topped the R&B charts for four weeks in the fall of 1973, became the group's only Number One pop hit, and was a certified million-seller.

Gladys and the Pips upped the tempo on their next single, the drum- and bass-laden "I've Got to Use My Imagination." The song marked the pairing of the group with the production team of Kenny Kerner and Richie Wise, who recently took the rock group Stories to Number One with "Brother Louie."

Gladys and the Pips came close to achieving the same success as "I've Got to Use My Imagination" topped the R&B charts for a week early in 1974, hit number four on the pop charts, and became another million-seller.

By the end of 1973, Gladys Knight and the Pips had their finest commercial year, selling close to 7.5 million singles and albums. Nominated for four Grammy Awards, they won two: "Neither One of Us (Wants to Be the First to Say Goodbye)" was deemed best pop vocal performance by a duo, group, or chorus; and "Midnight Train to Georgia" won for best R&B vocal performance by a duo, group, or chorus.

In the spring of 1974 Gladys and the Pips enjoyed their third straight Number One R&B hit and million-seller with the beautiful "Best Thing That Ever Happened to Me." Written by Weatherly in 1971, the song became a Number One country hit for Ray Price two years later. When producers Kerner and Wise recorded "Best Thing That Ever Happened to Me" with Gladys and the Pips, they kept the country-and-western flavor. However, it was Gladys' heartfelt interpretation of what was arguably their finest Weatherly-penned recording that gave their version its magic.

Led by the success of "Midnight Train to Georgia," "Best Thing That Ever Happened," "I've Got to Use My Imagination," and "Where Peaceful Waters Flow," the *Imagination* album went gold. By 1974 Gladys Knight and the Pips had reached the pinnacle of their success and became household names. They appeared on all of the major television shows and drew rave concert reviews at many of the country's prestigious show places, including the Waldorf-Astoria in New York and the Flamingo Hilton in Las Vegas.

Gladys and the Pips were paired with Curtis Mayfield for their next album, the soundtrack for the popular movie *Claudine,* which starred Diahann Carroll and James Earl Jones. Mayfield, the former creative force and lead singer of the Impressions, was a natural choice for producer after he achieved staggering success with the soundtrack to 1972's "blaxploitation" movie *Superfly.* Working with Mayfield, whose hits with the Impressions were targeted strictly to the black community, also assured Gladys and the Pips that success with their middle-of-the-road tunes from *Imagination* would not result in them losing their black audience. The *Claudine* soundtrack, released in the spring of 1974, yielded three notable songs and was certified gold. The lead single was "On and On," a complete departure from the songs on *Imagination*. Led by a funky guitar intro, Gladys' gritty vocals, accompanied by the prominent backing of the Pips, propelled this hard-driving dance track to number two on the R&B charts for four weeks in the spring of 1974. The song also hit number five on the pop charts and was the group's fourth consecutive million-seller. "On and On" was backed by the soulful ballad "The Makings of You," originally recorded by Mayfield in 1970. Although Gladys and the Pips' version never charted as a single, this solo Gladys recording was one of the finest moments of her tenure on Buddah. One of the more popular songs from the soundtrack was the melodic "Make Yours a Happy Home." Inexplicably, the song, which served as the film's finale, was not released as a single until 1976, when it reached number 13, after the group began to lose some of its steam.

In the fall of 1974, Gladys and the Pips released *I Feel a Song*. The title track, co-written by Tony Camillo and his writing partner Mary Sawyer, was recorded by three other artists — the Stairsteps, Linda Carr, and Sandra Richardson — before hitting paydirt with Gladys and the Pips. The group's version of "I Feel a Song (In My Heart)" had a defiant Gladys praising a new love while saying goodbye to an old one. The song topped the R&B charts for two weeks late in 1974. However, in relation to the group's previous four releases, "I Feel a Song" was a disappointment on the pop charts, only reaching number 21.

Gladys and the Pips followed "I Feel a Song" with "Love Finds Its Own Way" early in 1975. This track was strictly a pop ballad that surprisingly failed to generate much interest on the pop charts (number 47). However, the song did reach number three on the R&B charts, mostly due to the group's long-standing reputation.

The next move for Gladys and the Pips was to cover "The Way We Were," a huge hit in 1973 for Barbra Streisand. The song received widespread acclaim whenever the quartet performed it live, which prompted Buddah to have them record it. The Pips' version was included in a medley with the standard "Try to Remember," and was recorded live at the Pine Knob Music Theater, located just outside of Detroit. When released as a single in the spring of 1975, "The Way We Were/Try to Remember" was targeted to the R&B audience (number six), although it did manage to score well on the pop charts also, peaking at number 11.

On the strength of "I Feel a Song (In My Heart)" and "The Way We Were/Try to Remember," the *I Feel a Song* album became the group's fourth straight gold LP.

As a testament to their widespread appeal, Gladys and the Pips were chosen to headline a four-week summer variety show on NBC-TV in 1975. Each week the group sang a number of their hits and joined guest stars in musical and comedy routines.

Later in 1975 the group released the *2nd Anniversary* album. This new LP gave them two R&B hits, with the funky "Money" reaching number four and the heartfelt, melancholy "Part Time Love," written by David Gates of Bread, also reaching number four. However, neither of these songs, particularly the former, came close to matching the consistent pop success the group achieved just 18 months earlier.

In the fall of 1976 Gladys made her acting debut in *Pipe Dreams*, a film produced and co-starring her then husband Barry Hankerson and gospel star James Cleveland. The movie, which used the unlikely setting of the Alaskan oil pipeline for a romantic drama, was heavily financed by Gladys and turned out to be an economic disaster, leaving her heavily in debt. The Pips were not featured in the film but joined Gladys for eight songs on the soundtrack, including "So Sad the Song," which peaked at number 12 in the fall of 1976.

Chart success for Gladys and the Pips began to falter in the mid- to late 1970s as the songs they generated during this period did not quite match their material from earlier in the decade.

Also negatively impacting the group was the change at this time in musical taste from soul towards disco. However, hit records became something of an afterthought for the group as they concentrated on the more lucrative cabaret circuit. For the rest of the decade their only song to crack the R&B top 10 was "Baby Don't Change Your Mind," released in the spring of 1977. This sugar-coated, disco-flavored track marked a reunion of the group with Van McCoy, who produced tracks for Gladys and the Pips in 1964 when the group was recording for Maxx Records.

Also contributing to the group's recording letdown was the financial disarray of Buddah Records, which made a deal to have the label distributed by Arista Records. In April 1978, Gladys filed a $23 million lawsuit against Buddah Records, its president Art Kass, Arista Records, and its president Clive Davis. The suit reportedly charged the defendants with breach of contract and conspiring to interfere with Gladys' attempt to terminate her contract. The matter was further complicated when Gladys Knight signed as a solo artist with Columbia Records in the summer of 1978. This brought a counter-suit from Buddah and Arista against Gladys and CBS (Columbia's parent company), charging breach of contract.

While the cases were under suit, Gladys and the Pips were restricted from recording together, although they could continue to perform live. Gladys recorded a solo album entitled *Miss Gladys Knight,* and with the permission of Buddah, the Pips recorded two albums for Casablanca Records, *At Last . . . The Pips* and *Callin.'* However, none of these releases generated much interest.

In the spring of 1980, marathon meetings were held with representatives of Gladys, Buddah, Arista, and Columbia and an agreement was reached. The agreement called for Buddah to receive a settlement in return for them dropping the lawsuit against Gladys and Columbia. Buddah also agreed to release the Pips, who were never part of the suit.

Gladys and the Pips celebrated their return to recording together with the release of *About Love,* their Columbia debut, in the summer of 1980. The album was written and produced by Nick Ashford and Valerie Simpson, with whom the group had briefly worked at Motown resulting in their 1969 hit, "Didn't You Know (You'd Have to Cry Sometime)." By 1980 Ashford and Simpson were one of the hottest R&B production teams in the industry, having produced Chaka Khan's solo debut, "I'm Every Woman," in 1978 and rejuvenated Diana Ross' recording career with an updated sound on her 1979 album *The Boss.*

The first single from *About Love* was "Landlord," a warm, mid-tempo track, somewhat unfashionable in the age of disco. With its catchy lyrics, the single rose to number three on the R&B charts in the summer of 1980. Ironically, the album's more up-to-date song, the danceable "Taste of Bitter Love," was the second single released and had only moderate success, peaking at number 38. Led by these two singles, *About Love* was a success with the black audience. The album also served as the proper vehicle for Gladys Knight and the Pips to re-establish themselves with the public after the confusion created by the lawsuits at the end of the previous decade.

Ashford and the Simpson were unable to duplicate the success of *About Love* on the group's next album, 1981's *Touch.* Although *Touch* lacked a solid hit like "Landlord," the album did yield some notable songs and gave the group moderate hits with the bouncy, Motown-flavored "I Will Fight" in the fall of 1981 and "A Friend of Mine" early in 1982.

The group's 1983 *Visions* album was perhaps their finest since the *Claudine* soundtrack and brought Gladys and the Pips back to contemporary hit-making status. For this album, the group worked with producer Leon Sylvers and members of his Silverspoon Production staff. At the time, Sylvers was highly in demand, having been responsible for a string of R&B hits earlier in the decade by Shalamar, the Whispers, and other artists on Dick Griffey's Solar label. Sylvers took responsibility for the production of half of the album, while Gladys and Bubba Knight, along with Sam Dees, produced the other half.

The album's first single, "Save the Overtime (For Me)," co-written by Gladys and Bubba, topped the R&B charts for a week in the spring of 1983, their first R&B chart-topper since 1974's "I Feel a Song," and spent an astounding 25 weeks on the charts. This infectious dance track, full of catchy hooks, made the group current and re-established them with the younger record-buying public.

Despite its huge success with the black audience, "Save the Overtime (For Me)" failed to generate any success on the pop charts, and even today is regarded by pop music critics as a "minor" hit. The crossover gap in music, which narrowed in the late 1960s and early 1970s, had widened by the start of the 1980s. Success on the R&B charts in 1983, no matter how great, did not automatically translate into pop radio airplay. Perhaps the greatest example of this was George Clinton's "Atomic Dog," which topped the R&B charts for four weeks that spring but failed to crack the pop 100. The only black artists to reach the summit of the pop charts in 1983 were pop superstars Michael Jackson ("Billie Jean" and "Beat It") and Lionel Richie ("All Night Long").

Gladys and the Pips followed with "You're Number One (In My Book)," a beautiful, melodic, mid-tempo track which gave the group another solid hit, peaking at number five in the summer of 1983. Further enhanced by the underrated "When You're Far Away," and "Hero" (later known as "Wind Beneath My Wings"), which the group co-produced with Dees, the *Visions* album achieved gold status, the group's first album in eight years to achieve this distinction.

Gladys and the Pips again utilized Sylvers for their *Life* album in 1985, which also included several of their own productions. However, this effort failed to generate much interest, although "My Time" did crack the R&B top 20.

In the fall of 1985, Gladys took a break from recording to play opposite Flip Wilson in the short-lived CBS sitcom *Charlie and Company*. In the show Gladys played Wilson's wife, a schoolteacher and mother of three. Unfortunately this sitcom received widespread criticism as a "carbon copy" of NBC's highly successful *The Cosby Show*, which debuted the previous season.

Later that year Gladys, along with Stevie Wonder and Elton John, contributed vocals to Dionne Warwick's anthem for AIDS research, "That's What Friends Are For," which topped both the pop and R&B charts. Attributed to "Dionne and Friends," the song won a Grammy for best pop vocal performance by a duo, group, or chorus.

In 1986 Gladys and the Pips signed with MCA Records. Their first MCA single, "Send It to Me," generated moderate success when released at the end of that year. A year later, the release of "Love Overboard" gave the group their biggest hit since "The Way We Were/Try to Remember" 12 years earlier. Produced by the Midnight Star creative team of Reggie and Vincent Calloway, this percussion-driven dance track shot up the R&B charts until it rested at Number One early in 1988. "Love Overboard" also reached number 13 on the pop charts and won a Grammy for best R&B vocal performance by a duo or group with vocals. After the success of "Love Overboard," the group released another dance song, "Lovin' on Next to Nothin'," as a follow-up. This perky track did well on the R&B charts, peaking at number three in the spring of 1988, but failed to generate any pop interest. "Love Overboard," "Lovin' on Next to Nothin'," and a third single, the ballad "It's Gonna Take All Our Love," were included on the group's MCA debut album, *All Our Love*.

Despite their initial success on MCA, Gladys and the Pips did not record a follow-up album. In 1990 the three Pips left the music business to pursue other interests. After initial contract haggling with MCA because the original contract was signed with the Pips, Gladys signed with the label as a solo artist. Her 1991 MCA solo debut, *Good Woman*, topped the R&B charts and yielded the number two R&B hit "Men" and the moderately successful "Where Would I Be."

In 1994 Gladys released her latest solo album, *Just for You*, which gave her hits with a remake of Boyz II Men's 1992 smash "End of the Road" and the up-tempo "Next Time." The album was certified gold, surprising since the majority of her fans are not avid record buyers. Having recorded for nearly 40 years, either as a soloist or with the Pips, and surviving disco, rap, and various definitions of crossover, a gold record for Gladys Knight at this stage of her career is merely icing on the cake. Given the contribution she has made to modern popular music, this incomparable artist has secured her status as a legend.

Jean Knight

New Orleans native Jean Knight recorded a series of songs in the early 1970s centered around men who "messed over" women, and gave Stax Records one of their biggest hits with her 1971 smash "Mr. Big Stuff."

Born in New Orleans, Jean Caliste (Knight is her stage name) began singing in the early 1960s in small clubs on weekends. In 1965 she cut her first record, a remake of Jackie Wilson's "Doggin' Around." Cajun music king Huey Meaux released the song on his Jetstream label and brought Knight to Houston to record one more single for Jetstream and three for his Tribe label. Although none of the songs sold well, they enabled Knight to enhance her reputation around the New Orleans and Mississippi region.

Her big break came when she met arranger/producer Wardell Quezerque, a former trumpet player in David Bartholomew's band in the '50s. Quezerque had now developed something of a track record in New Orleans, having arranged 1965's "Teasin' You" by Willie Tee and "Iko Iko" by the Dixie Cups.

Knight remembers, "I met Wardell through some songwriters I knew and they called me to tell me they had some material they wanted me to hear. At the time I had gotten kind of aggravated — going to work every day and spending my money to buy outfits to wear to all of these little gigs and it wasn't paying off too much. So, I was kind of putting the singing on the back burner until I could see some real money coming out of this. I told them I wasn't too interested in singing anymore unless I was recording. The next time anybody heard me I was going to be on wax. They had four songs they wanted me to hear. I played the songs and I picked out 'Mr. Big Stuff,' but I didn't like the melody. The next day I went to [songwriter] Joe Broussard's house and Wardell was there. He told me he wanted to meet me because I had a unique sound in my voice. He let me work with Albert Savoy, another songwriter who had nothing to do with the writing of 'Mr. Big Stuff.' [Savoy] kind of programmed me. He said, 'Jean, everybody knows you're flip and sassy. Just approach the song like you're sacking a guy out.' So, I just took it and went with it."

Quezerque made arrangements with Tommy Couch and Wolf Stevenson of Malaco Productions for four of his artists, including Knight, to record in their studio in Jackson, Mississippi on Sunday, May 17, 1970. The first artist up was King Floyd, who recorded several self-penned songs. Next up was Knight, who included "Mr. Big Stuff" in her set. Initially no one was interested in leasing the sides from Quezerque. Couch and Stevenson formed the Chimneyville label to release Floyd's "What Our Love Needs." The song was slow taking off until a deejay started playing the B-side, "Groove Me." "Groove Me" caught on and was picked up for national distribution by Atlantic's Cotillion Records. By the beginning of 1971 it was at the top of the R&B charts. Following the success of "Groove Me," several record companies began bidding for Quezerque's other sides, Knight's "Mr. Big Stuff" included. He eventually placed the song with Memphis-based Stax Records.

"[The success of 'Groove Me'] gave me so much confidence because King Floyd recorded just before me," says Knight. "He had to go to a gig so they decided to let him go ahead of me. I really had high hopes about 'Mr. Big Stuff.' I had no idea when the record would come out but I just felt real good about it. I took only two takes of the record. We had rehearsed a lot in New Orleans before we went to Mississippi to do that.

"They sent out all of this stuff to different companies, preferably Atlantic Records, Stax, and Capitol. Atlantic Records took 'Groove Me,' and when they did, Stax wanted to hear whatever else they had. When Stax heard 'Mr. Big Stuff' they took it. By the time Stax took 'Mr. Big Stuff' Atlantic wanted to hear it but Stax already had it. I was kind of glad I was with Stax because they weren't as big a company as Atlantic, and I felt they would be able to give more of a concentrated effort towards me."

"Mr. Big Stuff" was released on Stax Records in the spring of 1971 and quickly became a smash hit. The reggae-flavored dance track with the catchy "oh, oh, yeah . . . ooh" background chirps topped the R&B charts for five weeks, reached number two on the pop charts, and sold over two million copies.

"It was unbelievable," says Knight. "You almost had to pinch yourself to see if this is real. I went everyplace, all across the country, and just about every major city in the country. I'm a Catholic by faith and I do pray very hard. We make things called novenas to St. Jude, and St. Jude is the saint of impossible things. I had made a novena to St. Jude that, through Jesus Christ, I would be able to get a record that would be big enough to get me some gigs right around New Orleans and pay off some little bills I had. I wasn't asking for anything big. And I got that a hundred times greater."

An album entitled *Mr. Big Stuff* featured several standouts, including "Don't Talk About Jody," an answer to Johnnie Taylor's recent hit "Jody's Got Your Girl and Gone"; "You City Slicker"; and the soulful ballad, "A Little Bit of Something (Is Better Than All of Nothing)."

The success of "Mr. Big Stuff" had Jean Knight primed for stardom. Also at that time, Stax Records had become a hit-making machine, having had monumental success with the Staple Singers, the Dramatics, Isaac Hayes, Johnnie Taylor, Rufus Thomas, and the Emotions. However, Knight was unable to capitalize fully on her situation due to conflicting managerial interests between Stax and her management in New Orleans. Unlike the other artists on the Stax roster whose music was created in-house, Knight came to Stax with "Mr. Big Stuff" already completed. Because Quezerque and Malaco Productions were predominantly responsible for the success of the song, they, not Stax, assumed control over the direction of Knight's career.

She explains, "I had some one-on-one talks with [Stax president] Jim Stewart. I was at the Grammy Awards in New York and he said, 'We have some more publicity stuff coming out on you but our hands are tied.' They didn't get much cooperation from the other end, Wardell and Malaco, the people who were controlling things for me. They didn't let Stax do some of the things that they wanted to do. Stax was a great company for me. If they had a little more authority I think they would've done much more, but because they didn't have me lock, stock, and barrel, that held things off."

The follow-up to "Mr. Big Stuff" was "You Think You're Hot Stuff," a song similar in vein to its predecessor in lyrical theme, melody, and background chirps. Written by the same "Mr. Big Stuff" team of Joe Broussard, Ralph Williams, and Carrol Washington, "You Think You're Hot Stuff" cracked the R&B top 20 but only reached the lower portions of the pop charts.

"That [song] wasn't my idea," says Knight. "When you're a fresh star like that, it's not much say you have. Everybody's got everything already programmed for you. Stax had a really good song for me called 'Cold, Bold and Ready.' It was hot and I was so fired up to do that song but when I got back to New Orleans, Wardell said, 'No,' they had their own songs. So I think that was a bad move. My thing is, I don't care who writes the songs. If it's a hit, it doesn't matter. But they were trying to keep everything within this little circle of songwriters they had in New Orleans. It kind of turned me off because I knew that song could've been another big hit, but they stopped all of that."

"Carry On," released in 1972, was Knight's final chart entry for the Stax label. For the rest of the 1970s Jean Knight remained in virtual obscurity. She label-hopped, recording for Staff, Dial, Chelsea, Open, and Ola. She resurfaced in 1981 on Isaac Bolden's Soulin' label with "You Got the Papers (But I Got the Man)," an answer to Richard "Dimples" Fields and Betty Wright's controversial hit "She's Got Papers on Me."

"I was with producer Isaac Bolden at that time," says Knight. "He told me there was a song out by Richard 'Dimples' Fields and Betty Wright. I had heard of a man's song, 'She's Got Papers on Me,' but I never heard Betty's part. He thought it would be a great idea if we could answer it. Initially, I didn't know whether I would answer him or her. I listened to the tape again and decided I would answer her. It took me about a half-hour to 45 minutes to really get it going, and I sat there and wrote this little talking part. [Bolden] got it leased with Atlantic Records and it was a hit."

In 1985 Rockin' Sydney had a hit with "My Toot Toot," which received the majority of its airplay on country stations. Soulin' Records had Knight cover the song, giving it more of a soulful flavor, and the song became a big hit in New Orleans. Malaco Records attempted to buy Knight's master but Soulin' eventually licensed it to Atlantic, which released it on their Mirage label. Meanwhile, Malaco had Denise LaSalle cover Knight's version. While Knight's version received more airplay in the States, LaSalle's version became a British top 10 hit.

The following year Knight's name resurfaced again when rap outfit Heavy D and the Boyz had their debut with a cover of "Mr. Big Stuff." "I thought that was good," says Knight. "What it always does is wake you back up. It always brings attention back to the person who actually did it because anyone who would hear his [version] with the little background 'oh, oh, yeah,' they think about Jean Knight and the original 'Mr. Big Stuff.'"

The legacy of "Mr. Big Stuff" was apparent in 1994 when filmmaker Spike Lee used the entire song in his film, *Crooklyn*. Today, when she is not working as a nurse, Jean Knight still performs regularly in and around the New Orleans and Gulf Coast area, and is completing work on an album.

She says, "I might get four good gigs a month; *good* gigs. I could do a lot more but I don't just take anything. I'm choicy about what I take."

The Main Ingredient

The sleek and smooth sound of the Main Ingredient created some of the best music in the early 1970s that combined the elements of pop and soul. The group initially showed promise at the start of the decade with "You've Been My Inspiration" and "Spinning Around" before lead singer Don McPherson died of leukemia. McPherson was replaced by distinctive vocalist Cuba Gooding. It was with Gooding and hits such as "Everybody Plays the Fool" and "Just Don't Want to Be Lonely" that this New York City trio enjoyed their greatest success, becoming one of the premier vocal groups of their day.

Enrique "Tony" Silvester, Luther Simmons, Jr., and Don McPherson first organized in the mid-'60s in the Harlem section of New York City where they grew up. Tony Silvester recalls, "We were all friends from the time we were kids. We worked together at a supermarket and used to sing on the street corner. [McPherson and Simmons] had a group with another guy named Miller, but he could never hit the note. I used to go to rehearsals with them and they would always say, 'Tony, sing Miller's parts so he can see how it's supposed to be done.' After about the third rehearsal, it dawned on them, 'Why are we trying to get Miller to sing the part when Tony can sing it?' We went out and bought this *old* piano from an old man, Mr. Weiser, who must've been about 80 years old. All we had was $100 but he liked us and he threw in the free delivery. We put it in my house and that's when we started writing the tunes. Thanks to that old man, we got a shot."

Originally known as the Poets, the trio was signed to Mike

Stoller and Jerry Leiber's Red Bird label in 1965 and released one single called "Merry Christmas Baby" later that year. With a new name, the Insiders, they were signed to RCA in 1967 by R&B A&R director Buzzy Willis (a former member of the Solitaires). Their one RCA single, "I'm Better Off Without You," failed to generate any interest and the group decided on another name change. They finally settled on the Main Ingredient after Silvester read the list of ingredients on a Coke bottle.

The group started appearing on the charts in 1970 with the beautiful ballad "You've Been My Inspiration." Highlighted by McPherson's high tenor on lead, perfectly interwoven with the background harmonies of Simmons and Silvester, the song reached number 25 on the R&B charts. The group maintained its upward momentum with a remake of the Impressions' 1964 hit "I'm So Proud" and the ballad "Spinning Around (I Must Be Falling in Love)," the latter becoming their first top 10 R&B hit. Other notable songs from their two albums, *Main Ingredient L.T.D.* and *Tasteful Soul*, were the up-tempo "Can't Stand Your Love" and "Magic Shoes," and ballads "I'm Better Off Without You" (a rerecording of their Insiders cut) and "Make It With You," a cover of the Number One pop hit by Bread.

During the run of their next single, the powerful "Black Seeds Keep on Growing," McPherson got sick and was unable to tour with the group. His spot in the lineup was taken over by Cuba Gooding, a fellow New Yorker who sang with the Main Ingredient before they recorded professionally.

Gooding remembers, "The four of us had sung together from the time we were teenagers, although they were about three to four years older than I was. We did it in our spare time when we were teenagers and young adults. Each of us had different jobs. Don worked with the fire department and I was a salesman, always on the road.

"When I was on the road, the group was signed by RCA through Buzz Willis. I sang background for them and filled in for Don when he was sick. 'Black Seeds Keep on Growing' was Don's last song with the group. I sang background on the record and took the lead when we went on the road because he couldn't travel. We were friends and as friends we thought that we'd always be together. In 1970, when he was too sick to go on the road and I filled in for him, it never crossed anyone's mind that he wouldn't be back. I was having fun and was content to be making $250 – $350 a week."

However, as McPherson's condition worsened, it was apparent that he would not be returning. Gooding recalls, "We were appearing at P.J.'s in California when we got word that Don was critical. We flew to New York to see him and back to California to finish the set, and while we were on stage he died. That was *tremendous.*"

Donald McPherson died of leukemia on July 4, 1971, five days before his 30th birthday. Cuba Gooding became a permanent member of the Main Ingredient at a time when most stand-up R&B groups were dominated by the falsetto sound on lead vocals, as exhibited by his predecessor McPherson. RCA executives initially doubted whether Gooding had a commercial sound to compete with the likes of William Hart of the Delfonics and Russell Thompkins of the Stylistics.

Gooding notes, "RCA wanted to break up the group right after Don's death because they didn't feel he could be replaced. We kept on singing because there were still four months to go on the contract and I became the principal. [RCA] had doubts as to whether my voice was commercial but Luther, Tony, and I didn't."

The addition of Gooding did mark a dramatic change in the sound of the group. With McPherson's tenor previously at the helm, the backing vocals of Silvester and Simmons were an integral part of the group's sound. While this sound helped the Main Ingredient become R&B mainstays, their success on the pop charts was limited. Despite RCA's initial apprehension about the commercialism of Gooding's voice, his vocals would soon come to dominate all future Main Ingredient songs; the harmonies of Silvester and Simmons were pushed further to the background.

The Main Ingredient achieved their major breakthrough on their next album, the appropriately titled *Bitter/Sweet*, which contained the good-natured "Everybody Plays the Fool." Gooding says, "Soon after Don's death we recorded 'Everybody Plays the Fool' and it became a smash success, much to the surprise of RCA. 'Everybody Plays the Fool' climbed the pop charts before it did the R&B charts. It didn't surprise me, though, because I always considered it to be a pop record." The group's first million-seller, "Everybody Plays the Fool" eventually reached number three on the pop charts in the fall of 1972, spent three weeks at the number two spot on the R&B charts, and was nominated for a Grammy for best R&B song.

Gooding described the experience of the group progressing from moderate R&B stars to superstar status after the success of "Everybody Plays the Fool." "It was a lot of fun. We took it for granted. When 'Everybody Plays the Fool' came out we started appearing on *Soul Train, Midnight Special, American Bandstand* and were traveling all over the world. It was a star-studded experience. After 'Everybody Plays the Fool' we just assumed that we would always have hit records.

"We did everything ourselves in regards to production and engineering. We even did our own choreography, that's why you never saw us move around too much. Our manager wasn't a music industry person but he was a businessman so, financially, we were cool. We would walk the streets with our pockets full of money looking for ways to spend it . . . clothes, cars, jewelry, hotels. None of us were into drugs. We believed that we were too successful or trying to be successful to get involved with something of that nature. However, everything we did, we did in the proper context of what we were supposed to do. We're talking about three guys from Harlem now all of a sudden hanging out in California."

The follow-up to "Everybody Plays the Fool," the ballad "You've Got to Take It (If You Want It)," a top 20 R&B hit, and the mid-tempo, Latin-flavored "No Tears" added to the success of the *Bitter/Sweet* album.

The success of *Bitter/Sweet* and particularly the pop success of "Everybody Plays the Fool," a complete contrast to their previous hits, did have its drawbacks as the Main Ingredient came close to losing its core audience. To solve this dilemma RCA had the group record their next album, *Afrodisiac*, strictly for the black audience. Gooding explains, "Once we crossed over with 'Everybody Plays the Fool' people didn't realize that it was the same Main Ingredient. They were saying, 'We don't sing black anymore,' or 'We don't sound black.' So, for our next album, *Afrodisiac*, RCA had us going strictly black, and they made a *big* mistake by putting a naked black woman on the cover — and it *bombed*."

He further adds, "RCA was not marked for black music. We were the only black artists on the label with the exception of Charley Pride, whose music I don't really consider 'black.' RCA didn't know how to market the *Afrodisiac* album and they made the mistake of the black woman on the cover. They were able to market 'Everybody Plays the Fool' because it's not considered a black record. A wonderful song that Stevie Wonder wrote for us, 'Girl Blue,' got no promotion at all." With little promotion, the melancholy "Girl Blue" stalled at number 51 on the R&B charts in the fall of 1973.

The Main Ingredient rebounded in the spring of 1974 with *The Euphrates River* album, which the trio themselves produced. The album's first single, the bass-laden "Just Don't Want to Be Lonely," was the group's second million-seller, reaching the top 10 on both the pop and R&B charts. Like the group's previous million-seller, "Just Don't Want to Be Lonely" contained an opening monologue by Gooding, which would soon become a trademark on all of the group's hits. He says, "I always thought that it would add a personal note to the song. Singing a song is like telling a story and I felt that the dialogue in the beginning set up the story."

The second single, "Happiness Is Just Around the Bend," was a deviation from the group's trademark pop/R&B ballads. Released almost as an afterthought, this dance track with a killer bass line, along with the Hues Corporation's "Rock the Boat" and George McRae's "Rock Your Baby," is considered to be one of the first big disco hits. "Happiness" was a top 10 R&B hit and was the group's third biggest success behind their two previous million-sellers. Unfortunately, disco brought about the demise of several of the stand-up groups. Despite being produced by the Main Ingredient themselves, the success of "Happiness," and to a lesser extent, the funky "California My Way," did little to convince the music industry that the group could survive the disco era.

Gooding explains, "We were considered a ballad R&B stand-up group. Disco was supposed to be for the likes of Donna Summer. With 'Just Don't Want to Be Lonely' doing as well as it did, it was almost incidental that 'Happiness Is Just Around the Bend' was released. The feeling was that 'Just Don't Want to Be Lonely' had already sold a million copies, it's already gone gold. They looked towards 'Happiness Is Just Around the Bend' just for us to make personal appearances on TV shows. Buzz Willis, who is black, was in a token situation at that time as vice-president. These people at RCA were lawyers, CPAs, and Harvard graduates. They only knew the business of business and not music."

In 1974 charter member Tony Silvester left the group to fulfill his dream of becoming a top producer. He went on to become an important producer in the disco era, working with such artists as Sister Sledge, Linda Lewis, and Ben E. King on his 1975 hit, "Supernatural Thing." Silvester's exit ended a period of turmoil within the group that had been brewing over the years.

"I just said, 'To hell with it,' and I just departed," Silvester says. "It was still my group but I let them work. My deal with them was that I got a third — even though I wasn't singing with them — that allowed them to still use the name. That was the deal. I went on to make money doing what I'm doing now."

Carl Thompkins replaced Silvester for the *Rolling Down a Mountainside* album. The title song gave the group their final top 10 R&B hit, peaking at number seven in the spring of 1975. After the release of the *Shame on the World* album a year later, the group disbanded on friendly terms.

Gooding states, "RCA offered more money for me to be the lead singer. With them it didn't matter who the other two were. They didn't realize that Luther [Simmons] created the whole Main Ingredient sound and had a hand in one-third of the production. This is something that Luther agonized over and we both knew that it wouldn't be the Main Ingredient without Tony [Silvester]. I knew then that there really was no more future with the group but RCA gave us more money to do the *Rolling Down a Mountainside* album. We eventually got back together. We would always break up and get back together after a contract. Never did we not honor a contractual agreement."

Unlike several of their contemporaries, the Main Ingredient recognized the importance of taking care of the business end of show business. They formed the LTD (Luther-Tony-Donald) corporation and later LTC (Luther-Tony-Cuba) to protect their business interests.

Gooding explains, "We were involved in all areas of the 'industry,' if you can call it that, with the exception of publicity. That was one hat that just didn't fit. We handled management, production, you name it. It was to our advantage because, financially, we were able to do well. We watched what was going on and, because of it, I think we did a little better than several other groups during that era who operated strictly out of the 'I just want to sing' mode. We have a suit now against RCA for past royalties. They'll find some money but they won't find a whole lot."

After the Main Ingredient disbanded, Cuba Gooding signed with Motown Records as a solo artist amid much speculation that he used the Main Ingredient as a stepping-stone to a solo career. However, Gooding dismisses this theory. "I used to just pray that I could get in the Main Ingredient and become a member of the group. I was a solo artist in the beginning and Tony [Silvester] would help me to perfect my show. But it was always important for me to be a part of the group. Coming from 116th Street in Harlem and being on stage as a part of the Main Ingredient and singing million-seller records . . . it was like I died and went to heaven. It wasn't until after three albums when I realized that I could be a solo artist. But I knew it would only happen after the vehicle would no longer work."

Despite critical acclaim and high expectations, Cuba Gooding had an uneventful career at Motown Records, a company undergoing something of a hit famine at that time. Only one of his singles, "Mind Pleaser," cracked the top 100 on the R&B charts.

Looking back at his career at Motown, Gooding says, "Motown wasn't my first choice. I wanted to sign with Capitol or Columbia but nothing happened there. Motown was the first company who offered me a sensible deal but Motown was not the company I should have been with. There was a long line of artists in the company who were waiting all these years to have hit records. In front of them you had Smokey Robinson who was the vice-president of the company. To top that off, Rick James and I were signed to Motown on the *same day*. Of course he released his 'You and I' which became a smash so I didn't have a *chance* at Motown."

The Main Ingredient reformed in 1979 as the Main Ingredient featuring Cuba Gooding but with little fanfare. Their single, "Think Positive," released in 1980, only reached the lower portion of the charts before the group disbanded again. Gooding had a sizable hit in 1984 with a remake of "Happiness Is Just Around the Bend" on the Streetwise label. He reunited with Tony Silvester in 1989 and the group added Jerome Jackson for the *I Just Wanna Love You* album on Polygram, which produced a hit with the smooth, mid-tempo title song. In 1991 the trio again disbanded, with Silvester going back into production and Gooding to a solo career.

Cuba Gooding's name reappeared in the spotlight that year when his son Cuba Gooding, Jr. starred in the movie *Boyz 'N the Hood*, one of the most successful films of 1991.

His solo career also got a boost in 1991 when Aaron Neville had a top 10 pop hit with "Everybody Plays the Fool." Gooding says, "I wasn't surprised that it became a hit. I wanted to redo it myself but couldn't talk anybody into doing it so it was kind of like egg all over everybody's faces when his version became a hit. I was happy and flattered because Aaron didn't do too much different [from the original version]. The only thing different is that he doesn't do any talking in the beginning, but basically the riffs and the moves are the same. When his version started climbing the charts, they started playing our version and it helped to keep my career from dying."

In 1993 Gooding released his latest album, *Meant to Be in Love*. He currently performs live an average of twice a month before enthusiastic audiences; his energy and charisma have made him a favorite throughout the world. He says, "I don't think any male singer has ever reached his peak unless he has learned to interact with the audience. I learned to entertain from watching *The Ed Sullivan Show* and *Hit Parade*. When I would do amateur shows I was competing with kids. Everybody loves kids so in order for me to win I knew I had to get involved with the audience. That's my style. That's what I do best and what I'm most proud of. With the Main Ingredient we had very little choreography. We would just stand there and hold a mike. Being able to sing and talk with the audience helped keep the Main Ingredient afloat."

In 1994 Gooding reunited with Silvester and Simmons, a situation Silvester says will occur periodically, but not on a permanent basis due to Silvester continuing to be a top producer and Simmons living in California.

"[The reunion] is by popular demand," Silvester says. "It's difficult for me to go backwards but I don't mind doing it. [The Main Ingredient] was the first thing I created so it's a situation like it's your baby. You always want to keep your baby alive. Your first baby is something that you want to cherish and keep alive. The Main Ingredient is established but every opportunity that you get, you want to give it a little juice to keep it going."

The Manhattans

With a recording career that has spanned more than 30 years, the Manhattans created some of the finest romantic ballads in the history of soul music. Led by Gerald Alston's gospel-infused tenor and Winfred "Blue" Lovett's heartfelt monologues, this New Jersey-based group was virtually the only one of its kind to achieve any significant success during the disco era of the mid-1970s. The Manhattans initially recorded for a series of small labels in the 1960s and enjoyed only marginal success. When original lead singer George Smith died in 1970, Alston took his place. The group's fortunes changed when they moved to Columbia Records in 1973 and were paired with arranger/producer Bobby Martin. There followed a string of hits, including "There's No Me Without You," "Kiss and Say Goodbye," and "I Kinda Miss You," which made the Manhattans one of the classiest and most beloved R&B stand-up vocal groups of all time.

The original members of the Manhattans grew up in Jersey City, New Jersey. Winfred "Blue" Lovett (bass) first got together with Edward "Sonny" Bivins (first tenor) and Richard Taylor (baritone) in a group called the Statesmen while they were all serving in the Air Force in Germany in the late 1950s. When they returned to the States, Lovett and Taylor formed the Dulcets with George Smith (lead) and Ethel Sanders. In 1961 the quartet recorded an unsuccessful single, "Pork Chops," for the New York-based Asnes label. When the Dulcets disbanded later that year, Lovett, Taylor, Smith, Bivins, and second tenor Kenny Kelly formed a group and decided to call themselves the Manhattans.

"Blue" Lovett remembers, "The name Dulcets meant 'beautiful tones' and that just didn't sound right. We chose 'Manhattans' because it was the name of a cocktail. Also, we were all from New Jersey, and that was close to the borough of Manhattan, so we wanted something that would also allow us to identify with the New York-Manhattan image, not just the image of alcohol."

In 1963 the quintet came to the attention of Bobby Robinson's Enjoy Records. Recording under the name Ronnie and the Manhattans, they released the unsuccessful "Come on Back." The Manhattans got their first break in 1964 when Barbara Brown, a former singer with Newark-based Carnival Records, recommended the group to label owner Joe Evans, who caught their performance at an Apollo Theater amateur night contest. Although the Manhattans finished third that night, their reception was strong enough to convince Evans to sign them to his label.

The group was unsuccessful in 1964 with their first two Carnival releases: "For the Very First Time," a rock-and-roll flavored track; and "There Goes a Fool," a light, mid-tempo pop tune. Their luck finally changed in early 1965 when the Lovett-penned, New Orleans-styled "I Wanna Be (Your Everything)" placed at number 12 on the R&B charts. The group followed with "Searchin' for My Baby," a perky song similar in production to Marvin Gaye's "Hitch Hike"; it reached number 20 that spring. The B-side to "Searchin'" was "I'm the One That Love Forgot," a sorrowful doo-wop ballad, which became quite popular in the northeast and established the Manhattans as soulful balladeers.

Over the next two years, the quintet had moderate success on the R&B charts with the haunting "Follow Your Heart," the sweet, mid-tempo "Baby I Need You," the pleading ballad "Can I," and "I Betcha (Couldn't Love Me)." After two failed singles in 1967 — "Alone on New Year's Eve" and "Our Love Will Never Die" — the quintet released "When We're Made as

One," which reached number 31 on the R&B charts that summer. Written by George Smith and Joe Evans, this heartfelt ballad was arguably the Manhattans' best song of their Carnival tenure, and was unarguably Smith's finest moment as lead singer of the group.

In search of greener pastures, the Manhattans left Carnival in 1969 and signed with Deluxe Records, a Nashville-based subsidiary of King. Lovett recalls, "We felt that we weren't getting enough exposure being with a small independent company like Carnival. There were times when we'd have a song out and would perform in the eastern cities to promote it. We would go from city to city, and by the time we got to . . . Atlanta, the song was already off the charts. So we saw our move to Deluxe as a way of reaching for bigger and better things."

The group's move to Deluxe did not immediately improve their fortunes. Their three releases in 1970 — "It's Gonna Take a Lot to Bring Me Back," "If My Heart Could Speak," and "From Atlanta to Goodbye" — were only mildly successful. During a tour of southern black colleges in 1970, the Manhattans appeared on a show at North Carolina's Kittrell College with a group called the New Imperials (no relation to Little Anthony's quintet), which included student Gerald Alston. At the time, lead singer Smith was seriously ill. Alston, a Henderson, North Carolina native, impressed the Manhattans so much with his Sam Cooke-inspired tenor that he was asked to join the group, but he declined.

He recalls, "I met the Manhattans during my first year at college. They were performing [at Kittrell], and the original lead singer [Smith] was sick. They needed a sound system and my band had one. I set it up and was testing it out, and they heard me sing. That's when they told me that George was sick. They took my name and asked me to sing on the show, which I did. His illness got worse and they got back in touch with me the following week."

When George Smith died a short while later in 1970 from spinal meningitis, Alston agreed to take his place.

"George Smith's death was a shocking loss to us," says Lovett.

"We had grown up with him and had performed professionally for about five or six years with him as our lead singer. All of a sudden it was the end of what we thought would be a lifetime situation."

With Alston's tenor brought to the forefront of the Manhattans, the quintet charted early in 1972 with "A Million to One." Later that fall the group had their biggest hit to date when "One Life to Live" reached number three on the R&B charts. The Manhattans were again faced with a roadblock when Deluxe went out of business in 1972. With James Brown having left the parent company, King, in the summer of 1971, the label found it difficult to remain competitive without the services of its number one breadwinner.

Toward the end of 1972, the Manhattans signed with Columbia Records, a move that proved to be the turning point in their career. In addition to now having the backing of a major label, the group was also put into the production hands of Bobby Martin, an arranger at Philadelphia's Sigma Sound studio and a protégé of Kenny Gamble and Leon Huff. The Manhattans collaborated with Martin at a time when the "Philly Soul" coming out of Sigma Sound studio was on the verge of becoming the dominant force in black music in the 1970s.

"Signing with Columbia was definitely the turning point in our career," says Lovett. "After we were with Deluxe for three years, James Brown left [King], and they really didn't have what it took to promote us. We had one song on Deluxe, 'One Life to Live,' that did very well for us. That song made us recognizable and got CBS interested in us.

"Once we signed with Columbia we hooked up with Bobby Martin, and that made all the difference in the world. At that time, Gamble and Huff had the Philly sound kickin' pretty heavy. Thom Bell was working with the Stylistics and with the O'Jays, and Bobby Martin did part of the O'Jays' first [Philadelphia International] album. Columbia made a direct deal for Bobby to do an album on us. It was a challenge to complete the album at Sigma Sound studio because everyone else was trying to get in there. For five or six weeks, it seemed like everyone was in line to get in there: the Spinners, the O'Jays, Teddy [Pendergrass] and the Blue Notes. Bobby would get three or four days booked and that's when he laid the tracks and we did our voices and everything else. Once you got in [Sigma Sound], you sometimes had to rush because if you didn't finish in time, it might be another month before you could get back in there."

The Manhattans made their Columbia debut in the spring of 1973 with the release of *There's No Me Without You*. The album's first single was the Bivins-penned title track, a ballad highlighted by Alston's superior lead and Lovett's talking bass bridge, which would soon become his trademark. "There's No Me Without You" reached number three on the R&B charts and gave the group their finest showing to date on the pop charts finishing at number 43. Martin updated the quintet's doo-wop style by backing their harmony with several musicians from the Sigma Sound house band, MFSB. Despite the similar R&B success of "One Life to Live" less than a year earlier, "There's No Me Without You" is generally considered to be the Manhattans' first significant hit, perhaps because this song was recorded for a major label and was able to make a small dent in the pop charts.

Commenting on the success of their Columbia debut, Alston says, "That was great! ['There's No Me Without You'] was our first hit! The group had been singing for over nine years and we had just seen the O'Jays and the Spinners finally break through after so many years. This was *our* breakthrough, and it was just an exciting time for us."

"'There's No Me Without You' was the song that got us set," adds Lovett. "It was our first song that did okay on the pop charts. Clive Davis, who was 'the man' at CBS at that time, liked what he heard. He put us out there and established our sound with the public."

Two other songs from the *There's No Me Without You* album made the R&B top 20 later in 1973: the haunting "You'd Better Believe It" and "Wish That You Were Mine"; the latter was a beautiful ballad written by Lovett. An underrated track from the album was "The Day the Robin Sang to Me," a smooth, mid-tempo song written by Kenny Kelly.

Toward the end of 1974, the Manhattans hit the R&B top 10 again and reached the pop top 40 for the first time with "Don't Take Your Love," a pleading ballad highlighted by Lovett's "begging" rap near the end. The group followed in the spring of 1975 with "Hurt," which reached the top 10.

A year went by before the Manhattans released their next single, "Kiss and Say Goodbye." Lovett, who wrote this song, never intended for it to be released by the group. He explains, "It's usually around the hours of two or three in the morning when I can do a lot of writing. It's been that way since day one. Sometimes songs would come to me when I was asleep or when I was on an airplane. If I was asleep, I had to get up and jot down the lyrics or else I would lose it. That's what I did on 'Kiss and Say Goodbye.'

"To me ['Kiss and Say Goodbye'] was a country song; nothing special, very simple. I envisioned it as a country tune for Glen Campbell or Charley Pride. CBS wasn't about to let that song get away, although they kept it in the can for about a year. They liked what we were doing but I was beginning to get a little concerned because they kept pushing ballad after ballad. When we recorded 'Kiss and Say Goodbye' they put in a country flavor. I was very dissatisfied with the production and I wanted to give it to somebody else. Of course, now it's another story."

Released in the spring of 1976, "Kiss and Say Goodbye" topped the R&B charts for a week, gave the group their crossover breakthrough by reaching the summit of the pop charts for two weeks, and became the second single in the music industry (behind Johnnie Taylor's "Disco Lady") to be certified platinum for sales of two million.

Lovett contends, "We had no idea that after more than 11 years, ['Kiss and Say Goodbye'] would become our first gold record; we had no clue. That song went to Number One on the pop charts with a bullet and became the song of the year. It was like a dream. You had to ask yourself, 'Is this really happening?' It didn't really sink in until three months after its release, when the song went platinum. For a while after that, it seemed like everything we touched was a hit."

Lovett's initial misgivings about recording "Kiss and Say Goodbye" and his surprise at the song's success are understandable. By 1976 disco music was firmly established. For a veteran stand-up R&B vocal group to record a country-flavored ballad during this time was considered career suicide. Virtually all of the dominant soul artists from the early 1970s either jumped aboard the disco bandwagon or were forced to go overseas to find work. However, the Manhattans did not suffer a decline in popularity during this period. The group remained true to their ballad form and enjoyed their greatest run during the disco era.

"It seems crazy that we were successful at that time," says Lovett. "We actually thought that CBS was trying to murder [our career] by releasing a country tune on us in the heart of disco. It was as if they were putting a noose around our necks."

Alston adds, "I don't know why we were successful during that time when some of the other groups fell off. I think that maybe after a while, people got tired of dancing and needed a change. It's like the song says, 'we never danced to a love song.' We just hung in there because we knew we could make it, and we didn't have to change to make it. We were just determined to do what we did best."

Right after the success of "Kiss and Say Goodbye," Richard Taylor left the Manhattans. He became a Muslim and changed his name to Abdul Rashid Talhah. The group continued on as a quartet after he left. Lovett explains, "When he left, we thought it would be a temporary thing for him to get his thoughts together and then he would come back, so we didn't immediately consider filling the spot. After about a year, we saw that he was serious about this, it was what he wanted to do, and he wasn't going to change his mind. We were still successful by leaving his spot open, so after we knew that he wasn't coming back, we just decided to survive without that fifth spot."

For the next two years, the Manhattans remained a fixture on the R&B top 10 with a string of ballads. These included the Lovett composition "I Kinda Miss You" (fall 1976), a heartbreaking ballad about a man pleading for his lady to come back home; "It Feels So Good to Be Loved So Bad" (spring 1977); the Alston-penned "We Never Danced to a Love Song" (summer 1977), a plea for a slight break from disco; and "Am I Losing You" (early 1978), which had a man questioning his lady's commitment to him.

After the success of "Am I Losing You," the Manhattans hit a slight lull for the remainder of the 1970s. The group parted with Martin and began recording in Chicago with Leo Graham, who was responsible for several of Tyrone Davis' hits in the 1970s, including "Turning Point." Graham brought the Manhattans back to the top with the country-flavored ballad "Shining Star," which became a top five hit on both the pop and R&B charts in the spring of 1980.

Lovett points out, "Sigma Sound was such a popular spot that after we recorded something, it might've taken another two or three months to get back in there. So, we had to find someplace else to record. Bobby Martin became a born-again Christian and he kinda just eased out. We ventured off to Chicago to meet Leo Graham, who did 'Turning Point' for Tyrone Davis. Leo liked what we were doing, but he wasn't a flyer. So, we flew out there to meet him and we decided to hook up.

"He added a little country flavor to 'Shining Star' and that was the secret to the song's success. It took us away from the typical R&B stand-up group sound, and that's what helped the song cross over. Being an R&B act, you usually have to go to the top of the black charts before you can hit the pop charts. But that wasn't the case with 'Shining Star.' It only had to go as high as number five on the black charts before the pop stations picked it up."

Graham and his writing partner, bassist Paul Richmond, gave the Manhattans top 20 success with the popular mid-tempo "I'll Never Find Another (Find Another Like You)" later in 1980 and "Just One Moment Away" in the summer of 1981.

The group then recorded in New York with producer Morrie Brown, who gave them a top 10 hit in the summer of 1983 with the up-tempo "Crazy." Further moderate hits for them included the ballad "Forever By Your Side" in the fall of 1983 and a re-make of Sam Cooke's "You Send Me" early in 1985.

In 1985 and 1986, Regina Belle, a college student at Rutgers University in New Jersey, toured with the Manhattans and worked with them on their *Too Hot to Stop It* and *Back to Basics* albums. Her recording debut was a duet with Alston on the Bobby Womack-produced "Where Did We Go Wrong?" late in 1986. By 1987 Belle had her own contract with Columbia. She later became one of the leading "quiet storm" divas of the late 1980s and early 1990s.

Lovett recalls, "We were working on two or three tunes with Morrie Brown and he had one tune that was supposed to fea-ture a female vocalist. He was looking for an edge, that pop or supper club sound. We were searching for the right vocalist for about three or four months and nobody really knocked us out. We finally found someone whom we liked and right before we made an announcement, [New York's WBLS 'quiet storm' deejay] Vaughan Harper called us and said that we had to listen to this young lady [Belle]. We decided to hold off on the announcement because, with the way he talked about [Belle], we thought that she may be a little better. Naturally when we heard her sing, we were very impressed and she ended up sing-ing with us for almost two years."

In 1988 lead singer Gerald Alston left the Manhattans for a solo career. He signed with Motown Records and had R&B success into the early 1990s with "Take Me Where You Want To," "Slow Motion," "Getting Back into Love," and a remake of Atlantic Starr's "Send for Me." According to Alston, "I felt that it was time to have a solo career and it was just something that I wanted to do. I debated over [going solo] for about three years before I did it. But the opportunity was there so I took advan-tage of it."

"[Alston going solo] had a big effect on us," says Lovett. "You take 17 or 18 years of life in a marriage and then it's gone, it can be quite a change. It's like losing a family member. When you have a strong singer, eventually he reaches a point where he wants to make a go of it on his own. I saw the handwriting on the wall, even as far back as 'Kiss and Say Goodbye,' so it didn't really surprise me."

Alston's place in the lineup was taken over by Roger Harris. He appeared on the group's 1989 Value Vue album *We're Back*. However, by now the Manhattans were well past their commercial prime. In 1991, "Blue" Lovett and Kenny Kelly retired and Harris worked as a backup singer for Alston. Sonny Bivins created a new lineup of Manhattans, adding Al Pazant, Harsey Hemphill, Charles Handy, and Lee Williams.

Alston's solo career at Motown and Lovett's retirement were both short-lived. The two reunited to form "the Manhattans featuring Gerald Alston and 'Blue' Lovett." This group also included Roger Harris. Although neither set of Manhattans have an active recording career, they remain popular attractions on the club circuit.

Lovett explains, "Having done this professionally for nearly 30 years, and also with Gerald leaving, [Kelly and I] decided to call it quits. After four years, Gerald said that his solo career wasn't what he thought it would've been. When you're out there by yourself, it can be quite demanding because everyone focuses on *you*. I was ready to give it one more shot and in talking to him, he said he felt it also. So, we decided to put it back together and also bring in Roger Harris. Sonny [Bivins] is performing with his other Manhattans, and Kenny [Kelly] decided to go to computer school. He just got tired of the business after 27 years."

Alston adds, "We figured it was time to get back out there and give it a try, so . . . here we are."

Harold Melvin and the Blue Notes

FEATURING
TEDDY PENDERGRASS

Led by the gruff, impassioned baritone of lead singer Teddy Pendergrass, Harold Melvin and the Blue Notes were one of the top soul groups of the early 1970s and were an integral part of the "Philly Soul sound" created by Kenny Gamble and Leon Huff. Initially a doo-wop unit in the late 1950s and a cabaret act in the 1960s, this Philadelphia-based quintet enjoyed their greatest run between 1972 and 1976, with Pendergrass out front on hits such as "If You Don't Know Me By Now" and "The Love I Lost." Pendergrass later achieved superstardom in the late 1970s and early 1980s as a solo artist.

The origin of the Blue Notes is in Philadelphia in 1954 with charter members Jessie Gillis, Frank Peaker, Bernie Williams, and Donald Brodie. Two years later the group recruited 16-year-old Harold Melvin, who previously had his own group, the Charmagnes. Soon afterwards, the Blue Notes competed in New York at the Apollo Theater's amateur hour. After winning for five straight weeks, they were signed to New York-based Josie Records and recorded "If You Love Me" in 1957. A few years later, as the senior members left the Blue Notes for other professions, Melvin was given the rights to the group's name.

By 1960, the Blue Notes consisted of Melvin, lead singer John Atkins, Bernard Wilson, and Lawrence Brown. The group had their first hit that year with "My Hero" on the Value label. For the remainder of the decade the quartet recorded for various labels including Landa and Chess, but with limited success. Only "Get Out" in 1965 on Landa reached the charts. However, the emphasis of the group was on building a strong nightclub act, not records. Initially working the "chitlin' circuit," the group received a boost when they signed with the William Morris Agency on the recommendation of Martha Reeves. The Blue Notes were then transformed from an R&B group to a lounge act singing old standards and other artists' songs. Venues increased in stature as the Blue Notes were now performing at nightclubs in Miami, Las Vegas, Puerto Rico, and Nassau.

In 1971 the group got their big break when they were invited by Melvin's childhood friend, noted producer Kenny Gamble, to join Philadelphia International Records, headed by Gamble and his writing and producing partner, Leon Huff. A reorganization of the Blue Notes brought the growling, gospel-influenced baritone of Teddy Pendergrass out front. Born in Philadelphia in 1950, Pendergrass began singing gospel music in Philadelphia churches at age three and was an ordained minister at 10. He would often accompany his mother, a nightclub performer, to her job at Skioles, a popular Philadelphia supper club. It was there where he first learned to play the drums. After a short career in a group called the Paramounts, and another in a group headed by a man claiming to be James Brown's brother, Pendergrass joined the Cadillacs, a local band in need of a drummer. While performing at a small club, he met Melvin, who was putting a band together to back up the Blue Notes. Pendergrass was hired and for the next six years played drums behind the Blue Notes.

It was during an impromptu performance in Puerto Rico where Melvin first became aware of Pendergrass' talent as a vocalist, and he soon had Pendergrass replace Atkins as lead singer. A fifth member, Lloyd Parks, was added and the lineup of Melvin, Pendergrass, Parks, Brown, and Wilson, now known as Harold Melvin and the Blue Notes, was signed to the Philadelphia International label.

Harold Melvin recalls, "We were in Puerto Rico and the club owner asked us to play a little longer set. I asked the musicians if they could play a couple of more tunes and they didn't mind. That's when I first heard Teddy sing. I knew then that I had something.

"At that same hotel in Puerto Rico where I first discovered Teddy's singing, Gamble called me and said he just made a deal with CBS and needed for me to get there as soon as I could. I told him that we had about two more weeks there and after I finished, I'd be at Philadelphia. When we flew in to Philadelphia, that's when me and Mr. Gamble sat down and decided what we were going to do and I started to get to work. That's how it came about. That's the kind of relationship we had."

The first song the group recorded was "I Miss You." Written and produced by Gamble and Huff and arranged by Thom Bell, this pleading ballad, which featured Pendergrass' growling baritone interwoven with the falsetto riffs of Parks, dented the R&B top 10 in the summer of 1972, peaking at number seven. An appealing factor of the song was the second part, containing a monologue by a one-time down-on-his-luck Melvin now trying to reconcile with his lady, spoken over the begging vocals of Pendergrass. This aspect allowed the song to be regarded as something of a black national anthem.

Despite the obvious singing talent of Pendergrass, his limited recording experience was cause for some creative thinking on the part of Melvin to complete the song.

He explains, "When we did 'I Miss You,' that was the first song Teddy ever recorded and I had to record him live. In other words, Teddy couldn't sing and just open up his voice with just a track playing. Teddy had to have girls around him and other people in the studio before he could take it and start singing. That's the only way he could actually feel the song. We went in and cut 'I Miss You' and he couldn't feel it. So Gamble asked me, 'What do you need to do?' I said 'Well, let me cut him live.'"

Having established themselves in the black market, Harold Melvin and the Blue Notes captured the pop audience with their next release, "If You Don't Know Me By Now." Again written and produced by Gamble and Huff, with the arrangement this time by Bobby Martin, this heartfelt ballad allowed Pendergrass' intense baritone to roam over the full orchestration of Philadelphia International house band MFSB. The song topped the R&B charts for two weeks in the fall of 1972, peaked at number three on the pop charts, and sold two million copies, netting them a Grammy nomination for best R&B group performance.

"I was surprised when ['If You Don't Know Me By Now'] crossed over that big," says Melvin. "Clive Davis at the time was the president of CBS. I remember one time, before it was released as a single, he took out a full page in *Billboard* magazine that said, 'By next week the whole world will be singing 'If You Don't Know Me By Now.' I just thought it was great publicity but it came true."

The Blue Notes followed their biggest seller with the triumphant ballad "Yesterday I Had the Blues," reaching number 12 on the R&B charts early in 1973. All three hits were included on the group's self-titled Philadelphia International debut album. The album was further enhanced by the Melvin-led "Ebony Woman," which showed traces of the group's cabaret past, and "Be for Real," featuring an opening monologue by Pendergrass about the dangers of putting on airs.

Led by the success of their debut album and particularly the success of "If You Don't Know Me By Now," Harold Melvin and the Blue Notes made the leap from virtual obscurity to the top of the R&B music world. "That just made me realize and think about all the time I put into the business and paying my dues," says Melvin. "Things didn't come easy for me and I didn't regret any of it. I wish more black acts had more to go through because these acts today aren't paying any dues. They don't have any training or know what the stage is about. They make that little money for a minute and then they're outta here. I'm still booked up every year. I owe that to the public and I appreciate it and I thank them."

With the group having monumental success with ballads, Gamble and Huff initially sought to keep the same formula for the Blue Notes' next release, "The Love I Lost." However, no one liked the original version and Gamble decided to speed up the tempo. The change worked as the sleek and smooth instrumental track behind Pendergrass' lead carried "The Love I Lost" to the top of the R&B charts for two weeks in the fall of 1973; it reached number seven on the pop charts and was the group's second million-seller.

"We did the first album all ballads, so we didn't want to do another album of all ballads," says Melvin. "People wouldn't want to see us if we were up there singing all slow songs, one after another. So about that time, the up-tempo songs just started to come in, and with the different chords and changes, those songs were right down our alley."

He further adds, "Everything we recorded was a true song. Those were songs that were happening in people's lives. These little pop songs weren't made up. They were true experiences that the guys in Philadelphia were going through."

Despite conscious efforts to add some variety to the tempo of the group's sound, "The Love I Lost" was one of only two up-tempo songs on the quintet's *Black and Blue* album. The second was the charging, straightforward "Satisfaction Guaranteed (Or Take Your Love Back)," a number six R&B hit in the spring of 1974. With the exception of the mid-tempo "Is There a Place for Me," the rest of the songs were ballads. One of the more popular was the Melvin-led, blues-flavored "I'm Weak for You," which was the B-side of "Satisfaction Guaranteed."

In the fall of 1974, Melvin and the Blue Notes released *To Be True*, which was arguably the group's finest album. By now Lloyd Parks had left and been replaced by first tenor Jerry Cummings, a Washington, D.C. native who previously sang with a local group, the Internationals. The album's debut single was "Where Are All My Friends." Written by Victor Carstarphen and the team of Gene McFadden and John Whitehead (who in 1972 gave the O'Jays their first massive hit with "Back Stabbers") this rousing track about friends leaving a sinking ship reached number eight on the R&B charts.

The group followed with "Bad Luck" in the spring of 1975. Again written by Carstarphen, McFadden, and Whitehead, this socially conscious track pointed to the recession era of Richard Nixon's presidency. "McFadden and Whitehead were two very talented guys," says Melvin. "I don't know what they were thinking about when they brought ['Bad Luck'] to me but I just knew it was the one." "Bad Luck" kept Melvin and the Blue Notes in the R&B top 10 by peaking at number four. The song also reached the pop top 20 (number 15). In addition to the lyrics, the song's popularity was aided by its danceable, up-tempo production, particularly on the second part of the track, played behind the ad-libs of Pendergrass. This was a critical asset for the group because "Bad Luck" was introduced during the initial stages of disco music. This has had a lasting effect on Melvin and the Blue Notes. Because of the success of "Bad Luck" and of "The Love I Lost" in 1973, the group today is able to perform at several venues featuring veteran disco acts.

"We came in on the front end of disco," says Melvin. "I guess it's alright but I didn't want to bank my career on it. I'm glad that we're a nightclub act and not a disco act but I'm glad that we did make a statement during disco."

He further adds, "The night we were cutting 'Bad Luck' and the part two rap where Teddy is talking about the President of the United States, that came to me in the studio when we started ad-libbing. That was my specialty. Any ad-libbing in any of the songs came from me."

The album's third single, "Hope That We Can Be Together Soon," introduced Sharon Paige, who shared lead vocals with both Melvin and Pendergrass on this ballad. Paige previously appeared at local talent shows in Philadelphia before landing an office job at Philadelphia International. Melvin recalls, "My valet, the road manager, knew her and told me he knew a girl who could sing and I had to meet her. I hadn't even heard her sing yet but she came to my office and I said that just by talking to her I could tell she could sing. So I signed her up. The very first song I showed her was 'Hope That We Can Be Together

Soon.'" The added attraction proved beneficial as "Hope That We Can Be Together Soon" topped the R&B charts for a week in the summer of 1975.

The success of "Hope That We Can Be Together Soon" was an added benefit to Melvin because he produced the majority of the song before Gamble and Huff applied their finishing touches. He says, "I took my own musicians into the studio. Mr. Gamble and Mr. Huff didn't even know I recorded it. They had no idea. I took my own musicians in and used my own money, cut the track, and put Teddy, Sharon, and myself on it. Joe Tarsia [Sigma Sound Studio owner] said to Gamble, 'You need to hear this stuff that Mr. Melvin is cutting over here.' By the time Gambs heard it when I finished he said, 'My God . . . Melvin, we've got to have that.' Then I put Sharon in the group and took her on the road with us for a little while at different one-nighters so the public could get used to her because no one really knew who she was. Then 'Hope That We Can Be Together Soon' came out. She was a great talent."

Other outstanding tracks on the album included the title track and "Pretty Flower," with the respective pleading, heartfelt leads of Melvin and Pendergrass, and the perfect harmonizing of the group on the ballad "Somewhere Down the Line." *To Be True* was certified gold, mainly on the strength of sales in the black markets, as neither of the album's singles (with the possible exception of "Bad Luck") achieved significant crossover success.

One other significant factor of the *To Be True* album was the group now being billed as "Harold Melvin and the Blue Notes featuring Theodore Pendergrass" as Pendergrass' lead was becoming more visible as the focal point of the group's sound. It was widely speculated at this time that Pendergrass wanted top billing in the group and settled on having his name mentioned as a featured artist. However, Melvin disputes this notion. He says, "Teddy never really wanted top billing. That was my idea of 'Harold Melvin and the Blue Notes featuring Theodore Pendergrass.' Nobody wanted to put his name anywhere. That was my doing. I just believed that the brother deserved it. He had been with me for awhile and had proven himself. A lot of people try to make negative things out of it. Teddy never came to me with anything like [having top billing]. We never had any problems on stage, we never had any problems, period."

Melvin and the Blue Notes began 1976 with the title song from their *Wake Up Everybody* album topping the R&B charts for two weeks and reaching number 12 on the pop charts. Again written by the team of Carstarphen, McFadden, and Whitehead, this socially-conscious track was virtually an exclusive Pendergrass recording. The song, which started off slow before building to a rousing finish, showcased the gospel influence of Pendergrass' voice. Despite the success of "Wake Up Everybody" and of "Bad Luck" a year earlier, Melvin expressed concern about the possibility of the group being labeled as a message group. "I never really wanted to get involved with the all-out message songs," he says. "I didn't think those songs would work for us and I didn't want for us to be a group that couldn't cross over. Gamble cut most of those message songs on the O'Jays."

The group followed with the energetic "Tell the World How I Feel About 'Cha Baby," which peaked at number seven. Other standouts from the album were "Keep on Loving You" and "Don't Leave Me This Way," the latter a massive hit the following year for Thelma Houston. Although Melvin was concerned about keeping his crossover audience, the *Wake Up Everybody* album, like its predecessor, achieved gold status mainly on the strength of sales in the black markets.

In 1976 Teddy Pendergrass severed his ties with Melvin and the Blue Notes. Initially there were two competing groups. Pendergrass, Wilson, Brown, and former member Parks were known as the Blue Notes featuring Teddy Pendergrass. This lineup lasted for only a few months before Pendergrass decided to go solo. Wilson, Brown, Parks, and former lead singer John Atkins recorded a little-noticed album entitled *Truth Has Come to Light* on the Florida-based Glades label before disappearing. Melvin formed a new set of Blue Notes with Cummings; Dwight Johnson, who also sang in Washington, D.C. with the

Internationals; Bill Spratley, who sang with Nat Turner's R
bellion in Virginia; and lead singer David Ebo, whom Melvin
discovered at Emerson's Bar in South Philadelphia.

While Pendergrass remained incognito for most of 1976,
Melvin and the Blue Notes signed with ABC Records. On his
decision to leave Philadelphia International, Melvin says, "I
didn't want any confusion. I didn't want any arguments between
Gamble and Teddy, and Gamble and me. I just said, 'I can make
it on my own. I'll be cool. I'll be over here. We're still friends.
There's no sense in messing up a friendship over [Pendergrass
going solo].' I walked out on a lot of money but I'm happy.

"You really don't replace somebody like Teddy. Teddy was
my sound. Teddy is a talent of his own. He's one of the best
talents I ever ran across. He could feel me instantly. All I had
to do was give him something and he had it. He had what a
star has. You have to be born with it. You can't just say you're
a star, you have to be born a star. Most singers don't possess
that special thing that Teddy had."

Melvin's new lineup got off to a good start early in 1977 with
the smooth, mid-tempo "Reaching for the World," featuring
alternate leads between Melvin and Ebo, peaking at number
six on the R&B charts. After the top 15 success of "After You
Love Me, Why Do You Leave Me," a sultry duet with Melvin
and Sharon Paige, later recordings on Source, MCA, and Philly
World were less successful.

After Pendergrass took a nearly year-long hiatus, he decided
to remain with Philadelphia International, despite receiving
offers from several other companies. Continuing to utilize the
creative services of Gamble and Huff, and the songwriters and
musicians who contributed to the success of the Blue Notes,
Pendergrass released four platinum albums in a three-year
period.

His solo career began with the release of his eponymous
1977 album. Only two singles from the album achieved chart
success: the up-tempo "I Don't Love You Anymore" reached
number five on the R&B charts in the spring of 1977, while the
ballad "The Whole Town's Laughing At Me" reached number

16 later that fall. However, numbers do not begin to tell the impact of this album. Strong favorites included the danceable tracks "You Can't Hide From Yourself" and "The More I Get, the More I Want," the latter containing openly sexual lyrics which would soon become his trademark. "Somebody Told Me," with its powerful socially-conscious message, was something of a continuation of "Wake Up Everybody." Perhaps the album's most sensuous ballads were the underrated "And If I Had" and "Easy, Easy, Got to Take It Easy," which helped lay the foundation for Pendergrass' strong female fan base that carried the album to million-selling status. Honors for the album included a Grammy nomination and a selection by *Billboard* for the Pop Album New Artist Award for 1977.

Pendergrass' next disc, *Life Is a Song Worth Singing*, would establish him as a *bona fide* superstar. The album's first single, the sensuous ballad "Close the Door," topped the R&B charts for two weeks in the summer of 1978. "Close the Door," which would become Pendergrass' signature song, was in context with him being regarded as R&B music's premier male sex symbol of this period. Affectionately known as the Teddy Bear, his "For Women Only" concerts attracted standing-room-only crowds that were 90 percent female. At these concerts, chocolate teddy bear lollipops were given out to women, and panties were regularly tossed on stage in his direction.

In addition to "Close the Door," the album's double-platinum success was generated by the straightforward "Only You," the second single released and one more commonly known by the phrase "you got what I want"; the lilting "When Somebody Loves You Back;" and the underrated ballad "It Don't Hurt Now."

In 1979, Pendergrass' third solo album, *Teddy*, continued the seductive theme created with "Close the Door." On the first single, "Turn Off the Lights," Pendergrass describes, among other things, taking a shower with a woman and later the two rubbing each other's bodies with oils. The follow-up, "Come Go with Me," was perhaps the zenith of his "begging," as he invited a lady over to his place.

Teddy Pendergrass showed no signs of slowing down at the start of the 1980s. He continued to have a string of hits, including "Can't We Try," "Love TKO," "Two Hearts" (a duet with Stephanie Mills), "I Can't Live Without Your Love," and "You're My Latest, My Greatest Inspiration."

On March 12, 1982, tragedy struck. While Pendergrass was returning home from a basketball game in Philadelphia, his Rolls-Royce sideswiped a metal guardrail, skidded across a two-lane street, ripped the bark off a tree, slammed into another tree, and pinned the passenger side of the car against a third tree. He was pulled from the wreck, had a severely injured spinal cord, and was hospitalized in critical condition. Initially paralyzed from the neck down, he gradually recovered partial movement, but was confined to a wheelchair.

After a long period of physical therapy, Pendergrass returned to recording. He left Philadelphia International and signed with Elektra-Asylum. His Elektra debut, *Love Language*, generated the hit "Hold Me," a duet with then-unknown Whitney Houston. Pendergrass continues to release albums on the Elektra label every two to three years. He has remained a consistent presence on the R&B charts, having hits with "Love 4/2," "Joy," "2 A. M.," and "It Should've Been You." In particular, 1988's *Joy*, with the Number One title track produced by Midnight Star's creative force Reggie Calloway, rejuvenated his career after a short lean period.

The legacy of the music created when Pendergrass was still with the Blue Notes was apparent in 1990 when British pop group Simply Red had a Number One pop hit with "If You Don't Know Me By Now." Melvin and Pendergrass later performed "If You Don't Know Me By Know" on *The Arsenio Hall Show*. Contrary to popular speculation, Harold Melvin and Teddy Pendergrass remain friends.

"[Teddy] still calls me," says Melvin. "Just before we did *The Arsenio Hall Show*, he called and said, 'I want you to come out to L.A. I need you.' He wanted me to come out and put together a little arrangement of 'If You Don't Know Me By Now.' He said, 'I had to call you because I wouldn't have had a career without you.' Still to this day, in the show, I'll say to the girls, 'I'm gonna tell Teddy y'all asked about him.'

"When the accident happened, I was one of the only ones to keep calling. [The hangers-on] all ran when everything fell down. I was the only one to help him build his ego back up. I used to go over to his house to rehearse his lungs, to strengthen them while he was cutting."

Although Harold Melvin and the Blue Notes no longer have a recording career, they continue to draw enthusiastic audiences around the country. As of 1995, the group consisted of Melvin, Dwight Johnson, and Donnell Gillespie. "We perform about two nights a week, minimum," says Melvin. "Sometimes we do four nights. That's consistent, right now, to this day. A lot of acts stopped working altogether. A lot of acts are out there ego-tripping and they out-priced themselves. You can't out-price yourself. You have to be thankful that you're still out here. You can't ask for more than the club owner or promoter thinks you can bring in. If you want to be a promoter and you book us somewhere and you don't make money, then we're no good to you. If you walk around with an ego and overprice yourself, you'll be right out of the market. If people don't see you, they'll forget you, so it's best to make a living and be visible than make nothing at all and have people forget about you. If you stay visible and hang around, that circle will come back around. I feel pretty fortunate that God has allowed me to still be here through all these years and through all the stuff that has gone on."

The Moments
(RAY, GOODMAN AND BROWN)

One of the more consistent love ballad groups of the 1970s, Harry Ray, Al Goodman, and Billy Brown, collectively known as the Moments, recorded a string of R&B hits which made them synonymous with romantic love songs. Led by ballads such as "Love on a Two-Way Street" and "Look at Me (I'm in Love)," the threesome, known as a ladies' group, garnered a strong following of young women who made up the core of their audience. Changing their name to Ray, Goodman and Brown in 1979, this New Jersey-based trio was the only one of its tenor dominated soft soul contemporaries to record consistently throughout the 1980s.

The original Moments, Mark Greene (lead), Richie Horsely, and John Morgan, came out of Washington, D.C. In 1968 they were signed to All Platinum Records, the New Jersey-based company founded in the late 1960s by Joe and Sylvia Robinson. Sylvia was the female half of the "Love Is Strange" (1956) duo Mickey and Sylvia. Led by Greene's falsetto, the group first charted in the fall of 1968 with "Not on the Outside," a pleading ballad, which made the R&B top 20. However, after two shows at the Apollo Theater, Sylvia Robinson fired all but Morgan. Greene and Horsely were replaced by Billy Brown (falsetto) and Al Goodman (bass). Brown, from Asbury Park, New Jersey, had been with Lenny Welch in the Broadways, and was later in the Uniques. Goodman, a Jackson, Mississippi native, was previously in the Corvettes and the Vipers.

He recalls, "I was with a group out of New York called the Vipers. Sylvia had a club up in the Bronx that used to have a talent show every Wednesday and I was there for a show. I won the show and Joe Robinson invited me out. I liked him from the jump because he was a regular kind of guy. We sat down in the studio and he said, 'Just keep coming. You can quit your day job and do some things around here while you enhance your career.'

"I had to sing with Sylvia, who came from Mickey and Sylvia. She had a song out called 'Do It to Me Baby' when Mickey was in France, and I sang his parts. So . . . I became a part of the little scam around there.

"When the guys got fired I was the first one hired to replace . . . somebody. Then they hired Billy, and the two of us, along with the third original member John Morgan, became the Moments."

After the spring 1969 release of "Sunday," a song similar to its predecessor, the Moments had their first top 10 R&B hit with the doo-wop-flavored "I Do" later that summer. The combination of Goodman, Brown, and Morgan lasted for only six months as Morgan's spot was taken over by John Moore, Sylvia Robinson's brother-in-law. After the Motown-flavored ballad "I'm So Lost," the group had their fourth top 20 R&B hit, "Lovely Way She Loves," which featured a cameo appearance by Sylvia Robinson.

The Moments' next single would be their breakthrough. Released in the spring of 1970, "Love on a Two-Way Street," about a man who is broken-hearted after his lover walks out on him, topped the R&B charts for five weeks and rose to number three on the pop charts. Written and produced by Sylvia Robinson, this sweet soul classic was the Moments' first gold single.

As "Love on a Two-Way Street" was climbing the charts, Moore left the group. His place was taken by Harry Ray, a tenor singer from Long Branch, New Jersey, who fronted a local group called the Establishment. Ray joined the Moments three days before the beginning of a cross-country tour with the Temptations.

He previously stated, "I auditioned with my group because I knew Billy Brown from Asbury Park. We had competing bands and did a couple of shows together when we were coming up in high school. Meanwhile, 'Love on a Two-Way Street' was climbing the charts. When I auditioned, [Brown] wasn't there; Al was there. I didn't know [Moore] was gone. I just happened to pick the right day and the right time."

Goodman adds, "Harry was auditioning with the Establishment and I heard his voice. I'm the one who pulled Harry in and said, 'Hey, man, come with us; forget about the Establishment.' Three days of rehearsal and he knew everything that we did. Maybe a little nervousness would come out but that was it."

The success of "Love on a Two-Way Street" took the Moments from virtual obscurity to the top of the R&B music world. "At that time we were all crazy . . . I guess because our dream had come true," says Goodman. "All of us had wanted to be in show business and had reached the dream we desired. We thought it was great but then Joe Robinson kept our heads on straight so we didn't get caught up in the drug scene. I enjoyed it."

Harry Ray became lead singer of the Moments almost by default. He made his debut as lead singer on the group's next single, a cover of the Ink Spots' classic "If I Didn't Care." Billy Brown explains, "The first song Harry recorded with the Moments was 'If I Didn't Care.' I was supposed to sing it but I was having problems with my throat. It was somewhat of a blessing in disguise for us. Eventually, I imagine that Harry would have gotten around to doing some recording but at that particular time he wasn't. He was sort of a victim of circumstance."

Brown sang lead on "All I Have," which in the fall of 1970 became the group's third straight top 10 hit. Over the next few years, Brown and Ray alternated leads.

Although the All Platinum roster featured the talents of Lonnie Youngblood, the Ponderosa Twins Plus One, and the late Linda Jones, the company was built around the Moments as the trio became the label's only consistent hitmaking act. Each member also wore several hats. Al Goodman was an engineer, promotion man, and head of A&R with Brown as his assistant, while Harry Ray was in charge of album covers.

Goodman notes, "The Moments pretty much carried the company but we didn't know anything about the business at that time so we didn't know what we were carrying. It was just fun for us. If we knew then what we know now, things would've been different. Joe Robinson told us just a short time ago that we were the only thing he had to keep the doors open; that's how so many guys got fired. Anytime someone did anything to the Moments, he had to let him go because that was the only thing he had to keep the doors open. When guys came in with bad habits he said, 'Y'all got to get rid of that.' We really didn't know about the load that we had on us."

Harry Ray stated, "We were the only guys who could go in [the studio] by ourselves, without the producers or anybody, and do our own thing. We'd have two other guys on background but we didn't need anybody else in there. If they said, 'Put out a record by next Friday,' it was done."

Throughout the early 1970s, the group's reputation for love songs grew as a string of romantic ballads kept the Moments on the charts. "We tried to get our biggest hits on ballads and keep ballads as our mainstay," says Goodman. "After awhile people wouldn't accept us for anything else. We would try to record a good up-tempo song and they wouldn't even consider it. They said, 'Forget about this, you guys are balladeers. This stuff here, this is not you. Give it to the Isley Brothers 'cause it's not you.'"

Brown adds, "We were taught by Joe and Sylvia Robinson, when you're winning with something, stick with it until it fails. That was our philosophy all through those years."

Among the highlights of the Moments' songs during this period were "Lucky Me," "To You with Love" (1971), "Just Because He Wants to Make Love (Doesn't Mean He Loves You)" (1972), "Gotta Find a Way," "Girl, I'm Gonna Miss You," and the mid-tempo "My Thing" (1973). These songs became minor R&B hits but achieved limited success on the pop charts.

The group's crossover fortunes changed in the fall of 1973 with the release of "Sexy Mama." Although credited to the Moments, Harry Ray's voice is the only one from the trio that is featured on the song. This aptly titled single with its sensuous rhythm track was the Moments' biggest hit since "Love on a Two-Way Street," peaking at number three on the R&B charts and climbing to number 17 on the pop charts.

Goodman explains, "[Harry and I] wrote the song. Basically, Harry Ray was the writer. I put a couple of lines in but Harry had most of the song. We actually wrote the song for Sylvia and it was called 'Sexy Daddy.' She had just done 'Pillow Talk.' And somehow Joe thought ['Sexy Mama'] was too syrupy. Harry and I cut a track on the song. We came into the studio at ten o'clock that night when nobody was there and we recorded it. I was the engineer, Harry was the artist, and we recorded it straight out in one take. We knew it was a hit the next day because all of the secretaries came in and they were finger-popping up and down the hall. When we put it out, the first place that picked up the record was a big station in Canada called CKLW. Once they picked it up, the monster stations picked it up and it became number one for two weeks.

"I was surprised that WABC [New York] didn't play it at that time. That was the only station we couldn't get to play it. We were close to 900,000 [in sales]. We felt that if WABC had picked it up, we would've gotten the other 100,000."

After the release of "Sweet Sweet Lady" and the moody "What's Your Name" in 1974, the Moments recorded the disco-flavored "Girls" with their labelmates the Whatnauts as the disco boom began to pick up steam. Despite its limited chart success (number 25 R&B), "Girls" remains one of the group's more popular songs.

Goodman says, "When we did the record 'Girls,' believe it or not, 'Girls' didn't do as particularly well black as it did white. We played a lot of the discos and whites loved it. That's when a lot of whites really got into the Moments."

The Moments returned to their ballad tradition in the spring of 1975 with the release of "Look at Me (I'm in Love)," which became their second Number One R&B hit. Goodman explains the origin of the song, "I wrote that song for Harry when he was getting married back in 1974. He came to me in Atlantic City and told me that he wanted to get married, which I thought was ironic because, at that time, Harry and Billy had women chasing them down the streets. I asked him, 'Why is it that a guy who has women chasing him wants to get married?' and he said 'Look at me, I must be in love.' So, I wrote the song. We ended up performing it at Harry's wedding, my wedding, and Billy's wedding."

Like its predecessor, "Girls," the Moments recorded a French version of "Look at Me (I'm in Love)." Goodman recalls, "The whole idea came about because they were trying to break us into France. We had broken Europe so big but yet we never broke in France. We had every place else there sewed up; Japan, Turkey, England, but no France. At the time, Barbara Baker, a young lady from France, became a part of Joe Robinson's company. Joe Robinson had an idea because Barbara Baker's husband was French and he was also a record producer, so we cut the two songs in French. Naturally it wasn't the same. The story was the same but the words weren't the same."

With the rise of the disco era, the majority of the stand-up vocal groups suffered and the Moments were no exception. As Billy Brown explains, "We were hurt a lot by disco. When it came in there was nothing happening for us. In order for us to get work, we had to go out of the country."

The Moments' biggest success during this period was the cool, elegant "With You" in the fall of 1976. Sung by Harry Ray in a deep tenor, this mellow ballad reached number 14 on the R&B charts. "I Don't Wanna Go" in 1977 and "I Could Have Loved You" the following year were the trio's last top 20 hits as the Moments.

When All Platinum Records was beset by financial and distribution problems due to a major slump in the industry, the trio cut their ties with the label in 1977. When they left All Platinum, they also left behind their name since the label owned the copyright.

The group has mixed emotions about their eight-year relationship with All Platinum. "We always lived pretty good, basically because of the three of us, not because of anybody else," says Goodman. "We went out on the road, we got our money, and we preserved ourselves, so we did live pretty good during those years but we didn't live as well as we *should* have."

He further adds, "I don't preach it but I'm a religious person. I'll forgive anyone for anything. I didn't say I'll forget but I will forgive. What we didn't know we learned later on. We got somewhat of an education."

After a two-and-a-half-year absence from recording, the trio changed their name to Ray, Goodman and Brown and signed with Polydor Records in 1979. "[The name change] wasn't a big problem because on stage we always used our names, Billy Brown, Al Goodman, and Harry Ray," says Goodman. "When the name change came about, it was at a time when we wanted to get rid of that stigma of Moments . . . Delfonics . . . that sort of thing. We said that if we have to change, let's change to something where we'll always be identified and that nobody can ever take from us."

The first release from their self-titled Polydor debut was "Special Lady," which became the group's third Number One R&B hit. This doo wop-flavored ballad also reached number five on the pop charts and was certified gold in the spring of 1980. More important, the success of "Special Lady" gave Ray, Goodman and Brown a new identity apart from the love ballad groups of the early 1970s who had their recording careers stalled by the rise of disco.

Harry Ray previously explained, "When the Moments faded out and we became Ray, Goodman and Brown, we got very lucky to get a new record label in '79. We got a three-album deal with Polydor and we became current all of a sudden. The first record under Ray, Goodman and Brown, 'Special Lady,' was a million-seller. These other groups haven't had that. They had a reign for awhile but they never had a hit song that they recorded in the late '70s.

" 'Special Lady' and 'Inside of You' opened us up to a wider audience because of crossover. We got a lot of coverage just from 'Special Lady,' so it broadened us. In 1970 'Love on a Two-Way Street' was a million-seller but after that we had two that were top 10 ['Sexy Mama' and 'Look at Me'] and the rest were 18, 20, high in the 20s on the R&B charts; they never went pop."

Spurred by "Special Lady" and the second single, "Inside of You," a beautiful ballad with Billy Brown on lead, the *Ray, Goodman and Brown* album went gold. Both singles begin and end with *a cappella* street harmonies reminiscent of the late '50s.

Goodman explains, "We had the songs written already. Vince Castellano, who was the producer, came in and said, 'Hey, you guys can sing. Let's try something in the hallway.' We tried it in the hallway and it sounded good so we put it on the record. No one else had done the *a cappella* thing for so long. Usually all you hear is straight-laced recording; you don't hear the fun time we had in the recording. When it came out it made it look like it was an intimate thing between Billy, Harry, and I. You can really hear the closeness because we're talking with each other and singing. It gave the recording a little more meaning."

The pop success of the *Ray, Goodman and Brown* album, and particularly "Special Lady," did have its drawbacks as Polydor had the same aspirations for the group's follow-up album, *Ray, Goodman and Brown Two*. The first single, a remake of the Platters' 1956 classic "My Prayer," was targeted strictly to the pop audience.

Brown recalls, "The first week . . . Bam! 'My Prayer' went straight to the pop charts. The second week not one black station would touch it."

Goodman adds, "[The black stations] played 'Happy Anniversary.' That's the song they should've put out in the first place. You put that one out first, then you come with a 'My Prayer' to ease it in. We sold the album but it confused the hell out of the charts." Although relegated to secondary status by the record company, "Happy Anniversary" became a top 20 R&B

hit for Ray, Goodman and Brown while "My Prayer" had limited success on the pop charts.

In the spring of 1981 the group received a boost when Stacy Lattisaw had her biggest hit with a cover of "Love on a Two-Way Street" that spent four weeks at the number two spot on the R&B charts.

Goodman says, "When Stacy had her 'Love on a Two-Way Street' out they backed it up with the Moments' 'Love on a Two-Way Street.' We didn't write it but it gave the group new life. You can't work on the same show — we've experienced that — unless you sing the song together. The first time we worked together [with Stacy Lattisaw] it was all teeny-boppers and they didn't know we had recorded the song; they thought we stole it. We tried to talk [Stacy's management] into letting us do it together but they refused."

After the *Stay* album in 1982, Harry Ray left the group to pursue a solo career. Goodman and Brown found a replacement in Kevin Owens, a backup singer for Luther Vandross, and continued to use the name Ray, Goodman and Brown for live performances. Ray's career began and ended with a little-noticed solo album (*It's Good to Be Home*) and the single "Sweet Baby." The following year he rejoined the group, replacing his own replacement.

Ray, Goodman and Brown had a revival in 1986 with the release of the *Take It to the Limit* album on EMI Records. The title track, a doo-wop ballad which featured all three members sharing the lead, was the trio's first top 10 R&B hit since "Special Lady," peaking at number eight.

"'Take It to the Limit' opened us up to a younger audience because we were able to do a tour with Freddie Jackson," says Goodman. "Freddie had a different audience from what we had and we were able to do an eight-month tour with him. During that tour we were able to play for a younger audience.

"We worked with Stacy [Lattisaw] again after the Freddie Jackson tour when we had been through that market of teen-agers and 18 and up and, at that point, they knew that we recorded 'Love on a Two-Way Street.' Again we asked if she wanted to do it together and her management said 'No,' but this time she *should* have [performed it]."

In 1988 Ray, Goodman and Brown released *Mood for Lovin'* but got little promotion and as a result achieved limited commercial success.

While Ray, Goodman and Brown shopped for a record label, they continued to tour throughout the world. Tragedy struck the group in 1992 when lead singer Harry Ray unexpectedly died from a massive stroke on October 1, at the age of 45. "That hypertension is a serious thing for blacks," says Goodman. "They preach it every day. Harry had some problems in the past but he cleaned up those problems and in cleaning up those problems, a lot of things didn't show up. With hypertension, every time he went to the doctor it was like . . . right on. So . . . I guess he felt that his problems in the past were what was causing it but it wasn't. When you got it, you got it . . . But it was sudden. We talked to him that Wednesday morning and that Wednesday evening . . . He was all prepared to leave town that weekend, so it was very sudden. He had no plans for what happened. His clothes were in the car to take to the cleaners, he was going to get a haircut, then he was coming [to my place].

"Harry drank that Ultra Slim Fast and that must've shot his blood pressure straight to the ceiling. That was the only thing in his system. Harry had gained a lot of weight. Every bad habit that he had, he put down. It took him a year to clean up his whole life and I mean his *whole* life; his attitude, his belief in God, everything. We say now that God had a purpose for Harry because He gave him time to clean up his life before He came and got him. That's the way we look at it."

Ray's place in the lineup was initially taken by Clifford Perkins, a former member of the 1970s soul group Soul Generation ("Body and Soul," "Million Dollars"), and later by Kevin Owens, before the position was finally secured by Wade Elliott. Despite the absence of a current record, Ray, Goodman and Brown are able to perform an average of four to five times a month before their legion of fans.

"Even though you don't record, you want to keep a certain image about yourself," says Goodman. "That's one thing Ray, Goodman and Brown have been able to maintain, a certain image. We work a lot, about four to five times a month. I guess we've had enough records in the past to sustain us and the kind of act we've had has kept us in some pretty good rooms. That's one of the keys. When you don't work, people tend to find something else to do but we've been lucky that we can still work.

"I also attribute it to the fact that we haven't burned any bridges in this industry. We haven't messed over anybody. So the promoters have been nice to us even when we didn't have a record out. Also, with a lot of our friends in the music business, we continually look out. Blue [Lovett] of the Manhattans, Marshall [Thompson] and the Chi-Lites, they turn us on to different clubs and we in turn mention clubs to them and talk to the club owners about them. We don't want that type of music, Manhattans, Chi-Lites, Stylistics, Blue Magic, to die. We as black people sometimes let our music die. Whites don't do that. A guy can be 75 years old and still sing country and western. As soon as we turn 35, they're ready to give up on us in the music business. This is *ours*. R&B is ours, so we have to keep that going and I do everything I can to keep the guys out there."

New Birth

One of the more creative and exciting soul ensembles of the early 1970s, New Birth started as a touring band that, after eight years, began recording and had a string of hits with their innovative cover versions of other artists' songs, such as Bobby Womack's "I Can Understand It" and Jerry Butler's "Dream Merchant." Although most of the group's hits were sung by Leslie Wilson and Londee Loren, New Birth employed the talents of four vocalists who could assume the lead, and was a popular force in the soul music field between 1972 and 1976.

The origin of New Birth was in Louisville, Kentucky in 1963 under the guidance of Harvey Fuqua, a former Motown songwriter and producer, and Tony Churchill. The original concept was a touring company of four acts consisting of 17 people who could perform separately or as part of a fifth group called New Birth, Inc. The acts included eight musicians known as the Nite-Lighters; four female vocalists called the Mint Juleps; four male singers called the New Sound; and soloist Alan Frye. The four acts would perform individual sets and then join together for the show's grand finale. After a number of years of touring and numerous personnel changes, this eventually led to two groups, the instrumentalist Nite-Lighters and the vocal portion, New Birth, which consisted of Londee Loren, Bobby Downs, Melvin Wilson, Leslie Wilson, Ann Bogan (formerly with the Marvelettes), and Frye.

In 1971 Fuqua joined RCA Records and set up his own independent production and talent company. Through Fuqua both groups became affiliated with RCA. The Nite-Lighters were first to strike a hit in the summer of 1971, with "K-Jee" reaching the R&B top 20. New Birth gained notice later that year with the powerful, sparkling vocals of Londee Loren on "It's Impossible," a cover of the Perry Como classic, which reached number 12. In 1972 the Wilson brothers and Bogan branched off to form Love, Peace and Happiness and had a moderate hit with a cover of Gladys Knight and the Pips' "I Don't Want to Do Wrong."

The groups were together as a single unit for their debut *Birth Day* album in 1973. Their first release was a cover of Bobby Womack's recently recorded soul classic "I Can Understand It." Adding a gritty and funky flavor to the multitextured production of the song's arrangement, New Birth began their custom of recording their own versions of other artists' songs. The experience New Birth garnered from their lengthy touring over the years gave them an indication of what songs would receive favorable acceptance. "I Can Understand It" reached number four on the R&B charts in the spring of 1973 and cracked the pop top 40.

Melvin Wilson explains, "I didn't like the songs that were presented to us so I started picking songs I thought we could do better. I had been working with each [vocalist] for a long time. By working with each of the vocalists, I was able to determine who sang lead. What we had to do was be able to sound the same on the record as we did on the road. I had to make sure each one of the individuals sang a part that fit them and that they were happy singing. By doing it on the road it gave me a chance to record them. If they appealed to the audience live, then we would go ahead and cut them. That's how I did those cover songs. I did them on the road before I ever laid them down, and the response was fantastic."

The group followed with "Until It's Time for You to Go," a mystical, sensuous, bass-laden cover of an obscure Elvis Presley single of 1972 written by Buffy Sainte-Marie. The song was recorded during an apparent feud between the group and Fuqua, and as a result, the vocals of Sue Say and not Londee Loren are on the track. "There was a discrepancy with the management," says Wilson. "Harvey was in the process of trying to do another group. He would always go and try to get other people and put them on the album. The group was going to leave. What Harvey was going to do was just replace them with another group. Sue Say is the one who sang the song 'Until It's Time for You to Go.' Londee just reproduced it on stage. Harvey cut it on Sue Say and she was under the impression that she would be singing with us, which did cause a slight problem down the road."

Despite the controversy surrounding the production of the song, "Until It's Time for You to Go" reached number 21 on the R&B charts later that summer and remains a favorite of New Birth fans. Adding to the popularity of the album was "Got to Get a Knutt," a comical, frantic track that slows down just enough to be in tune with Loren's orgasmic panting.

The group had more production input on their follow-up album, *It's Been a Long Time.* All of the vocal arrangements were done by Melvin Wilson, who also co-wrote several tracks with keyboardist and trombonist James Baker. The album's first release was the Wilson and Baker-penned, sensuous title track ballad. " 'It's Been a Long Time' does a lot for me," says Wilson. "During the time we were trying to get into the music business I lost my family, my wife and my children, so the song had something to do with that. It was the reason how the song came about."

Led by the emotive vocals of Leslie Wilson and the understated riffs of Loren, "It's Been a Long Time" became their second top 10 R&B hit, peaking at number four in the spring of 1974. The group followed up with a cover version of "Wild Flower," a top 10 pop hit the previous year for the Canadian one-hit-wonder group Skylark. Arranged and conducted by the entire group, New Birth was able to turn this much-covered ballad into a soul classic. The relatively moderate success of "Wild Flower," peaking at number 17 on the R&B charts in the summer of 1974, does not accurately reflect the importance of the song to the group. Of all of New Birth's singles, "Wild Flower" is arguably the song with which the group is most identified. The R&B audience, unfamiliar with the obscure Skylark, generally assumes that New Birth recorded the original version. A sleeper selection from the album, the smooth "Keep on Doin' It," helped the *It's Been a Long Time* album achieve the same critical success as its predecessor.

An added contributor to New Birth's popularity was their stage presentation. Their show began with 11 members on stage dressed in space-age costumes that glistened through the fog enveloping them. As the smoke cleared and the lights came on, an enormous "egg" was revealed. Out of the egg, which symbolized "new birth," popped Loren to begin the show.

"Our stage presentation was the only thing that we can definitely say we had control over," says Wilson. "Anything else that had to do with contracts and different stuff like that, it didn't seem as if we had a lot of control over that. But how we presented ourselves to the public was important because of word of mouth, and if we put on a good show, then the people would come back to see you. My uniforms were $1,000 apiece for the ones you see back at the time when we were working with the egg, so you know I was spending money, but I had to do that to make my dream come true."

It was in the best interest of the band to promote themselves through their spectacular stage presentation. The success of New Birth on the charts did not adequately reflect their level of popularity with the music audience, as evidenced by the relatively moderate success of "Until It's Time for You to Go" and "Wild Flower." New Birth, like the Main Ingredient and the Friends of Distinction before them, fell victim to RCA's inability to market black music properly.

Wilson points out, "RCA didn't have a good R&B anything in there. They just didn't know what they were doing when it came to black music. They could handle someone like Sam Cooke or people who were contemporary and could cross over, but just for black music I didn't see anything. I didn't understand how other people and other groups were getting things played and getting things done and we just couldn't. They stopped a song that people wanted to hear and was rising on the charts, 'Don't Blame the Young Folks for the Drug Society.'

When I was in Love, Peace and Happiness they just killed that. They said, 'We can't have that kind of language,' although there was nothing vulgar. That's just the way they were. There are things being said on records now that you couldn't do back then. I never knew why the songs didn't get any play. I just knew that we were struggling hard, doing the best we could, gigging night after night, and nothing was happening."

New Birth seemed to be going through the motions on their next two releases, "I Wash My Hands of the Whole Damn Deal" and "Coming from All Ends," and the results were indicated by the lowest chart showing of their career. After performing together for several years and experiencing a string of hits, it became inevitable that with a 12-member band, different members would seek different musical directions. Wilson notes, "It was difficult dealing with such a large personnel because you had different moods and different people and also Harvey [Fuqua] had certain things, so all of these were separated into what they thought they should have had and what they thought they were going to accomplish.

"It was easier for me to make it work when we were in a position where we were starving; when we were in a position where we didn't have anything going for us. We had a manager and we had Harvey. Harvey was acting as the advisor of the group and he also was the producer. He had signed contracts but we never saw any front money. We never saw anything and we couldn't understand why we weren't getting anything. It was easier for me to deal with them once we were out there in a starving position. They had to have someone to follow. When the hits started coming later on and we started to get some play, that's when they wanted to do their own thing."

By 1975, New Birth left Harvey Fuqua and RCA and joined Buddah Records. By now the group consisted of Loren, brothers Melvin and Leslie Wilson, and Frye as vocalists, backed by James Baker (keyboards), Robin Russell (drums), Carl McDaniel and Charlie Hearndon (guitars), Leroy Taylor (bass), Robert Jackson (trumpet), Austin Lander (baritone sax), and Tony Churchill (tenor sax and vibes). Their Buddah debut, *Blind Baby,* surprisingly featured 11 new songs and only one remake. However, it was the one remake, a cover of Jerry Butler's 1963 hit "Dream Merchant," that became the smash hit. With the production of Wilson and Baker changing very little from the original, New Birth took "Dream Merchant" to the top of the R&B charts for one week in the summer of 1975. It also crossed over to become their second top 40 pop hit.

"That really felt good," says Wilson. "It made us feel like we had a chance. I always liked 'Dream Merchant' because I always liked the version that Jerry Butler, one of my favorite singers did. He was inspirational to me, just listening to his records when I was trying to get into the music business."

New Birth's tenure at Buddah was short-lived despite having a Number One hit. The group joined Buddah at a time when the label was concentrating on black music. Veteran R&B artists such as Barbara Mason with "From His Woman to You" and Gladys Knight and the Pips with "The Way We Were/Try to Remember" continued to have success on the label. However, Buddah released a series of recordings by new artists, most of which were unsuccessful. This only accelerated Buddah's financial problems, which would lead to the label's downfall at the start of the 1980s. By 1976, New Birth was on the Warner label.

At this time disco was in and New Birth, along with several traditional soul and funk bands, faded as they failed to adapt to the funkier style of the later 1970s' self-contained funk bands. Their two-year tenure on Warner Brothers was uneventful, giving the group only a modest showing on the charts. "We wanted to make another rise but the music industry seemed to change it," explains Wilson. "Disco was coming in so fast; that put us in a bad position. It seemed like our time was up before we could really make our next comeback."

After the mildly successful "I Love You" on the Ariola label in 1979, New Birth decided to call it quits. When the band broke up, various members continued to be active in other areas of the music business while others left completely. The Wilson brothers continued to remain active, albeit sporadically, while Londee Loren pursued a nursing degree. Melvin Wilson recounts, "I had been doing some songs, just writing and presenting songs to different local artists. Leslie had been working and did an album with LTD after Jeffrey [Osborne] left. We did things in bits and pieces. I never really completely left."

In 1994 Melvin Wilson revived New Birth with his brother Leslie, and two new singers, Barbara Wilson and Paulette Williams. "New Birth is down to four artists now," says Wilson. "Londee was with us for a minute but she's working to be a nurse so we lost contact with her. She was supposed to be with us but she had another career so she wasn't interested in the business anymore. We're in the process of trying to get it back together now. We did a show with the Emotions at the Cotton Club in Los Angeles [in early September 1994] and we got a standing ovation. It was like we had never left because the things were happening like they always had been. Right now I'm just trying to make sure that we do it right because I don't want to let the people down when I get there."

The Ohio Players

The Ohio Players, led by their eccentric lead vocalist and guitarist Leroy "Sugarfoot" Bonner, enjoyed immense success in the mid-1970s with an innovative blend of R&B, jazz, and funk played to sexual lyrics on such tracks as "Fire" and "Skin Tight." However, the grooves on some of their other hits were so powerful that the lyrics hardly mattered, as evidenced by the success of "Love Rollercoaster" and "Who'd She Coo." A self-contained group where each member contributed to every song, this seven-member unit from Dayton, Ohio was one of the hottest record and concert attractions in the music industry for one funky stretch between 1973 and 1976.

The history of the Ohio Players begins in 1959, when singer-guitarist Robert Ward formed a group called the Ohio Untouchables. It included Levar Frederick (bass) and Cornelius Johnson (drums). Clarence Satchell (saxophone, flute), Marshall Jones (bass), and Ralph "Pee Wee" Middlebrook (trumpet) were soon added. The group provided the vocal backing for the Falcons and their new lead singer, 19-year-old Wilson Pickett, on their 1962 hit "I Found a Love." The Untouchables released their own single "Love Is Amazing" on the Detroit-based LuPine Records to local success. Ward left the Untouchables in 1964 for a short-lived solo career on Lupine and Groove City. He was replaced on guitar by Leroy "Sugarfoot" Bonner, but in this period the band remained relatively inactive. In 1967, Satchell and Jones recruited some local Dayton, Ohio musicians, reformed as an octet, and called themselves the Ohio Players. The newly formed ensemble worked as the house band for Compass Records and recorded demo tapes on their own time. The group cracked the R&B charts for the first time early in 1968 with "Trespassin'." After a follow-up single, "It's a Cryin' Shame," failed to chart, the Ohio Players were signed by Capitol Records in Los Angeles, aided by a Compass-recorded demo tape. Their one Capitol album, *Observations in Time,* went nowhere and the Capitol contract expired without any success.

The Players' next move was to pool $400 for a trip to Nashville to record their next album, *Pain,* for Top Hit, an independent Dayton label. The funky title track, basically a forum for each band member to display his musical ability, became a minor R&B hit and the album was picked up by Detroit's Westbound label. The Ohio Players at this time consisted of Satchell, Jones, Middlebrook, Bonner, Greg Webster (drums), Bruce Napier (trumpet), Marvin Pierce (trumpet, vocals), and Walter "Junie" Morrison (piano, vocals).

In 1973 the Ohio Players released *Pleasure,* which contained the novelty song "Funky Worm." Featuring the voice of Morrison as the aged Granny singing about a graveyard worm, "Funky Worm" topped the R&B charts for a week in the spring of 1973, was a top 20 pop hit, and sold over a million copies. After the *Ecstasy* album, also released in 1973, the Ohio Players left Westbound and signed with Mercury Records. By the time the band moved to Mercury Records there had been more personnel changes. Jimmy "Diamond" Williams came on board a year earlier as the band's drummer. Also, lead singer Morrison decided to stay at Westbound, where he embarked on a solo career and later joined the group Parliament/Funkadelic. Morrison was replaced on keyboards by Billy Beck. The loss of the lead singer and keyboard player (Morrison) did not deter Mercury from signing the group.

Jimmy Williams recalls, "We called Walter Morrison 'Junie' and Junie was the lead vocalist and keyboard player of the group during the Westbound start. He was basically the musical director and he added quite a lot in terms of the writing aspect. He was also the Granny in 'Funky Worm.' He was an artist and an incredible musician and he contributed a lot to the group.

"There was a contract dispute with Westbound where the Ohio Players said that Westbound had not given them any royalties. That was the reason why we initially left. We said, 'We're not getting paid, so we're outta here.' Polygram accepted that situation and said, 'Well, if you're not getting paid, we'll take you on.'

"There was never any apprehension at all as far as Mercury was concerned. Although Junie decided to stay at Westbound, they were very much interested in the group. The replacement guy that we got was Billy Beck who was also an incredible musician, so there was no hesitation."

The Players' first effort for Mercury was the summer 1974 release of *Skin Tight*, an album that took only one week to record. As was their norm, the band went into the studio without any prepared material or preconceived notions. Each member also contributed to each song, whether writing lyrics or contributing to the melody line. Williams explains, "There was always something that you planned on but it used to be the norm of the group in most instances we would go in the recording studio with an open mind and just go in there and jam and see what we came out with and made songs out of it."

Guitar player and vocalist Leroy "Sugarfoot" Bonner adds, "I like things live. I'm not into synthesizers. It's robotic . . . it's not human. I made up stuff while I was up there [in the studio]. If I felt like saying 'excuse me' on a record, I said it."

The result was a gold album, which in three months outsold their three Westbound albums combined. The first release, the mostly-instrumental "Jive Turkey," was a top 10 R&B hit. However, it was the title track that served as the impetus for the album's success. Featuring the nasal, almost snarling vocals of Sugarfoot for much of the song, the bass- and horn-driven "Skin Tight" reached number two on the R&B charts in the fall of 1974; it was a top 20 pop hit and the Ohio Players' second gold single. "Walter [Morrison] decided to quit the group after *Ecstasy*, which left us without a singer," says Sugarfoot. "Rather than hire someone else, I said 'I can sing it.' The very first time I opened my mouth it was a gold record."

Skin Tight contained only six songs averaging seven minutes each in length. In addition to the two chart hits, the album's appeal was aided by the popular "Heaven Must Be Like This," a soft, dreamy ballad which infused the band's jazz roots with their customary funk, and the sensuous ballad "It's Your Night/Words of Love." The *Skin Tight* album topped the R&B charts and became the band's first gold album.

The Ohio Players followed *Skin Tight* with *Fire*, released in November 1974. Continuing their trademark of highly erotic sleeve pictures, the cover of *Fire* featured a nude model wearing a fireman's helmet and entwined in a fire hose. "[The album covers] were a collaboration between us and the record company," explains Williams. "Our idea was, if you can get somebody to look at the cover, and can catch their eye, maybe you can catch their ear secondly. First you have to catch their eye because there are so many albums on the rack at the record store. So, to be a little bit different, it was a good thing. What we decided to do was put some sensuality and some nice-looking black women to portray our album covers and that got us the look. Then, hopefully, after they posted the album cover on the walls, they took the album out and played it. That was the essence behind that."

Sugarfoot adds, "*Playboy* and *Players* were 'our' magazines, so we hired the models from *Playboy* and the *Playboy* photographers. It was a very catchy thing. People buy *Playboy* to look at the pictures, they don't buy it to read it. People open up to the center, look at it, and put it back on the shelf. We needed something that would attract people to us in the same way."

The music of the *Fire* album took the Ohio Players to the pinnacle of their success. The title track was the first released from the album. Built upon an infectious dance groove and featuring the use of fire engines for sound effects, the single reached the top of the R&B charts for two weeks early in 1975 and was the group's first Number One pop hit and third million-seller. The following year "Fire" earned the Ohio Players a Grammy nomination for best R&B performance by a group or duo.

The album was certified gold in two weeks and, in addition to rising to the top of the R&B charts, *Fire* topped the pop charts for a week, a remarkable feat for a mid-'70s R&B/funk band. The album's second release, the ballad "I Want to Be Free," with its repeated "shoop-shoop" hook, became the Ohio Players' fourth consecutive R&B top 10 hit, peaking at number six in the spring of 1975. However, "I Want to Be Free" failed to crack the pop top 40. The success of *Fire* on the pop charts is a testament to the popularity of the title track. None of the album's remaining five songs were released as singles, nor were any of the tracks consistent with any songs receiving pop top 40 airplay in 1975.

"At the time it was always a surprise for any black group to cross over and hit the pop charts," says Williams. "To hit them was one thing and to be on top of them was always something else. At that time it wasn't being done by too many black artists, bands in particular. It was very rewarding and very surprising that our songs were able to do that.

"It's good when you have the black public behind you buying your material, but when you start to sell to the white public also, it just adds a plus. When you get on the airlines with your music and Casey Kasem is saying you're in the top 10 and you're hearing it on TWA and United Airlines . . . It gave us a lot of publicity and a lot of recognition throughout the world."

Despite the rarity of this feat, Sugarfoot was not surprised. He says, "White folks, believe it or not, have been wanting to be funky all their lives. They just needed an excuse and there we were. We were there to give them that excuse. I'm glad that they have this soul because it made my job a hell of a lot easier. We sold most of our records to the white audience and that's what I'm most grateful for because crossover back in those days was unheard of. If something is good, it doesn't matter whether it's black or white."

The success of *Fire* made the Ohio Players one of the hottest record and concert attractions in the music industry. The band toured constantly.

"[The success] was absolutely marvelous on one end and on the other end I guess it was also some detriment involved," says Williams. "We were playing on the road a long time. Certain things like your family you don't see much of, but it was great for the band. We toured a lot, we saw a lot of places and things we'd never seen before. That part of it was absolutely marvelous. For a few years we were out on the road for about 300 days in a year . . . That was a lot."

Late in 1975 the Ohio Players released *Honey*. The cover of the album, which won the group a Grammy for best album cover, featured a nude model tasting honey right out of the jar. On the inside cover, she was wearing nothing but honey. Despite their erotic covers, the Ohio Players were spared any flak from feminist groups. Williams points out, "If you go to an art museum and look at some of the art that's on the walls from some of the most famous artists and sculptors, you see that they depict the human body as the human body is. We didn't do anything on the verge of *Hustler* magazine — not to discredit the magazine. We tried to be a little bit more tasteful in our presentation of the black woman. I don't think there's anything wrong with what we did in our portrayal of her. Most of the comments were, 'Hey, that's a nice-looking chick,' and always from the guys, 'Do you know their numbers?' We didn't have people picketing our houses and feminist groups saying, 'Tear up the album.'"

The first single released from *Honey* was "Sweet Sticky Thing," a song that starts off softer and jazzier than most of the Players' other hits, before building to a funky climax. "Sweet Sticky Thing" topped the R&B charts for a week in the fall of 1975. It was back to uninterrupted funk late in 1975 on the second single, "Love Rollercoaster," which became the group's second simultaneous Number One pop and R&B hit and fourth million-seller. The song, originally inspired by a bumpy plane ride, became controversial after a deejay in Berkeley, California started a rumor that a woman (model Ester Cordet) was killed in the studio during the recording of the track. To help them sell more records, the band took a vow of silence on the matter.

The "death scream" was actually a screech by Beck during a guitar break before the second verse. The band increased the funk on "Fopp," which also made the R&B top 10 in early 1976. Aided by these three releases, the *Honey* album reached number two on the pop charts and was the Players' third straight platinum album.

The group had their fifth and final R&B chart topper in the summer of 1976 with the perky "Who'd She Coo," inspired by the phrase "Hoochie Coo." Like most of the Players' previous hits, "Who'd She Coo" was a success on the strength of its track, not its lyrical content.

With the Ohio Players at the peak of their success, the disco phenomenon was beginning to rise and funk bands, along with stand-up vocal groups, suffered. Williams notes, "I think all groups were hurt by disco. Not only this group but it hurt the world. It took music to such a bland point. The music that we created was kind of syncopated and to go where you have that 'doom-doom-doom-doom-doom' throughout the music was stagnant. I think it not only hurt groups but also the music industry.

"Disco was so methodical . . . so confined. It was a problem getting booked. All of the major clubs that were happening . . . There was a club out in L.A. called Oasis, a fabulous club, and there were a lot of clubs that were really happening but they weren't hiring bands anymore. Bands didn't have anyplace to play although there were great venues that we could've played in. It kinda put us out of work."

The group's two subsequent singles, "Far East Mississippi" and "Feel the Beat (Everybody Disco)" early in 1977 were their first Mercury recordings not to reach the top 10. In the late '70s the traditional funk of the Ohio Players began to lose its popularity to the newer funk bands such as the Commodores, Con Funk Shun, and George Clinton's Parliament/Funkadelic, groups who were earlier influenced by the Ohio Players.

Williams points out, "The Ohio Players have been able to receive and take things from other bands. It's just a part of the music. You listen, you learn, if you like, sometimes you take and make it a part of what you're doing. We've been fortunate that we've written things and have done things that people enjoy and if they want to use it or borrow it, it was fine.

"Recently [former Con Funk Shun lead singer] Michael Cooper was on BET [Black Entertainment Television] and he said, 'I have to give Sugarfoot his credit and the Ohio Players. I love that band. Those are my guys.' If somebody as an artist gives you the accolades and says that you have been an influence, that's a good thing. He did a remake of 'Skin Tight' and his 'shoop-shoop' song ['Shoop Shoop (Never Stop Giving You Love)'] . . . I think we might have contributed to that."

The Ohio Players had their final top 10 R&B hit in the summer of 1977 with the instrumental "O-H-I-O." In 1979 they moved to Arista Records for a one-shot album, *Everybody Up.* The following year the group temporarily broke into rival units, with Sugarfoot, Jones, Middlebrook, and Pierce remaining as the Ohio Players, and Beck and Williams forming a group called Shadow. In the 1980s the Players label-hopped to Accord (*Young and Ready,* 1980), Neil Bogart's Broadway (*Ouch!,* 1981; *Tenderness*), and Chip Wilson's Track (*Back,* 1988), but with limited success.

Today only Sugarfoot and Williams remain from the group's peak years. Rounding out the Ohio Players are bassist Darwin Dortch, keyboardist Ronald Nooks, and second guitarist Clarence "Chet" Willis (formerly of Shadow). Still a top concert attraction, the group performs an average of once a month. Williams says, "Marshall [Jones] has a studio in Dayton that he's doing some work with for other artists. Satch isn't playing. Pee-Wee is playing a little bit. Marvin Pierce is a doctor in Australia.

"We try to stay busy as much as we can but it varies. Sometimes we'll work every weekend, sometimes we're working once a month. It depends on our schedule."

THE OHIO PLAYERS.
Rear: Leroy "Sugarfoot" Bonner, Jimmy "Diamond" Williams, Marvin Pierce, Billy Beck
Front: Ralph "Pee Wee" Middlebrook, Marshall Jones, Clarence Satchell (Courtesy *Blues and Soul* magazine)

THE MANHATTANS.

Rear: Edward "Sonny" Bivins, Kenny Kelly, Richard Taylor

Front: Winfred "Blue" Lovett, Gerald Alston

(Courtesy of Showtime Archives [Toronto])

THE MAIN INGREDIENT.
(L-R) Luther Simmons, Cuba Gooding, Tony Silvester
(Courtesy *Blues and Soul* magazine)

ISAAC HAYES.
(Courtesy *Blues and Soul* magazine)

Above: HAROLD MELVIN & THE BLUE NOTES. (L-R) Lawrence Brown, Lloyd Parks, Bernard Wilson, Harold Melvin, Teddy Pendergrass (Courtesy *Blues and Soul* magazine)

Right: JEAN KNIGHT. (Courtesy *Blues and Soul* magazine)

GLADYS KNIGHT & THE PIPS. (L-R) Edward Patten, Merald "Bubba" Knight, William Guest, Gladys Knight
(Courtesy *Blues and Soul* magazine)

THE MOMENTS. Billy Brown, Harry Ray, Al Goodman (Courtesy *Blues and Soul* magazine)

The O'Jays

Led by the rugged, intense lead of Eddie Levert and the smooth tenor of Walter Williams, the O'Jays have enjoyed enormous success for more than two decades and were a major component in helping establish Kenny Gamble and Leon Huff's "Philly Soul sound" as the dominant force in black music in the 1970s. The group first came to prominence with a series of message songs, most notably "Back Stabbers" and "For the Love of Money," before softening their sound and scoring with a string of love songs, such as "Darlin' Darlin' Baby" and "Forever Mine," later in the decade. By remaining at the summit of the parade of stars on the Philadelphia International label, this trio was arguably the most successful R&B vocal group of the 1970s.

Natives of Canton, Ohio, Eddie Levert and Walter Williams knew each other from elementary school and, as the Levert Brothers, sang in a gospel duo on a local radio station. In 1958, while attending McKinley High School, they hooked up with William Powell, Bobby Massey, and Bill Isles to form the Triumphs. A local songwriter gave the group some songs — "The Story of My Heart," "(Do the) Wiggle," "That's the Way I Feel," and "Lonely Rain" — and the quintet went to New York to audition for Decca Records. When Decca passed, King Records president Syd Nathan signed the group to his label in 1959 and renamed them the Mascots. They cut the four singles on King but none were released at that time. However, the group was taken under the wing of Cleveland disk jockey Eddie O'Jay, who honed their stage act to professionalism and gave them career guidance. In appreciation of their mentor's guidance, the group changed their name to the O'Jays. O'Jay put the group in touch with Detroit producer Don Davis. They recorded "Miracles" for the small Daco label in 1960 and leased the song to New York's Apollo Records. This prompted King Records to release "The Story of My Heart" in the fall of 1960 and "Lonely Rain" early in 1961, but both songs got lost in the shuffle.

O'Jay then sent the group to Little Star Records in 1963, where they met owner H.B. Barnum, a former member of the 1950s R&B group the Dootones. Barnum fine-tuned the group's harmonies and made a deal for them with Imperial Records. In the summer of 1963 the O'Jays' self-penned ballad "Lonely Drifter" became their first chart entry. The group continued recording for Imperial through 1966 and had moderate success with "Lipstick Traces (on a Cigarette)," "Let It All Out," and "Stand in for Love." They also did backing for Nat "King" Cole and Lou Rawls. When Imperial was acquired by Liberty, the O'Jays were transferred to the company's Minit subsidiary, but had little success. With the group having achieved only minimal success with their recording career, Isles quit in August 1966 to work as a songwriter, and the remaining quartet returned to Cleveland.

After the O'Jays appeared at the Apollo Theater, deejay Rockee Gee suggested they do some demos with producer Richard King, which eventually got them a recording deal with Bell Records. Working with producer George Kerr, the O'Jays scored two hits with the ballads "I'll Be Sweeter Tomorrow (Than I Was Today)" and "Look Over Your Shoulder." However, they were unable to find a hit formula with their next three singles.

In 1969 the O'Jays again played the Apollo, this time with Philadelphia-based quartet the Intruders, who were scoring a string of hits on Kenny Gamble and Leon Huff's label, Gamble Records. The Intruders recommended the O'Jays to Gamble and Huff with an eye towards signing them to a record deal. The O'Jays did link with Gamble and Huff's independent production company and signed with their Chess-distributed Neptune label.

Walter Williams remembers, "We were working the Apollo and the Intruders were on the show. Gamble and Huff came up to see the show and that's when we met and talked. At the time we had just left the Bell label. They came up to see us and they liked what they saw. They said they would come into Cleveland, which they did, and sat down with our managers and worked out a recording deal."

The O'Jays' first release on Neptune was "One Night Affair." Written and produced by Gamble and Huff, and aided by the haunting arrangements of Thom Bell and Bobby Martin, "One Night Affair" made a solid showing on the R&B charts in the summer of 1969, peaking at number 15. During the next year, three of their releases charted, including the bouncy and joyful "Deeper (in Love with You)," and "Looky Looky (Look at Me Girl)." However, before the O'Jays could build on this foundation, the label folded when Chess Records owner Leonard Chess died. They were briefly reunited with Barnum, but singles on Saru and Little Star were unsuccessful.

Meanwhile Gamble and Huff regrouped to set up their own Philadelphia International label and got a distribution deal with a major company, CBS. When they contacted the O'Jays about joining the new label, the quartet was reluctant, still remembering the unfortunate events from their Neptune days. Eddie Levert went to Philadelphia alone to talk to Gamble and Huff, and the producers initially suggested to Levert that he sign as a solo artist. However, he was only interested in working as part of a group. After more prodding, Williams and Powell, along with Levert, accepted Gamble and Huff's invitation, despite also receiving offers from Motown and Invictus. However, Massey could not be persuaded to join. He felt the group should be writing and producing their own material. He left the O'Jays in 1971 and later produced a top 15 R&B hit with a remake of Sam Cooke's "You Send Me" for the Ponderosa Twins + One.

Williams recalls, "We were somewhat reluctant to go back with Gamble and Huff because there was no follow-up on the product that we had out with them [on Neptune]. We had a song called 'Deeper [in Love with You]' which made a little noise and it sounded like it would be a nice hit for us, but I don't think the promotion was what it should have been. We did do *The Johnny Carson Show* when Flip Wilson was hosting to further it somewhat, but it didn't get all of the exposure that we felt it should have gotten. Then the Chess situation fell apart and we came back to Cleveland and we got into some independent writing and producing.

"Gamble was inbetween label deals at the time and then he finally hooked up with CBS. He called us to come back and we were reluctant to go back, and he called Eddie and talked to Eddie a lot, and he called me a couple of times. I think what really made us go back was that he kept calling. Finally we decided we would go back and at least hear the songs that he had. We got an offer from Norman Whitfield at Motown. All of the Undisputed Truth stuff is what he wanted to do on us but we declined to sign with him because we decided to go back with Gamble and Huff.

"We lost a member along the way, Bobby Massey, who was disenchanted with the situation and decided to quit the group. He wanted to write and produce everything, all of the songs. He wanted more involvement. *We* wanted more involvement but we realized [Gamble and Huff] were better writers and producers, or at least better known at the time, and we settled to let them write and produce."

The first song the O'Jays recorded for Philadelphia International was "Back Stabbers." Gene McFadden and John Whitehead, who in 1979 would have their own smash hit with "Ain't No Stoppin' Us Now," co-wrote "Back Stabbers" along with Huff. At the time McFadden and Whitehead were in a group called the Epsilons and wanted to have first crack at the song but Kenny Gamble declined, thinking it would be a good fit for the O'Jays, the first group signed to the Philadelphia International label.

Ironically, "Back Stabbers" was a song the group was rumored to have initially disliked. Williams explains, "Gamble and Huff, McFadden and Whitehead presented the song to us, and normally what they do is play the track and sing the song, right there live, physically sing it for us. ['Back Stabbers'] was a different twist from the stuff we had been doing in the past. It's not that we didn't like the song, it was just different. What happened was that it was typed out lyrically on a sheet of paper and as I intended to put the paper on the desk it airplaned and floated off onto the floor, and they said, 'Hey, he threw my song on the floor!' That was not the case. It just actually missed the desk and went onto the floor. But I did like the song. Once we put it with music, anybody could've heard that it was really a huge record."

Produced by Gamble and Huff, "Back Stabbers" opened with a piano flourish that introduced their Philly soul sound that would dominate R&B music throughout the mid-1970s. The song, a warning about false friends, featured the intense and rugged lead of Eddie Levert, sung over the lushly orchestrated, yet rhythmic and sophisticated arrangement of Thom Bell. With these components, a complete departure from the O'Jays' previous releases, "Back Stabbers" topped the R&B charts in the fall of 1972; it was the first Number One R&B hit for Philadelphia International. The song also crossed over to number three on the pop charts, sold a million copies, and netted the group a Grammy nomination for best R&B song of 1972.

The O'Jays followed "Back Stabbers" with the entertaining, Latin-tinged "992 Arguments." Although similar in melody to "Back Stabbers," and again produced by Gamble and Huff and arranged by Thom Bell, "992 Arguments" only reached number 13 on the R&B charts and failed to crack the pop top 40; normally an impressive showing for an O'Jays record, but it was a fall from grace compared to the monster success the group achieved with "Back Stabbers."

The O'Jays rebounded with their biggest hit, "Love Train," which topped both the pop and R&B charts early in 1973 and became their second million-selling single. This universal call for brotherhood received Grammy nominations for best R&B song and best R&B performance by a group or duo. The group changed the tempo a bit on their next release, the Williams-led

"Time to Get Down," a sleeper hit for the O'Jays despite spending two weeks at the number two spot on the R&B charts. All four singles were included on the group's debut PIR album *Back Stabbers*. A fifth song, "Sunshine," a gospel-infused ballad featuring the gut-wrenching, emotive lead of Levert, was overlooked at the time of the release of *Back Stabbers,* perhaps because the song served as the B-side of the title track, and also due to the song being a deviation from the group's newfound reputation for delivering songs carrying strong social messages. However, as time passed, "Sunshine" has become a soulful classic for the O'Jays' legion of fans.

"We were diversified," says Williams. "We were able to growl if you needed it, and we were able to sing a soft, pretty ballad if you needed it. We were flexible and we were really thankful for that. I think it had to do with our gospel background."

Aided by two million-sellers and three other solid tracks, the *Back Stabbers* album achieved gold status.

With the success of *Back Stabbers*, and particularly the title track and "Love Train," the O'Jays were chosen by Gamble and Huff to be their messengers about the complexities of life. This was best exemplified on the group's next album, *Ship Ahoy*, which delivered messages of varying kinds. The haunting title track was a 10-minute tale recounting how the black man came to America. Gamble and Huff originally wrote "Ship Ahoy" for the movie soundtrack for *Shaft in Africa* but it was never used. The album's first release was "Put Your Hands Together," a rousing, joyous, gospel-flavored track, which made the pop top 10 and spent two weeks at the number two spot on the R&B charts early in 1974. The album's gem, however, was "For the Love of Money" which made both the pop and R&B top 10 in the spring of 1974 and was the group's third million-selling single. Led by its funky guitar intro and hard-driving bass line, "For the Love of Money" delivered a powerful message about the temptations of greed, touching on subjects ranging from crime to prostitution. The song later received Grammy nominations for best R&B song and best R&B performance by a group or duo. With its timeless lyrics, "For the Love of Money" remains arguably the most popular of the O'Jays' hits from the 1970s, despite other songs being more successful.

"Singing the message songs had to do with our delivery, the way we could deliver a song," says Williams. "When we lived in Canton, Ohio, my father was the choir director and my stepmother was the organist and pianist, so we were used to singing hard, gospel-type delivery, and that's what these kinds of message songs needed. 'For the Love of Money,' 'Give the People What They Want,' 'The Rich Get Richer,' 'Survival,' all of these songs had a hard, gospel-type flavor or pounding sound to drive it home and that's what it needed. Gamble would always state that we were the messengers. He wrote it and produced it but we were actually the messengers."

An unrecognized track from *Ship Ahoy* was the subtle and melodic "Now That We Found Love." The song later achieved enormous success for reggae group Third World in 1978 and for rapper Heavy D in 1992, almost to the point where it is forgotten that the O'Jays recorded the original version. Further aided by "You Got Your Hooks in Me," and "Don't Call Me Brother," a message song similar in theme to "Back Stabbers," the *Ship Ahoy* album outsold its predecessor and achieved platinum status.

As successful as the O'Jays were on vinyl, their popularity was further enhanced by their stage presentation. Having had hits with message songs, up-tempo workouts, and ballads, the trio could display all facets of human emotion. Their nonstop energy highlighted Eddie Levert's natural grace as a dancer, perfectly interwoven with Walter Williams' and William Powell's sense of style. The end result showed the time, care, and dedication invested to make their presentation come across with top precision. A rousing version of "For the Love of Money" typically ended their concerts in the mid-70s. This was captured on a live album in 1974, *The O'Jays Live in London*, recorded on their first UK and European tour; it became the group's third gold album.

"I think our stage presentation added to our popularity and also to our longevity," notes Williams. "Your live performance is *you.* That's what keeps you around. As long as you can satisfy these ticket buyers I think you can stay in the mainstream of the game. Once Motown moved to the West Coast, our choreographer Cholly Atkins had the time to deal with us and that's when he started teaching us all of these things. We had learned and just visually watched the Motown acts and other acts on stage and tried to get it ourselves, but we were missing a lot of things. We had the raw talent but when we got with him, he worked it out and that's what kept it going.

"What we do is get with Cholly every year before touring and we work out a show and we rehearse that show in Las Vegas, usually at the Maxim Hotel, six to eight weeks every day except Sunday. When we leave his rehearsal hall, we know we've got a good show and the more you do it, the better you get at it. We're prepared to come out and do a good show. It's a difference than just going out there singing your records. You have to have an act these days, and if you have an act, it's more than likely you'll be around a lot longer than those people that just go out and sing their records. You have to put a little more into it.

"Cholly is still a slavedriver but he's a very knowledgeable old man and you love him to death. He beats you bad but he makes you appreciate the business you're in. He makes you come out of there feeling like you're one of the best at it and you have to respect that."

The O'Jays extended the concept of their message songs to militancy with the release of their next single, "Give the People What They Want." The group's first funky tune, this hard-core plea for freedom, justice, and equality topped the R&B charts for a week in the spring of 1975. Perhaps due to the song's upfront militancy as opposed to the lighter and universal messages of "Love Train" and "For the Love of Money," "Give the People What They Want" failed to make a serious dent in the pop charts. Eddie Levert's gospel-infused lead on "Let Me Make Love to You" fueled this sensuous, pleading ballad's rise to the R&B top 10 later that summer. Like its predecessor, "Let Me Make Love to You" failed to cross over to the pop charts as that segment of the music audience was still unfamiliar with the O'Jays' balladeer style. Both songs were included on *Survival,* which became the group's fourth gold album, most likely on the strength of sales in the black market. A third song from the album, "Rich Get Richer," despite its smooth, danceable melody, told a powerful tale of the rich preying on the poor.

Williams points out, "Some of our songs like 'For the Love of Money' crossed over because it was universal. Everybody should have been able to relate to the money part. I wasn't surprised that 'Love Train' crossed over because it related to the whole world. I was somewhat surprised that 'Survival' crossed over but 'Rich Get Richer' . . . I was surprised got airplay at all because at one point it didn't. I thought the political message was *so* big and it named very influential families like the Mellons and the Gettys, Howard Hughes, and the DuPonts. So, for a minute I thought somebody had gotten to the FCC and told them 'Don't let that record be played,' and it wasn't for awhile, and then it just burst onto the scene because people wanted to hear it."

By 1975, disco music was the dominant force in the industry and many veteran R&B performers, including some on the Philadelphia International label, fell by the wayside. However, the O'Jays were able to maintain their hit-making streak throughout the disco period. The foundation for their durability during this era lay perhaps with the release of the vibrant "I Love Music," the group's contribution to disco, which topped the R&B charts late in 1975, brought them back to the pop top 10 (number five), and became their fourth million-selling single.

I think the success of 'I Love Music' helped us to survive disco," says Williams. "It was right at the beginning of disco when 'I Love Music' came out, and it was a big hit for us. Being that it was in the disco vein I think it got a lot of play in the clubs. It was the same when we followed with 'Message in Our Music.' The club scene was as big as the radio scene then. I think 'Love Train' a little before the disco scene helped set it up."

At the high point of the O'Jays' career, group member William Powell was forced to step down at the beginning of 1976.

He had had cancer diagnosed and his health had been deteriorating for a year to the point where he could no longer stand the rigors of the road. After a long battle with cancer, Powell died on May 26, 1977 at the age of 37.

"That was a difficult situation," recalls Williams. "William Powell somehow . . . and I guess no one ever knows how you contract cancer, and he was in and he was out. A lot of people don't know that William had a drug problem as well, and that didn't help. Perhaps, I don't know which came first, but he would do the drug thing to keep the pain down on the cancer thing, and then not be able to perform as well as he should or not be as coherent. Doing a lot of choreography and doing a lot of cues, you can't do drugs because your mind just won't let you function the way you should function. So when it really got bad for William around '75, that's when we started looking around and we were lucky to find a guy like Sammy Strain."

Sammy Strain, a 12-year veteran of Little Anthony and the Imperials, was brought in after a lengthy search. Initially the O'Jays considered bringing in a younger person who needed a break. However, on the advice of Cholly Atkins, they were convinced to go with a more experienced artist. Williams recalls, "Between Smokey Robinson, and Otis [Williams] with the Tempts, they both recommended Sammy. We got Cholly Atkins to set up some interviews for us in L.A. and we interviewed some guys. We didn't do a national campaign, we just decided to go out to one of the musical capitals like L.A. or New York. We ended up doing it in L.A. and we got some guys who were recommended to us to come by. Cholly gave them some steps and things to do and he really crossed up a lot of their minds with the steps. I think some of the guys left show business completely after dealing with Cholly. Sammy passed the test with flying colors, and he was an old pro anyway. He'd been with Little Anthony for 12 or 13 years and for whatever reason they had broken up and he retired. He joined the group in '75 and we went out on tour in '76."

By the time the O'Jays went on tour in 1976, their single "Livin' for the Weekend" was climbing the charts. "Livin' for the Weekend" started off slow with blues overtones before going through its up-tempo workout and returning to a slower, jazzier finish. The song gave the O'Jays their fifth Number One R&B hit, spending two weeks at the summit that spring. Surprisingly not released as a single, but used as the B-side to "Weekend," was the popular "Stairway to Heaven," a gospel-infused ballad which built and built until, by the end of the song, Levert and Williams had you feeling like you were in a Baptist church.

It was almost incidental that the song "Family Reunion" was released as a single, and this was reflected by its modest chart success in the summer of 1976. However, "Family Reunion" cannot be judged by its chart showing, as this track has become a holiday favorite over the years and has enjoyed eternal staying power on the radio. All four songs were included on the *Family Reunion* album, which went platinum. Despite being in the enviable position of having a string of gold and platinum albums, the O'Jays never felt any pressure to top the success of previous albums.

Williams says, "At the time I wasn't the writer or the producer; I was the guy who would learn the songs that we chose and would go in the studio and put them on tape. That was *easy*. That was not a hard job. I was not in competition with myself. Each song was different. I sing the way I sing. Sometimes you would sound like, 'That's the same run I used on the last song,' but it's a different song. In my opinion that's why people bought it, to hear what you do. You have to try to give it to them the best you can. I will never be in competition with myself because then I might as well stay at home. It's a mental thing I don't think you can shake."

The O'Jays released *Message in Our Music* in the fall of 1976 and had a Number One R&B hit with the disco-flavored title track. The trio achieved the same lofty status late in 1976 with its follow-up, "Darlin' Darlin' Baby (Sweet, Tender, Love)." This song differed from several of their previous hits in that it was a romantic love song. So as not to get redundant with their message songs, the O'Jays were presented with product that allowed them to switch between love songs and message songs.

Williams explains, "When we would go to Philadelphia there were probably three or four teams of writers — Gamble and Huff, Gary Gilbert, Bunny Sigler, Phil Terry, Dexter Wansel, Cynthia Briggs, Thom Bell, Linda Creed — all of these people presented songs when we went there and being that we were getting hit albums, they would save their best stuff for us. We would have to go through a hundred songs of all of the known great writers and then some of the guys that were underlings trying to get in. We would have to go through songs for days trying to pick the right songs and 'Darlin' Darlin' Baby' just happened to be one of the songs that we liked. It was just a good song. I don't think there was any conscious effort to get away from message music. It was just a transition that took place."

Led by the title track and "Darlin' Darlin' Baby," *Message in Our Music* achieved gold status on the strength of the group's loyal black audience, as neither of these Number One R&B songs were sizable pop hits.

The O'Jays released *Travelin' at the Speed of Light* in the spring of 1977; it made gold status but yielded only one hit single, "Work on Me," a number seven R&B hit that summer.

The trio rebounded in 1978 with their next effort, *So Full of Love*. This aptly-titled album was a complete departure from the group's previous efforts because it contained no message songs. *So Full of Love* was the group's fastest-selling disc, making the platinum level in just six weeks. The success of the album can be attributed to the first single, "Use Ta Be My Girl," the O'Jays' biggest hit since 1973's "Love Train," as it topped the R&B charts for five weeks and returned them to the pop top 10 (number four) for the first time in three years. With its "shoop-shoop" background throughout the song, "Use Ta Be My Girl" displayed the influence of the great doo-wop singers on the trio.

"[The background] just seemed to be something that worked," says Williams. "Gamble and Huff would leave it up to us to do our own background. We would go back to the hotel — we usually stayed at the Warwick or close by — we'd have another rehearsal and make up our own background. Then we'd rehearse our leads as well before going into the studio to put them down on tape. We would get with Gamble and Huff before going in to see if they liked the background, and then if there were any changes that they wanted to make, we'd make them right there on the spot. The doo-wop era was the era that we grew up in as kids and we loved the doo-wop groups. I'm sure there was some influence there from the Coasters, the Drifters, Platters, Little Anthony, the Teenagers; all of these people influenced us greatly."

Producer Thom Bell provided the O'Jays with two cuts: "Brandy," which was the second single released and was a moderate hit later that summer, and "This Time Baby," written by Leroy Bell and Casey James, who enjoyed a disco hit themselves later that year, "Living It Up (Friday Night)," as Bell and James. The following year a disco cover of "This Time Baby" was a sizable hit for veteran R&B singer Jackie Moore. An unrecognized track from the album was "Cry Together." This heartfelt ballad, featuring a spoken intro by Levert, although never released as a single, has proven to be a fan favorite over the years and is still used in a medley form when the O'Jays perform.

The O'Jays released *Identify Yourself* the following year and again achieved platinum status, mostly on the strength of black sales. The album's first release, the light-hearted "Sing a Happy Song," reached R&B number seven in the fall of 1979 but failed to crack the pop top 100. After the moderate success of the sweet, mid-tempo "I Want You Here with Me," the group released the album's strongest track, "Forever Mine." Continuing their recent trend of romantic love songs, this ballad reached number four on the R&B charts late in 1979 and made the pop top 30 as that segment of the audience finally accepted this new aspect of the O'Jays' sound.

By the end of the 1970s the O'Jays had established themselves as arguably the most successful R&B vocal group of the decade. With Philadelphia International Records clearly the dominant force in black music in the 1970s, accumulating 17

Number One R&B hits, the O'Jays were at the very top. Beginning with "Back Stabbers" in 1972, 15 of their singles reached the R&B top 10, with eight reaching Number One.

Williams says, "That was a high that was unreal because it seemed like everything they did or touched turned to gold, and we were a main horse in that stable. I say it like that because we weren't the only ones who were getting gigantic hits. Thom Bell and Gamble and Huff were doing the Delfonics, Tommy was doing the Spinners, Gamble and Huff were doing Harold Melvin and the Blue Notes, the Intruders, Jerry Butler, Wilson Pickett, and they were doing the O'Jays. *Everybody* was on the charts. Everybody was selling gold and platinum. Lou Rawls even snuck in there and got a couple of big ones. All of that was great and we were at the top of it, and it lasted a good 10 years. And that was a tremendously long run. So that was a great feeling. Today even when we work, those very same songs are in the show and get the biggest response. We're talking 10, 15, 20 years ago for some of those songs. 'Back Stabbers' and 'Love Train' . . . that was '72, '73. It's '95 now. So I'm very proud to have been a part of that. That's a part of history at some point. That'll be a part of something people my age or older or a little younger can look back and say to their better half, 'They're playing our song,' and feel real good about it."

The O'Jays opened the 1980s on a high note with "Girl Don't Let It Get You Down" peaking at number three that summer. The group then went into a tailspin, disappearing from the airwaves. Although they remained a top concert attraction, their albums and singles generated little impact on the charts or in sales. The O'Jays' most impressive efforts during the early 1980s were "Your Body's Here with Me (But Your Mind's on the Other Side of Town)" (1982), "Extraordinary Girl" (1984), and "Just Another Lonely Night" (1985). Although changing trends in the black music field were a factor, Williams points to another reason why the group suddenly went cold.

"We got in trouble," he says. "We did some things we shouldn't have done but because of ignorance, that's what got us into those things. We went to South Africa and once we got over there we found out what it was about and how devastating it was going to be on our career for going. It hampered airplay, especially with the black jocks, and it was just a bad scene for us.

"We had no idea going to South Africa would do that to us. It was out of ignorance. We were offered a lot of money but we had no idea what was going on over there. Once we got over there the tour broke down because we weren't the kind of blacks that would cater to and buckle under to what was going on over there. When we got off the plane they made us honorary white citizens and that was like a big slap in the face. We were ready to turn around and come back home right then, and keep the money. We had to get out of there because it got a little crazy and we came back here and there were problems for going.

"From the press conferences we had when we got back we found out that Randall Robinson from TransAfrica did not approve and Jesse Jackson did not approve of us going. And I think it hurt our airplay, and you have to have airplay. If you don't get it, then you're not exposed and people don't know that you have new product. It hurt us for a good while and we kissed a lot of behind to get back into good graces."

By 1987, the O'Jays had paid enough dues and returned to the top of the R&B charts for the first time in nine years with "Lovin' You," a Williams-led ballad that was actually written in the '70s. The title song from their *Let Me Touch You* album was released as a follow-up later in 1987 and gave the O'Jays their second consecutive top 10 R&B hit (number five). *Let Me Touch You* was the trio's final album on Philadelphia International Records, ending a successful 15-year relationship with Gamble and Huff.

Williams explains, "For some reason, and I still don't know today other than Gamble being accused of being too black and saying too many things about white society, but for some reason they stopped getting hits and stopped getting airplay and stopped getting their product distributed like it should have been. That hurt all of the artists and acts that Gamble had, not just us. We had dropped from selling platinum, and a million, 750,000, down to selling 150,000, 200,000, and you can't stay in business doing that. You never get in a recouped position. It costs anywhere from $350,000 to $500,000 to record an O'Jays album and before you can earn royalties, they have to recoup the recording budget. So it was probably time to part company although we're still close friends. I talk to them at least every two or three months. I still love them. I learned a lot there. I learned about writing, I learned about producing, and more important, I was able to *sustain* myself as a writer and producer and an artist."

The O'Jays were able to build on the success of *Let Me Touch You* and keep their sound fresh with the emergence of Eddie Levert's two sons Gerald and Sean, along with their long-time friend Marc Gordon, who formed the group Levert in the mid-'80s. As a trio, Levert had a dozen top 10 R&B hits between 1986 and 1993, with five of them, including "Casanova" and "(Pop, Pop, Pop, Pop) Goes My Mind," reaching Number One. Gerald has enjoyed further success as a solo artist; his 1991 album *Private Line* produced two R&B chart-toppers: the title track and "Baby Hold on to Me," a duet with his father. As the O'Jays became increasingly involved in the production end of their music, they often employed the services of Gerald Levert and Gordon.

Williams points out, "They came along at a time when the flame was flickering somewhat. When they came along, people didn't know whether or not we were them or they were us but when they found out, they knew that they were from our camp because of Gerald sounding so much like Eddie and the influence that was there. He's always been around us when we rehearsed and wrote songs. Gerald's always been a hard worker and very attentive, so I think our influence helped him get into the business and get a good foothold and I think what they've done, Levert and Gerald [as a solo artist], together has helped the O'Jays to stay alive."

The O'Jays reemerged on the EMI label in 1989 with *Serious.* Williams and Levert wrote and co-produced much of the material on the album, including the hit ballad "Serious Hold on Me." Later that spring, the group scored their 10th R&B chart-topper with "Have You Had Your Love Today," featuring an interlude by rapper Jaz. In 1991 the O'Jays released *Emotionally Yours*, their finest album in years. Standouts included "Don't Let Me Down" and the ballad "Keep on Lovin' Me," both co-written and co-produced by Levert and Williams. The album also included an R&B version and a gospel version of Bob Dylan's "Emotionally Yours," the latter containing an all-star choir featuring the likes of Phyllis Hyman, Evelyn "Champagne" King, Will Downing, and members of Levert. This led to an appearance in the following year's all-star tribute concert for Dylan at Madison Square Garden.

Despite the string of hits achieved by the O'Jays in the 1970s, they find their albums more satisfying now because of their behind-the-scenes control. Williams says, "I feel good because we work hard at writing it and producing it. I don't know if it'll ever compare to what we did in the past because those were great songs, but that was of another time and another era. I think, and I hope and pray that it does come back to an era of doing good music again. I'm proud of what we're doing today and I think the more we do it, the better we'll get at doing it. We're at a point now where we want to give something back. We want to develop young artists and get them on the right road to true artistry, to know how to put a good show together and go out and entertain people; help [the audience] for one moment to forget about their problems."

In 1993 Nathaniel Best replaced Sammy Strain, who returned to Little Anthony and the Imperials. Later that year the group released *Heartbreaker* and had a sizable hit with "Somebody Else Will." Today the O'Jays remain a top concert attraction, performing predominantly in the summer months. They continue to release albums on the EMI label about once every other year. After more than 30 years in the music industry, the O'Jays have no plans to slow down.

"You gotta have heart for this," says Williams. "You gotta have a real love for this. There were times when we would go out for seven or eight months out of the year and my children were growing up and I wouldn't see them and I'd miss them and probably missed some important times in their lives when they were growing up. Once we didn't have to work as hard and as much, we got a chance to spend a little time at home, but you find out that when you come home and you get time to spend at home, you prefer to be on the road. You get tired of sitting around at home, you don't know what to do with yourself so I think it's kind of an equal thing and it has balanced out over the years. We don't work nearly as much as we used to. We probably, other than the months of June and July, do anywhere from two, three, or four jobs a month. We just go out and work enough to keep a decent cash flow going and pay bills and keep going in other areas.

"I'll keep at it as long as I'm physically able. I love it. You know what happens when we retire: we die. As long as I'm physically able to do this and I'm not harmful to myself by doing it, I'll be out there. I think I'm helpful to myself because it keeps the arteries open and the blood pumping good and as long as I don't have any other problems that'll hinder me from doing it, I'm gonna do it."

Billy Paul

A jazz-infused singer for much of his career, Billy Paul made a transition to soul music in the early 1970s and had several hits. Best remembered for his 1972 classic "Me and Mrs. Jones," Paul, through his collaboration with Gamble and Huff, was an important artist in the early development of the Philadelphia International label.

Billy Paul was born Paul Williams on December 1, 1934 in Philadelphia. At an early age his strongest musical influences were female vocalists. He points out, "I liked to listen to Nina Simone, Nancy Wilson, Sarah Vaughan, Ella Fitzgerald . . . and Johnny Mathis, although he was male. I was mostly interested in them because of their range."

Williams was singing on Philadelphia radio station WPEN at age 11 thanks to his childhood friend, comedian Bill Cosby. "We grew up as kids together," he says. "We were working at a club together, Bill Cosby, myself, and Lola Falana, for about eight dollars a night. We were doing this show called *The Kiddie Hour*. We were all trying to help each other make it. Bill Cosby and I went to college together at Temple and he's still a great friend of mine."

At 16, Paul Williams changed his name to Billy Paul at the suggestion of a female manager, due to several other entertainers named Paul Williams. The following year he played the Club Harlem in Philadelphia and was on the same bill as Charlie Parker for a week. "Charlie Parker is my jazz influence," he says. "He was the man who taught me execution; how to modulate. He taught me how to control my notes. I'm a balladeer and I always liked to listen to him play ballads . . . 'Stella By Starlight' and 'Just Friends.'"

Paul entered Temple University as a music major. He later studied at the West Philadelphia Music School and the Granoff Music School. He says, "Growing up in the Philadelphia ghetto helped me to focus on the fact that if I wanted to get out, I had to get on with my education and make something of myself; not to sit there and feel sorry for myself or sit there and be stuck in that mindset. It helped me realize that if I wanted to get out of the ghetto, I had to succeed and make something of myself."

Paul's recording debut was "Why Am I" on the Jubilee label in 1955. After a stint in the military, he briefly joined Harold Melvin and the Blue Notes and also the Flamingos, while continuing to build a reputation in Philadelphia as one of the top jazz stylists around.

In 1967, Paul met Kenny Gamble at the Cadillac Club in Philadelphia. That collaboration led to Paul's self-produced album *Feelin' Good at the Cadillac Club* on Gamble Records. The album, a jazz-oriented concept piece with a heavy piano and percussion arrangement, displayed his talent as a jazz stylist, particularly on "Just in Time" and "That's Life." However, despite receiving widespread critical acclaim, the album did not fare well commercially.

For the *Ebony Woman* album on Neptune, Kenny Gamble and Leon Huff gave Paul an updated soul sound. He explains, "I think that transition came about because in the early '70s, everyone was listening to love music and message songs. I was one of the first that was trying to do that, and I was doing a lot of things like Jefferson Airplane, Bob Dylan, and the Doobie Brothers; making messages for black people."

The album included a perky, almost salsa-flavored version of Simon and Garfunkel's "Mrs. Robinson" and a cover of Michael Legrand's "The Windmills of Your Mind." Fueled by the title track and the ballad "Let's Fall in Love All Over Again," the *Ebony Woman* album entered the R&B charts, but Neptune was distributed by Chess Records, and after Leonard Chess' death, the label folded.

When Gamble and Huff regrouped to form Philadelphia International Records, they signed many of their former artists, including Billy Paul. His first album on Philadelphia International was 1971's *Goin' East*, which extended his transition into soul music. "I was always on top of [the transition] but it took me about two or three years to get comfortable with it," he says. "At the time I was going through a phase where I doubted myself. I didn't know how good Billy Paul was."

It was Paul's next effort that proved to be his breakthrough. Released in the fall of 1972, the timeless, soulful ballad "Me and Mrs Jones," with its lush Philadelphia sound, topped the R&B charts for four weeks and was the first Number One pop single for the Philadelphia International label, holding the top spot for three weeks. Paul contends, "I knew it was a hit when I first heard it. When most people heard it, they just flipped over it. I did Operation Breadbasket with Jesse Jackson before it was released and I got a standing ovation. That sort of told me something. Also, Roberta Flack and other singers were out there and Roberta Flack told me, 'That's gonna be a number one smash.'"

The multi-million-selling tale about a steamy extramarital affair won Paul a Grammy for best male R&B vocal performance, and the song was also nominated for the year's best R&B song. The success of the single made a seemingly over night sensation of Billy Paul at the age of 38. He says, "I woke up one day and saw number one across the board. I wasn't ready for that. I had to make an adjustment all at once. You lay down one night and nobody knows you, you wake up the next day and your song is number one all over the world. That's a helluva adjustment. It took me awhile because I didn't know how good I was. I had to learn that; some of it the good way, some of it the hard way. I don't fault anybody but I learned it.

"I could've done better but I think I was able to handle [the success]. Being at the age I was, I was able to maintain it more than if I had been a little younger, say 21 or 22. There's a great possibility I may have gone off the deep end."

At this time, the bearded singer became just as well known for his wide assortment of hats as he was for "Me and Mrs. Jones." He explains, "I always had luck with records when I wore hats. It's a Philadelphia thing. When you cut a hit record in the studio, everybody wore a hat. It definitely became my trademark."

Led by "Me and Mrs. Jones," the album *360 Degrees of Billy Paul* was certified gold and won acclaim as one of the best albums of 1972. Ironically, "Me and Mrs. Jones" was the last song to be placed on the album. In addition to "Jones," standouts included a remake of the Carole King classic "It's Too Late," a slower, jazz-infused cover of Al Green's "Let's Stay Together," the smooth "Brown Baby," and the haunting "I'm Just a Prisoner," an explicit tale about the ills of the penal system.

The surprising follow-up to "Me and Mrs. Jones" was the arrogant, almost irritating "Am I Black Enough for You?," a song completely out of character for Paul. He says, " 'Am I Black Enough for You?' was not my decision, it was CBS' and Kenny Gamble's decision. I always felt that was a bad song. That was the thing that hurt me. That was the wrong song to follow 'Me and Mrs. Jones.' I was very upset. It damaged me and I was bitter about it for a long time." "Am I Black Enough for You?" only reached the lower portion of the pop charts and did not fare much better on the R&B charts, peaking at number 29.

Paul followed the *360 Degrees* album with *War of the Gods* in 1973. He says, "After the success of *360 Degrees* there was a lot of pressure to come out with a follow-up. *War of the Gods* was a very spiritual thing that I wanted to do. How I got turned on with *War of the Gods* was because of Marvin [Gaye] and *What's Going On*. It was a political statement. I think *War of the Gods* would be timely now because of the genocide with the young killing each other. There's only one God and we can't kill each other off."

Paul had a hit with the stimulating "Thanks for Saving My Life," his second top 10 R&B hit, peaking at number nine in the spring of 1974. After having mild success on the R&B

charts later in 1974 with the uptempo "Be Truthful to Me" and in 1975 with the ballad "Billy's Back Home," a song similar in melody to "Me and Mrs. Jones," Billy Paul returned to controversy in 1976 with "Let's Make a Baby."

He explains, "I wrote 'Let's Make a Baby' at a time when me and my wife were trying to make a baby. It's a very controversial song because a lot of people thought that I was telling young people to fornicate, but I was saying it for myself. It's a very beautiful song. I do believe in abortion to a certain extent but I don't believe in getting rid of kid after kid after kid." Despite its controversy, the majority of the song's content was about childhood and not sex. "Let's Make a Baby" gave Paul his final top 20 R&B hit, charting at number 18.

In 1977, Paul had mild success with the album *Let 'Em In*. The title song, a remake of the Paul McCartney hit a year earlier, opened with a speech by Malcolm X and ended with one by Martin Luther King, Jr. Other standouts were the danceable "How Good Is Your Game," with its effective use of female background vocals, "I Trust You," and "Without You," a cover of Nilsson's 1972 Number One pop hit.

After a period away from recording, Billy Paul returned with *Lately* on the Total Experience label in 1985 and *Wide Open* on Ichiban in 1988, but with little fanfare.

In 1992, he reunited with Gamble and Huff to begin work on a jazz album, tentatively entitled *Prayer Dance*. He says, "I've been in music since I was eight years old. I perform in Brazil, Peru, England, and Japan. I perform all over the world. I can honestly say that it's my life now. I'm older now and can accept that this is what I want. This is what I'm going to do."

Freda Payne

A cabaret-style singer with a jazz background, Freda Payne made a transition into the pop/R&B field, where she achieved stardom in the early 1970s. Best remembered for "Band of Gold" and the anti-war "Bring the Boys Home," Payne was an important part of the early success of Holland-Dozier-Holland's post-Motown Invictus label.

Freda Payne was born in Detroit and as a child was encouraged to study the piano, which later extended to singing. She recalls, "I started piano lessons when I was five. My mother took me to the Detroit Institute of Musical Arts and I was taking piano lessons. I didn't ask. It was one of those things that she did and I took it as, oh, well, this is something that she wants me to do and I guess this is part of my cultural training as a young girl. That's basically what she meant by it. She had no idea and she never really had any intentions of me being in show business whatsoever. That was the last thing on her mind.

"As a result of my piano training, that led me into singing because it was my piano teacher who really first became aware of the fact that I had a voice, other than just the norm. She was sort of just testing my voice out. We were having an upcoming recital and she was testing my voice out for a group to sing in a vocal ensemble which consisted of about four or five singers. She said, 'Oh, Freda, you have such a nice voice. I'd like you to do a solo as well.' So I sang a solo in addition to the song that we were doing as an ensemble.

"My mother invited all of her friends to the recital and everybody was so impressed because prior to that, my younger sister

Scherrie was the one who always performed for everybody. She was always that kind of gregarious person and I was extremely shy and withdrawn; I never exposed any talent. No one was aware of any exceptional talent that I had. So when I sang at the recital everybody started saying, 'Oh, we didn't know Freda could sing. Where did she get this from? We thought Scherrie was the only one.' From that point on it sparked something inside of me like a little light that said, 'Aha! This is how I can excel.'

"Then I started entering talent contests and I started winning. I was on a local TV show called *Ed McKinsey's Local Dance Hour*. It was almost like *American Bandstand* but it was more than that. Whoever was appearing in the nightclubs in Detroit at the time would appear on the show. They also had kids dancing and then they had a talent contest. I appeared on his show and I won the talent contest. Then I appeared about three to four months later and I won again. From that point on you couldn't stop me.

"By the time I was about 14 I auditioned for the *Ted Mack Amateur Hour*. I won the audition and then I was a contestant on the show. I won second place and as a result of that I got a write-up in *Jet* magazine. This was my first write-up."

Payne's local success drew the attention of Berry Gordy, who sought her out to sign to his Motown label when he was beginning to build his music empire. However, her mother balked at Gordy's restrictive contract. Payne explains, "I was Berry Gordy Jr.'s first female protégé but I never went with the Gordy organization, nor did I ever sign with Motown. Back then the rules were a little different and Motown wasn't into artists negotiating their contracts. My mother was more into business. It wasn't so much that she was a business whiz but she was an extremely bright person. She just had good common sense. Her attitude was, 'Okay, if you're getting 10 percent and they're getting 15 percent and somebody else is getting another 20 percent, what does that leave my daughter?' That's what happened to the artists. They'd get the stardom, they'd get the fame, but what happens is that somebody has to pay for all of this. Then when the money comes back, they get it. You don't have anything but your fame. You always have to go to them and say, 'I need money for this, I need money for that.' And everything is in the company's name. If you read different biographies on different stars, it's all been spelled out over and over again."

Upon graduating from high school, Payne performed with Pearl Bailey and later Duke Ellington, who offered her a job with his orchestra. However, Payne refused because of certain unfavorable terms in the 10-year contract proposal. She spread her talents to the Broadway stage, where she was an understudy for Leslie Uggams in *Hallelujah, Baby!* She later took a job with Quincy Jones and toured extensively with his band.

She remembers, "Right after I finished high school I had the luck to meet Duke Ellington. How I met Duke Ellington was, his son Mercer was in town. Mercer and a friend of our family had met at a cocktail party. He told Mercer about me and he wanted Mercer and his father to hear me sing. So they arranged it. They took me to Duke Ellington and he played for me and I sang. He said he really felt I had a great future and he wanted me to sing with his band. I did sing with his band and after that he offered me a 10-year contract. That never did come to pass because there were some things that we wanted to change in the contract and he wasn't willing to change.

"From that point on I went to New York at 18 and I met Quincy Jones. He invited me to appear with him in a show at the Apollo with his big band, Billy Eckstine, and Redd Foxx. I appeared with him at the Apollo twice. One year I sang with him and then the next year he asked me and I sang with him again."

Payne began her recording career on Impulse Records. She later released two albums on MGM as a member of Bob Crosby's Bobcats and also recorded with ABC-Paramount. Meanwhile, Motown's legendary writing and producing team Holland-Dozier-Holland left the label in 1968 and formed the Invictus and Hot Wax labels. While in Detroit in 1969, Payne was approached by the Holland brothers, whom she knew from high school, about signing to their Invictus label.

Signing with Invictus marked a change in musical direction for Freda Payne. Originally a jazz singer with a taste for cabaret songs, she made the change to R&B and pop. Payne says, "It was a case of me making a decision to go more pop. I was more of a cabaret-type singer or Broadway singer; I sang more jazz. My first recording was a jazz recording on Impulse. What happened was that I was approached by Brian Holland and he inquired as to what my status was. I told him I didn't have a manager right now. I just got released from the last label I was on, which was ABC-Paramount. He asked, 'Would you like to come with us? We just left Motown. We formed a new label and we're calling it Invictus and we'd love to work with you.' So, I went to Detroit and sat down and talked with them. Eddie asked, 'Are you willing to go in our direction because we don't want you to sound like Nancy Wilson or Betty 'Be-bop' Carter. We want you to do it our way.' I had already made up my mind that that's what I wanted to do. When they produced me, I sang the way they wanted me to sing."

Payne's first single on Invictus, "The Unhooked Generation," joyfully spoke of being single again and was a moderate success, peaking at number 43 on the R&B charts early in 1970. But it was her second single that would become her signature song. Released in the spring of 1970, "Band of Gold" sold five million copies and made Freda Payne an international star. "Band of Gold," about a husband's impotence on his wedding night, is a song that Payne was initially apprehensive about singing. She says, "When I first looked at the lyrics I said, 'What?! What is this 'we stayed in separate rooms'? I would never do that.' So they said, 'Don't worry about what you would do, just sing it.'"

"Band of Gold" was a number three pop hit that stalled at only number 20 on the R&B charts. Because of its across-the-board success and Freda Payne's lack of a gospel background, "Band of Gold," despite the track's killer drumbeat, was never considered an R&B or "soul" record. However, Payne disputes this classification. She says, " 'Band of Gold' is a black record. What made 'Band of Gold' such a success was that it appealed to everybody. Sometimes if you appeal to the soul or R&B element and don't appeal to the white element, you kinda limit yourself."

Payne's next single, the sweet, mid-tempo "Deeper and Deeper" (released later that fall), had her singing in a low, slightly bluesier tone. The song reached number 24 on the pop charts and became her first top 10 R&B hit, peaking at number nine. After "Cherish What Is Dear to You (While It's Near to You)" became a hit in 1971 (number 11 R&B), Payne's next big hit, "Bring the Boys Home," became the center of controversy. A rare black anti-war song, "Bring the Boys Home" was released during the height of the Vietnam War. The song's lyrics, which described the war as senseless and offered suggestions of how to end it, offended the U.S. government, which banned the song from all U.S. military bases in Vietnam.

Payne recalls, "Before it was released I had a close associate who told me I would have a problem with the Republican administration concerning 'Bring the Boys Home.' This person wasn't with the record company, he was my road manager; he was working for me. The record company and the producers never mentioned anything about it. They may have thought it but they never thought it would be a problem. We did get a telegram from the U.S. government saying that the record had been banned from being played in South Vietnam.

"It was somewhat disappointing to me because I thought that was very narrow-minded of them. Actually I thought it would be opposite, meaning that I had been personally approached by Vietnam vets, both black and white, who told me the song really helped them. They said the song really helped them emotionally. When they were really down, they would hear the song and it would make them feel good and help them get through."

Despite or perhaps because of its controversy, the song reached number three on the R&B charts in the summer of 1971, was a number 12 pop hit, and became Freda Payne's second gold record.

The exuberant "You Brought the Joy," released in the fall of

1971, was Payne's last top 30 R&B entry, peaking at number 21. Further releases included "The Road We Didn't Take"; the smooth, mid-tempo "Two Wrongs Don't Make a Right"; and an 11-minute "I'm Not Getting Any Better." These songs had Payne leaning more towards her more comfortable cabaret style. As a result they achieved limited commercial success on the pop and R&B charts. By 1973 Invictus and Hot Wax began experiencing cash-flow problems, coupled with lawsuits and counter-lawsuits with several of its artists, including Freda Payne. The labels soon folded.

Despite the superstar status achieved by Payne from her 1970 and 1971 hits, particularly "Band of Gold," her tenure at Invictus Records was not always pleasant. "It was hectic," she says. "It was really hectic. When I was with Invictus, they were controlling my career but I wasn't quite happy with the way it was being handled. People said 'Oh, wow! You're making it, you've got hit records, you're a star . . . ' but didn't know what was going on behind the scenes. Personally I was quite unhappy."

After leaving Invictus, Payne remained a popular club attraction. She later recorded for ABC/Dunhill Records and Capitol Records in a style that reflected her jazz origins. Her only singles to enter the R&B charts were "It's Yours to Have" (number 81) in 1974, "Love Magnet" (number 85) in 1975, and "In Motion" (number 63), the latter released on the Sutra label in 1982. Because of her absence from the pop/R&B charts, there was some speculation that she was in a period of semi-retirement. However, Payne refutes this.

"I've never retired," she says. "It's just that you haven't heard from me. There's never been a year that I haven't been singing or working; sometimes not as much but I've always been singing and performing."

In 1981 Payne accepted an offer to host *For Today's Black Woman*, a nationally syndicated half-hour talk show. "I was being managed by Charles Huggins over at HUSH Productions, who was also handing his wife Melba Moore. He said that he had a program and wanted to know if I wanted to do it. They asked Melba Moore to do it but she already had too many commitments. First they had to talk me into it. I didn't want to do it. I said, 'Gee, there's no music. It's all talk and that's not my thing. I'm not a talk narrator, I'm a performer.' He said, 'It'll be different, it'll be educational, it'll really increase your popularity.' So I did it and it really worked out quite well. It really did all of those things."

While continuing to perform in clubs, Payne branched out into theater. As a result, she is often called on to do tours of the musical *Sophisticated Ladies.* While performing throughout the world an average of five or six months a year, Payne adapts her stage act according to the musical taste of her audience.

She says, "I'm sort of a versatile type of person. When I do a tour in the U.K., I gear my show to more of an R&B and rock kind of taste but I still do my other stuff. [In the U.S.] I do a lot of Duke Ellington material. I do what I really consider fun material. And also I do 'Band of Gold' and 'Bring the Boys Home,' some of the oldies. I just put on a good show and sing to the best of my ability."

The Spinners

Led by the twin lead vocals of Philippe Wynne and Bobbie Smith, and the production of Thom Bell, the Spinners were an integral part of the Philly Soul sound that dominated black music in the 1970s. With a string of hits about the variations of love — falling in love, motherly love, lost love — this quintet enjoyed tremendous success between 1972 and 1976.

The Spinners started their recording career in the early 1960s on Tri-Phi Records. They later toiled at Motown for most of the decade with only sporadic success. The group's fortunes changed when they moved to Atlantic in 1972 and were paired with Bell. Thus began an incredible run of hits, including "I'll Be Around," "Could It Be I'm Falling in Love," and "Mighty Love," which made them one of the most popular and successful vocal groups in the history of modern black music.

The Spinners, originally known as the Domingoes, formed in the Royal Oak Township section of Ferndale, Michigan in 1955. The charter members were Bobbie Smith (tenor), Henry Fambrough (baritone), Pervis Jackson (bass), Billy Henderson (tenor), and C. P. Spencer. The quintet initially started singing on street corners and at youth centers and school dances. They later "graduated" to local clubs, and made a name for themselves by winning the Top Amateur Vocal Group award in Detroit in 1957. By now a name change was in order due to the moniker "Domingoes" sounding too much like the more established group, the Flamingos. The name "Spinners" was chosen in reference to the big Cadillac hubcaps called "spinners" that adorned Smith's car.

The group earned a strong reputation around Detroit, particularly after winning the amateur award. This led to a contract with Anna Records, a label owned by Gwen Gordy (Berry's sister). It was here the Spinners met Harvey Fuqua of the Moonglows. With a string of hits on the Chess label, including "Sincerely" (1954), "Most of All" (1955), and "Please Send Me Someone to Love" (1957), the Moonglows were perhaps the most respected vocal group of their day. By 1958 the original quintet split up. Fuqua then formed a new set of Moonglows that included Chuck Barksdale of the Dells, and Marvin Gaye, then a member of a Washington DC teenage group, the Marquees. However, after two unsuccessful singles in 1959, this group disbanded. Chess Records owner Leonard Chess then sent Fuqua to Detroit to help Gordy run the Anna label, which Chess distributed. Once at Anna, Fuqua took the Spinners under his wing, teaching them how to sing five-part harmony and rehearsing them for a year. By now Spencer was gone and his spot was taken by George Dixon. Anna Records soon closed down and Fuqua started his own Tri-Phi and Harvey labels in 1961. That same year, he married Gwen Gordy.

In the spring of 1961, the Spinners released a Fuqua-Gordy composition on Tri-Phi entitled "That's What Girls Are Made For." Fuqua had molded the Spinners to be so much like the Moonglows that he was often mistaken for singing lead on this ballad, though it was actually Smith. The song reached number five on the R&B charts and cracked the pop top 30. However, the Spinners were unable to benefit from this success. Like most black-owned independent labels, Tri-Phi faced distribution problems. Fuqua was able to use his clout as a former Moonglow to get the roster's songs played on the radio, but could not get enough records into stores around the country to capitalize on this exposure. Over the next year and a half, the Spinners released five more singles on Tri-Phi: "Love (I'm So Glad) I Found You," "What Did She Use," "She Loves Me So," and "She Don't Love Me," the last credited to "the Spinners and Bobby Smith." However, the only song to chart was "Love (I'm So Glad) I Found You." By now Edgar

Edwards had replaced Dixon.

In 1963 Fuqua merged his record labels with Motown. The Spinners, along with Jr. Walker and the All-Stars, Shorty Long, and Johnny Bristol, were brought into the fold. The group's first release on Motown was "Sweet Thing" in 1964. Produced in the same bouncy, gospel-flavored, hand-clapping mold that soon became known as "the Motown sound," it was a style that the quintet was unaccustomed to, and the song failed to chart. The Spinners fared better the second time, cracking the R&B top 10 in the summer of 1965 with the up-tempo "I'll Always Love You." The group then followed with "Truly Yours," a heartbreaking song despite its sweet melody, which reached number 16 in the spring of 1966.

In 1967 Edwards left the Spinners. His spot was filled by G. C. Cameron, who became the primary lead singer. Cameron, born in Mississippi and raised in Detroit, joined the Spinners at the suggestion of Dennis Edwards, soon to become lead singer of the Temptations. However, Cameron's presence did not immediately improve matters. The group's 1967 release "For All We Know" and their 1968 release "Bad Bad Weather (Til You Come Home)," the latter a Temptations-flavored, mid-tempo track featuring thunderstorm sound effects, failed to chart.

The Spinners were switched to Motown's VIP subsidiary in 1969 and were produced by Johnnie Bristol. However, their fortunes did not change. Their first three VIP singles — "In My Diary" (1969), a tribute to the Moonglows, "At Sundown," and the controversial "Message from a Black Man" (both 1970) — failed to chart. Stevie Wonder took over production of the group and gave them their biggest Motown hit, "It's a Shame." Co-written by Wonder and his future wife, Syretta Wright, the song reached number four on the R&B charts in the summer of 1970 and cracked the pop top 20. The success of "It's a Shame," a glorious tune despite its heartbreaking lyrics, was beneficial for both parties involved. At the time, Wonder was in the process of negotiating a new contract with Motown and was seeking total artistic freedom. His success with the Spinners served as a vehicle to showcase his production talent. Wonder also penned the group's follow-up, "We'll Have It Made," which reached number 20 on the R&B charts early in 1971.

That same year, the Spinners' contract with Motown expired. Having joined the label from an outside source (Tri-Phi), the Spinners were never considered part of the Motown family, and were continually lost in the shuffle. During their eight years at the company, they released nine singles with only "It's a Shame" becoming a bona fide hit. Their smooth Moonglows-influenced style was in sharp contrast to the strong, driving, drum- and bass-dominated "Motown sound." As a result, the Spinners were shifted around to various producers and were often given second-rate material to record. The quintet was regularly featured as an opening act on Motown package tours, but they often moonlighted by performing whatever jobs the company needed done, even chauffeuring for the label's "true" stars or working in the shipping department. Realizing that they would never escalate to Motown's A-list, the Spinners decided to move elsewhere.

When the Spinners left Motown, they also left behind their lead singer, Cameron, who opted to stay with the label for a solo career. Cameron's solo career was relatively uneventful. His 1974 solo album *Love Songs and Other Tragedies* and a 1977 duet album with Syretta Wright, *Rich Love, Poor Love*, were commercial failures. Perhaps his finest moment as a solo artist was "It's So Hard to Say Goodbye to Yesterday" from the 1975 film *Cooley High*.

Cameron recommended his friend Philippe Wynne (real name Philip Walker) as his replacement in the Spinners. Wynne, a Cincinnati native born in 1941, had previously sung with the Pacesetters, a local group led by Bootsy Collins. He later worked with Joe Tex at the Twenty Grand in Detroit before moving to Europe and joining the Afro Kings, a group of Liberian musicians in search of a vocalist. Wynne stayed in Europe with the Afro Kings for two years, performing around the military bases and at small clubs. When he returned to the

States, he went back to Detroit and met the Spinners. It took Wynne only the first few lines of one song to convince the group that he was the man to fill Cameron's spot.

The Spinners received considerable interest from Stax and Avco, but Aretha Franklin, a long-time friend of the group, put them in touch with Atlantic Records. Although the other offers initially seemed more lucrative, the quintet signed with Atlantic towards the end of 1971.

Early in 1972, the Spinners cut four tracks with former Motown producer, Jimmy Roach: "(Oh Lord) I Wish I Could Sleep," "I Just Gotta Make It Happen," "Mr. Big Man," and "You Sure Are Nasty." However, Atlantic's promotion department told label president Henry Allen that the songs were not up to par. The group was then snapped up by producer/arranger/writer Thom Bell.

Whether working independently or alongside Kenny Gamble and Leon Huff, Bell was a major player in establishing the Philly Soul sound that would dominate black music in the 1970s. Having produced nearly all of the Delfonics' hits in the late 1960s and the Stylistics' smashes in the early 1970s, he was one of the hottest creative talents in the music industry. In 1972, Henry Allen approached Bell with an offer to produce any artist on the Atlantic roster, and he decided on the Spinners. A former pianist in the house band at Philadelphia's Uptown Theater, Bell remembered the group from their performance at the Uptown after the success of "That's What Girls Are Made For."

Bell was noted for his ethereal, string-filled brand of soul, and this was the perfect match for the velvet-smooth sound of the Spinners' pre-Motown days. The primary beneficiary of Bell's production was Bobbie Smith. With Smith having previously lost his lead spot to Cameron during the group's final years at Motown, the Spinners were led to believe that his light tenor was not strong enough to carry the lead. Bell's laid-back arrangements allowed Smith to sing in a comfortable manner and not strain his vocals as he did on some of the group's Motown recordings.

Due to the money spent on the Roach sessions, Atlantic only budgeted enough for Bell to produce four songs for the Spinners. One of the four was an Yvette Davis composition, "How Could I Let You Get Away." In the summer of 1972, this lush, laid-back ballad was selected as the group's first Atlantic release. However, radio deejays preferred the flip side, "I'll Be Around," and this song got the push as the A-side. Whereas "How Could I Let You Get Away" sounded like something Bell might have produced for the Stylistics, "I'll Be Around" was entirely different. Led by its guitar-dominated arrangement and the underlying conga playing of Larry Washington, this smooth dance track, with Smith on lead, was an instant smash and the group's biggest hit. "I'll Be Around" became the Spinners' first Number One R&B hit, topping the charts for five weeks in the fall of 1972. The song also crossed over to number three on the pop charts and became the group's first million-seller. Although relegated to B-side status, "How Could I Let You Get Away" is regarded as one of the group's hits and is always included on any greatest hits package.

Toward the end of the year, the Spinners followed their gold success with "Could It Be I'm Falling in Love," arguably their most romantic single ever. Produced again by Bell, the song was written by twin brothers Mervin and Melvin Steals, who had been sending Bell material for quite some time. This gentle, mid-tempo track, with Smith carrying the majority of the lead, featured the prominent female backing vocals of Carla Benson, Yvette Benton, and Barbara Ingram. "Could It Be I'm Falling in Love" topped the R&B charts for a week early in 1973, reached number four on the pop charts, and was the group's second million-seller. The success of the song was an added boost to the confidence of the quintet. With their previous hits, "That's What Girls Are Made For" and "It's a Shame," spread out over a spotty career of unfulfilled promises, the Spinners were still skeptical after the success of "I'll Be Around." When their follow-up achieved the same lofty status, it gave them assurance that they were close to reaching the big time.

The quintet pulled the hat trick when their next single, "One of a Kind (Love Affair)," became their third straight million-seller and Number One R&B hit, topping the charts for four weeks in the spring of 1973. This bouncy, mid-tempo track was written by Richmond, Virginia native Joseph Jefferson, who would write several of the Spinners' hits over the next three years. "One of a Kind" was noteworthy for having Smith and Wynne share lead vocals. The styles of the two tenors were distinctly different — Wynne was a gospel-infused shouter while Smith was warm, laid-back, and smooth. However, Wynne toned his vocals down for much of this song, and it was difficult to distinguish his voice from Smith's until the former took over towards the end.

Bell teamed up with his primary writing partner, Linda Creed, for the socially-conscious "Ghetto Child." This composition was an attempt to pull the Spinners away from the love theme, just as the pair had done the previous year for the Stylistics with "People Make the World Go Round." The easy-listening "Ghetto Child," prominently featuring the baritone of Henry Fambrough, reached number four on the R&B charts in the summer of 1973.

Led by the three million sellers ["I'll Be Around," "Could It Be I'm Falling in Love," and "One of a Kind (Love Affair)"], "How Could I Let You Get Away," and "Ghetto Child," the Spinners' self-titled Atlantic debut album was certified gold and was perhaps their finest.

The Spinners followed their successful debut with the release of *Mighty Love* early in 1974. The first release was the title track, co-written by Jefferson and relative newcomers Charles Simmons and Bruce Hawes, and it topped the R&B charts for two weeks. Although "Mighty Love" did not fare as well on the pop charts (number 20) as its million-selling predecessors, the song had great impact because Philippe Wynne was out front as the focal point of the group. Wynne sang in a smooth, laid-back tenor for the first half of the song (the part actually released as a single), as he again shared the lead with Smith. However, for the next two and a half minutes he sang like a man possessed; ad-libbing, stammering, stuttering, babbling, and scatting as the other four Spinners chanted the title phrase in support. Wynne's improvisations on "Mighty Love" carried over to his stage presentation. The Spinners were always a slick, choreographed act on stage, having worked under the guidance of legendary choreographer Cholly Atkins and honed their skills on numerous Motown package tours in the 1960s. However, the bespectacled Wynne's onstage antics added another dimension to this. Skipping across the stage, going into the audience, and often acting out the lyrics of the songs, an ecstatic Wynne would often end the group's concerts in a typical James Brown fashion of having to be torn away from the microphone and pulled offstage by his singing partners.

The group followed "Mighty Love" in the spring of 1974 with "I'm Coming Home," a joyous song that had Wynne singing at his gospel-infused best. It was as if his exuberance from "Mighty Love" had carried over to this number. Here he sang of returning to his rural roots after an inability to adjust to the city. Written by Bell and Creed, this keyboard- and conga-driven track reached number three on the R&B charts, cracked the pop top 20, and remains arguably the Spinners' most underrated hit. The flip side of "I'm Coming Home" was the popular "He'll Never Love You Like I Do," a sweet, melodic track that stressed the importance of love over material possessions. Wynne and Smith again traded leads on this song, which by all accounts was strong enough to stand on its own.

Dionne Warwick joined the Spinners for the summer release of "Then Came You," which became a million-seller and the first Number One pop hit for both parties. Warwick had known Bell since the early 1960s, when she appeared at the Uptown Theater. She expressed a desire to work with him and he suggested a duet between her and the Spinners. Pairing Warwick with the group was mutually beneficial. She introduced the Spinners to the lucrative cabaret circuit by featuring them as the opening act on her five-week summer theater tour of Las Vegas. They in turn brought her back to her black roots after she had previously moved into the pop mainstream. Although a duet album was planned, nothing came of it and no future duet singles were produced.

Later that fall the Spinners released "Love Don't Love Nobody," which reached number four on the R&B charts and made the pop top 20. Here a melancholy Wynne delivered a sermon on the dues one pays when going through the stages of being in love. Sung and spoken over the course of seven minutes, Wynne turned this Jefferson-Simmons composition into a much-covered soul classic. The song remains one of his finest moments as a Spinner.

Led by "Mighty Love," "I'm Coming Home," and "Love Don't Love Nobody," the *Mighty Love* album was the group's second gold LP.

"Then Came You" was featured on the group's third Atlantic album, *New and Improved*, and helped propel the LP into top 10 and gold status. A second single from the album was "Living a Little, Laughing a Little," a Bell-Creed composition along the same "tears of a clown" theme as Blue Magic's "Sideshow" from the previous year. A joyous, gospel-infused ballad, "Living a Little, Laughing a Little" reached number seven on the R&B charts early in 1975. However, this song petered out at number 37 on the pop charts, the group's first Atlantic single not to achieve any significant crossover success. The same was true of their next 45 "Sadie," a top 10 R&B hit in the spring of 1975, which only managed to reach number 54 on the pop charts. However, numbers do not fully tell the story here. Written by the same "Mighty Love" team of Jefferson, Simmons, and Hawes, this warm ballad featured Wynne reflecting on the memory of the strong matriarchal figure in his life. The track has gone on to become a perennial Mother's Day favorite for African-Americans.

The quintet improved their fortunes on the pop charts in the fall of 1975 when "They Just Can't Stop It the (Games People Play)" reached number five. The song also gave the Spinners their fourth Number One R&B hit. Originally released as "Games People Play," Atlantic Records reissued this single with the unorthodox title to differentiate it from another single at that time with the same name. Thom Bell's arrangement of this bouncy song gave all five Spinners a chance to sing lead. "Games People Play" was the lead track from *Pick of the Litter*, the group's fourth straight gold LP. Other strong songs from the album were "Love or Leave," a spirited carbon copy of "Mighty Love" that reached number eight on the R&B charts early in 1976; and the ballads "I Don't Want to Lose You" and "Sweet Love of Mine."

The Spinners released *Happiness Is Being with the Spinners* in the summer of 1976, which became their fifth gold album. The lead single from this disc was "Wake Up Susan," which reached number 11. However, the album's success was triggered by "The Rubberband Man." A hard-driving yet somewhat silly song, "The Rubberband Man" topped the R&B charts for a week in the fall of 1976 and spent three weeks at the number two spot on the pop charts behind Rod Stewart's "Tonight's the Night."

The gold success of "The Rubberband Man" marked the end of Philippe Wynne's tenure with the group, as he left at the beginning of 1977 for a solo career. Wynne's departure ended a long period of conflict between him and the other Spinners, and also between him and Bell. Like many groups before and since, the Spinners were faced with a situation where the lead singer thought he was bigger than the group. And like several lead singers before and since, Wynne would discover that the public was familiar with the Spinners, not Philippe Wynne. His solo career got off to a decent start on Cotillion Records with "Hats Off to Mama," something of a continuation of "Sadie," which reached number 17 on the R&B charts in 1977. He was later featured on Funkadelic's 1979 hit "(not just) Knee Deep." Wynne's career was spotty after this triumph. His album on George Clinton's Uncle Jam label and one on Sugar Hill Records received scant notice. Wynne did not surface again until "Wait 'Til Tomorrow" became a minor hit in 1983. On July 13, 1984, as he jumped off the stage into the audience to begin his third encore at Ivey's, a nightclub in Oakland, Philippe Wynne suffered a massive heart attack and died at the age of 43.

Billy Henderson recruited John Edwards to take Wynne's place in the Spinners. Edwards, a St. Louis native, previously recorded as a solo artist for various small labels such as Twin Stacks and Aware. However, his solo success had been marginal. In addition to facing life without the contribution of Wynne, the Spinners, like several of their soul contemporaries, had to adjust to the arrival of disco. They continued to have moderate success for the remainder of the decade with the smooth "You're Throwing a Good Love Away" (spring 1977), "Heaven on Earth (So Fine)" (fall 1977), "If You Wanna Do a Dance" (summer 1978), and "Are You Ready for Love" (spring 1979). With their smooth brand of soul being somewhat dated by now, the Spinners felt that it was time for a change. After their 1979 album *From Here to Eternally* failed to generate any noise, the group parted amicably with Thom Bell.

The Spinners then hooked up with disco producer Michael Zager, whose Mike Zager Band had solid disco hits in 1978 with "Let's All Chant" and "Love Express." Zager brought the Spinners back to the top in the fall of 1979 with a remake of the Four Seasons' "Working My Way Back to You" blended in a medley with "Forgive Me, Girl." Despite the quintet's initial apprehension about singing an oldie, the song became the group's seventh and final gold single, reaching number two on the pop charts and number six R&B. In the summer of 1980, the Spinners followed up in similar fashion, blending a remake of Sam Cooke's "Cupid" with "I've Loved You for a Long Time." The formula worked again as this medley was a top five hit on the pop and R&B charts.

The quintet continued to turn out albums and singles into the mid-1980s but their commercial years were behind them. Their last chart entry was "Right or Wrong," which reached number 22 on the R&B charts in the spring of 1984. The Spinners left Atlantic in 1987 and did not appear on disc again until 1989 with a little-noticed album on Fantasy's Volt label.

Despite a stalled recording career, the Spinners remain in-demand live performers. Unlike many of their soul contemporaries of the early 1970s, the quintet often performs in lucrative show places on the cabaret circuit. Part of the reason for this can be traced to the grooming they received from Motown's Artist Development classes in the 1960s, and also to the business acumen of their manager Buddy Allen. However, their universal appeal lies in the sophistication and passion they pour into their songs.

The Staple Singers

A gospel group for much of their career, the Staple Singers, led by the gritty, emotional contralto of Mavis Staples and the blues-style guitar playing of "Pops" Staples, achieved international acclaim as one of the top groups in American popular music during the early 1970s. With the success of songs such as "Respect Yourself" and "I'll Take You There," the Staples expanded the boundaries of gospel, reaching larger audiences with their message of peace, love, and brotherhood.

Roebuck "Pops" Staples was born in Winona, Mississippi in 1915. He started singing and playing the guitar on the plantation where he was raised. As a teenager, he began performing at local dance parties, and later sang with a local spiritual group called the Golden Trumpets. In 1935 he moved to Chicago with his wife and their first two children, Pervis and Cleotha. Once in Chicago, Pops began training his kids in gospel music. He explains, "I'm a self-taught guitar player. There were 14 in my family, seven boys and seven girls. I'm the 13th child. We used to sing on the farm when we got through picking cotton. We had no radio, no television, nothing. My brothers and sisters had children before I was born; they were that much older than me. I was a little kid and we would get out there and sing to amuse ourselves until bedtime. That motivated me and really made me bring my family together when I got married and had children. We weren't trying to make stars out of ourselves, we were just singing around the home like we did [when I was a kid]."

Pops officially formed the Staple Singers in 1951 with son

Pervis and daughters Cleo (alto) and Mavis (contralto, lead). They sang at Holy Trinity Baptist Church in Chicago and in 1952 cut their first record, "They Are They" backed with "Faith and Grace," for their own Royal label. In 1953 the Staples signed with the United label, where they recorded "Sit Down Servant." Two years later they signed with the larger Vee-Jay label in 1955. Pops built the sound of the group around Mavis' raspy, booming, emotional voice, balanced by his own low-voiced, almost understated singing. At Vee-Jay, the Staple Singers became a major attraction on the gospel circuit, particularly after the release of the smash hit "Uncloudy Day." Released in 1957, the song sold 36,000 copies in a few months (remarkable for a religious record). Over the next few years they made several gospel albums on the Vee-Jay label, and in 1962 *Downbeat* magazine presented the Staple Singers with the New Star Award for "the most promising vocal group of the year." It was the first time the award was ever given to a gospel group.

Leaving Vee-Jay in 1962, the Staples began to mix folk music with gospel, recording first for Riverside before moving to Columbia in 1964. In 1967, the group had their first pop chart single with the Larry Williams-produced "Why (Am I Treated So Bad)" and a cover of Buffalo Springfield's "For What It's Worth."

At this time, the Staples were making a gradual shift from traditional gospel to message songs. Mavis points out, "We made a transition from strictly gospel to message songs and we did that because of our relationship with Dr. King. We were in the movement; we marched and sang. We were actually singing his messages. We started out singing songs like 'Washington Is Watching You,' 'When Will We Be Paid for the Work We've Done,' and 'Freedom's Highway.'"

Pops adds, "We considered ourselves a message group. We'd sing about what's happening to the people now and what we need now. We were trying to set up something constructive to take to the people."

The Staple Singers made an important move in July 1968 when they signed with Stax Records in Memphis. The Staples had known Al Bell, the vice-president of Stax and a powerful figure in black music at that time, since his days as a disk jockey in Arkansas in the 1950s. "Stax wanted me to sign with them because they felt I had something they would like to have," says Pops. "They asked me to sign and I signed."

Their first two albums for the company, *Soul Folk in Action* and *We'll Get Over*, were produced by house-band guitarist Steve Cropper, and failed to generate much interest. In 1971, Bell took over production and added a contemporary sound to the group's lyrics. Also at this time Pervis left for the military and was replaced by his sister Yvonne (soprano). Bell gave the Staple Singers their first R&B hit in April 1971 with a rousing, joyous cover of Bobby Bloom's "Heavy Makes You Happy (Sha-Na-Boom-Boom)" from their third Stax album, *The Staple Swingers*. The chart success of "Heavy Makes You Happy" (a number six R&B hit) caused the group to receive considerable flak from gospel traditionalists who accused the Staple Singers of "selling out" to secular music.

Mavis says, "We caught flak from the church people because our records were played across the board. They weren't listening to the lyrics of our songs. They just heard the Staple Singers being played on the R&B stations and said we were going to the devil."

Pops adds, "Our music was still gospel. Any time you sing the truth, it's gospel. It was gospel then and it's gospel now. We were singing the truth. Edwin Hawkins with 'Oh Happy Day' was one of the first contemporary gospel groups to come out along with the Staple Singers. We were singing contemporary gospel music. We were telling people what they needed to know and telling them the truth. To me that's what gospel is.

"We didn't consider ourselves singing rhythm and blues. We worked with Dr. Martin Luther King and said, 'If you can preach it, we can sing it.' So, we went out singing protest songs against what we were going up against. The rhythm and blues disk jockeys heard it and said, 'Wow, this needs to be heard,' and they started playing it on their stations. The gospel people, some of them are the biggest devils in the church, and they raised more hell, talking about, 'Don't be playing the Staple Singers. They ain't gospel.' They went against us. Some people are just so narrow-minded. But after they found out that the Staple Singers meant good, trying to bring the world together in peace and love, they came back and started to buy it up. That's when we started selling millions."

An added benefit to the group's success was their appearance in a concert in Ghana that was attended by over 100,000 people and included other acts such as Wilson Pickett, Roberta Flack, and Ike and Tina Turner. A film of the concert, called *Soul to Soul*, was released in 1971.

"It was a great feeling being out there and trying to bring things back together and everything," says Pops. "It was really a great thrill for us to be out there, a new group doing that kind of work when there were so many other top, heavy, or what they call superstars that were there to do it, and they asked us to do it. I'd never been to Africa before and never knew what it would be like. It was a whole different feeling when I got to Africa. It felt like I was at home. It just felt like a whole different thing. I didn't know it could feel like that. There were tears in my daughters' eyes and we just rejoiced."

Mavis adds, "In time, we've visited at least 16 different countries in Africa and each one was a different experience. I loved all of West Africa. We've been to Johannesburg twice and our experience there was different because we saw our brothers and sisters but we felt good that we were able to take such a strong message to them. But West Africa, I could have stayed there. I didn't really have to come back here."

After "You've Got to Earn It" peaked at number 11 on the R&B charts in the summer of 1971, the Staple Singers released the album *Bealtitude: Respect Yourself.* The title song, "Respect Yourself," was the group's breakthrough. Featuring the understated, almost thin lead of Pops with Mavis' heavy, gritty voice as a counterpart, the song spent two weeks at the number two spot on the R&B charts and was the Staple Singers' first top 20 pop hit, peaking at number 12. "Respect Yourself" sold over a million copies and netted the group a Grammy nomination.

Sixteen years later, television's *Moonlighting* star Bruce Willis had a hit with his cover version of the song.

The success of "Respect Yourself" came almost as an afterthought to Pops. He explains, "I wasn't trying to be successful in the pop field. I wasn't shooting at being successful at anything. I was just trying to do what we felt could make people down in their hearts feel good. That's what we were trying to do. We weren't trying to be successful. It just turned out that way."

It was the follow-up that made the Staple Singers the number one group in the country and, more important, established Mavis Staples as the focal point of the group. Released in the spring of 1972, the bass-dominated, reggae-flavored "I'll Take You There" topped the R&B charts for four weeks and was the group's first Number One pop hit. The song was nominated for a Grammy for best R&B performance by a group and eventually sold two million copies.

Mavis describes the feeling of being at the top of the music world during this time. "It felt good but it was more like an added blessing because we felt like that before when we were singing strictly gospel. With 'I'll Take You There' and 'Respect Yourself' we made a transition to do message songs so that they could be played across the board and could reach young adults. We felt really good about it because we never expected to go that far in our career. We never did start singing to make a career out of it. We just happened to make a record and the people across the world loved it and bought it up."

Pops is a little more philosophical about becoming a superstar. "Everybody is somebody. I'm just as much as anybody, no more than anybody else. Superstars, or what they call the stars, I don't think much of because I'm trying to do something to help people along the way. I receive my award from God above. It doesn't make too much difference to me about awards and things that they're giving out. A lot of them are phony anyway. I like the pure things and that's what's going to come from God. He's blessed me to be able to do the things that have to be done. I wasn't trying to be a star."

The Staple Singers maintained their popularity throughout the next year with the funky "This World," a number six R&B hit, and the joyous, foot-stomping "Oh La De Da," a number four hit in the spring of 1973. During the run of their next single, the title track from their *Be What You Are* album, the group appeared in the movie *Wattstax*, along with Isaac Hayes, Richard Pryor, and Rufus Thomas.

In the fall of 1973, the second release from *Be What You Are*, the reggae-tinged "If You're Ready (Come Go with Me)," became the group's biggest hit since "I'll Take You There." The million-selling call for brotherhood was a top 10 pop hit and was the group's second Number One R&B hit, topping the charts for three weeks. Early in 1974, the Staple Singers followed this success with the easy-listening "Touch a Hand, Make a Friend," the zenith of their quest for brotherhood.

Pops recalls, "I was trying to bridge the gap between black and white but the hardest thing to do is bridge the gap between black and black. That's what I always say, we need to stick together. Together we stand, divided we fall."

The group followed this success with the title track from the *City in the Sky* album, a number four R&B hit in the summer of 1974. The follow-up, "My Main Man," was to be their last release on the Stax label. Stax Records collapsed in 1975 and the Staple Singers signed with Warner Brothers.

Pops explains, "Stax had lost out and they couldn't do us anymore. They just lost whatever they were doing. Warner wanted us to sign with them and we had to keep going; we couldn't stop."

The Staples' first album under their new association with Warner was the soundtrack for *Let's Do It Again*, the hit comedy starring Bill Cosby and Sidney Poitier. Produced by Curtis Mayfield and released on his Curtom label (which was distributed by Warner), the album was the Staples' all-time best seller. The title song stayed at the Number One spot on the R&B charts for two weeks in the fall of 1975 and was the group's second Number One pop hit. "Let's Do It Again" was at that time the biggest-selling single to date for Warner Brothers Records.

"Working with Curtis Mayfield was great," says Pops. "He was very good for the Staple Singers. He made one of the biggest hits we ever had with 'Let's Do It Again.' He's a good writer and producer, just a very fine man."

Despite the success of the single, Pops admits to having problems with its lyrics. "I didn't think about it at the time; I'm naive. I wasn't thinking about any 'do it,' whatever they were talking about doing. But that's what made it sell so big. What happened was that Bill Cosby and Sidney Poitier said, 'That last particular song you did was alright. Let's do it again.' That's where the title 'Let's Do It Again' came from. So many funny things have come up about that song, I wasn't even thinking about it but there was a lot of controversy about that song. That's the hardest one for me to get out of. I wasn't thinking about what I was doing when I did it. It was the same with 'I'll Take You There.' We were talking about 'I'll take you to heaven' but when I found out anything, they were talking about take you to breakfast, take you to a movie, take you to the motel, everything [but what we meant]. We were talking about going to heaven and they just took it the other way. Anyone who wanted to go there, that's who bought it. ['I'll Take You There'] sold millions and millions of it."

Mavis adds, "Our only secular song is 'Let's Do It Again.' The rest of them we sing in church. That's the only one we won't sing in church."

The follow-up, "New Orleans," also from the *Let's Do It Again* soundtrack, peaked at number four on the R&B charts early in 1976 and was to be the Staple Singers' final top 10 hit.

Mayfield produced the group's next album, *Pass It On*, which yielded the hit single "Love Me, Love Me, Love Me" later in 1976. After *Unlock Your Mind* in 1978, the Staples recorded for Private I in the 1980s. Their most successful effort was the *Turning Point* album in 1984, which yielded three impressive singles, "H-A-T-E (Don't Live Here Anymore)," "This Is Our Night," and a cover of the Talking Heads' "Slippery People."

Although the Staples were unable to attain the level of success they achieved a decade earlier, their songs from the 1970s became hits for other artists. In 1985 the Oak Ridge Boys had a Number One country hit with their cover version of "Touch a Hand, Make a Friend" and gospel duo BeBe and CeCe Winans featuring Mavis Staples had a Number One R&B hit in 1991 with "I'll Take You There."

"I'm thankful that some young people can take on where we left off and thought enough of the song and what we were doing to keep it alive," says Pops. "I think it's beautiful. I hope that they'll pick up some more of our songs and keep them alive."

Mavis, who previously cut solo albums for Volt (a Stax subsidiary), Curtom, and Warner, signed to Prince's Paisley Park label in 1987 and recorded *Time Waits for No One*, co-produced by Al Bell and Prince. In 1993 she released her second Paisley Park album, *The Voice.*

Pops, who had done two singles at Stax, recorded a self-titled gospel album for the I Am label in 1987. In 1992 he signed with Point Blank Records for the release of *Peace to the Neighborhood.* Pops won a Grammy in 1995 for his second Point Blank album, *Father Father,* which included a cover of the Impressions' 1965 hit "People Get Ready." He says, "I'm trying to carry the message on. I have more young people that like Pops Staples now. Staple Singers music is just as new now as it was when we first started because our music is timeless. I don't care about the trends. I'll just go on singing my timeless message songs."

The Stylistics

Led by the distinctive high tenor of Russell Thompkins, Jr. and the production and songwriting team of Thom Bell and Linda Creed, the Stylistics recorded some of the finest soft-soul music of the 1970s. Turning out a string of ethereal love songs including "Betcha By Golly, Wow" and "You Make Me Feel Brand New," this Philadelphia quintet enjoyed enormous popularity and was a consistent presence near the top of the pop and R&B charts between 1971 and 1974. With five gold singles and three gold albums to their credit, the Stylistics were the most successful love ballad group of their era.

The Stylistics were formed in 1968 out of a combination of two groups from Benjamin Franklin High School in Philadelphia. Russell Thompkins, Jr. (lead and tenor), Airrion Love (first and second tenor), and James Smith (bass) sang with the Monarchs, while Herb Murrell (lead and baritone) and James Dunn (baritone) sang with the Percussions. After graduation, members of both groups went to college or joined the armed services. One of the teachers at Benjamin Franklin came up with the idea of putting the remaining five (Thompkins, Love, Smith, Murrell, and Dunn) together to form one group. Robert Douglas, the guitarist in the group's backup band Slim and the Boys, chose the name Stylistics.

The group worked the local club scene in Philadelphia, playing places such as the Cadillac Club, the Blue Horizon, the Imperial Ballroom, and the Starlight Club, and also in the Allentown and Bethlehem area. The following year they recorded "You're a Big Girl Now," a song written by Douglas and their road manager, ex-Monarch Marty Bryant, for the local Sebring label.

Herb Murrell remembers, "We were performing at a club in Philly called the Racka Poom-Poom. Our road manager Marty Bryant said, 'I've got these people from this record company coming down to check y'all out. They might be checking to see if they can record you.' Being a young group, we never thought twice about it. The idea of recording was exciting but we were just used to working. They came along and liked what they saw and they took us in the studio to record 'You're a Big Girl Now.'"

The song became a local hit but Sebring was not equipped for national distribution. The group and the song were then brought to Avco Records. Murrell explains, "Bill Perry, the person who owned Sebring Records at that time, tried to get national distribution for 'You're a Big Girl Now' and he took it to Avco Embassy, which had Embassy Pictures. The record company came under the same grouping. They put it on a nationwide distribution plan as far as New York, D.C., Baltimore, Atlanta ... and the record itself took off. From there they came up with the idea that they wanted an album done. We never envisioned that it would go as far as it did or the things that evolved from doing 'You're a Big Girl Now.'"

With the introduction of Russell Thompkins' high tenor to the record-buying public, the teeny-bopper "You're a Big Girl Now" became a hit at the beginning of 1971, reaching number seven on the R&B charts. The Stylistics soon became the top priority of recently hired producer/writer Thom Bell, fresh off his string of hits with the Delfonics. Bell and his writing partner, Linda Creed, would produce a series of best-selling singles for the Stylistics over the next three years.

"Working with Thom Bell was a very good learning experience, a very good musical experience," says Murrell. "Because we were young we didn't know much about the business. In terms of music I think we all grew because, with his greatness and the things that he accomplished, his knowledge of music passed onto the group. It wasn't like just going into the studio and turning out songs. We were learning."

In the summer of 1971 the Stylistics' second single, "Stop, Look, Listen (To Your Heart)," with its haunting melody, further established the group's presence on the R&B charts by reaching number six. It was the group's third single that brought them to the pop market. Released in the fall of 1971, the lush "You Are Everything" became the group's first simultaneous top 10 pop and R&B hit and the first of five gold singles. The Stylistics followed with "Betcha By Golly, Wow," arguably their most romantic single ever. With its smooth melody, this much-covered classic was a number three pop hit, spent two weeks at the number two spot on the R&B charts, and became the group's second gold single. With their consistent success on both charts in the States and overseas in England, the Stylistics became international superstars in less than three years.

"Things kind of happened fast for us," says Murrell. "Right after 'You're a Big Girl Now' came 'Stop, Look, Listen' and then 'You Are Everything.' We were working on the road at the time. The records were taking off and they started putting us into different markets. During the time when the songs were coming out we went on a 46-one-nighter tour with James Brown, which really gave us a lot of exposure. So we were on tour during the time that these songs were coming out. As each one came out we would add it to the show. In terms of success or being stars, that never really crossed our minds."

With the Stylistics' reputation for soft-soul ballads firmly intact, they branched out with the socially conscious "People Make the World Go Round." Murrell points out, "There were a lot of things going on in the '70s such as the Vietnam War still being prominent. The song itself, the whole aspect and idea of it, came from Linda Creed. Being aware of the things that were going on with people and events in the world at that time, it was good timing for that song. We were noted for love songs but during the time that we did ['People Make the World Go Round'], to be able to have a song that made a statement about what was going on in the world, because there was a lot going on in the world, was a good song for the group to do at that time."

Led by its hypnotic, sensuous bass line, "People Make the World Go Round" was popular with the black audience and reached number six on the R&B charts in the spring of 1972. However, the group's diversity did not catch on with the pop market, as "People Make the World Go Round" only reached number 25 on the pop charts and broke the Stylistics' string of top 10 pop hits and gold singles.

The Stylistics' self-titled debut album was certified gold. Furthermore, the success of the album established a foundation that would make the Stylistics the most successful tenor-dominated love ballad group of the early 1970s. "I think the very first album did it," says Murrell. "It presented so many hit songs. One song from the album came out and became a hit. Next thing, they put out another one and that became a hit and so on. In terms of making a statement as far as the group was concerned, I think the very first album did it. There were other albums along the way that were good but I think the impact came from the very first one."

The Stylistics followed their debut with the equally successful *Round 2* album late in 1972. The first two singles, "I'm Stone in Love with You" and the melancholy, ultra-slow "Break Up to Make Up" gave the Stylistics their third and fourth gold singles and two more simultaneous top 10 pop and R&B hits. A third single, a salsa-tinged remake of the Dionne Warwick hit "You'll Never Get to Heaven (If You Break My Heart)," reached number eight on the R&B charts in the spring of 1973. Further aided by the popular "You're As Right As Rain," "Peek-a-Boo," and "Children of the Night," *Round 2* became the Stylistics' second gold album.

During the run of the *Round 2* album, the group had the privilege of headlining at New York's prestigious Copacabana. Murrell recalls, "It was a big thing to work the Copa. Once we found out that we were going to do the Copa, we hired the late Honi Coles to choreograph the show for us. He worked us; he worked us *hard*. I think it was one of the big stepping-stones in our career. During the time that we were working there, we were honored with the fact that Stevie Wonder stopped by to see us and he came onstage to sing a song with us. So working the Copa was definitely one of the highlights of our career."

The Stylistics followed this success with the title song from the *Rockin' Roll Baby* album, an up-tempo track recorded primarily to enhance their slow-paced live performances. Murrell explains, "During the time we were working with Thom Bell all of our songs were ballads and we didn't have anything to offset our show. We had always mentioned it to Thom Bell and Linda Creed that we needed something that was more up-tempo than doing a lot of slow songs. We were known for [ballads] so we couldn't get around doing that, but we still needed something up-tempo; not just a song that was recorded by somebody else to put in the show, but something of our own. Linda Creed came up with the idea, which was a good offset for all of the stuff that we were doing."

Despite the change in musical tempo, "Rockin' Roll Baby" peaked at number 14 on the pop charts late in 1973 and was the Stylistics' ninth consecutive top 10 R&B hit. For the follow-up, the group moved back to their ballad tradition. "You Make Me Feel Brand New," which would become their biggest success and fifth million-selling single, spent two weeks at the number two spot on the pop charts. Released in the spring of 1974, "You Make Me Feel Brand New" featured the baritone of Airrion Love for much of the song rather than Thompkins' familiar tenor.

Murrell explains, "To have Airrion sing lead was Thom Bell's idea and it also came about through the writing of Linda Creed. They said that they have this song and the way they wrote and constructed it, Airrion would start it off and Russell would come in. Once we heard the song and the lyrical content of it, it was fantastic. The idea of moving Airrion more to the forefront and introducing his voice to the record-buying public actually started on the beginning of 'You Are Everything' and it took off from there."

The success of "You Make Me Feel Brand New" was a fitting finale to the collaboration between the Stylistics and Thom Bell. Bell officially left Avco to work primarily with the Spinners, but there were rumors that there was friction between him and the Stylistics. However, Murrell disputes this claim. "Over the years people always thought that we, the Stylistics, said, 'We don't want to work with Thom Bell anymore,' but that's not true. The whole thing came about between Thom Bell and the record company. They wanted Thom to produce two albums a year on the group, and with his schedule, he couldn't live up to that. So, contractual-wise, between Thom Bell and the record company, that's how the split came down. But for years people always thought that it was something that the group wanted . . . There was success there. It worked good. We had one of the best producers and arrangers and one of the best songwriters around at that time in Thom Bell and Linda Creed. One would be a fool to walk away from Thom."

With the departure of Thom Bell and Linda Creed, Hugo Peretti and Luigi Creatore (H&L), along with Van McCoy, took over production. McCoy, who also favored lush arrangements, kept the same formula as Bell for the *Let's Put It All Together* album. Spurred by the title track, which became a number eight R&B hit in the summer of 1974, *Let's Put It All Together* was the group's third and final gold album.

The follow-up album, *Heavy,* had the Stylistics leaning more towards the disco sound that was starting to become popular towards the end of 1974. While the group's black audience bought it, the Stylistics would never again match the pop success of their string of ballads from the early part of the decade. The first single released from *Heavy,* the eerie "Heavy Falling Out," gave the group their 12th straight top 10 R&B hit, peaking at number four late in 1974 (only "Betcha By Golly, Wow" and "Rockin' Roll Baby" have done better). However, "Heavy Falling Out" only peaked at number 41 on the pop charts, the Stylistics' lowest showing since their debut, "You're a Big Girl Now." A second single, the lush "Hey Girl, Come and Get It," with its bossa nova flavor, remained popular with the disco audience.

Murrell points out, "Disco was not only a hurting thing for the Stylistics, it hurt a lot of stand-up groups. It changed the music scene drastically, especially with the club scene. Whereas groups were very prominent before disco came in, as soon as disco hit, all of these groups subsided. Club owners went from hiring groups to just playing records. We were fortunate to be able to get songs during that era that became hits in other parts of the world. It affected our record sales here in the U.S. and it all happened during the time of the split with Thom Bell.

"The producers at that time, Hugo and Luigi from H&L Records, started doing everything themselves as far as producing. First they brought in Van McCoy, so that kind of moved us into that disco era. It affected our record sales [in the States] but, in turn, our record sales around the world started picking up from songs like 'Hey Girl, Come and Get It' and 'Heavy Falling Out.'

"Disco wasn't something that we didn't want to do and the songs we did at that time all had the disco attitude. I think the attitude of the public or the attitude of program directors of the radio stations, they were just locked in with us doing love songs. To all of a sudden try to get into this thing called the disco bandwagon, I think it was a combination of too many things going on at that time; the split with Thom Bell, a new kind of sound happening with things that Van McCoy was doing, and people moving more towards that dance thing, not associating the dance thing with Stylistics music. All of these things played a part in us being hurt by disco."

In 1975, the ballad "Thank You Baby" became the group's final top 10 R&B hit, peaking at number seven. Hugo and Luigi changed the Stylistics' direction, giving them a cabaret sound to capitalize on the growing European market. When the *Best of the Stylistics* album was released in 1975, Polygram, which distributed Avco internationally, heavily promoted the album on British television and radio. As a result, the album went to Number One and was reportedly the biggest seller ever for a black vocal group. "Can't Give You Anything (But My Love)," a number 18 hit in the States, shot to the top of the British charts in the summer of 1975. Further minor hits included "Star on a TV Show," "Na-Na Is the Saddest Word," "Funky Weekend" (a funk track completely out of character for the group), and the ballad "The Miracle." With the emphasis in popular music shifting from the tenor-dominated sound, the baritone of Airrion Love was featured with more regularity as an answering lead to Thompkins' falsetto. "You Are Beautiful," a ballad dominated by Love and similar in melody to "You Make Me Feel Brand New," was the Stylistics' final release on Avco before switching over to the producers' new H&L label.

In 1978 the Stylistics moved to Mercury Records, where they released *In Fashion* (1978) and *Love Spell* (1979). Despite high expectations, the group's tenure at Mercury was not a successful one. Only two singles, "First Impressions" (number 22) and "Love at First Sight" (number 93), cracked the R&B charts.

Murrell says,"[Being at Mercury] was something that we had high hopes on but it just never got off the ground. We did two good albums with Teddy Randazzo. With that whole project we had a chance, especially with the first album. We went up to Teddy's house in upstate New York and we stayed up there for two weeks. We lived the music day and night. We would go to the studio and cut at night and come back to the house and sit around and listen to everything and put everything in perspective and say, 'Okay, let's go back tomorrow and do this right here with that song.' It wasn't a situation where we went into the studio one night, cut three songs and went back the next night, cut four songs and then walked away from the project. Unfortunately, for whatever reason, Mercury never did anything with it."

The Stylistics moved to Gamble and Huff's Philadelphia International label in 1980 for *Hurry Up This Way Again.* Murrell recalls, "When the Mercury thing did not work out we were looking for another record label and, at this time, because of the success that Kenny Gamble was having with Philadelphia International Records and the strong distributorship with Columbia Records that he had, that's what we needed. We needed someone who could put the material out. In all of those years we were still cutting music but it wasn't being put out there, and PIR, with their collaboration with Columbia Records, they offered that."

The album's elegant title track gave the Stylistics their first hit in five years and opened them up to a younger audience. Unfortunately the group was unable to fully capitalize on the success of "Hurry Up This Way Again." Murrell explains, "People got the news that we were still around and it also gathered a new market. It was good, it was fresh. The whole project of working with Dexter [Wansel] was good. When the *Hurry Up This Way Again* album came out it let everybody know, okay, yes, the Stylistics are still around; they're still making music. But unfortunately, at the same time, they were having problems at Philadelphia International.

"There was another song on that album that should've been the follow-up to 'Hurry Up,' a song called 'Maybe It's Love This Time.' They didn't follow up on it so subsequently the album just died. We came back with the *Closer Than Close* album where we got back with Thom Bell and Linda Creed, but they only did half of the album so the album was too diverse. We never had a chance to get too much out of that album. But then, it can all be attributed to the problems that were going on at Philadelphia International and it happened around the time that Teddy [Pendergrass] had his accident. Of course Pendergrass was the mainstay at Philadelphia International so, once again . . . timing."

By this time the Stylistics were down to a trio as both James Smith and James Dunn left the group. Murrell explains, "James Dunn left the group in 1977. He had ideas that he wanted to do things his way, other than what was conducive to what the Stylistics were about, so we wished him well in whatever he wanted to do and he left.

"James Smith had the same idea so he left in 1980. I see them all the time. At least once or twice a week we'll get together and talk old times and what they're doing in their lives."

In 1984 the Stylistics signed with the independent Streetwise label for the *Some Things Never Change* album. However, Streetwise was mired in lawsuits over then teen sensation New Edition, and as a result, the album's two singles, the title track and "Give a Little," received little promotion. Murrell says,

"Once again a fresh sound, still in the vein of what the Stylistics are about but something fresh working with Maurice Starr. Streetwise Records, for whatever reason, didn't do what they were supposed to do as far as promoting the material. So, once again you have material that's there but it's just sitting there. Early in our career, if you got airplay, that sold records. Now we've moved into the video aspect. If a company is not set up to do that, then you might as well not do anything because everything now is visual. We didn't do the video [with Streetwise] so that didn't help us at all."

"Let's Go Rocking (Tonight)," released the following year, was the group's last chart single to date.

While the Stylistics shopped for a record deal, they continued to perform throughout the world. In 1991 they signed with Amherst Records (which bought out the Avco catalog) for the release of the *Love Talk* album, but unfortunately the album was issued with little fanfare. "[*Love Talk*] did okay but it could've done better," says Murrell. "Once again, there was no video. We signed with Amherst at the time when they had MCA as their distributor. The whole thing looked good because we now had a company with the ability to put the music in our markets. But then shortly after signing and going into the studio, for whatever reason, their distribution deal with MCA fell apart. Once again, a new album with no video."

As the Stylistics set their sights on going back into the studio, the trio celebrated their 25th year performing together in 1993. Murrell notes, "At this point in time, we're very fortunate to be able to still perform because so many groups that started are not around anymore, which is sad because there were a lot of good groups, a lot of good music. As the work comes in we do it. On the average we work about eight months out of the year. After being together for 25 years, we're very fortunate to be able to do what we do.

"We'll keep it up as long as it lasts. You still see the light at the end of the tunnel, and as long as you see that light you keep striving for it. With the grace of God, as things keep working for you, you keep doing it."

The Temprees

A male trio from Memphis, the Temprees were a captivating falsetto-lead love ballad group of the early 1970s, known for their innovative interpretations of earlier songs. Although the group was unable to maintain a consistent presence on the charts, they were able to gain quite a following of fans attracted to their rich sound and live performances.

The Temprees formed in junior high school in the mid-1960s in their native Memphis, Tennessee. The trio consisted of Jasper "Jabbo" Phillips, Harold "Scotty" Scott, and Deljuan Calvin. The group initially began drawing attention by performing in their hometown. As their reputation grew, a close association with Booker T. and the MG's drummer Al Jackson brought them to the attention of Stax producers Josephine Bridges and Tom Nixon. After hearing the Temprees perform at a Memphis club called the Showcase, Bridges and Nixon signed the trio to their Stax-distributed We Produce label.

Jasper Phillips remembers, "All of us grew up together. We were just kicking around the neighborhood, going to each other's houses and we just started singing together in junior high school. We got to be pretty good in the city, doing a lot of club things. We grew up around Al Jackson from Booker T. and the MG's and a couple of the Mad Lads. Through them, Jo Bridges and Tom Nixon of Stax Records came out one night and checked us out, and from then it was on. They signed us to We Produce, which was Josephine and Tom Nixon's label and a subsidiary of Stax. They were trying to get their own production."

The Temprees made their recording debut in 1970 at a time when there was a heavy influx of falsetto-dominated love ballad vocal groups. However, their first songs to generate any noise were the up-tempo "My Baby Love" and "Explain It to Her Mama"; the latter cracked the R&B charts in the spring of 1972. For their fifth release, the Temprees covered the Shirelles' 1961 hit, "Dedicated to the One I Love." Producers Bridges and Nixon added a heavy orchestration and slowed down the arrangement to give the song a haunting flavor. With Phillips and Scott continuously interjecting "ooh baby" throughout Calvin's lead performance, "Dedicated" became the Temprees' biggest hit, peaking at number 16 in the fall of 1972.

"[The cover version] was the idea of Deljuan Calvin and Tom Nixon," says Phillips. "We just wanted to reach back and get something and do something our own way with it. We had a strange way of doing a lot of things. We really got into slow ballads. It was just the Temprees' way. We would do a lot of other people's stuff like the Delfonics, a lot of other groups, but it was a certain type of technique we put on it."

"Dedicated to the One I Love," "Explain It to Her Mama," "My Baby Love," and the ballad "I'm for You, You for Me" were included on the group's highly acclaimed debut album, *Lovemen.*

The Temprees received a boost that year when they were among the Stax artists selected to go to the L. A. Coliseum to perform and subsequently be filmed for the movie *Wattstax.* "That was amazing," says Phillips. "It just made you feel good to see all of those people and all of the acts and everybody enjoying themselves. Everybody got along well."

The Temprees were in a unique situation of remaining popular despite a less than glorious presence on the recording charts. This can be partially attributed to location. Philadelphia was the hotbed of falsetto-lead ballad groups of that period, led by the Delfonics, and later the Stylistics and Blue Magic. Residing in Memphis, the Temprees suffered from the inability of Stax/We Produce to market their sound, and the group got lost in the shuffle of several of the label's top acts who were able to capitalize on the Memphis sound. The exposure the performance in *Wattstax* brought the Temprees was an added benefit, by exposing them to an audience unfamiliar with their recordings. Phillips notes, "We did a lot of live stuff. When we performed in a certain area, we always went back because, live, we came off pretty good. We got into the audience and did our own thing. We made friends, got in good with the jocks, and everything was nice."

On the Temprees' second album, *Love Maze*, in 1973, William "Norvell" Johnson replaced Calvin on some of the cuts. The album's finest track was the title song, a ballad written by Harold Scott. Other highlights included a cover of the Carpenters' "Let Me Be the One" and a speeded-up version of the standard "At Last." When the Temprees recorded their third album, *Temprees 3*, Stax was mired in financial difficulty that would eventually lead to the label's collapse. As a result, the Temprees' third effort received little promotion. Although the group was still ballad-oriented, the standouts from the album included a remake of Redbone's 1974 hit "Come and Get Your Love," and "I Love, I Love," a beautiful mid-tempo track co-written by Phillips and Scott.

Adding to the group's drop in popularity was the shift in the preference of music lovers to disco music. The Temprees parted company with We Produce and released two disco-oriented songs on the Epic label but met with limited success. Only one of the releases, "I Found Love on a Disco Floor," managed to reach the charts.

"We really had a thing for ballads," says Phillips. " 'I Love, I Love' was just a case where we had just started to get into that up-tempo thing because we were trying to reach all aspects, but the ballads were really our first love."

He further adds, "Disco hurt us. We were prone to ballads, slow things. Our up-tempo stuff was . . . mediocre. It just never did take off, to me it didn't. Disco kinda tore a hole in the thing that we were doing. We tried a couple of disco tunes and it really didn't take off well. The material wasn't right for us. We didn't get the chance to stretch out into anything because the time was so short."

The group finally called it quits in 1976. Phillips formed an act called Kilo, but with little impact. He later worked with Al Green and producer J. Blackfoot. "We broke up around '75 or '76," says Phillips. "That was right after the Epic thing. We just decided to give it up. We were having management problems; that was the biggest thing that made us get out of it. We just really fell out with that. Everybody just figured it was time to let go. If something else came behind it we would've jumped on it but after the years passed, nothing happened. I got into a project with some other guys called Kilo. We did that through Fantasy Records with David Porter. Then I started working with J. Blackfoot and Al Green in the '80s. The other guys went into other little things. Some of the guys started working jobs. We still keep in contact and we're hoping to do other things."

The original Temprees remain close despite Scott living in Washington, D.C. while Phillips and Calvin reside in Memphis. The members are writing songs and are looking for an opportunity to record again. Due to health problems, Jasper Phillips is unable to perform regularly. "Deljuan [Calvin] and I stay very close," he says. "We have a catalog that we're still stacking up and we're hoping to put it out. I haven't been doing anything for the last four years because I'm a kidney patient so that's what has really slowed me down. I have dialysis three times a week. I still do a little work in the city and I still go out every now and then with Al [Green]. We're still staying in contact with each other. Hopefully we can get something to happen. Everybody's still ready to go back to work. We're working on it but it takes some time to put it together but as soon as we can, it'll be on."

The Three Degrees

A female trio from Philadelphia, the Three Degrees achieved popularity in the early 1970s with their soothing, sweet-soul sound, and a high-polished, professional stage routine that allowed them to perform in such prestigious places as New York's Copacabana and Caesar's Palace in Las Vegas. Primarily a cabaret act, the trio's versatility allowed them to appeal to the soul audience with hits such as "I Didn't Know" and their revival of the Chantels' "Maybe." Although the Three Degrees attained success in America, the trio, best known for their international smash hit "When Will I See You Again," achieved their greatest superstardom in Europe and Japan.

The Three Degrees started in Philadelphia in the early 1960s. The original members were Linda Turner, Shirley Porter, and Fayette Pinkney. Beginning their career performing at local engagements in the Philadelphia area, the group soon came to the attention of writer-producer Richard Barrett. Barrett had previously managed Frankie Lymon and the Teenagers and the Chantels, producing a string of hits for both groups, including the Chantels' 1958 smash hit "Maybe." By 1965, Barrett was working in the A&R department at Swan Records; he arranged for the Three Degrees to be signed to the label. His first production for the trio was "Gee Baby (I'm Sorry)," which became a local hit. When Swan collapsed in 1966, Barrett took over the group's management and produced several more songs for them, including "Look in My Eyes," originally written for the Chantels. During this time there were several more personnel changes in the group, including the addition of Helen

Scott and former Chantel Sandra Goring. However, by 1967 the lineup was set. Pinkney remained, and added to the group were Sheila Ferguson, a solo singer who cut records for various independent labels like Landa, Jamie, and Swan; and Boston native Valerie Holiday.

Valerie recalls, "I met Richard Barrett through a friend of mine, Frank Hatchett. At the time he had three other ladies. We talked for awhile and discovered that we had quite a bit in common. When the opportunity came, I joined. I had a solo career going at the time but I wasn't interested in traveling alone. I was looking to move further along in the entertainment field and I saw this as an opportunity to advance."

When Swan folded, the Three Degrees moved to Warner Brothers, and later to Metromedia. After a record with Neptune, a label owned by Kenny Gamble and Leon Huff, the group was signed to Roulette Records. The trio had their first big hit in 1970 with a remake of the Chantels' "Maybe." For the cover version, the Three Degrees added a rap at the beginning of the song, spoken over an eerie, almost bluesy melody. Singing with a deep-rooted passion and intensity, the trio added an adult flavor to what was originally a teenage anthem.

Valerie explains, "All of us, along with Richard, came up with the rap. We were with Roulette at the time and we needed to find a way to make the song different from the original version. We came up with the rap because there were no female groups at that time doing anything of that nature. We were trying to build our image so we needed something like that. We did [the rap] in one take."

The novelty worked as "Maybe" peaked at number four on the R&B charts in the summer of 1970 and became a top 30 pop hit. "I think it was the rap that made 'Maybe' a hit," says Valerie. "We were already working throughout the eastern coast but [the success of] 'Maybe' gave us a lot of recognition. It was a real lift. After 'Maybe' we were able to work larger clubs at the time, like the Club Harlem, so it lifted us up a notch."

Being able to perform "Maybe," particularly the rap, on stage enhanced the group's already polished nightclub act. Valerie points out, "Our performance was our strong point. At the time we weren't really into recording; we hadn't reached the teen market yet. Performing was what we knew best, so we concentrated on developing a complete show where we could tell jokes and really entertain the audience."

After "Maybe" the Three Degrees followed with "I Do Take You" in the fall of 1970, their second top 10 R&B hit, and "You're the One" the following year. Their final releases for Roulette, "There's So Much Love All Around Me" and "Tradewinds," met with only moderate success.

A breakthrough for the group came in 1973 when they signed with Gamble and Huff's Philadelphia International label. Having started Philadelphia International Records less than two years before, producers Kenny Gamble and Leon Huff were red-hot, having produced smash hits for the O'Jays, Harold Melvin and the Blue Notes, and Billy Paul.

"Signing with Philadelphia International was a turning point in our career because of their distribution with CBS," notes Valerie. "Also, Gamble and Huff were great songwriters and producers so that was a definite plus. They were very creative and easygoing. All over in Europe, Gamble and Huff were known for quite some time. After we recorded our first album we went to Europe to promote it."

The first release was "Dirty Ol' Man," a song that, because of its title, was originally banned in England. Perhaps because of the controversy, "Dirty Ol' Man" was a gold single in Japan, Holland, and Belgium. "I wasn't surprised that 'Dirty Ol' Man' was banned in England because they have a very religious type of background," says Valerie. "I don't think they understood the concept of what was being said. It turned out to be an advantage by being banned because it caught on in the rest of Europe and became Number One in Holland, so it won out in the end."

Despite "Dirty Ol' Man" being a smash overseas, it had only moderate success in the States. At the same time "Dirty Ol' Man" was released, the Three Degrees were featured at the end of another hit, "TSOP (The Sound of Philadelphia)" by Philadelphia International house band MFSB. This instrumental track, which topped the pop and R&B charts in the spring of 1974, served as the theme song for TV's *Soul Train*.

The next single by the Three Degrees would become their signature song. Released in the fall of 1974, the warm, lilting "When Will I See You Again" became a top five hit on the pop and R&B charts and was certified gold. In Britain the song was also enormously popular, reaching the Number One spot and becoming the country's top-selling record in 1974.

"That was a very exciting time, to put it mildly," says Valerie. "We were so groomed in what to do and what not to do that our heads never became too large. We managed to keep both feet on the ground. When the song became a hit we saw it as an opportunity to make it further in our career, to reach more people and go to more places. We were able to perform in countries that we had only read about in books. ['When Will I See You Again'] was also a big hit in England and that allowed us to perform before royalty, so it was a very exciting time for us."

As popular as the Three Degrees were in America, it was overseas where they enjoyed a long run of chart hits. "When Will I See You Again" was first introduced in the summer of 1973 at the Tokyo Music Festival in Japan and became a big hit in America only after becoming a giant hit in Japan. At one time, the group was responsible for 50 percent of all foreign records sold in Japan. Part of the reason for the lack of equal success in America was the fact that the group was largely inaccessible to the American public.

Valerie explains, "When 'When Will I See You Again' came out we were working concert dates overseas. The demand for us became so big that we were constantly working. Before we would finish one tour, another one had already been booked. We were constantly out of the States so we couldn't fully capitalize on the song being a hit here. Had we been able to perform on TV or in supper clubs, I think our success here would've been equal, but the bookings made it impossible. We did do a couple of things here but as a whole, we just didn't have the time."

The Three Degrees followed their smash hit with "I Didn't Know," which became a top 20 R&B hit in the spring of 1975. Arguably the group's most soulful recording for the Philadelphia International label and most popular song with the younger market, "I Didn't Know" did not realize its fullest potential, particularly coming behind "When Will I See You Again." Valerie points out, "I think it's possible that after the experience with 'When Will I See You Again' and us not being available to work [in America], the record company backed off after that. There was probably the feeling of, 'Why bother to put a big push behind them if we can't get them over here?'"

The group had moderate success in the States with "Take Good Care of Yourself" in 1975 and a remake of the Intruders' "Together," which made them international stars and the queens of the cabaret circuit. Between 1974 and 1979, five of the trio's releases reached the top 10 in England. A change to the Ariola label in 1978 saw the Three Degrees return to soul with "Giving Up, Giving In," but future songs like "Women in Love" and "My Simple Heart" proved the group to be more successful in their easy-listening cabaret style.

While the group's recording career stalled, they continued to play the international cabaret circuit throughout the '80s. In 1976 Fayette Pinkney left and was replaced by Helen Scott, an early member of the group in the '60s. In 1984 Sheila Ferguson left, and after a lengthy search, her spot was taken by Cynthia Garrison.

Valerie Holiday-Christie, who still performs with the Three Degrees, explains, "At the time we were working so much that life began to get dull and unhappy. It was just work, work, work. Fayette wanted a bit more, and that just wasn't possible. She decided to get married and we had to replace her with Helen Scott. This was in '76.

"Sheila had gotten married and had twins. It was difficult for her to be home with the twins while we were constantly on the road. With a group situation, other people's livelihood depends on you, and handling both situations became a difficult thing to do, so she left in '84.

"It took some time to fill that slot. After performing for so long, everything becomes somewhat second nature; you just don't pick it up. To find someone who could sing and dance was not easy. We would bring people in and find someone who could sing but couldn't get the dancing down, or someone who could dance but couldn't sing. Singing is most important because the harmony is the focal point of the Three Degrees. If you can't harmonize, we can't use you.

"We went through about four or five people and we were starting to get discouraged because we were constantly shifting people in and out. Publicly, it made the group look unstable, like we didn't know what we were doing. Fans were beginning to ask, 'Who's here this time?' We continued looking and, through our tour manager, we met Cynthia Garrison in late '89. Talent-wise and personality-wise, she turned out to be the perfect person."

With the personnel firmly intact, the Three Degrees perform on the international cabaret circuit an average of 10 months out of the year. The group recently entered the *Guinness Book of World Records* for being the longest-running female group.

"I like what I do," says Valerie. "Plus the money is attractive, I have to say that. You go with what you feel. Normally we need a two- to three-week break between tours. The most we'll tour is six weeks at a time, and two weeks is the minimum. The body goes through withdrawal. The one absolute day we won't work is December 25. I still enjoy performing. There are things you have to put up with, but it's gotten to a point where it's satisfactory. Being able to perform has been very pleasant."

THE THREE DEGREES.
(Courtesy Showtime Archives [Toronto])

BOBBY WOMACK.
(Courtesy *Blues and Soul* magazine)

BARRY WHITE.
(Courtesy *Blues and Soul* magazine)

Above:
THE SPINNERS.
(L-R) Henry Fambrough,
Bobbie Smith,
Philippe Wynne,
Billy Henderson,
Pervis Jackson
(Courtesy *Blues and
Soul* magazine)

Right:
THE STAPLE SINGERS.
(standing) Cleo,
Yvonne, Mavis
(seated) Roebuck
"Pops" Staples
(Courtesy Fantasy Records)

Opposite page bottom:
THE STYLISTICS.
(L-R) James Dunn,
Herb Murrell, Russell
Thompkins, Jr.,
Airrion Love,
James Smith
(Courtesy *Blues and
Soul* magazine)

Above: THE WHISPERS.
(standing) Walter Scott, Leaveil Degree,
Nicholas Caldwell, Wallace "Scotty" Scott
(seated) Marcus Hutson
(Courtesy *Blues and Soul* magazine)

WAR. (Courtesy *Blues and Soul* magazine)

THE O'JAYS. Eddie Levert, William Powell, Walter Williams
(Courtesy of Showtime Archives [Toronto])

War

With a combination of rock, soul, jazz, Latin, and blues influences, War created an innovative body of music in the 1970s that exceeded all musical definition and racial barriers. With cultural messages an intrinsic part of their songs, particularly "Slippin' into Darkness," "The World Is a Ghetto," and "Why Can't We Be Friends," this Los Angeles-based septet attracted a multiracial international following to become one of the more successful bands of their era.

The roots of War are in the South Central Los Angeles area where four of its members grew up. Harold Brown (drums and percussion) was raised in Long Beach, B.B. Dickerson (bass and vocals) was raised in Harbor City, Lonnie Jordan (keyboards and vocals) grew up in Compton, and Howard Scott (guitar and vocals) was raised in San Pedro.

Howard Scott recalls, "In high school we started our first band, called the Creators, in 1962. I guess when we started we liked to play music. We never thought it would end up here. When I started playing guitar I never thought that a guitar could take you so far and meet so many people just by being in music."

Lonnie Jordan adds, "[At the time] I was 14 years old. Howard lived right around the corner from me in Compton where I made my rounds all the time. I was a young buck at 14. The original piano player, Stan, left at an early stage. I went in there and started playing and it's been history ever since."

As the Creators, the band began to gain a local reputation performing in small clubs in the area, and got a recording agreement with the small Dorey Records label. After a few singles including "Burn, Baby, Burn," "Lovely Feeling," and "That's What Love Will Do," the group temporarily disbanded when Howard Scott was inducted into the army. During this time, the fate of the group was in limbo. However, one by one, they drifted back together.

Scott explains, "When I left, the band had a golden opportunity as the Creators. We built the Creators all the way from high school to the point where we were getting ready to go into some of the highest clubs in Los Angeles. Unfortunately, I had to go off into the cold war and by the time I came back, the band had disbanded and Lonnie was in Santa Barbara. I was kind of brokenhearted because I had high hopes that when I got back out, at least I could fall back on something that was still rolling. But when I got back out it was like, 'Let's start this thing all over again . . . from scratch.'"

Jordan adds, "Half of the band was still playing off and on but by the time [Howard] came out, he, my mother, I think the whole world came and saved me in Santa Barbara because I was to go into boot training for highway patrol. They took me and we went back to L.A. and we put the forces back together again."

In 1968 the group reformed as the Night Shift and added Charles Miller (saxophone and clarinet). Also at this time, Dickerson left and was replaced by Peter Rosen. The following year they added Thomas "Papa Dee" Allen (percussion), a Wilmington, Delaware native who moved to the Los Angeles area and became acquainted with some of the members in the Night Shift. In 1969 the band was performing at the Rag Doll, a San Fernando Valley club, as a backup band for football star Deacon Jones.

Scott remembers, "In '68 when I got out of the service we formed a new group. We said, 'Let's give it one more shot.' Rather than go back to the same name we originally had, we got the Creators together, added Charles Miller and called ourselves the Night Shift. We had a 10-piece band in the Night Shift and we were playing local clubs in L.A. We made it to the high point of that, which was playing behind number 75, Hall of Famer for the Los Angeles Rams, David 'Deacon' Jones."

Meanwhile, Lee Oskar, a harmonica player from Copenhagen, had become friends with former Animals lead singer Eric Burdon ("House of the Rising Sun," "Please Don't Let Me Be Misunderstood") and they decided to form their own group. Rosen invited Burdon, Oskar, and music industry executive Jerry Goldstein to come by and see the Night Shift. Goldstein's past credits included co-writing and co-producing the Angels' 1963 Number One pop hit "My Boyfriend's Back" and "Hang on Sloopy," a 1965 Number One pop hit for the McCoys. After the show Oskar got on stage and jammed with the group and everyone involved agreed to use the Night Shift as the nucleus for Burdon's new group.

"Eric Burdon came down to hear us play," recounts Scott. "Lee Oskar and Jerry Goldstein were with him. Eric Burdon needed a band. We were working. He and Lee Oskar were out of work. They were pounding the pavement on Sunset Boulevard asking for spare change. The Night Shift was probably making $20 to $30 a night, which was a lot of money in those days. We got together with Eric and Lee, let three of our horn players go, and kept Charles Miller with Lee Oskar."

Everyone involved also agreed that the name Night Shift had become outdated and needed to be changed. Scott explains the origin of the name War. "Shortly after our meeting we knew there was no way we could go on as Eric Burdon and the Night Shift. It took two days to come up with a name. We had Eric Burdon and . . . and . . . and . . . and. The first name they came up with was Velvet Oven. We knew Velvet Oven would only last three to four years and then it would be over. This was during the Vietnam conflict and a lot of people were going off to the war and coming back in body bags. The main thing in that whole situation with the nation was 'power of peace.' The most unpopular phrase you could say at that time was 'war.' The word 'war' drew attention to us because we were playing music and we had a war within ourselves with the music."

Burdon's association with the band was one in which he initially wanted just to blend in. However, because of his previous success, this was virtually impossible. "When Eric saw us he knew he wanted to be in the band," says Jordan. "He knew that was it beyond a shadow of a doubt. Plus Eric wanted to be in the band as a trombone player. He didn't want it to be Eric Burdon and War. He just wanted it to be War and he become a part of the band. It couldn't work out that way because all of his fans knew who he was. It ended up being Eric Burdon and War anyway even though he tried to hide behind us."

Scott adds, "The talent in Night Shift coming into War was so respected by Eric. He had never been in a band like this before. He grew up on black music. This was his first black band and he respected that a lot, so he was kind of apprehensive to come right out and say, 'I'm Eric Burdon, the big pop star.'"

After a year of touring, the band recorded *Eric Burdon Declares War,* released on MGM in 1970. Taken from it was "Spill the Wine," which would reach number three on the pop charts and become a gold single. The album also contained musical tributes to jazz reed player Roland Kirk ("The Vision of Rassan") and Memphis Slim ("Blues for Memphis Slim"). By this time, Dickerson was back in the group, replacing Rosen, who died of a drug overdose.

Burdon and War continued to tour extensively throughout the U.S. and Europe and released their second MGM album, *The Black Man's Burdon,* in 1971. During a European tour, an exhausted Burdon dropped out and returned to Los Angeles, leaving War to finish the tour dates on their own. At the end of the tour, Burdon and War decided to go their separate ways. Through the efforts of their manager Steve Gold, War signed a recording contract with United Artists Records in 1971.

Their first album without Burdon was simply entitled *War* and contained the gospel-infused "Lonely Feeling," which reached number 38 on the R&B charts in the spring of 1971. Other notable songs included "Sun Oh Sun" and "Fidel's Fantasy," a dark look at Castro's Cuba. Although the *War* album did not fare well commercially, it did showcase the band's promise for the future.

For the follow-up album, *All Day Music,* War created a balance of achieving commercial success while still maintaining their Latin and R&B sound. The album's first single, the easy-listening title track with its steady Latin-infused beat, made the R&B top 20 in the fall of 1971. The next single, "Slipping into Darkness," released early in 1972, was the first of War's message songs, which would become their trademark throughout the decade. Scott says, " 'Slipping into Darkness' is a song about people losing themselves. You can lose yourself to drugs, you can lose yourself to a woman . . . anything. But when you lose yourself there's still hope somewhere."

With the combination of its lyrical content and funky, infectious, bass-laden beat, "Slipping into Darkness" became the group's first simultaneous top 20 pop and R&B hit and first "solo" gold record. Further enhanced by the haunting ballad "That's What Love Will Do" and the funky "Get Down," the *All Day Music* album achieved platinum status and sold nearly two million copies.

War's next album, *The World Is a Ghetto*, would become their masterpiece and establish the group as international superstars. The album's thought-provoking title track reached number three on the R&B charts and number seven on the pop charts early in 1973. Scott points out, "We came up in the streets of Los Angeles and we had the opportunity to see a lot and we wrote about what we saw. Papa Dee Allen was the oldest member of the group. He was more of a philosopher and was very well aware. When we look at a thing like 'The World Is a Ghetto,' the situation in '73 is still the same in '93. The world is still a ghetto, it's still the same thing; it's still polluted. Nothing has changed."

The album's next single, "The Cisco Kid," was equally successful (number two pop, number five R&B in the spring of 1973) and more important, gave War a strong Latino following. Jordan says, "I grew up in Southern California and the bottom line was that there was nothing but Latinos and brothers."

Scott adds, "When I was growing up in California, you'd turn on the TV and most of the people on TV were Anglos like Hopalong Cassidy and John Wayne, and then you would see these two Hispanic guys, Cisco and Pancho. In my eyes, as a kid, I could relate more to them being Western heroes, so I wrote about the Cisco Kid rather than Roy Rogers."

Other outstanding tracks from the album included "City, Country, City," a 13-minute instrumental blend of easy listening and funk, and the haunting "Four Cornered Room." " 'Four Cornered Room' is a song about somebody sitting back and thinking," explains Scott, "just taking time to think about something and just thinking within yourself. At one point 'Four Cornered Room' was the number one song in the L.A. County Jail."

Both "The Cisco Kid" and "The World Is a Ghetto" were certified gold. The latter record went on to top the pop charts for two weeks and become the best-selling album in 1973, with sales of over three million copies. Sitting atop the music world put War in an enviable position of trying to come up with an appropriate encore.

Scott remembers, "The beginning was like this big nursery rhyme story . . . with Eric Burdon and flying around the world to exotic places and making tons of money. I personally enjoyed it. When our first hits started coming down, we were on a roll and everybody was making money at the time. Anytime you can ride around L.A. in a '71 Mercedes, carefree, listening to your songs on the radio and the money's coming in, you think there's no end to this. This is the world. You're enjoying the world as it is.

"It was great in the beginning to feel like that but as in all stories, reality sets in. Once you get into a groove and you put out an album that sells a million copies, and then you put out another one which outsells that, you come to the point of saying, 'What do you do after that?' Now you come to the reality of 'How do you top your last album?' The thing about it is, what if you don't top it? Is your career over?"

War's encore performance was the *Deliver the Word* album, released in the fall of 1973. Spurred by "Gypsy Man," a top 10 pop and R&B hit, and "Me and Baby Brother," *Deliver the Word* scored gold and sold over a million and a half copies.

In addition to the group's paramount success as a recording act, War was also becoming a hot concert attraction. This was captured in *War Live,* recorded during a four-night engagement at Chicago's High Chaparral Club in 1974. In addition to the War standards, a previously unrecorded instrumental, "Ballero," was included on the live set. Like its predecessors, the *War Live* album sold more than a million and a half copies.

The year 1975 saw War release *Why Can't We Be Friends*, the band's fifth straight gold album. The good-natured, reggae-flavored title track was the album's first single and sold over a million copies while reaching the top 10 on both the pop and R&B charts in the spring of 1975. The Latin funk track "Low Rider" was equally successful as a follow-up later that fall, topping the R&B charts for a week. Featuring other outstanding tracks, such as "Leroy's Latin Lament" and the ballad "So," *Why Can't We Be Friends* sold over two million copies.

After the release of the easy-flowing "Summer" in 1976, War left United Artists over a conflict regarding direction and marketing of the band's music. "We had gotten too big at United Artists," says Scott. "[The only other artists] they had were Bobby Womack and Ike and Tina Turner. What I think United Artists did after we started rolling so big was that they started putting together groups to stop us, to halt that. It gave a lot of people a chance to make some money, like the Brass Construction. They signed them up and said, 'War's getting too big, let's bring out Brass Construction. War's still too big, let's get another group.' Bam! Here comes Mandrill. They put Mandrill in there. We had gotten so big at United Artists that it actually got out of hand."

The agreement between War and the record company was for the band to move elsewhere but to deliver a final album to United Artists to be released on its subsidiary Blue Note jazz label. The result was *Platinum Jazz*, released in 1977. Featuring the hit single "L.A. Sunshine," the album became the first certified gold seller in the label's history.

War signed with MCA and moved into the disco medium with the release of "Galaxy" late in 1977. Despite the success of the single (the band's final top 10 R&B and top 40 pop hit), the move into the disco territory was one that War was not comfortable with. Scott recalls, "When War went through the fatalistic disco era, people said, 'What's wrong with you guys? War is supposed to be giving a message. Everybody's waiting for War to say a message. You guys are supposed to be making social statements, not songs like 'Shake Your Booty' and the whole disco thing. What's up with that?' That got me thinking about the message of War. We got all caught up in the mix of disco and I personally was unhappy about it."

The late '70s brought personnel changes within the group. B.B. Dickerson left in 1978 for a solo career and was replaced on bass by Luther Rabb, formerly with the R&B group Aalon. Ron Hammon (also from Aalon) joined as War's second drummer and Pat Rizzo joined in 1979 to replace Charles Miller. Miller was stabbed to death the following year. While the disco-flavored "Good, Good Feelin'" became a minor hit in the spring of 1979, several members of the band began to venture into solo projects. Lee Oskar released his self-titled solo debut album on United Artists in 1976, followed by *Before the Rain* (1978) and *My Road Our Road* (1981) on Elektra. Lonnie Jordan also released solo efforts, *Different Moods of Me* (MCA, 1978) and *The Affair* (Boardwalk, 1982).

War signed with RCA in 1982 and received a boost with the release of the *Outlaw* album. Both "You Got the Power" and the title track became top 20 R&B hits. However, despite this revival, War was still uncomfortable with the disco sound.

"Again we were just playing music," says Jordan. "We weren't trying to really do a disco thing, but then Luther [Rabb], our bass player, was trying to do the disco thing. That's why we don't have a bass player anymore. Luther was older than all of us and he thought that we should go along with what's going on today which, at that time, was still disco. What we did was say, 'Well, let's just go in the studio and play.' Luther started playing this bass line and it ended up being a disco groove. So, we said, 'Well, let's put some lyrics to it and see how it comes out.' Then the media and the record company started liking it. They said, 'Oh, that's good. You're keeping up with today's things.' To me it wasn't us and to this very day it still isn't us."

Scott adds, "War has always been innovators. We have always

set the pathway instead of following the pathway. During the disco thing we kinda did follow along with the disco beat. We finally said, 'Well, this is what everybody else is doing so let's do this.' *Outlaw* was the only album we did for RCA. That was a very short relationship."

War remained relatively quiet for the remainder of the decade although they did continue to perform live. Brown left War in 1984 and the band decided to go with Hammon as the solo drummer. During a 1988 club date at California's Talk of the Town, percussionist "Papa Dee" Allen suffered a fatal heart attack while performing "Gypsy Man."

A continuing trend of the band's music being sampled by rap artists led to a sudden rise of interest in the past classics of War. This culminated in the 1992 release of *Rap Declares War*, a collection of the best of these samples. Two years later War had a minor hit on Avenue Records with "Peace Sign."

"[The sudden interest] has been going on for awhile," notes Jordan. "We never stopped playing. We were performing for awhile, we just didn't make any records. It's been almost like a world cult or following. We're one of the most sampled groups around. It just seems to be getting bigger."

Scott adds, "The reason there's so much interest in War right now is because after 12 years, the entire War catalog is back out. They had to make sure there was a demand for it. There was a demand for it because it wasn't there. The European people and people all over the world were asking, 'Where's War?' We were traveling around low-key, keeping our band together and making some money. We were just keeping it together until the point when we could reintroduce the whole catalog and come with our new campaign. We thought it would only take two years but it actually took us 10 years to get that together. It took a lot more planning but we were finally able to do that."

The Whispers

L ed by the sound-alike tenors of twins Walter and Wallace "Scotty" Scott, the Whispers have been turning out quality soul music for more than 30 years. Recording for a series of small Los Angeles-based labels in the 1960s and mid-1970s, the Whispers persevered for 14 years before topping the charts in 1980 with "And the Beat Goes On." That song laid the foundation for this quintet to become virtually the only R&B stand-up vocal group to achieve consistent success through both the disco and rap eras.

Identical twins Walter and Wallace "Scotty" Scott were born in Fort Worth, Texas and moved to Los Angeles at an early age. They made their performing debut at age five as the Scott Twins, singing "Me and My Shadow." At a talent contest at Jordan High School the Scotts met the Eden Trio: Nicholas Caldwell, Gordy Harmon, and Marcus Hutson. While waiting to go on, the five teens began harmonizing together and after the talent show decided to form a group.

In 1964, through Harmon, the group came to the attention of Lou Bedell, owner of Dore Records. He liked their soft sound and named them the Whispers. Nicholas Caldwell remembers, "Gordy Harmon was singing with a group called the Superbs, that, at that time, was already signed to Dore Records. When he heard Scotty, myself, and Walter sing, he fell in love with it. So he told Lou Bedell, 'You gotta hear these guys.' He brought us in and we sang for him and Lou Bedell went crazy. Gordy quit the Superbs and joined this group with this soft sound. The Whispers' name actually came from Lou Bedell.

We were trying to find a name at that time and he said, 'You guys sing like a whisper,' and it was like, 'That's it!' "

The Whispers recorded five singles on Dore: "It Only Hurts for a Little While," "Never Again," "The Dip," "As I Sit Here," and "Doctor Love." Although none of these singles charted nationally, they sold well in southern California.

In 1968, Walter Scott attended a Curtis Mayfield concert and met nightclub owner and concert promoter Dick Griffey, who said he could make the Whispers the biggest group in the business if given the chance to manage them. Walter recalls, "I happened to be out one night with my wife. We were seeing a Curtis Mayfield concert and after the concert we were on our way out and this big guy [Griffey] comes toward me. I thought he was a football player; big, big guy, six feet, big wide shoulders, and he said, 'Your group, whether you know it or not, is probably the best vocal group that's out here of all time, but only if I manage y'all.' For years we had heard this before and I just laughed.

"For almost three months Dick Griffey would call me religiously and we would have two-hour conversations on the phone and this was before I took it back to the others. He basically said things to me that we had no idea took place. He told me about royalties, publishing, what your worth is, how much money you generated. We never heard this before. We were always curious and of course we wanted to know, but, being younger, we were more interested in being famous. Dick would say to me, 'Famous ain't where it's at, staying power is where it's at.' So finally I told the guys about Dick and they met him and he told them basically the same thing, 'It's going to take three to five years but I think I can make you the biggest group in the country.' This man exuded confidence. You might call it arrogance because if you don't know Dick he comes off like that, but he just believes what he says. Right away we weren't committed because, like me, the others heard the same thing before, but we finally agreed to let Dick come in and manage us along with another guy who was already managing us.

"What really impressed us about that was that I really didn't know how long it took [to be successful] but I never heard anybody put a time limit on it. He came across knowing what he was really talking about and he revealed to us things that, right today, if an artist asks a record company about they either get a 'No comment,' or they'll move on to another subject because they don't want you to really know what your true worth is. So for a guy to tell us this just to open our eyes, we were very impressed and went on to form a relationship that lasted close to 20 years."

Wallace adds, "I have to give Dick credit from an administrative standpoint. Thank God he was able to get us away from the glitter part. You are impressed by the glitter, the limos . . . everything you shouldn't be impressed by and, luckily for us, someone came along. We always knew right from wrong and we had basic common sense but, like everybody else, we were from humble beginnings. We were raised in the projects like a lot of acts and we had no idea about the administrative end. Dick Griffey sat us down and told us where it's at."

The Whispers began recording for the local Soul Clock label in 1969 and scored regionally with the ballad "Great Day." The summer release of the follow-up, "Time Will Come," written by Caldwell and Harmon, gave them their first chart appearance at number 17. Their fourth single for Soul Clock, the melancholy "Seems Like I Gotta Do Wrong," broke them into the R&B top 10 the following year, peaking at number six.

By 1970, the Whispers had signed with the Chess-distributed Janus label. At Janus the Whispers suffered from the limited resources of a small label unable to properly promote their music outside of California. Over the next four years eight of the group's 12 singles charted. Some of their more impressive releases were the ballads "There's a Love for Everyone," "Your Love Is So Doggone Good," and "I Only Meant to Wet My Feet." Although none of these singles were smash hits, they did help the group build a loyal following. Griffey, who handled the biggest concerts of any black promoter in Los Angeles, often featured the Whispers as the opening act on his shows.

"We have some very loyal fans," says Caldwell. "Early on we did a lot of touring across the country with no hit records. We have an awful lot of fans. I think we have the most loyal fans in the world. There was a time when the records weren't coming as constantly as we would have liked them to, and we still were able to survive. With our strong suit being ballads, there's always time for love."

In 1973 Leaveil Degree, who for a time sang with the Friends of Distinction, replaced Harmon after the latter ruptured his larynx in a car accident. Two years later Griffey and television's *Soul Train* host Don Cornelius formed Soul Train Records and added the Whispers to the roster. At the time of the move to their manager's new label, disco was a dominant force in the music industry and many of the stand-up vocal groups fell by the wayside. It appeared as if the Whispers' career might be over before fulfilling Griffey's aspirations for them to be the number one group in the country. However, the formation of Soul Train Records proved to be the beginning of the turning point in the group's career. The Whispers jumped aboard the disco bandwagon in 1976 and returned to the top 10 with the Norman Harris-produced "One for the Money." After the beautiful ballad "Living Together (In Sin)" became a moderate hit later in 1976, the Whispers enjoyed their second top 10 record on the Soul Train label with an up-tempo and sophisticated cover of Bread's 1970 Number One pop hit "Make It with You" in the summer of 1977. However, the collaboration between Cornelius and Griffey was short-lived as Cornelius continued to concentrate on television. When Soul Train Records was dissolved in 1978, Griffey took the Whispers, Shalamar, and Carrie Lucas and formed Solar (Sounds of Los Angeles Records) Records.

"Soul Train was really a new experience for Dick," explains Caldwell. "He and Don Cornelius co-owned that. But I think he really learned a lot about the skill and the transition, and then when it became Solar he was able to implement, unhampered, his thoughts."

Walter Scott adds, "When Soul Train took off it was basically a deal between Don Cornelius and Dick Griffey. Don Cornelius had his television industry which was most important to him, and rightfully so. Dick Griffey's priority was records, so that really wasn't a good combination. When they decided to break that off and it became Solar Records, it was a full-fledged record company. Dick wasn't like most record company owners; he got involved. He would stay up all night at a recording session and when he wanted to hear somebody, he got on the plane himself, much like an early Berry Gordy, whom he patterned himself after. He really could tell you what a good song was. That's what made Solar what it was and it's a shame that it couldn't keep up."

The Whispers got off to a good start on Solar, reaching the top 10 in the spring of 1978 with the rhythmic "(Let's Go) All the Way," which showcased the quintet's tight harmony. The group nearly reached the same level with their next single, "(Olivia) Lost and Turned Out," a popular ballad which would remain a fan favorite for years to come despite the song being about prostitution. Although the Whispers did have occasional top 10 success, album sales were faltering due to disco still being in its heyday and the group sticking to its almost outdated ballad formula.

"That was very disheartening when disco came in because it put a lot of groups who were in good standing and powerful out of business," says Wallace. "People were going into garages and creating these tracks and the next thing I knew . . . Gloria Gaynor, Donna Summer, Chic. It just put you . . . all of a sudden you find yourself out of the mainstream. A lot of groups really didn't know how to deal with that, so they were out of the business. We, like everybody else, survived it because we stuck to our guns. We always believed that we could continue. In 1978, '79 we got caught in the middle. We didn't know what disco was. We were in the middle of doing an LP and we finished it and it really didn't have any disco on it and nothing happened. That was scary. You have an album that sells *nothing*, you won't be around too long."

Things began to change for the better later in 1979 beginning with "A Song for Donny," dedicated to soul great Donny Hathaway, who had recently died. The song was actually a cover of

Hathaway's perennial holiday favorite "This Christmas," with new lyrics added by fellow Solar recording artist and Griffey's wife Carrie Lucas. Part of the single's proceeds went to the Donny Hathaway Scholarship Fund. "From a vocal standpoint he probably was one of the greatest R&B vocalists and musicians that ever lived," says Walter. "When [his death] happened [Solar] wanted to find a way to keep Donny Hathaway alive, so we decided to create the Donny Hathaway Scholarship Fund. That was our way of letting people know how these types of artists should be remembered. I really wish the younger people today had more of a memory and a respect for these people because they are the backbone of what we do, and that was the intent. He meant a lot to us."

The Whispers ended the decade with their biggest hit ever, the disco-flavored "And the Beat Goes On." Produced by the Whispers with Griffey and Leon Sylvers III, "And the Beat Goes On" topped the R&B charts for five weeks in the spring of 1980, broke into the pop top 20, and was a million-seller. "Our greatest feeling was the night we had the playback of 'And the Beat Goes On,'" says Degree. "It was almost like we had been working as longshoremen for a month. When we heard the end result in its entirety, completed, we *knew*. 'And the Beat Goes On'. . . when we finished it, if you couldn't hear that, then something was wrong. It was no doubt in our minds, and that's the way most hits are."

"Ain't nothing like that first hit," adds Wallace. "We were on stage and all of a sudden the lights went off, the band stopped playing and we were wondering what was going on. And we looked around and a representative from RCA walked out with five gold albums, our first. That meant everything. We had come close time and time again. It happened so fast we thought it was a joke but it was true. We thought it was for another Whispers. It was the greatest feeling in the world. That was after about 14 years and *finally* we had a hit record."

The Whispers were in the right place at the right time, being on the Solar label and working with Leon Sylvers. Formerly a member of the Sylvers, his teen-sensation family group, Leon began working with Solar in 1978. At the start of the 1980s he was one of the hottest producers in black music, fresh off of co-writing and producing Shalamar's Number One gold single "The Second Time Around," which reached the R&B summit two weeks before "And the Beat Goes On" topped the charts. Solar Records was in the process of becoming a force in black music during the early part of the decade. Virtually every artist on the roster enjoyed success: Shalamar, Lakeside ("Fantastic Voyage," "I Wanna Hold Your Hand"), Carrie Lucas ("Dance with You," "Career Girl"), and Sylvers' own group Dynasty ("I've Just Begun to Love You," "Here I Am"). Despite being a veteran stand-up vocal group, the Whispers, due to the enormous success of "And the Beat Goes On" and their association with the Solar label, were able to dispel any temptation on the part of observers to label them as has-beens. With "And the Beat Goes On" as their foundation and with Leon Sylvers continuing to be their creative force, the Whispers enjoyed enormous success in the 1980s, unequaled by any of their vocal group contemporaries.

As a follow-up to "And the Beat Goes On," the Whispers returned to their more familiar ballad turf with the release of the Caldwell-penned "Lady," which peaked at number three on the R&B charts later that summer. Led by the success of these two singles, their self-titled album topped the R&B charts, crossed over to the pop top 10, and achieved double-platinum status.

With the Whispers finally atop the music industry, they still suffered from the relatively limited resources associated with the independent status of Solar Records. Walter Scott explains, "Solar was a small company with a limited ability to do a promotion thing. That's why had we been with CBS or Warner Brothers it would've been on the charts much sooner. Then again, that tells you about the charts. We weren't expected to do well. The expectation of the Whispers in 1979 wasn't that great. We just had a hit that cut through all of that. The album went double platinum. We didn't know that it had a life left for almost another six months. We never had a tune that debuted in December and in February it was gold. That's why we thought it was a Whispers from Europe or somewhere else because it never happened to us.

"But being at a small company . . . we had the biggest song in 1980 and we weren't nominated for a Grammy. You have the biggest hit . . . *bona fide* and we didn't get nominated for a Grammy, American Music Award, nothing. That tells me that some of the things that are supposed to go on to perpetuate [the nomination], do not."

The Whispers had three successful singles in 1981, led by "It's a Love Thing" which spent three weeks at the number two spot on the R&B charts. Later in the year Solar moved its distribution from RCA to Elektra/Asylum. The first Whispers album handled by Elektra/Asylum was the gold *Love Is Where You Find It*. It gave the group two more uncharacteristic up-tempo hits in 1982 with "In the Raw" and "Emergency." The following year the group had back-to-back top 10 hits with "Tonight" and "Keep on Lovin' Me."

Beginning in 1984, production of the group's music was shifted to Reggie Calloway, the creative force behind Midnight Star, who was signed to the Solar label. Calloway kept the Whispers in the top 10 with the funky "Contagious." The Calloway-produced follow-up, "Some Kinda Lover," was co-written by Kenny "Babyface" Edmonds, a member of the Cincinnati group the Deele, who, through Midnight Star, was signed to Solar. The Whispers recognized the potential of the novice Edmonds and his writing and producing partner Antonio "L.A." Reid, and allowed them to write and produce a song for the group's next album. The result was the 1987 release of "Rock Steady," the Whispers' biggest hit since "And the Beat Goes On," topping the R&B charts for a week and entering the pop top 10 for the first time in their career.

"We met Babyface through Reggie Calloway of Midnight Star," says Walter Scott. "The Deele were signed to Solar through them, and Babyface and L.A. were just trying to get their songs exposed. We had a song written by Kenny that Reggie was producing, called 'Don't Keep Me Waiting.' How we really saw the talent with Kenny was that we heard Reggie's production, which was good, then we heard Kenny's production and it was clear from what you heard from Kenny that he was incredible. He was just as bad then as he is now. He just hadn't been exposed to the world."

Wallace adds, "Kenny, because he was so good at doing the kind of music that we do well, the other people weren't accepting that. Early on, the Deele were sort of into that Prince or the Time funk sound. That's what they wanted to do; everybody except Kenny. Kenny wanted to do good R&B and we recognized that, but the group didn't want to go that direction. Afterwards, the Deele saw what our songs did and they started to soften their sound with 'Two Occasions,' which was on their first gold album."

"Rock Steady" was one of two songs produced by L.A. and Babyface for the Whispers' *Just Gets Better with Time* album, the other being the sensuous ballad "In the Mood," which made the R&B top 20 in the fall of 1987. Further enhanced by the title track, "No Pain, No Gain," and "Give It to Me," a beautiful ballad written and produced by Caldwell, *Just Gets Better with Time* achieved double platinum status and was perhaps the group's finest album.

Following a split with the Solar label, the Whispers reemerged on Capitol Records in 1990 with *More of the Night*, which gave them three top 10 R&B hits: "Innocent," "My Heart Your Heart," and "Is It Good to You." While the group remained a unit, the Scott twins cut a duet album, *My Brother's Keeper*, in 1993 and had a sizable hit with a remake of the Intruders' "I Wanna Know Your Name." Currently operating as a quartet consisting of the Scott twins, Caldwell, and Degree, the Whispers still maintain a loyal following and manage to reach gold or near gold status with their album sales. In 1995, the group released their latest album, *Toast to the Ladies*.

"As long as we can do good work and give our audience what they deserve, which is good music, we'll keep it up," says Caldwell. "The key is not to flatter yourself. When it's over you will know it's time to bow out, but with performing, as long as we can perform and do a credible job and keep the standards that we set for ourselves, we'll keep on doing this."

Barry White

A multi-talented writer, producer, and singer, with arguably the most distinctive bass voice in the history of popular music, Barry White was one of soul music's most successful artists in the 1970s. White's hit-making formula consisted of romantic songs delivered with a masculine sensitivity. He became known as "The Maestro of Love," as these songs were usually introduced with a steamy pillow-talk rap, and were backed by a lavish orchestral arrangement of swirling strings and lush keyboards.

White recorded sporadically in the 1960s while he developed his writing and producing skills. His first major triumph occurred in 1972 when he wrote and produced Love Unlimited's "Walking in the Rain with the One I Love." A year later White launched his successful solo career. Soon came a string of hits, including "I'm Gonna Love You Just a Little More Baby," "Never, Never Gonna Give Ya Up," and "Can't Get Enough of Your Love, Babe," which would greatly influence the disco era and later the 1990s soul of Britain's Lisa Stansfield and Soul II Soul. As a solo artist or as a writer and producer for Love Unlimited and his 41-piece ensemble, the Love Unlimited Orchestra, White sold close to 100 million records between 1972 and 1978. After a cool period in the 1980s, the artist made a grand comeback in the 1990s when his 1994 hit album *The Icon Is Love* returned him to his rightful place at the top of the R&B music world.

Barry White was born September 12, 1944 in Galveston, Texas, but his family moved to Los Angeles when he was six months old. His earliest musical influence was his mother, who majored in music in college and had a solid background in classical music. White began playing the piano at the age of five. At age eight, he joined the choir at the local Greater Tabernacle Baptist Church. Two years later, he became the choir's organist and later served as its assistant director. White's early teens were marred by his involvement with local gangs. Running afoul of the law, a 15-year-old White spent four months in juvenile hall for stealing tires off a Cadillac. Upon his release, he resolved to straighten his life out, dedicating it to music. White was soon asked by some friends he knew from junior high school to join a vocal group called the Upfronts. He sang bass on the group's first single, "Little Girl," released in 1960 on the Lummtone label, but it was unsuccessful. Over the next two years, the Upfronts played small clubs around Los Angeles and cut five more songs for Lummtone, but unfortunately they also failed.

White later joined the Atlantics, who recorded a single on Rampart Records in 1962 entitled "Home on the Range"/"Let Me Call You Sweetheart," which went nowhere. He sang backup on four songs with a surf band called the Majestics, and also recorded material as Lee Barry that was never released. Despite all this activity, White's aspirations were to be a writer, producer, and arranger, not a performer. One of his first successes as an arranger was "Harlem Shuffle," a minor hit in 1963 for duo Bob (Rolf) and Earl (Nelson). When Earl Nelson dissolved that partnership to record "The Duck" as Jackie Lee in 1965, White toured with him as his arranger, drummer, and road manager.

In 1966 White joined Bob Keene's Mustang-Bronco company. This move gave him his first legitimate opportunity to woodshed in the studio and learn all the facets of production and engineering, such as how to work the control booth as well as various tricks of mixing and mastering. He emerged as a full-fledged producer and rose to the top of the label's A&R department. In this capacity White produced the Bobby Fuller Four's second album, *Let Her Dance*. He also cut a single by himself entitled "All in the Run of a Day," which sank without a trace. White fared better as a producer for Viola Wills on "Lost Without the Love of My Guy" and for Felice Taylor on

"I'm Under the Influence of Love," both of which did well in England. In 1967, White gave Taylor two more UK hits with "It May Be Winter Outside (But in My Heart It's Spring)" and "I Feel Love Comin' On."

Of greater importance to White during his tenure at Bronco was his collaboration with Gene Page, an arranger known for his lush orchestrations. Their initial contact went back to 1963 when they worked on Bob and Earl's "Harlem Shuffle" together. When White was given his opportunity to record for Bronco, Page was the first person he hired. A Los Angeles native with a classical music background, Page began his career as a studio arranger after having won a scholarship to study at the Brooklyn Conservatory in New York. His first triumph was as a string arranger for the Righteous Brothers' 1965 hit "You've Lost That Loving Feelin'." That same year he arranged hits for Dobie Gray ("The 'In' Crowd") and Solomon Burke ("Got to Get You Off My Mind"). After Page worked with White at Bronco, he later became the artist's right-hand man, collaborating with him on nearly all of his hits in the 1970s.

In 1968, Bronco Records folded. For the rest of the year, White did independent production, working with artists such as Malcolm Hayes on Okeh Records, Larry Marks on BMC, and Brendetta Davis on Liberty. He also wrote and produced for Hanna/Barbera's *Banana Splits* children's television show.

At a 1969 recording session White met a female trio of back-up singers, Diane Taylor and sisters Linda and Glodean James, who would become Love Unlimited. Linda and Glodean were born in Long Beach, California but grew up in San Pedro, where they first sang in their church choir. When they joined their school choir, they became friends with Taylor, a Buffalo, New York native now living in Compton, California. The James sisters and Taylor formed a group in the early 1960s and called themselves the Croonettes. The trio performed at local parties and weddings, but broke up after high school graduation. The Croonettes reformed and met White at this recording session after another singer, Andrea Sprewell, had asked them to do background vocals on an album that White was producing for her. White was immediately attracted to the trio's high-pitched harmonies; he became their manager and mentor and renamed them Love Unlimited. He then started writing and producing for the group, and designed a three-year plan to make them successful.

In 1971, White completed Love Unlimited's first album and got the trio signed to MCA's Uni Records. The head of Uni was Russ Regan, whom White knew from 1966 when the former was with Loma Records, a Warner subsidiary. Love Unlimited's debut single, the romantic ballad "Walkin' in the Rain with the One I Love," featured many of the production elements that would become White's trademarks: the lavish orchestral arrangement, the soaring strings, and the heavy emphasis on keyboards. Led by the trio's superior harmonies, Glodean's breathy spoken vocals, and White's 13-word cameo appearance as the male voice on the telephone, "Walkin' in the Rain" became an instant hit. The single reached number six on the R&B charts in the spring of 1972 and was a top 20 pop hit and a million-seller.

Meanwhile, White wrote "I've Got So Much to Give" and "I'm Gonna Love You Just a Little More Baby," and planned to find a male vocalist to record them. Larry Nunes, White's spiritual advisor and business partner, listened to the demos and persuaded the writer/producer to record the songs himself. White had no interest in singing, but after much prodding from Nunes, he finally conceded. By now he had completed an entire album.

Early in 1973, Russ Regan left Uni to become head of 20th Century Records. Three days later, White got Love Unlimited out of their contract with Uni Records and brought them and himself to 20th Century. However, there were some executives at 20th Century who initially did not like White's album, which contained only five songs, ranging in length from six to over eight minutes each. They thought the album contained too few songs, and that the songs were too long. It took the enthusiasm of Elton John, then pop music's reigning superstar, to convince the label that the album would sell.

The first single from the album (entitled *I've Got So Much to Give*) was an edited version of the seven-minute "I'm Gonna Love You Just a Little More Baby." The song was marked by its sensuous lyrics, its lush instrumental track, and White's deep bass voice, the latter at its most effective on the steamy rap at the introduction and on moans and murmurs sprinkled throughout this hypnotic track. White's deep bass and his passion for lush instrumental tracks had music fans asking, "Who is this new singer who sounds like Isaac Hayes?"

Comparisons between Hayes and White were inevitable, due to both artists having deep voices and favoring lengthy, heavily orchestrated, string-filled songs containing raps. Although the comparisons were valid, neither artist would publicly admit to it. In some circles, however, music critics accused White of being merely a carbon-copy of Hayes. This was an unfair accusation for White, who spent nearly a dozen years behind the scenes learning his craft before hitting paydirt. Nevertheless, the charge of trying to cash in on Hayes' successful formula remained with White, and despite his astounding success in the 1970s, he did not receive critical acclaim during his commercial prime.

Fortunately for White, record buyers did not critique his music in the same manner as the so-called experts. "I'm Gonna Love You Just a Little More Baby" became the fastest selling single to date for 20th Century Records. The song topped the R&B charts for two weeks in the spring of 1973, reached number three on the pop charts, and was a million-seller. White's breakthrough hit also netted him Grammy nominations for best male R&B vocal performance and for best new artist.

The steamy monologues on "I'm Gonna Love You Just a Little More Baby" laid the foundation for White's status as a sex symbol in the 1970s, despite his girth. However, it was the follow-up, "I've Got So Much to Give," which solidified this status. Over eight minutes in length, this sensuous track contained a laid-back piano riff interwoven with White's obligatory rap and his most lavish arrangement ever, which gave the song claim as arguably his finest ballad. "I've Got So Much to Give" reached number five on the R&B charts in the summer of 1973 and made the pop top 40. The chart position of this song was indicative of White's career. His legacy was built on love songs; he often claimed that half of the world made love while listening to his records. However, during the height of his career, very few of his ballads were released as singles; none achieving any significant pop success. This was epitomized by the nearly six-minute "I've Found Someone," which prominently featured the background vocals of Love Unlimited. This ballad from the *I've Got So Much to Give* album was never released as a single, yet it remains one of White's more popular songs and was included in an edited version on his first greatest hits package.

Led by "I'm Gonna Love You Just a Little More Baby," "I've Got So Much to Give," and "I've Found Someone," *I've Got So Much to Give* was certified gold. The album also included an eight-minute cover of the Four Tops' "Standing in the Shadows of Love," White's tribute to Holland-Dozier-Holland (who wrote and produced the original version).

In the fall of 1973, White avoided the sophomore jinx when his second album, *Stone Gon'*, was certified gold. Like its predecessor, this disk contained five lengthy songs. The album's success was triggered by "Never, Never Gonna Give Ya Up," a smooth, bass-laden dance track which reached number two on the R&B charts for two weeks, cracked the pop top 10, and was his second million-seller. White stayed in familiar territory for the follow-up, "Honey Please, Can't Ya See." This dance track, with its killer drumbeat, peaked at number six on the R&B charts early in 1974 and remains one of White's more underrated hits, perhaps due to the song's relatively poor showing (number 44) on the pop charts. The remaining songs on the album were ballads: "You're My Lady," "Hard to Believe That I Found You," and "Girl It's True, Yes I'll Always Love You." White introduced each of these slow jams with a pillow-talk rap aimed at women. Whether showing appreciation for his lady's presence in his life or reassuring her of his love, White expressed himself in a tender manner. This male sensitivity was rarely heard in R&B music up to that point, and it proved to be a highly marketable formula.

White joined Isaac Hayes, Marvin Gaye, Al Green, and Stevie Wonder in a select group of black artists who could generate album sales in mass quantities. To enhance the commercial appeal of his albums, White always included one or two lengthy slow jams, hidden gems that his fans, particularly women, came to expect when purchasing his LPs.

In addition to successfully launching his solo career, White still had time to write and produce for Love Unlimited. He formed a 41-piece band called the Love Unlimited Orchestra to back the trio on their 1973 20th Century debut album, *Under the Influence of . . . ,* which went gold and rose to number three on the album charts, then the highest position ever for a female group. The LP's first single was "Yes, We Finally Made It," which only reached the lower portion of the charts in the summer of 1973. Then came their remake of "It May Be Winter Outside (But in My Heart It's Spring)," a song White wrote and produced for Felice Taylor in 1966. Like Taylor, Love Unlimited had only moderate success in the States with "It May Be Winter Outside," but fared better in England. The success of the album was due to a smooth instrumental track that would become known as "Love's Theme," perhaps the first-ever combination of classical music with a soulful dance beat. The track was originally composed as an introduction for the vocal number "Under the Influence of Love." It became a sensation with the dance club deejays, who played all eight minutes of the two songs. This created demand for a release of the prelude tune performed by the Love Unlimited Orchestra. When released as a single later in 1973, "Love's Theme" became a top 10 R&B hit and topped the pop charts for a week early in 1974.

The idea of producing the Love Unlimited Orchestra as a separate entity was not initially accepted by 20th Century, which questioned the commercial appeal of an orchestra. After much persistence, however, White was able to convince the label of his ability to sell symphonic soul. At the beginning of 1974, the Love Unlimited Orchestra's *Rhapsody in White* album was released, which contained "Love's Theme" and went gold. The title track, something of a continuation of "Love's Theme," became the second single from the disc to chart. As was the norm with White's albums, *Rhapsody in White* contained hidden treasures, which were never released as singles but would be regarded as some of his most memorable material. Among them were the hypnotic, yet lushly romantic "Baby Blues," which featured White's infamous introductory rap about baby blue panties; and "Midnight and You," a smooth groove that maintained its sensuality despite twice building to an intense, somewhat funky bridge.

White returned to his own career in the summer of 1974 with the release of *Can't Get Enough*, which topped the album charts and became his third gold disc. The album's first single, "Can't Get Enough of Your Love, Babe," contained all the essential ingredients of White's hit-making formula. However, the production of this dance track was not quite as direct or as funky as his previous two releases, "Never, Never Gonna Give Ya Up" and "Honey Please, Can't Ya See." Perhaps it was this laid-back subtlety that gave the song its edge. "Can't Get Enough of Your Love, Babe" became White's biggest hit, topping the pop top 100 for a week in the fall of 1974 (his only Number One pop hit). The song also became his second Number One R&B single, topping the charts for three weeks.

White ended 1974 with the release of "You're the First, the Last, My Everything," a perky, up-tempo track that topped the R&B charts for a week early in 1975 and reached number two on the pop charts behind Elton John's remake of "Lucy in the Sky with Diamonds."

At the beginning of 1975, Barry White was successfully represented on the charts by all three of his performing entities. In addition to his own *Can't Get Enough* still riding high, Love Unlimited was on the charts with *In Heat*, which White wrote and produced. The album's lead single, the piano- and string-driven ballad "I Belong to You," topped the R&B charts for a week early in the year; a surprise showing for a ballad during the initial stages of disco. White was also on the charts with the Love Unlimited Orchestra's *White Gold*. From this album the smooth dance track "Satin Soul" fared well on the pop and R&B charts, and the album became the ensemble's second gold LP.

In the spring of 1975, White had his third straight simultaneous Number One R&B and top 10 pop hit with the up-tempo "What Am I Gonna Do with You," an ode to his successful career (the "you" being his music). The song was the first single from the album *Just Another Way to Say I Love You*, which went gold. White maintained his good standing on the R&B charts with the follow-up, "I'll Do for You Anything You Want Me To," which reached number four that summer. However, this song was somewhat bland compared to its predecessors and that showed on the pop charts; it only reached number 40. The album also contained one of White's more popular bedroom songs, the haunting "Love Serenade." Although not a ballad, this bump-and-grind jam was arguably White's most directly sexual track. "Love Serenade" was never released as a single, but because of its underground popularity was placed on White's first greatest hits package.

By 1976, the fine precision of 20th Century Records was beginning to unravel. Too much success in such a short period of time led to internal conflicts, which caused Russ Regan to leave. White, having been responsible for five gold singles and seven gold albums on the label in only three years, was inexplicably overlooked after the departure of Regan. His early 1976 single "Let the Music Play," a joyous song despite its melancholy lyrics, reached number four on the R&B charts. However, this slowed-down disco track was only mildly successful on the pop charts. The spring release of "You See the Trouble with Me," again in the disco vein, reached number 14 on the R&B charts but was his first single to miss the pop top 100 completely. White remained on the R&B charts throughout the year and early into 1977 with "Baby, We Better Try to Get It Together" (number 26), "Don't Make Me Wait Too Long" (number 20), and "I'm Qualified to Satisfy You" (number 25). However, these showings were pale in comparison to his hits just 18 months before. Neither of his 1976 albums, *Let the Music Play* and *Is This Whatcha Wont?*, achieved gold status.

White returned to the top 10 with a bang in the summer of 1977 with "It's Ecstasy When You Lay Down Next to Me." It topped the R&B charts for five weeks, reached number four on the pop charts, was a million-seller, and remains arguably his signature song. The pulsating rhythm at the beginning of this cut nixed any need for an opening rap. Led by the bass and strings, the production built to a point where White's vocals were almost anti-climactic. It was reported that he was originally advised by his closest associates to leave the song as an instrumental. Although White did not give in to this suggestion, he knew that the instrumental track gave the song its magic. Compared to his previous hits, where he occasionally strained his voice, White softened his vocals on this mid-tempo dance track, and it was perhaps his best effort as a singer.

"Ecstasy" was the first single from *Barry White Sings for Someone You Love*, arguably his finest album. The second release was "Playing Your Game, Baby," which reached number eight on the R&B charts early in 1978. White again softened his voice on this song, perhaps his most laid-back groove ever and a perfect lead-in to "Ecstasy," which followed in sequence on the album. Rounding out the first side was the popular "You're So Good, You're Bad," a steady instrumental track that featured White and Love Unlimited repeating the chorus. A third single released from the album was the joyous "Oh What a Night for Dancing," which reached number 13 on the R&B charts and surprisingly cracked the pop top 30 in the spring of 1978. Led by these four songs, plus the romantic ballad "You've Turned My Whole World Around," *Barry White Sings for Someone You Love* was certified platinum.

Shortly after the release of this album, 20th Century Records was basking in the success of the *Star Wars* soundtrack. As a result, the label relied less on White, the man who put them on the musical map. Late in 1978 he released *The Man*, one of his finest albums and one that achieved platinum sales despite being targeted strictly to black audiences. Only two songs from the album were issued as singles: the relentless, hard-driving "Your Sweetness Is My Weakness," which spent three weeks at the number two spot on the R&B charts in the fall of 1978 but failed to crack the pop top 40; and a remake of Billy Joel's "Just the Way You Are," which reached number 45 on the R&B charts in early 1979. The latter was the lowest chart position of White's career and an indication of how little effort 20th Century put into promoting the album. *The Man* contained several outstanding tracks, some which should have been issued as singles and whose strong reputation lives on. Most notable were "It's Only Love Doing Its Thing"; the exuberant, Latin-tinged "Sha La La Means I Love You"; and the beautiful, lilting "September, When I First Met You." The latter two received considerable airplay despite never being released as singles.

Toward the end of 1978, White signed a $14 million deal with CBS and was given his own label, Unlimited Gold Records. His first album on his new label was *The Message Is Love*, which went gold and contained the moderate hits "Any Fool Could See (You Were Meant for Me)" and "It Ain't Love, Babe (Until You Give It)." However, by now White's career started to cool, due in part to the anti-disco backlash that was beginning to consume the music industry toward the end of the 1970s. Over the next four years, White would release four more solo albums on Unlimited Gold: *Shoot Music* (1980), *Beware* (1981), *Change* (1982), and *Dedicated* (1983). However, none of the albums were nearly as successful as his 20th Century material. His finest efforts during this period were the rhythmic "Sheet Music" (spring 1980), "Love Makin' Music" (summer 1980), a cover of Jesse Belvin's "Beware" (fall 1981), and the perky "Change" (summer 1982).

Unlimited Gold also released two albums by Love Unlimited: *He's All I've Got* (1977) and *Love Is Back* (1979); and three by the Love Unlimited Orchestra: *Let 'Em Dance* (1981), *Welcome Abroad* (1981), and *Rise* (1983). However, these were commercial failures. By the end of the 1970s, Love Unlimited had broken up. Glodean James (whom White married in 1974) did a duet album with White in 1981, entitled *Barry and Glodean*, that charted two singles: "Didn't We Make It Happen, Baby" and "I Want You," Linda James got married and left the country, and Diane Taylor died in 1985 after a long battle with cancer.

When the CBS contract ran out in 1983, White took a break from recording and touring. He updated his home studio, RISE (Research in Sound Excellence), with innovative technology and tried to raise $10 million to finance his own record label. When that deal fell through at the last minute, he signed with A&M Records in 1986.

In the fall of 1987 White released his A&M debut, entitled *The Right Night and Barry White*. The artist was now working with a new set of musicians, including his godson Chuckii Booker, who in 1989 had a Number One R&B hit with "Turned Away"; keyboardist Jack Perry; and former Raydio guitarist Charles Fearing. The album's first single, the exhilarating, perky "Sho' You Right," brought White back to the R&B top 20 in the fall. Early in 1988 he also had a moderate hit with "For Your Love (I'll Do Most Anything)." One of the album's most appealing songs was the ballad "Who's the Fool." Despite White now working with new musicians and updating his sound, this nearly seven-minute smoldering ballad was vintage Barry White and contained all the production trademarks of his early hits: the seductive rap, the lavish orchestration, and the heavy strings. *The Right Night and Barry White* was not a particularly huge seller. However, the album served its purpose by reintroducing White to music fans.

White fared better in 1989 with the release of *The Man Is Back*, which included a popular remake of Jesse Belvin's "Goodnight My Love." However, events taking place overseas had a greater impact on his career. British fans, who have long had a tendency to savor forgotten American musical genres, created a demand for the soul sound of the early 1970s. In the spring of 1989 British soul band Soul II Soul introduced a combination of string-filled reggae rhythms and dance. This new sound gave them great success in the States with "Keep on Movin' " and "Back to Life," two of the biggest R&B singles of the year. Band leader Beresford Romeo, better known as Jazzy B, publicly acknowledged White as being one of his biggest influences. Also at this time, British pop group Simply Red had a huge hit with a cover of White's "It's Only Love Doing Its Thing."

In the spring of 1990 White anchored "The Secret Garden," a track from Quincy Jones' *Back on the Block* album. White's contribution to this song probably did more than anything else to introduce him to a younger record-buying audience. "The Secret Garden" also featured Al B. Sure!, El DeBarge, and James Ingram. However, it was White's rap, particularly at the beginning of this sensuous ballad, which propelled it to Number One on the R&B charts for a week and had music listeners calling radio stations and requesting "the new Barry White record." Barry White was all of a sudden current again. "The Secret Garden" was replaced at the top of the R&B charts by "All Around the World," the solo debut from British blue-eyed soul singer Lisa Stansfield. One of the biggest R&B and pop singles of 1990, Stansfield's string-filled hit included a spoken intro similar to White's, and was basically an update of the "Philly Soul" sound of the 1970s. Like Jazzy B before her, Stansfield publicly acknowledged White as having been an influence on her music. In 1992 Stansfield and White re-recorded "All Around the World" together to release as the B-side of her single, "Time to Make You Mine."

White released his third A&M album, *Put Me in Your Mind* in the fall of 1991. With his name still fresh in the minds of record buyers, he went to number two on the R&B charts with the title song. Early the following year, he had a top 30 R&B hit with "Dark and Lovely," a duet with Isaac Hayes.

In 1994, the man who rarely received critical acclaim during his commercial prime in the 1970s was finally given his well-deserved recognition. In the spring, White was presented with the Soul Train Lifetime Achievement Award. Later that fall he made a return to the top with *The Icon Is Love*, a critical and commercial success that became his first platinum album in 16 years. To enhance the album's appeal, White was teamed with several of R&B music's hottest producers, including Jimmy Jam and Terry Lewis, Chuckii Booker, and Gerald Levert. Levert co-wrote the first single, "Practice What You Preach," a warm and somewhat down-home ballad, which topped the R&B charts and was one of the biggest hits of the year. Further stand-outs included the second single, "Come On," a song similar in production to "It's Ecstasy When You Lay Down Next To Me"; the up-tempo Jam and Lewis-produced "I Only Want to Be with You"; and the 10-minute "Whatever We Had, We Had," a heartfelt ballad in which White addressed his divorce from his wife Glodean.

The success of *The Icon Is Love* coincided with urban radio beginning to embrace the classic soul of the 1960s and 1970s. It is only fitting that Barry White is simultaneously revered for his music of yesterday and today and that this multi-talented writer/producer/arranger/conductor/singer is finally getting his just due as a musical genius.

Bobby Womack

A prolific songwriter, singer, and guitarist whose career has spanned four decades, Bobby Womack had an important influence on the development of postwar black music. With roots in gospel music, Womack was able to parlay his talents as a writer and guitarist in the mid-1960s into a significant career as a soul artist. In the early to mid-1970s he scored with a series of hits, such as "Woman's Gotta Have It" and "Lookin' for a Love," sung in his raspy, almost gravelly tenor. After a brief dry spell at the end of the decade, Womack made a tremendous comeback in the early 1980s with "If You Think You're Lonely Now." With several of his songs being covered by artists ranging from the Rolling Stones and Janis Joplin to George Benson and Chaka Khan, Womack created a body of work ranking among the finest in modern music.

Born in Cleveland, Ohio in 1944, Womack got his first exposure to music in church. He and his four brothers, Cecil, Curtis, Harry, and Friendly, Jr., formed the Womack Brothers under the guidance of their father, Friendly Womack, Sr., a singer and guitar player with a quartet called the Voices of Love. The brothers toured the country, appearing on religious shows with other notable gospel groups such as the Five Blind Boys, the Caravans, and the Pilgrim Travelers. When the Womack Brothers opened for the Soul Stirrers at a local gospel show in 1953, Bobby came in contact with their lead singer, Sam Cooke, who was just beginning to branch out into secular music.

In 1961 the Womack Brothers were signed to SAR Records, a label owned by Cooke and his manager, former Pilgrim

Travelers singer J. W. Alexander. Cooke convinced the Womack Brothers to branch into secular music and change their name to the Valentinos. The following year, under their new name, the group had a hit with "Lookin' for a Love," originally the gospel melody of "Couldn't Hear Nobody Pray," to which SAR writer Zelda Samuels wrote new lyrics. In addition to having the brothers open up for him, Cooke recruited Bobby as his guitar player. This stemmed from a night when Cooke's guitar player did not show up and Bobby, then 16 years old, filled in and impressed Cooke so much that he fired two of his guitar players and replaced them with Bobby.

"Sam Cooke had a helluva influence on me," says Womack, "not only because he was a great singer but because he was a great person. He would be the epitome of what the newcomers today would call a star. Sam was the kind of person who made you feel like you were him and he was you. He did it so well. I would ask him how could he do that. His idea was if somebody's a fan and they love you so much and all you have to do is sit there and talk to them for a few minutes . . . turn it on. He said, 'I enjoy singing. Bobby, they have nothing else going. When they come from that show, they go back to that daily pressure, the system. I feel lucky to be able to throw that party for them and get paid for it.' That to me was something I always dug."

Soon after Bobby left Cooke's band in 1963, he wrote and recorded "It's All Over Now," which became the Valentinos' last chart entry. The Rolling Stones had a moderate hit with their version, recorded in 1964. After Cooke's death in 1964, the Valentinos remained together for another year, recording unsuccessfully for the Checker label. By the mid-1960s Bobby's career as a session guitar player and songwriter was beginning to blossom. Among the artists he backed were Ray Charles, Aretha Franklin, Joe Tex, and King Curtis. He also wrote the hits "I'm in Love," "I'm a Midnight Mover," and "Ninety-Nine and a Half (Won't Do)" for Wilson Pickett. During this time Bobby began taking steps toward a solo career and recorded briefly for Him, Chess, and Atlantic, but without any success.

In 1968 Bobby scored his first chart entry on Minit Records with "What Is This," a gritty, Southern-soul track exemplifying his stay in Memphis working with Chips Moman. He continued to have moderate success with soul versions of the pop songs "Fly Me to the Moon" and the Mamas and the Papas' "California Dreamin'." A songwriting collaboration with Darryl Carter, an engineer at Moman's American Sound Studios, helped Bobby achieve better quality and greater success on "How I Miss You Baby" and "More Than I Can Stand." In 1970 Minit Records was absorbed by its parent company Liberty, and Womack was switched over to that label. The following year Liberty was closed by its owners, TransAmerica, and the roster was moved to United Artists.

The move to United Artists proved to be a major breakthrough for Womack's solo career. He was given the artistic freedom to produce his own album and the result was the highly acclaimed *Communication* released late in 1971. Continuing his penchant for covering pop hits, he gave soulful readings to James Taylor's "Fire and Rain" and Ray Stevens' "Everything Is Beautiful." On another cover, a bluesy take on the Carpenters' "(They Long to Be) Close to You," Womack delivered a long monologue about being pressured to make his music sound more commercial. Aside from the four songs he covered on the LP, including the traditional gospel song "Yield Not to Temptation," Womack wrote three original songs. The album's biggest hit was "That's the Way I Feel About Cha," a bluesy ballad which Womack again opened with a monologue. With a theme of bringing the grim realities of the ups and downs of being in love to the forefront and removing the frills of unrealistic romance, "That's the Way I Feel About Cha" cracked the pop top 30 and reached number two on the R&B charts early in 1972. More important, the track laid the foundation for Womack's reputation as a down-home philosopher about everyday life.

He says, "My songwriting inspiration comes from growing up in the ghetto, being a project child, and seeing events like people fighting. You work all day, there's love through the week, then on the weekend you get drunk and try to kill each other. Everybody knew of a neighborhood drunk. He was a normal guy, good person, had a family and all that, but on the weekend his only release was to get as much alcohol as he could, come staggering home and argue with his wife; just be crazy. It comes from different things like people falling in and out of love, me watching my parents go through ups and downs, and changes. Sometimes the pressure built so high that you thought they hated each other. They just had to find some release. They didn't drink or have a different outlet that people normally do to use to relax because they were churchgoing people, but they would explode on each other. It's just everyday life like that, that my songwriting comes from."

Womack followed *Communication* with *Understanding* later in 1972. Like his previous album, Womack recorded *Understanding* both in Memphis at American Sound Studio and in Muscle Shoals, Alabama. At Muscle Shoals, Womack utilized top session players, including drummer Rodger Hawkins, guitarists Jimmy Johnson and Tippy Armstrong, bassist David Hood, and keyboardist Barry Beckett. One of the key songs from the album was "I Can Understand It," which inexplicably was never released as a single. Highlighted by Hood's hypnotic bass and the effective use of female background singers, "I Can Understand It" has become a soul classic and was a major hit for New Birth the following year.

The first single released from *Understanding* was "Woman's Gotta Have It," a warning to a man who was taking his wife for granted, which Womack co-wrote with Darryl Carter and Linda Cooke Womack (Sam's daughter). Recorded at American Sound, personnel on the track included Mike Leech on bass, Reggie Young on guitar, Hayward Bishop on drums and percussion, Bobby Wood on piano, and Bobby Emmons on organ. With emphasis on Leech's bassline, "Woman's Gotta Have It" was Womack's first Number One R&B hit, topping the charts in the spring of 1972. As a follow-up, United Artists released Womack's cover of Neil Diamond's 1969 hit "Sweet Caroline (Good Times Never Seemed So Good)." The song had moderate success on the R&B charts, perhaps on the strength of Womack's two previous hits. However, black radio deejays played the flip side, "Harry Hippie." When the label flipped the single, "Harry Hippie" became the hit, reaching number eight on the R&B charts early in 1973 and giving Womack his first certified gold single. "Harry Hippie" had special meaning to Womack because the song was an ode to his brother Harry, who was found stabbed to death two years later.

He explains, "Harry was the bass player and tenor for the brothers when we were the Valentinos. He lived a very carefree life. As a child he always said he wanted to live on an Indian reservation. We used to joke about it, but when we got older he was the same way. He always thought I wanted the materialistic things and I said, 'I just want to do my music. My music put me into that comfortable territory.' He didn't want the pressure. We used to laugh and joke about the song when I'd sing it. When he was brutally killed in my home, it was by a jealous girlfriend who he'd lived with for five years. She fought a lot, violence. And in our home it was considered to be worth less than a man to fight a woman, so he didn't fight back and she stabbed him to death.

"At the time I was in Seattle doing a gig and he was going to join me when we got back. Previously I had hired a new bass player because I felt it would help [Harry's] relationship with his spouse if he wasn't on the road. And that turned out to be very sour. He ended up losing his life behind it. At that time ['Harry Hippie'] wasn't a joke anymore; I had lost a brother. I still do that song in his honor today."

In 1973 Womack took time out to record the soundtrack to *Across 110th Street*, one of the period's more outstanding "blaxploitation" films. The album's title track, recorded with his backup band Peace, gave Womack his fifth straight top 20 R&B hit in less than two years. Despite having a successful track record that included two consecutive self-produced albums, United Artists was reluctant to give Womack the assignment. He says, "My company was doing a lot of recording and I was really hot at the time. I approached them and asked, 'Why do y'all keep going outside to hire people to do your soundtracks when I'm number one?' They asked, 'Bobby, have you ever done soundtracks before?' and I said, 'No, I ain't ever gonna do one if you don't give me a shot.' So I complained that I would leave the company and go somewhere better where somebody else would utilize my talent and let me go ahead instead of trying to console me. When it came around they came to me and said, 'Okay, you have your chance to do a soundtrack.' I knew they didn't want me to do it because at that time I was getting ready to go on tour. They let me see the movie one time with no music, but they wouldn't give me a [copy of the] film to be able to go on the road and remember what I saw. Plus they said I had to finish it in two weeks. You know they didn't want me to do it but that gave me the incentive to show them.

"Fortunately the movie was about Harlem. There's a ghetto in every city. I could write that with my eyes closed. So, I wrote the songs and never saw the movie again until it came out. I not only finished it but I got it out there and they said, 'We're sorry that we did that because if you had an equal opportunity, think what you could've done with it.' Now, if they told me to write about war in two weeks I wouldn't have been able to do that. It's a whole different ball game. I haven't been there."

Womack followed the soundtrack with the *Facts of Life* album, which gave him a two-sided hit with "Nobody Wants You When You're Down and Out" and "I'm Through Trying to Prove My Love to You." The former, a smooth, mid-tempo track, somewhat up-beat given its theme, rose to number two on the R&B charts in the fall of 1973 and remains a song Womack considers "a very true song to me, along with 'Harry Hippie.'"

For his next release, Womack returned to his very first hit, and cut a remake of the Valentinos' 1962 "Lookin' for a Love." In 1971, "Lookin' for a Love" became the first hit for the Boston-based rock group J. Geils Band. Two years later Womack re-recorded the song almost as an afterthought while sorting through several original songs to be placed on his next album.

Later convinced by associates that his new version would be a hit, Womack gave his album the title *Lookin' for Love Again* and released the title track as the first single. The remake was more heartfelt and good-natured than most of Womack's previous songs about the realities of everyday life, and gave him his second Number One R&B hit, topping the charts for three weeks in the spring of 1974. Perhaps it was the song's good-natured flavor which allowed it to become Womack's only top 10 pop hit, and second certified gold single.

At a time when most singles to reach the summit of the R&B charts at least cracked the pop top 10, Womack enjoyed very limited crossover success. With his raw, gritty, soulful voice, drawing from the soul superstars he worked with in the previous decade, and the themes of his songs drawn predominantly from the ghetto experience, Womack's appeal was almost exclusively to the black audience.

"I'm proud to be a soul singer," he says. "I'm not proud of the way soul music has been treated but with every other thing, they take it, steal it, and say they did it. They take your song that you sell, maybe a million copies in the black market, and it won't reach their stations unless it's done by white people. My music is just a symbol of what Aretha [Franklin], Sam Cooke, Otis Redding, and others have done."

The second single from *Lookin' for Love Again*, "You're Welcome, Stop on By" reached number five on the R&B charts in the summer of 1974 and soon became identified as a classic in the repertoire of Rufus and Chaka Khan, although the group never released it as a single.

Womack's consistent chart presence in the early 1970s took him to superstar status. However, along with the triumph came signs of him beginning to become a victim of the dark side of the entertainment industry. "I was flying very high," he says. "I was doing all the wrong things. I was partying, getting high, hanging out. It was just like somebody had turned up the volume. I was already doing it when I was a kid and they were praising me as the new bishop, like the youngest bishop in the neighborhood or in the gospel field. I was always the greatest thing that ever happened. When you're born and people are surrounding you like that, you just get used to it. So, when they turned it up louder, I started doing it more. I never considered myself as being number one. I was still thinking it was James Brown, Sam Cooke, and Jackie Wilson, and they had moved over and gave me a slot. So, when the volume turned off, I was still there. It's what I do. I can always do that. That's why I pass on to people, if you can find something that you love to do, you'll never work a day in your life."

Womack's career began to take a slight dip during the mid-1970s. The funky "Check It Out" was his only hit in 1975, peaking at number six. A year later, returning to his production trademarks of an effective use of female background singers and emphasis on the bassline, Womack took "Daylight" to number five. "Daylight" proved to be his final hit on the United Artists label. After a dispute over the title of a collection of country and western songs, *B.W. Goes C&W* — Womack's own title had been *Move Over Charley Pride and Give Another Nigger a Chance* — he left the label.

"I left United Artists because they were afraid of me being in control of my own life. I said, 'Why shouldn't I? I bring the songs, I write them, I sing them, I produce them, and I publish them.' Plus United Artists wanted to produce me and put me on the shelf and say, 'Give me another hit like the other one. Make it sound like the other one or something close to it.' They wanted to hear the old Bobby Womack. I did it a couple of times and I thought about it but I said, 'Hey, I'm not there today. That was done yesterday so why should I do it again when I'm going further?'

"I cut a country and western album and that pissed them off. They said I had gone crazy. Charley Pride was the only other [black artist] doing country and western. I thought that was another avenue for me to channel."

During the mid-1970s many of the independent labels folded or were swallowed up by the majors due to a loss in popularity of the artists on their roster, thanks to disco. Many of the top performers from earlier in the decade signed with major labels (e.g., the signing of Tyrone Davis, Johnnie Taylor, and Bill Withers by CBS/Columbia). After leaving United Artists, Womack also signed with Columbia. During his brief stay on the label, he turned out two self-produced albums, *Home Is Where the Heart Is* (1976) and *Pieces* (1977), neither of which achieved commercial success. Womack's problems mounted during his tenure with Columbia, including being lost in the shuffle of the many artists on the label's roster, and almost being caught up in a political scheme with a company executive he refuses to identify.

"It was a political move on the part of a gentleman who was in the business, who now is out of the business because his mind was distorted. He came to me and signed me and told me he wanted me to do a benefit for all of the people in Africa, babies that didn't live to be a certain age. I said I didn't mind doing a benefit. He said, 'If you do this I will give you a million dollars.' I told him he didn't have to pay me but who's going to profit? I want to see if the money goes there. He said I couldn't watch over his shoulder so I asked if I could put somebody on the board of directors. He said no, so I decided not to do the benefit. Then he took the album, put it in the can and didn't do anything with it. And I made my decision, I don't need a platinum album if I have to sell somebody down who's already down."

Womack finished the decade on Arista with the little-noticed *Roads of Life* album in 1979. By the start of the 1980s, his career was flagging. Black popular music was still dominated by disco and self-contained funk groups like the Commodores, Parliament/ Funkadelic, and Slave. Traditional soul artists had become relics. Also at the root of Womack's problems was a drug addiction.

"I'm not a saint. I've fallen down but when I fall, I fall on my back. If I can look up, I can get up. There are some people who believe everything you say. That's why when I got drunk I got drunk in my own chambers. I'm on my own time then. But I respect you enough to not come on stage that way because I wouldn't want some kid to say, 'I wanna be just like you and come on stage drunk.' That would be sad to me. I'd do a Dr. Jekyll and Mr. Hyde; always walk out on my g.p., fall down behind the curtain. But I don't have that problem 'cause I'm still here. I've weathered the storm. I've had bouts with drugs but . . . life is a drug. The system is a drug."

Womack's career began to take a turn for the better in 1980 with the help of George Greif, manager of the Crusaders. Greif recruited Womack as a vocalist on several songs for Crusader Wilton Felder's solo album *Inherit the Wind*.

The following year, Womack signed a contract with Beverly Glen Records, a new label started by former ABC Records vice president Otis Smith. His first release on the new label was *The Poet*, which proved to be the comeback of all comebacks. Sticking with his soul roots, which was still unfashionable in the age of disco, the first single, "If You Think You're Lonely Now," gave Womack his first hit record in six years. This track, which would become Womack's signature song despite all of his earlier success, contained all of the elements of his hits from the previous decade: the opening monologue, the down-home production flavor, and the effective use of female background vocals. "If You Think You're Lonely Now" reached number three on the R&B charts early in 1982 and brought Womack back to superstar status after years of being considered a has-been. Adding to the success of *The Poet* was the follow-up, "Where Do We Go from Here." An underrated hit from the album, it was released almost as an afterthought and its modest chart success (number 26) does not accurately reflect its popularity. Ironically, the album's two more contemporary tracks, "So Many Sides of You" and "Lay Your Lovin' on Me," were never released as singles.

Two years later, Womack followed up with the equally impressive *The Poet II* album. The album's biggest hit was the ballad "Love Has Finally Come at Last," a duet with Patti Labelle, another traditional soul legend, herself experiencing something of a hit famine at the start of the decade but was now fresh off a Number One hit, "If Only You Knew." British publication *Blues & Soul* named *The Poet II* best album of 1984 in its prestigious annual poll. In addition, Womack was named best male vocalist, best songwriter, and best live performer. Although Womack received recognition in the States for his accomplishments, he has always been regarded as a *bona fide* superstar in Europe.

"I was popular in Europe because I was a foreigner there. All of the music that the Europeans have taken from America was black music and they became very famous with it. These artists were real enough to say, 'If you like what we do, listen to the original.' They always gave us props for being there. These white kids heard the B.B. Kings, Sam Cookes, Otis Redding, Wilson Pickett, Bobby Womack. Living in this country you're only as good as your last record. What happened was that we went to Europe and it was like Jimi Hendrix going to Europe. They found a place for us. There the music is the Bible, and we were at the forefront of it. That's what made it what it is. Here it's like fast food music. You're only as good as your last record. There they still like songs I cut 15 years ago, and they come out in droves to hear it, so that made a difference."

However, all was not well with Womack's new success. In between the release of *The Poet* and *The Poet II*, Womack took label owner Otis Smith to court, claiming that he received no royalties. At the time of signing the contract with Beverly Glen, Womack was at a low and considered Beverly Glen to be his only chance at recording again. The restrictive contract made no financial guarantees to Womack, beyond an initial advance and forbade him from working on any other label, either as an instrumentalist or background singer.

"Being at Beverly Glen was like being back in slavery before I got here, by being whipped by my own brother. The only thing that came out of it that did people good was my music. I never got paid on it and I never forgot it."

In 1985, free from his legal hassles, Womack again collaborated with Wilton Felder for the latter's second album, *Secrets*, and scored with "(No Matter How High I Get) I'll Still Be Looking Up to You," a duet with Altrina Grayson. Later that year he signed with MCA and recorded the highly acclaimed *So Many Rivers*. The album's debut single, "I Wish He Didn't

Trust Me So Much" reached number two on the R&B charts for two weeks that fall, and was followed up by "Let Me Kiss It Where It Hurts." The disc fared even better in England, where many critics named it the number one release of 1985. The following year he worked with the Rolling Stones on their new album *Dirty Work*, singing a duet with Mick Jagger on the hit "Harlem Shuffle." Later that year he reunited with Chips Moman for *Womagic* but met with little success, as did his 1989 Solar album *Save the Children.*

In the mid-1980s, Womack's brother Cecil and sister-in-law Linda began a recording career as Womack and Womack on the Elektra label, and had their biggest hit in 1984 with "Baby I'm Scared of You." Already a successful songwriting team, the duo previously wrote several songs for Teddy Pendergrass, including "Love TKO" and "I Can't Live Without Your Love."

After a period away from recording at the beginning of the 1990s, Bobby Womack released *Resurrection* in 1994 on Rolling Stone Ron Wood's Slide label. "*Resurrection* is just another album and another phase in my life," he says. "I paid more attention to the music business than the business of life. My family and myself suffered dearly for it because I was always out there trying to make somebody else happy when I wasn't giving it at home. Resurrection means born again and I'm glad that I can say I'm born again and to try to do it right this time, not just for everybody else but for me to grow with it."

In a recording career that has spanned nearly 35 years, Womack has created an important body of music and earned himself a permanent place in the annals of soul music. Reflecting on how he has been able to survive in the music business despite the numerous ups and downs of his career, he says, "I've been able to survive because I was a part of the business that made the business. The only people who trip are the people who don't have my talent and try to find a way to rip me off. So, they put all the things with you that can tempt you; women, cocaine, booze, everything. And of all those things, you'll pick one of them. That will be your vice, and when they want to take you out, that's the vice they'll use. Well, I switched up on them so fast that they didn't know what to give me. It was fun seeing the movie. It's still fun seeing the movie. The only sad part is that I know more dead people than I do people who are living. They've taken my brothers out, sisters out, one way or another. I'd trip but I wouldn't trip too long. I like to walk and feel like I'm in control, not walk and run halfway and fall down . . . Ain't no drug that good.

"Everybody isn't that fortunate but I think I have the greatest job in the world; to be able to walk into a place, get everybody feeling the same way, good, for two or three hours so when Monday rolls around they say, 'Man, f— this. I'll deal with this and try to catch Bobby Womack again next week.' I'm a disciple. [God] gave me the talent to do this. When I leave I hope somebody else will want to be a soul singer. It's my whole life as it passes by me and from what I can remember, nothing has more depth."

Betty Wright

With her exuberant and soulful vocals, Betty Wright was a big part of Miami's soul music scene in the 1970s. Beginning with her biggest hit, 1971's "Clean Up Woman," Wright built a successful career around songs warning about "the other woman." With her steady run of hits throughout the decade, including "Baby Sitter" and "Secretary," Wright was instrumental in the early development of Henry Stone's TK Productions.

The youngest of seven children, Wright was born in Miami in 1953. She started singing at age three in her family's gospel group, the Echoes of Joy. When the group broke up so that the individual members could branch out on their own, Wright began performing at talent shows around Miami. At age 11 she was discovered by the songwriting and production team of Clarence Reid and Willie Clarke at a record store after winning a "Guess the Tune" phone-in competition on a local radio station.

She remembers, "I won a 'Guess the Tune' competition on WMBM. The prize was a record at Johnny's Record Rack. At the time I was only 11 years old. I went to the store with two of my older cousins to pick up my record and while I was there I started singing with the record that was playing. The next record was Billy Stewart's 'Summertime.' When I started singing along to that one, I began drawing a crowd. Willie Clarke and Clarence Reid were there and they asked me if I wanted to record in a studio. So, we later went to a small studio and recorded a few tracks."

Wright initially did background vocals on some of Reid and Clarke's productions for their local Miami label, Deep City

Records. In 1966, at age 12, Wright released her own Deep City single, "Paralyzed," which became a local success. Disenchanted with the distribution arrangements Deep City faced, Clarke sought out the services of Henry Stone. Stone headed Tone Distributors, which handled distribution in Florida for most of the top independent record labels. Stone also owned a series of small labels, including Alston, which was distributed nationally by Atlantic. He invited Clarke and Reid to work with him at Alston and bring the artists they had produced at Deep City. Wright was initially turned down by Stone because she sang in a monotone. However, she prevailed upon him and two weeks later he decided to give her a chance.

In 1968 Wright released the Clarke-Reid composition "Girls Can't Do What the Guys Do," a down-home track with lyrics that advised women to go along with the existing double standard between the sexes. Despite an initial lack of faith from Stone and Atlantic Records creative force Jerry Wexler, the song reached number 15 on the R&B charts that summer and cracked the pop top 40; one of her few singles to achieve any crossover success. With Wright being relatively new to the recording industry, she was unaware of the significance of scoring a hit at such a young age. As a result, she was not overwhelmed by her newfound success. "It was my third record so [the success] didn't really phase me," she says. "When it became a hit the gigs started getting better and the crowds and venues started getting larger. At the time I wasn't really serious about recording so it was never a feeling of, 'Oh, boy, I got a big hit!'"

Two years later Wright performed at the Spanish Fiesta in Caracas, Venezuela, where she was the only American performer and the only black performer. She was also the youngest performer at the Fiesta, and the only one to sing in both Spanish and English. "I actually became part of the festival on a dare," she says. "I took Spanish in school. Henry Stone had a deal in South America and asked me if I would like to try Spanish singing and go to the country. At the festival I was the only one to sing in both English and Spanish and that was the first time that happened."

After the mild success of "Pure Love" in the summer of 1970 and "The Way You Love" in the summer of 1971, Wright released "Clean Up Woman," which became her biggest hit. Ironically, she did not like the song when she first heard it. She explains, " 'Clean Up Woman' didn't sound like a song when I first heard it. Clarence Reid had me singing the song and it wasn't finished yet. He's eccentric and energetic like that. When I sang 'Clean Up Woman' I ended up humming part of it because there was no bridge."

By the time "Clean Up Woman" was finished and released as a single late in 1971, Betty Wright had a million-seller at the age of 18. Highlighted by the reggae-flavored guitar riff of Willie "Little Beaver" Hale and the mature theme — at least for an 18-year-old — of not taking a man for granted for fear of losing him to another woman, "Clean Up Woman" reached the pop top 10 and spent eight weeks at the number two spot on the R&B charts. With the success of "Clean Up Woman" came a slew of awards. In 1972 Wright received a Grammy nomination for best female R&B performance, and *Cashbox* named her best new female vocalist, and "Clean Up Woman" best single of the year.

"At the time [the success of 'Clean Up Woman'] was like being in the twilight zone, but the people around me were more affected by it than I was," she says. "It's an unfortunate story of how some people are. Many people stopped speaking to me, which bothered me because I'm a people person. When I recorded the song I was only 17 and I was concentrating on graduating from high school, so I wasn't really paying that much attention to it. I was working on a TV show [*The Now Explosion*] on weekends and was looking forward to going to college. At the time I became quite visual and I was supporting myself while most people my age were still living in the house with their parents. When the song started taking major leaps and bounds it just proved to be too much for everybody."

Wright followed "Clean Up Woman" with a two-sided minor hit, "If You Love Me Like You Say" backed with the moody "I'm Gettin' Tired Baby," in the spring of 1972, and with "Is It

You Girl," a song similar in production to "Clean Up Woman," which reached the R&B top 20 later that summer.

Her next big hit came toward the end of 1972 with "Baby Sitter," a song she co-wrote with Clarke and Reid. The inspiration for "Baby Sitter," about a 16-year-old baby sitter who takes another woman's husband, came to Wright while she was daydreaming. "Some women are so gullible to let these young, fine women keep their kids," she says. "One day I was daydreaming about baby sitting for a man and his wife and in the dream, the husband always comes home first so he can be alone with me. I took the idea to Clarence [Reid] and he thought it was a good idea for a song, so we got together and wrote it." The success of "Baby Sitter" returned Wright to the R&B top 10, peaking at number six.

Wright added a slice of funk to the laid-back, Caribbean-flavored "Miami sound" with her next releases, "It's Hard to Stop (Doing Something When It's Good to You)" and "Let Me Be Your Lovemaker," the latter a top 10 R&B hit in the fall of 1973. The following year she had another hit with "Secretary," a song in the same vein as "Clean Up Woman" and "Baby Sitter," with a warning about "the other woman." Wright's perky cover of "Shoorah! Shoorah!" late in 1974, while not a huge success (number 26 R&B), remained on the charts for more than five months; a feat not accomplished by any of her bigger hits. In the spring of 1975 Wright had a notable hit with the dance track "Where Is the Love," a song she co-wrote with Willie Clarke and K.C. and the Sunshine Band leader Harry Casey. The following year she won a Grammy Award as co-writer of the song.

By the time "Where Is the Love" came out, Henry Stone was heavily involved with the disco phenomenon. George McRae, who recorded on Stone's TK Records, enjoyed enormous success the previous summer with "Rock Your Baby," a song generally regarded as one of the first disco hits. Also at this time, K. C. and the Sunshine Band were triumphing in England with their TK releases "Sound Your Funky Horn" and "Queen of Clubs." Wright was instrumental in the early recording careers of both acts. She, along with Willie Clarke, saw George and his wife Gwen McRae ("Rockin' Chair") perform in Florida and advised Stone of their talent. Harry Wayne "KC" Casey initially came to Stone's TK Productions as a warehouseman. By hanging out at the studio after work, Casey came in contact with Wright, who took a liking to him and invited him to sing background on a few of her recordings and be an opening act at some of her live performances.

Ironically, disco was a music form Wright had mixed feelings about. She says, "Disco in itself is faceless dance music that doesn't really identify with what's happening. Music is about keeping a story line going. Disco didn't seem to follow any pattern. It's all about 120 beats per minute. I love dance music if it comes from the likes of Otis Redding, James Brown, or Wilson Pickett, but some of the dance music during that time was a joke. The artists never got a chance to show any talent. Take Donna Summer for example. She was at the top during the disco era but over the years she has proven she can also sing other types of music."

During the mid-1970s, Wright's career seemed to suffer from the small-company atmosphere at Alston and TK Productions. In the summer of 1975 K.C. and the Sunshine Band had their breakthrough when "Get Down Tonight" topped the pop and R&B charts. The band's two subsequent singles, "That's the Way (I Like It)" late in 1975 and "(Shake, Shake, Shake) Shake Your Booty" in the summer of 1976, reached the same lofty heights. When K.C. and the Sunshine Band got red hot, they were the only act the company could focus on. As a result, Wright's career got lost in the shuffle.

"I didn't feel great about it at the time," she admits. "Before K.C. started recording, I was using part of his band as my band. I was one of the first to see [K.C.'s] promise as an artist. I wish I could have been given a finder's fee. A lot of other people at the company didn't like him because they saw him as another case of a white guy singing soul music. I'm glad for his success but sorry that it came at my expense. For awhile my sister was with K.C. and the Sunshine Band."

Wright continued to record for Alston for the rest of the decade. Her biggest success was the well received *Betty Wright Live* album in 1978. From the album, the warm and soulful "Tonight Is the Night Pt. 1 (Rap)," a new version of her 1974 single, reached number 11 on the R&B charts. That year Wright also contributed vocals on Peter Brown's major disco hit "Dance with Me."

When TK Productions filed for bankruptcy and dissolved in the early 1980s, Wright signed with Epic Records. Her first Epic album, 1981's *Betty Wright*, included a collaboration with Stevie Wonder on "What Are You Going to Do with It." However, neither of her two albums on Epic were successful. Later in 1981 her angry rap at the end of Richard "Dimples" Field's controversial song, "She's Got Papers on Me," made the song a hit.

After briefly recording two disco-style songs for New York-based Jamaica Records and another for First String, she decided to form her own label, Ms. B Records. "People got scared of black music," she says. "The A&R people at record companies are afraid for you to sing anything that doesn't sound pop. They always want something to be in that light and airy mood. After putting up with it long enough I decided, if they won't put my music out on their label, I'll put it out on my own. A lot of people later lost their jobs when the songs on my label became successful. People from different A&R departments were calling me and nearly begging me not to say anything about them passing up the chance to sign me."

Wright's first success on her new label occurred in 1988 with *Mother Wit* and its hit single "No Pain, No Gain," which reached the R&B top 15 that spring. It was her highest chart showing in 10 years. The success of the single was surprising due to its warm and soulful flavor, by now archaic in the era of rap and new jack swing. With the tastes of teenagers usually dominating the charts, the success of "No Pain, No Gain" exposed Wright to a younger audience not familiar with her string of hits in the 1970s. She points out, "I started out at such a young age that when "No Pain, No Gain" came out, a lot of my fans didn't realize that I was as young or younger than they were. They thought I was in my fifties or sixties."

In 1989 Wright followed *Mother Wit* with *4U2NJoy*, which contained the moderate hit "From Pain to Joy." Still a top concert attraction, Betty Wright performs an average of eight times a month and continues to release albums on her own label, the most recent being 1994's *B-Attitudes.*

"Millie [Jackson] and I work as much if not more than most females who are singing," she notes. "Even when I didn't have hit records out I always had a strong following because people know that the show will be given my all. Maybe by the time I get up in my forties I'll stop. If it's in your bones you'll still do it. The Lord will be the One to tell me to stop."

Bibliography

BOOKS

Bronson, Fred, *The Billboard Book of Number One Hits*, Billboard, New York, 1988.

Cumings, Tony, *The Sound of Philadelphia*, Methuen, London, 1975.

Gaar, Gillian, *She's a Rebel, The History of Women in Rock & Roll*, Seal, Washington, 1992.

George, Nelson, *The Death of Rhythm & Blues*, Omnibus, London, 1988.

George, Nelson, *Where Did Our Love Go? The Rise and Fall of the Motown Sound*, Omnibus, London, 1985.

Greig, Charlene, *Will You Still Love Me Tomorrow? Girl Groups from the 50s On*, Virago Press Ltd., London, 1989.

Guralnick, Peter, *Sweet Soul Music*, Virgin, London, 1986.

Hardy, Phil & Dave Laing, *The Faber Companion to 20th Century Popular Music*, Faber, London, 1990.

Hildebrand, Lee, *Stars of Soul and Rhythm & Blues*, Billboard, New York, 1994.

Jancik, Wayne, *Billboard Book of One Hit Wonders*, Watson-Guptill Pub., New York, 1990.

Parales, John, Patricia Romanowski, *The Rolling Stone Encyclopedia of Rock & Roll*, Fireside, New York, 1983.

Pavletich, Aida, *Rock-A-Bye-Baby*, Doubleday and Company, New York, 1980.

Pruter, Robert, *Chicago Soul*, University of Illinois Press, Illinois, 1991.

Scott, Barry, *We Had Joy We Had Fun: The Lost Recording Artists of the Seventies*, Faber and Faber, Massachusetts, 1994.

Stambler, Irwin, *The Encyclopedia of Pop, Rock and Soul*, St. Martin's Press, New York, 1989.

Warner, Jay, *The Billboard Book of American Singing Groups. A History 1940 – 1990*, Billboard, New York, 1992.

Whitburn, Joel, *Top R&B Singles 1942-1988*, Billboard, New York, 1988.

White, Adam & Fred Bronson, *The Billboard Book of Number One Rhythm & Blues Hits*, Billboard, New York, 1993.

MAGAZINES AND NEWSPAPERS

Adderton, Donald and Edwina L. Rankin. "The O'Jays Celebrate 20 Years." *Jet* 11 August 1977 pp. 56-59.

"Al Green Tells Why He Honors Woman Who Killed Self Over Him." *Jet* 15 July 1985 pp. 14-16.

Aletti, Vince. "His Name in Lights: Al Green." *Rolling Stone* 2 March 1972 p. 32.

Allen, Zita. "Freda Payne: A Star Is Reborn 'Today's Black Woman.'" *Essence* March 1982 pp. 72-74+.

Bailey, Peter. "The Magic of the Blue." *Black Stars* June 1975 pp. 50-57.

Banks, Lacy. "The Emotions: They Sing to Satisfy Their Musical Hunger." *Black Stars* December 1977 pp. 40-47.

Banks, Lacy. "The Ohio Players: From Pain to Pleasure," *Black Stars* November 1974 pp. 62-69.

Barol, Bill and Vern E. Smith. "In the Name of the Lord." *Newsweek* 20 January 1986 p. 68.

Bartley, G. Fitz. "Al Green Sets the Stage for Superstardom." *Black Stars* July 1973 pp. 22-29.

Berry, William Earl. "Betty Wright 'Cleans Up' with New Pop Tunes." *Jet* 18 January 1973 pp. 60-62.

"Billy Paul: Me and Mrs. Jones." *Black Stars* March 1973 pp. 52-54.

"Billy Paul Speaks About War and God." *Black Stars* March 1974 pp. 20-22.

"The Bloodstone—A Natural High." *Black Stars* July 1973 pp. 68-71.

Bloom, Steve. "Gladys Knight in No Man's Land." *Rolling Stone* 30 June 1988 p. 23.

Brookins, Portia Scott. "The O'Jays: Getting It Together." *Black Stars* Debember 1974 pp. 40-48.

Brown, Geoffrey F. "The O'Jays Are Giving People What They Want." *Jet* 19 June 1975 pp. 58-62.

Browne, David. "All Aboard the British Soul Train." *Entertainment Weekly* 29 June 1990 pp. 28-32.

Burrell, Walter Price. "Backstage with the Stylistics." *Black Stars* February 1973 pp. 10-18.

Burrell, Walter Price. "Isaac Hayes: From Cottonfields to Superstar." *Black Stars* December 1972 pp. 12-21.

Burrell, Walter Price. "War Battles Peacefully onto Success." *Black Stars* November 1973 pp. 26-32.

Carson, Alan. "Al Green Turns Soul to Gold." *Black Stars* June 1975 pp. 36-47.

"Chi-Lites Admit Guilt in Tax Evasion Case." *Jet* 22 January 1976 p. 55.

Clark, Sue Cassidy. "The Fantastic Stylistics." *Black Stars* January 1974 pp. 58-63.

Clark, Sue Cassidy. "The O'Jays Reaching Further into the Minds." *Black Stars* March 1974 pp. 50-57.

Clark, Sue Cassidy. "The Spinners Are on the Move." *Black Stars* December 1973 pp. 42-48.

Collier, Aldore. "The O'Jays: Still Turning Out Hit Songs After 32 Years." *Jet* 21 August 1989 pp. 58-62.

Crouse, Timothy. "Presenting Isaac Hayes Superstar." *Rolling Stone* 17 February 1972 pp. 14-16.

DeLeon, Robert A. "Al Green Sings Again." *Jet* 12 December 1974 pp. 54-59.

"The Dells: The Longest Running Group in Pop History." *Black Stars* October 1975 pp. 6-10.

"Emerson, Ken. "The Spinners Work Their Way Back." *Rolling Stone* 24 July 1980 pp. 19-20.

"The First Family of Gospel." *Ebony* September 1965 pp. 79-85.

Fong-Torres, Ben. "Deputy Al Green's Recovery." *Rolling Stone* 16 January 1975 pp. 14-15.

Fong-Torres, Ben. "Gladys Knight and the Pips." *Rolling Stone* 6 June 1974 pp. 53-56.

"40,000 Notes at Womack's Fingertips." *Black Stars* February 1973 pp. 70-73.

"Freda Payne's Song Causes Pain for U. S. Army." *Jet* 28 October 1971 pp. 58-60.

"Garland, Phyl. "Soul to Soul." *Ebony* July 1971 pp. 79-89.

Goldberg, Michael. "Bobby Womack: A New Hit Proves It's Not Over Yet for the Man Who Wrote 'It's All Over Now.'" *Rolling Stone* 21 June 1984 p. 48.

Goldberg, Michael. "Ex-Spinner Collapses Onstage, Dies." *Rolling Stone* 30 August 1984 p. 33.

Harrington, Richard. "The Lazarus of Love." *Washington Post* 15 January 1995 pp. G1-G2.

Hendrickson, Paul. "The Spinners: Up from Motown." *Rolling Stone* 12 September 1974 p. 17+.

Higgins, Chester. "Jean Knight: New 'Big Stuff' of Show Biz." *Jet* 12 August 1971 pp. 56-59.

Higgins, Chester. "Staple Singers Sell Soul with a Gospel Beat." *Jet* 9 December 1971 pp. 56-59.

Hoerburger, Rob. "The Gospel According to Al." *Rolling Stone* 27 March 1986 pp. 27+.

Holden, Stephen. "Gladys Knight: The End of a Nightmare." *Rolling Stone* 7 August 1980 pp. 17-18.

Holden, Stephen. "Ray, Goodman and Brown's Moments in the Sun." *Rolling Stone* 29 May 1980 p. 22.

"Isaac Hayes Talks About His Third Comeback." *Jet* 9 March 1987 pp. 22-23.

Keeps, David. "The High Priest of Boudoir Soul." *New York Times* 9 July 1995 p. 29.

Kisner, Ronald E. "The Chi-Lites: Seen and Heard." *Black Stars* March 1972 pp. 54-57.

Kisner, Ronald E. "The O'Jays Revive Good Old Soul." *Black Stars* February 1973 pp. 50-52.

Little, Benilde. "Just Gladys." *Essence* October 1991 pp. 52-56+.

Lucas, Bob. "Billy Paul Rides to Stardom on Sex and Songs." *Jet* 22 January 1976 pp. 60-62.

Lucas, Bob. "The Staple Singers Are Doing It Again." *Black Stars* February 1976 pp. 36-47.

"The Magic Is Blue." *New Yorker* 11 August 1975 pp. 19-20.

McNeil, Dee Dee. "Bloodstone: International Music Ambassadors." *Black Stars* July 1979 pp. 60-63.

Morthlaud, John. "Millie Jackson" Musical Combat in the Erogenous Zone." *Rolling Stone* 3 April 1980 p. 26.

Murphy, Frederick D. "The Blue Magic Mystique." *Black Stars* April 1974 pp. 13-16.

Murphy, Frederick D. "Caught Up with Millie Jackson." *Black Stars* February 1975 pp. 6-10.

Murphy, Frederick D. "First Choice: Three Choice Cuts from Philly." *Black Stars* March 1974 pp. 43-48.

Murphy, Frederick D. "Harold Melvin, The Man Behind 18 Years of Blue Notes." *Black Stars* March 1977 pp. 12-17.

Murphy, Frederick D. "Philippe Wynne Spins off on His Own." *Black Stars* November 1977 pp. 72-74.

Murphy, Frederick D. "Sitting on Top of the World with the Spinners." *Black Stars* March 1975 pp. 20-28.

Murphy, Frederick. "Theodore Pendergrass Discusses His New Career." *Black Stars* August 1977 pp. 22-24.

Murphy, Frederick D. "Thoroughly Talented Millie Jackson." *Black Stars* May 1980 pp. 52-57.

Murphy, Frederick D. "T.P. Sex Symbol of the Year." *Black Stars* January 1979 pp. 34-37.

Murphy, Frederick D. "War: Still Tops." *Black Stars* January 1977 pp. 48-54.

Norment, Lynn. "How Tragedy Has Affected the Life of Al Green." *Ebony* October 1976 pp. 158-165.

Palmer, Robert. "Isaac Hayes: Black Moses Moves On." *Rolling Stone* 9 October 1975 p. 18.

Rhoden, Bill "The O'Jays: There's a Message in Their Music." *Ebony* September 1977 pp. 90-96.

Ritz, David. "The Long Day's Night of Barry White." *Essence* April 1992 pp. 76-77+.

Robles, Robert. "First Choice Keep on Truckin.' " *Black Stars* March 1978 pp. 52-55.

Samuels, Ashley. "Bobby Womack: The Man and His Music." *Black Stars* May 1979 pp. 20-25.

"The Sandpaper Soul of Isaac Hayes." *Rolling Stone* 14 May 1970 p. 24.

Simmons, Judy. "A Conversation with . . . Isaac Hayes." *Essence* July 1987 p. 33.

"The Temprees Create a Sound All Their Own." *Black Stars* November 1973 pp. 42-43.

"Three Degrees." *New Yorker* 1 March 1976 pp. 24-26.

Unger, Norman O. "TP: The Sexy Teddy Bear." *Black Stars* August 1979 pp. 42-46.

Wallace, Robert. "Gladys Knight Seeks Release from Buddah." *Rolling Stone* 29 June 1978 p. 9.

Wilding, Stephen. "Millie Jackson: A Lady As Great As Her Voice." *Black Stars* April 1978 pp. 14-17.

Wilding, Stephen. "The New Al Green." *Black Stars* May 1978 pp. 40-46.

Index

Abbey, John 130
ABC Records 115, 328
ABC/Dunhill Records 242
Acklin, Barbara 23
Across 100th Street 324
Adderly, Cannonball 87
After 7 5
Alexander, J. W. 320
All Platinum Records 183
Allen, Buddy 254
Allen, Henry 248
Allen, Thomas "Papa Dee" 288
Allison, Verne 44, 102
Alston, Gerald 163, 209
American Bandstand 155
Amherst Records 272
Amos Records 138
Anderson, T. C. 30
Angels 289
Anna Records 244
Apollo Theater 18
Argo Records 47
Arista Records 208
Armstrong, Tippy 322
Arsenio Hall Show, The 181
Ashford, Nick 143
Atkins, Cholly 220
Atkins, John 172
Atlantic Records 333
Atlantic Starr 170
Austell, Leo 22
Avco Records 264

B-Attitudes 339
Bacharach, Burt 108, 110, 112
Bailey, Pearl 238
Bailey, Philip 75
Baker, Anita 110
Baker, Barbara 188

Baker, James 196
Banks, Ron 57
Barksdale, Chuck 44, 102
Barnes, Edward 123
Barnum, H. B. 214
Barrett, Richard 277
Barrett, Vinnie 8
Bartholomew, David 147
Bass, James 98
Beatles 91
Beaton, Keith 7, 101
Beck, Billy 203, 209
Beckett, Barry 323
Bedell, Lou 297
Belafonte, Harry 87
Bell, Al 107
Bell, Leroy 225
Bell, Ron 3
Bell, Thom 33
Bell, Vincent 13
Belle, Regina 169
Belvin, Jesse 87
Benson, Carla 249
Benson, George 319
Benton, Yvette 249
Bernstein, Steve 7
Best, Nathaniel 229
Beverly Glen Records 328
Big East Entertainment/
    Spectrum Records 15
Bishop, Hayward 323
Bivins, Edward "Sonny" 161, 209
Black Entertainment Television
    208
Blackfoot, J. 276
Block, Paul 84
Bloodstone 1-6
Blue Magic 7-15
Bobby Fuller Four, The 307

Bogan, Ann 195
Bogart, Neil 208
Bolden, Isaac 151
Bonner, Leroy "Sugarfoot" 201, 209
Booker, Chuckii 316
Booket T. and the MGs 91
Bowen, Burt 22
Bowen, Jeffrey 17
Boyz 'N the Hood 159
Boyz to Men 145
Brass Construction 293
Braunstein, George 2
Bread 141
Bridges, Josephine 273
Briggs, Cynthia 224
Bristol, Johnny 134, 245
Brodie, Donald 171
Bronco Records 308
Brooks, Patti 87
Broussard, Joe 150
Brown, Barbara 162
Brown, Billy 183, 212
Brown, Del 22
Brown, Ghee 87
Brown, Harold 287
Brown, James 60
Brown, Jim 84
Brown, Lawrence 172, 211
Brown, Morrie 169
Brown, Peter 337
Brown, Samuel "Little Sonny" 118
Brunswick Records 23
Bryant, Marty 264
Buchanan, Michael 12
Buddah Records 137
Burdon, Eric 289
Burke, Solomon 307
Butler, Floyd 82
Butler, Jerry 110, 199

Caesar, Shirley 99
Cain, Randy 34, 103

Caldwell, Nicholas 285, 296
Calloway, Reggie 181
Calvin, Deljuan 273
Cameo Records 34
Cameron, G. C. 245
Camillo, Tony 140
Campbell, Glen 108, 166
Cannon, Donald 34
Capitol Records 12, 66, 242
Car Wash 112
Caravans 319
Carey, Mariah 75
Carnival Records 162
Carroll, Diahann 139
Carstarphen, Victor 175
Carter, Calvin 45
Carter, Clarence 18
Carter, Darryl 321
Carter, Johnny 46, 102
Castellano, Vince 190
Chairmen of the Board 16-21
Chalmers, Charles 93
Chambers, Roland 119
Chantels 277
Charles, Ray 82
Charlie and Company 144
Chess Records 44
Chess, Leonard 44
Chess, Marshall 52
Chi-Lites 22-32, 103
Chi-Sound Records 31
Chic 300
Chocolate Syrup 62
Churchill, Tony 194
Clarke, Willie 333
Claudine 139
Claunch, Quinton 91
Cleaves, Jessica 83
Cleopatra Jones 126
Cleveland, James 141
Clinton, George 252
Coasters 225
Cole, Nat King 87
Coles, Honi 266

Collins, Bootsy 247
Columbia Records 71
Commodores 207, 328
Cooke, Sam 87, 319
Cooley High 247
Cooper, Michael 208
Copacabana 77, 266
Cordet, Ester 206
Cork Jr., Roy 84
Cornelius, Don 299
Cosby Show, The 144
Cosby Bill 231
Cotillion Records 252
Couch, Tommy 148
Creatore, Luigi 268
Creed, Linda 224, 263
Crocker, Frankie 127
Crooklyn 151
Cropper, Steve 257
Crosby, Bob 239
Crusaders 328
Cummings, Jerry 175
Cuoghi, Joe 91
Custis, Eddie 17

Daniels, Richie 34
Daughtry, Eugene "Bird" 118
David, Hal 108, 110, 112
Davis, Brendetta 308
Danls, Carl 23
Davis, Clive 166
Davis, Don 59
Davis, Roderick 57
Davis, Theresa 71
Davis, Tyrone 168
Davis, Yvette 248
Dead Presidents 100
DeBarge, El 317
Deele 303
Deep City Records 333
Dees, Sam 143
Degree, Leaveil 285, 299
Delfonics 33-43, 103
Dells 44-56, 102

Deluxe Records 163
Demps, Larry "Squirrel" 57
Denver, John 87
Dickerson, B.B. 287
Dixie Cups 147
Dixon, George 245
Doobie Brothers 232
Doors 92
Dootones 214
Dorey Records 287
Dortch, Darwin 208
Double Exposure 79
Douglas, Robert 263
Downing, Will 229
Downs, Bobby 195
Dozier, Lamont 16
Draffen Jr., Willis 1
Dramatics 57-67, 101
Drifters 225
Dunn, Donald "Duck" 107
Dunn, James 263, 285
Durham, Roger 1
Dylan, Bob 229, 232
Dynasty 302

Earth, Wind and Fire 71
Ebo, David 179
Echoes of Joy 333
Echols, Ron 98
Eckstine, Billy 239
Ed McKinsey's Local Dance Hour 237
Ed Sullivan Show, The 160
Edmonds, Kenny "Babyface" 303
Edwards, Dennis 245
Edwards, Edgar 245
Edwards, John 253
Edwards, Robert "Big Sonny" 118
Elektra-Asylum Records 181
Eli, Bobbi 8
Ellington, Duke 238-239
Ellington, Mercer 239
Ellington, Robert "Duke" 57

Elliott, Wade 193
Ellis, Shirley 136
Elston, Harry 82
Emmons, Bobby 323
Emotions 68-75, 102
Enjoy Records 162
Evans, Joe 162
Excel Records 119

Facts of Life 129
Fairfax, Reuben 98
Falana, Lola 231
Fambrough, Henry 244, 284
Fantasy Records 67
Fearing, Charles 316
Felder, Winton 328, 330
Ferguson, Sheila 278
Fields, Richard "Dimples" 150
Fifth Dimension 83
First Choice 76-81, 103
Fitzgerald, Ella 231
Five Blind Boys 319
Five Heartbeats, The 42
Five Special 66
Five Stairsteps 69
Flack, Roberta 258
Flamingos 23
Fleming, Rochelle 76, 103
Flip Wilson Show, The 60
Florez, John 84
Floyd, King 148
For Today's Black Woman 243
Ford, Willie 59
Four Tops 16
4U2NJoy 339
Foxx, Redd 239
Franklin, Aretha 77, 247
Franklin, Melvin 24
Frederick, Levar 201
Freed, Alan 45
Freeman, Joel 111
Friends of Distinction 82-88
Frye, Alan 195
Funches, Johnny 44

Fuqua, Harvey 45
Fury Records 133
Futures 42

Gable, Bruce 7
Gamble Records 119
Gamble, Kenny 37
Garrison, Cynthia 281
Gates, David 141
Gaye, Marvin 93
Gaye, Philip 123
Gaynor, Gloria 300
Gee, Rockee 214
George, Langston 133
Gerald, Raeford 125
Gibson, Charlene 86
Gilbert, Gary 224
Gillespie, Donnell 182
Gillis, Jessie 171
Gold, Steve 290
Golden Trumpets 256
Goldstein, Jerry 289
Gooding, Cuba 152, 210
Gooding Jr., Cuba 159
Goodman, Al 183, 212
Gordon, Marc 228
Gordy, Berry 134, 137, 237, 244, 300
Gordy, Gwen 244
Goring, Sandra 278
Graham, Leo 168
Granoff Music School 232
Gray, Dobie 307
Grayson, Altrina 330
Green, Al 89-101
Greene, Mark 183
Greif, George 328
Griffey, Dick 297
Grimes, Howard 91
Guest, Annette 76, 103
Guest, Eleanor 133
Guest, William 133, 212

Hale, Jack 91

Hale, Willie "Little Beaver" 334
Hamady, Ronald 2
Hammer, M.C. 31
Handy, Charles 170
Hankerson, Barry 141
Harmon, Gordy 296
Harper, Vaughan 170
Harris, Adrienne 74
Harris, Jimmy Jam 317
Harris, Major 39
Harris, Norman 8
Harris, Ray 91
Harris, Roger 170
Hart, Wilbert 34, 103
Hart, William 33, 103
Hathaway, Donny 301
Hawes, Bruce 249
Hawkins, Edwin 258
Hawkins, Rodger 322
Hayes, Isaac 104-117, 210
Hayes, Malcolm 308
Hearndon, Charlie 199
Heavy D 219
Hemphill, Harsey 170
Henderson, Billy 244, 284
Henderson, Willie 28
Herring, Ursula 78, 103
Hester, Tony 59
Hi Records 89
High Chaparral Club 293
Hit Parade 160
Hodges, Charles 91
Hodges, Leroy 91
Hodges, Mabon "Teenie" 91
Hoffman, Stan 52
Holiday, Valerie 278
Holland, Brian 16
Holland, Eddie 16
Hood, David 323
Horsely, Richie 183
Houston, Cissy 138
Houston, Thelma 178
Houston, Whitney 181
Howard, William "Wee Gee" 59

Hues Corporation 157
Huff, Leon 56
Huggins, Charles 243
100 Proof Aged in Soul 19
Hunter, Clifford 133
HUSH Productions 243
Hutch, Willie 112
Hutchinson, Jeanette 68
Hutchinson, Joe 68
Hutchinson, Pamela 72
Hutchinson, Sheila 70
Hutchinson, Wanda 68
Hutson, Marcus 285, 296
Hyman, Phyllis 229

Ichiban Records 130
Imperial Records 214
Impressions 139, 153, 262
Impulse Records 239
Ingram, Barbara 40
Ingram, James 317
Ingram, Luther 126
Ink Spots 185
Intruders 118-123
Invictus Records 16
Isles, Bill 213
Isley Brothers 5
Isley, Ernie 5
Isley, Jasper, Isley 5
Isley, Marvin 5

J. Geils Band 325
Jackson, Al 91
Jackson, Freddie 192
Jackson, Jerome 159
Jackson, Jesse 227
Jackson, Mahalia 68
Jackson, Michael 144
Jackson, Millie 124-131
Jackson, Pervis 244, 284
Jackson, Robert 199
Jackson, Wayne 91
Jagger, Mick 330
James, Casey 225

James, Glodean 308
James, Linda 308
James, Palmer 90
James, Rick 159
Janus Records 51, 138
Jarrett, Buddy 98
Jasper, Chris 5
Jefferson Airplane 232
Jefferson, Joseph 249
Jerry Van Dyke Show, The 69
John, Elton 309
John, Mable 104
Johnny Carson Show, The 216
Johnson, Clarence 22
Johnson, Cornelius 201
Johnson, Danny 30
Johnson, Dwight 178
Johnson, General 16
Johnson, Jimmy 322
Johnson, Ricky 34
Johnson, Ruby 104
Johnson, William "Norvell" 275
Jones, Craig 66
Jones, Creadel "Red" 22, 103
Jones, Deacon 288
Jones, Gloria 136
Jones, James Earl 139
Jones, Joyce 77
Jones, Linda 186
Jones, Marshall 201, 209
Jones, Quincy 238
Jones, Tom 47
Joplin, Janis 319
Jordan, Fred 98
Jordan, Lonnie 287
Joseph, Quinton 28
Josie Records 171
Junior, Marvin 44, 102

K.C. and the Sunshine Band
    336
Kalimba Productions 71
Kasem, Casey 205
Kass, Art 138, 142

Kelly, Kenny 162, 209
Kendricks, Eddie 58
Kennedy, Harrison 17
Kerner, Kenny 138
Kerr, George 214
Kersey, Willie 30
Kiddie Hour, The 231
Kilo 276
King, Ben E. 157
King, Carole 234
King, Curtis 320
King, Evelyn "Champagne" 229
King Jr., Martin Luther 235, 258
King Records 213
King, Richard 214
Kirk, Roland 290
Knight, Gladys 132, 212
Knight, Gladys and the Pips
    132-146, 212
Knight, Jean 147-151, 211
Knight, Merald "Bubba" 133,
    212
Knox, Ken 20

Labelle, Patti 99
Lakeside 302
Lance, Major 23
Lander, Austin 199
LaSalle, Denise 151
Lathan, Stan 34
Lattisaw, Stacy 191
Leavill, Otis 23
Lee, Spike 151
Leech, Mike 322
Legrand, Michael 232
Leiber, Jerry 153
Lennox, Annie 100
Lester, Robert "Squirrel" 22, 103
Levert, Eddie 213, 228, 286
Levert, Gerald 317, 228
Levy, Len 51
Lewis, Linda 157
Lewis, Terry 317
Limbo, Sonny 138

Little Anthony and the
 Imperials 222
Little Star Records 214
Logan, Ed 91
Long, Shorty 245
Loren, Londee 194
Love Unlimited 308
Love Unlimited Orchestra 312
Love, Airrion 263, 285
Love, Andrew 91
Love, Barbara Jean 83
Love, Charles 1
Lovett, Winfred "Blue" 161, 209
Lowe, Sammy 46
Lucas, Carrie 300
Tymon, Frankie and the
 Teenagers 33

Mack, The 78
Mad Lads 273
Main Ingredient 152-160, 210
Malaco Productions 148
Malcolm X 235
Mandrill 293
Manhattans 161-170, 209
Marks, Larry 308
Martin, Bobby 120
Marvelettes 195
Masekela, Hugh 85
Mason, Barbara 199
Mason, Gene 90
Massey, Bobby 213
Mathis, Johnny 231
Maxx Records 134
Mayes, Lenny 62
Mayfield, Curtis 40, 260
Mays, Marguerite 134
Maze 65
MCA Records 145
McCoo, Marilyn 82
McCormick, Charles 1
McCoy, Van 268
McCoys 289
McDaniel, Carl 199

McDonald, Clarence 84
McFadden, Gene 175
McGill, Lucius 45
McGill, Mickey 44, 102
McKinney, Stan 29
McLemore, Lamonte 82
McMurray, Clay 136
McPherson, Don 152
McRae, George 157, 336
McRae, Gwen 336
Meaux, Huey 147
Melvin, Harold 171, 211
Melvin, Harold and the
 Blue Notes 171-182, 211
Men, The 113
Mercury Records 33
MFSB 119
Middlebrook, Ralph
 "Pee Wee" 201, 209
Midnight Special 155
Midnight Star 303
Mighty Clouds of Joy 68
Miller, Bobby 48
Miller, Charles 288
Mills, Stephanie 181
Mills, Ted 7, 101
Minit Records 321
Mitchell, James 91
Mitchell, Willie 89
Moments 183-193, 212
Montana, Vince 8
Montgomery, Glenn 122
Moody, Alvin 13
Moon, Harry 122
Moonglows 45, 244
Moore, Jackie 225
Moore, John 184
Moore, Melba 243
Morgan, John 183
Morrison, Walter "Junie" 202
Motown 4, 158
Ms. B Records 337
Murphy, James 123
Murrell, Herb 263, 285

Napier, Bruce 202
Nat Turner's Rebellion 39
Nathan, Syd 213
Nelson, Earl 307
Neville, Aaron 159
New Birth 194-200
New Edition 271
New Imperials 163
New Kids on the Block 41
Newman, Floyd 105
Nichols, Billy 125
Nilsson 235
Nixon, Tom 273
Nooks, Ronald 208
Nunes, Larry 309
Nyro, Laura 87

Oak Ridge Boys 262
O'Jay, Eddie 213
O'Jays 213-230, 286
Ohio Players 201-209
Okeh Records 39
Originals 5
Osborne, Jeffrey 200
Oskar, Lee 289
Owens, Kevin 191

Page, Gene 308
Paige, Sharon 176
Parker, Charlie 231
Parks, Gordon 111
Parks, Lloyd 172, 211
Parliament/Funkadelic 203
Patten, Edward 133, 212
Paul, Billy 231-235
Payne, Freda 236-242
Pazant, Al 170
Peaker, Frank 171
Pendergrass, Teddy 171, 211
Peretti, Hugo 268
Perkins, Clifford 193
Perry, Bill 264
Perry, Greg 19
Perry, Jack 316

Philadelphia International
    Records 270, 279
Phillips, Jasper "Jabbo" 273
Philly Groove Records 35
Pickett, Wilson 201, 258
Pierce, Marvin 202, 209
Pilgrim Travelers 319
Pinkney, Fayette 277
Pipe Dreams 141
Piper, Wardell 77
Platters 225
Point Blank Records 262
Poitier, Sidney 260
Polydor Records 116
Ponderosa Twins Plus One 186
Porter, David 70
Porter, Shirley 277
Powell, Petsye 87
Powell, William 213, 286
Pratt, Richard 7, 101
Presley, Elvis 21
Pride, Charley 156
Prince 262
Pryor, Richard 260

Quezerque, Wardell 147

Rabb, Luther 294
Rampart Records 227
Randazzo, Teddy 270
Rawls, Lou 214
Ray, Goodman and Brown 183
Ray, Harry 184, 212
Record, Eugene 22, 103
Red Label Records 74
Redbone 275
Redding, Otis 50
Reed, Eddie 22
Reed, Isaac 62
Reed, Larry 57
Reese, Della 46
Reeves, Martha 172
Regan, Russ 309
Reid, Antonio "L.A." 303

Reid, Clarence 333
Reynolds, L. J. 62
Rhodes, Donna 93
Rhodes, Sandra 93
Richie, Lionel 144
Richmond, Paul 169
Riperton, Minnie 71
Rizzo, Pat 294
Roach, Jimmy 62, 247
Roberson, David (Doc) 30
Robinson, Bobby 162
Robinson, Joe 184
Robinson, Randall 227
Robinson, Smokey 159, 222
Robinson, Sylvia 183
Rock and Roll Hall of
    Fame 100
Rogers, Curtis 90
Rolf, Bob 307
Rolling Stones 319
Rosen, Peter 288
Ross, Diana 71
Roulette Records 278
Roundtree, Richard 111
Rubens, Al 7
Ruby and the Romantics 111
Rufus and Chaka Khan 65
Russell, Robin 199

Sainte-Marie, Buffy 196
Salsoul Orchestra 79
Salsoul Records 79
Sam and Dave 106
Samuels, Zelda 320
Sanders, Ethel 162
Sanders, Sonny 28
SAR Records 319
Satchell, Clarence 201, 209
Savoy, Albert 148
Sawyer, Mary 140
Sawyer, Pam 163
Sawyer, Vernon 7, 101
Sawyer, Wendell 9, 101
Say, Sue 196

Schaffner, Katherine
    Anderson 136
Schlacter, Marvin 51
Scott, David 30
Scott, Dick 59
Scott, Freddie 92, 117
Scott, Harold "Scotty" 273
Scott, Helen 277
Scott, Howard 287
Scott, Wallace "Scotty" 285, 296
Scott, Walter 285, 296, 300
Sears, Kitty 5
Sebring Records 264
Shalamar 300
Shapiro, Brad 126
Shelton, James 23
Showmen 16
Sigler, Bunny 224
Sigma Sound Studio 164
Silvester, Enrique "Tony"
    152, 210
Simmons, Charles 249
Simmons, Luther 152, 210
Simmons, Russell 13
Simon and Garfunkel 232
Simon, Joe 128
Simone, Nina 231
Simply Red 101
Simpson, Valerie 143
Sims, Dupree 62
Sister Sledge 157
Skylark 197
Slave 327
Slim and the Boys 263
Sly and the Family Stone 36
Smith, Bobbie 244, 284
Smith, George 162
Smith, James 263, 285
Smith, Otis 64
Smith, Walter 12
Snoop Doggy Dogg 67
Solar Records 300
Sophisticated Ladies 242
Soul Generation 316

Soul Stirrers 68
Soul II Soul 305, 316
Soul to Soul 258
Soul Train 62, 155
Soul Train Records 299
Soulin' Records 151
Sparkle 112
Spencer, C.P. 244
Spinners 243-254, 284
Sport Records 58
Spratley, Bill 179
Spring Records 124
Stansfield, Lisa 317
Staple Singers 255-262, 284
Staples, Cleo 256, 284
Staples, Mavis 255, 284
Staples, Pervis 256
Staples, Roebuck "Pop" 255, 284
Staples, Yvonne 257, 284
Star, Mulaney 77
Starr, Maurice 272
Stax Records 59
Steals, Melvin 249
Steals, Mervin 249
Stepney, Charles 48
Stevenson, Wolf 148
Stewart, Curt 46
Stewart, Jim 105
Stewart, Rod 252
Stoller, Mike 152
Stone, Henry 336
Strain, Sammy 222
Streisand, Barbra 141
Stubbs, Levi 17
Stylistics 285, 263-272
Sugar Hill Records 252
Sullivan, Ed 137
Sullivan, Eddie 22
Summer, Donna 157
Superfly 78
Sure!, Al B. 317
Surfside Records 20
Swan Records 277
Swedien, Bruce 28

Sweet Inspirations 138
Sylvers, Leon 302

T-Neck Records 5
Talking Heads 97, 261
Tarsia, Joe 177
Taylor, Dallas 47
Taylor, Diane 308
Taylor, Felice 308
Taylor, Leroy 199
Taylor, Johnnie 327
Taylor, Richard 161, 209
Taylor, James 321
Ted Mack Amateur Show 237
Tee, Willie 147
Temprees 273-276
Temptations 10
Terry, Phil 118, 224
Tex, Joe 320
Third World 219
Thomas, Carla 104, 107
Thomas, Rufus 149
Thompkins Jr., Russell 263, 285
Thompkins, Carl 157
Thompkins, Samuel 42
Thompson, Marshall 22, 103
Three Degrees 277-283
Three Tough Guys 114
Toney, Johnny 98
Touff, Cy 27
Townsend, Robert 42, 54
Train Ride to Hollywood 4
Tri-Phi Records 244
Truck Turner 114
Turner, Ike and Tina 8, 258
Turner, Linda 277
20th Century Records 309

Uggams, Leslie 238
Undisputed Truth 216
Uni Records 309
United Artists Records 291
Unlimited Gold Records 315
Uptown Theater 10, 248

Vaughan, Sarah 46, 231
Vee-Jay Records 45
Vernon, Mike 2
Vietnam War 241
Virgins, Lee 90

Walker, Jr. and the
    All-Stars 245
Wansel, Dexter 224
War 286-295
Warner Brothers Records 199,
    260, 262, 278, 302, 308
Warwick, Dionne 33
Washington, Carroll 150
Washington, Dinah 47
Washington, Frank 42
Washington, Larry 248
Washington, Tom
    "Tom Tom" 28
Watson, Anthony 31
Watson, Stan 34
Wattstax 260
Wayne, Rod 14
We Produce 273
Weatherley, Jim 137
Webb, Jim 108
Webster, Greg 202
West Philadelphia Music
    School 332
Wexler, Jerry 106
Whatnauts 188
Which Way Is Up 112
Whispers 285, 296-304
White, Barry 283, 305-318
White, Maurice 68
Whitehead, John 175
Whitfield, Norman 24
Wilkins, Elbert 57
William Morris Agency 172
Williams, Bernie 171
Williams, Harry 1
Williams, Jimmy "Diamond"
    203, 209
Williams, Lee 170

Williams, Otis, and the
    Charms 45
Williams, Paulette 201
Williams, Ralph 150
Williams, Walter 213, 286
Willis, Bruce 259
Willis, Buzzy 153
Wilis, Clarence "Chet" 208
Wills, Viola 307
Wilson, Barbara 201
Wilson, Bernard 172, 211
Wilson, Chip 208
Wilson, Leslie 194
Wilson, Melvin 195
Wilson, Nancy 58, 231
Wilson, Ron 5
Winans, BeBe and CeCe
    262
Wingate Records 58
Wingate, Ed 58
Wise, Richie 138
Withers, Bill 327
Womack and Womack 330
Womack, Bobby 283, 319-331
Womack, Linda Cooke 323
Wonder, Stevie 78
Wood, Bobby 323
Wood, Ron 330
Woods, Danny 17
Woods, Georgie 76
Woods, James "Pip" 131
Woodson, Mary 96
Wright, Betty 332-338
Wright, Syretta 247
Wynne, Philippe 243, 284

Young, Paul 31
Young, Reggie 323
Young-Holt Unlimited 24
Youngblood, Lonnie 186
*Your Arm's Too Short to Box
    with God* 99

Zager, Michael 253

SONG INDEX

"A Heart Is a House for Love" 55
"A Letter to Myself" 28
"Ain't No Stoppin' Us Now" 216
"Am I Black Enough for You?" 234
"And the Beat Goes On" 296
"Armed and Extremely Dangerous" 77
"Ask Me What You Want" 124
"Baby Sitter" 332
"Back Stabbers" 216
"Back Up Train" 90
"Bad Luck" 176
"Band of Gold" 236
"Belle" 98
"Best of My Love" 72
"Best Thing That Ever Happened to Me" 139
"Betcha By Golly Wow" 265
"Break Up to Make Up" 266
"Bring the Boys Home" 236
"By the Time I Get to Phoenix 104
"Call Me (Come Back Home)" 95
"Can't Get Enough of Your Love, Babe" 313
"Cisco Kid, The" 292
"Clean Up Woman" 332
"Close the Door" 180
"Coldest Days of My Life, The" 27
"Come Go with Me" 180
"Could It Be I'm Falling in Love" 249
"Cowboys to Girls" 120
"Darlin' Darlin' Baby (Sweet Tender Love)" 223
"Dedicated to the One I Love" 274

"Didn't I (Blow Your Mind This Time)" 33
"Dirty Ol' Man" 279
"Do Your Thing" 111
"Doctor Love" 80
"Don't Ask My Neighbors" 73
"Dream Merchant" 199
"Every Beat of My Heart" 133
"Everybody Plays the Fool" 152
"Fire" 201
"Flowers" 72
"(For God's Sake) Give More Power to the People" 25
"For the Love of Money" 218
"Forever Mine" 225
"Four Cornered Room" 292
"Friendship Train" 136
"From Pain to Joy" 339
"Funky Worm" 202
"Galaxy" 293
"Get Up and Get Down" 60
"Ghetto Child" 249
"Girls" 188
"Give Me Just a Little More Time" 16
"Give the People What They Want" 220
"Give Your Baby a Standing Ovation" 44
"Going in Circles" 82
"Grazing in the Grass" 82
"Groove Me" 148
"Happiness Is Just Around the Bend" 156
"Harry Hippie" 323
"Have You Seen Her" 25
"Heavy Makes You Happy (Sha Na Boom Boom)" 257
"Help Me Make It Through the Night" 137
"Here I Am (Come and Take Me)" 95-96
"Homely Girl" 29

"Honey Please, Can't Ya See" 310, 312

"Hope That We Can Be Together Soon" 176

"How Can You Mend a Broken Heart" 93

"How Could I Let You Get Away" 248

"Hurry Up This Way Again" 271

"Hurts So Good" 124

"I Can Sing a Rainbow / Love Is Blue" 50

"I Can Understand It" 195

"I Can't Get Next to You" 92

"I Didn't Know" 277

"I Don't Wanna Lose Your Love" 71

"I Don't Want to Do Wrong" 136

"I Feel a Song (In My Heart)" 140

"I Heard It Through the Grapevine" 135

"I Kinda Miss You" 161

"I Love Music" 221

"I Miss You" 173

"I Stand Accused" 110

"I Wanna Know Your Name" 121

"I Want to be Free" 205

"I Wish He Didn't Trust Me So Much" 330

"If I Were Your Woman" 136

"(If Loving You Is Wrong) I Don't Want to Be Right" 126

"If You Don't Know Me By Now" 171

"If You Think You're Lonely Now" 328

"Ike's Mood" 111

"Ike's Rap" / "Hey Girl" 117

"I'll Always Love My Mama" 121

"I'll Be Around" 248

"I'll Take You There" 259

"I'm Gonna Love You Just a Little More Baby" 309

"I'm Sorry" 37

"I'm Still in Love with You" 94

"I'm Stone in Love with You" 266

"I've Got So Much to Give" 309

"I've Got to Use My Imagination" 138

"In the Mood" 304

"In the Rain" 60

"Inside of You" 190

"It Feels So Good to Be Loved So Bad" 168

"It Will Stand" 16

"It's a Love Thing" 303

"It's a Shame" 246

"It's All Over Now" 320

"It's Been a Long Time" 197

"It's Ecstacy When You Lay Down Next To Me" 314

"It's So Hard to Say Goodbye to Yesterday" 247

"Just Don't Want to Be Lonely" 152

"Kiss and Say Goodbye" 161

"L-O-V-E Love" 97-98

"La-La Means I Love You" 33

"Landlord" 143

"Let No Man Put Asunder" 80

"Let's Do It Again" 260

"Let's Make a Baby" 235

"Let's Stay Together" 92

"Letter Full of Tears" 134

"Livin' for the Weekend" 222

"Look at Me (I'm in Love)" 188

"Look of Love, The" 110

"Look What You Done for Me" 93

"Lookin' for a Love" 325

"Love and Happiness" 94

"Love Don't Love Nobody" 251
"Love Has Finally Come at
    Last" 329
"Love I Lost, The" 171
"(Love Is Like a) Baseball
    Game" 118, 120
"Love on a Two-Way Street" 184
"Love or Let Me Be Lonely" 86
"Love Overboard" 145
"Love Rollercoaster" 201
"Love Thang" 80
"Love TKO" 330
"Love Train" 217
"Love We Had (Stays on
    My Mind), The" 44
"Love Won't Let Me Wait" 40
"Love's Theme" 312
"Low Rider" 293
"Maybe" 278
"Me and Mrs. Jones" 233
"Midnight Train to Georgia" 138
"Mighty Love" 249
"Mr. Big Stuff" 147
"My Little Lady" 4
"Natural High" 1
"Neither One of Us (Wants
    to Be the First to Say
    Goodbye)" 137
"Never Never Gonna Give
    Ya Up" 311
"O-o, I Love You" 48-49
"Oh Girl" 27
"Oh What a Nite" 44
"On and On" 140
"One of a Kind (Love
    Affair)" 249
"Patches" 18
"Pay to the Piper" 16
"People Make the World
    Go Round" 265
"Player, The" 76, 78-79
"Playing Your Game, Baby" 314

"Practice What You Preach" 318
"Put Your Hands Together" 218
"Respect Yourself" 258
"Rock Steady" 304
"Rock the Boat" 157
"Rock Your Baby" 157
"Rubberband Man, The" 252
"Sadie" 251
"Save the Overtime
    (For Me)" 143
"Secretary" 332
"Sexy Mama" 187
"Shining Star" 168
"Show Me How" 70
"Sideshow" 9
"Skin Tight" 201
"So I Can Love You" 70
"Special Lady" 190
"Spell" 8
"Stay in My Corner" 44
"Stoned Out of My Mind" 28
"Stop, Look, Listen (To
    Your Heart)" 265
"Sweet Sticky Thing" 206
"Take It to the Limit" 192
"Take Me to the River" 97, 100
"Thanks for Saving My Life" 234
"That's the Way I Feel
    About 'Cha" 321
"Theme from *Shaft*" 111-112
"Theme from *The Men*" 113
"Then Came You" 250
"There's No Me Without
    You" 161
"They Just Can't Stop It the
    (Games People Play)" 251
"Tired of Being Alone" 92
"TSOP (The Sound of
    Philadelphia" 279
"Turn Off the Lights" 180
"Use Ta Be My Girl" 224
"Wake Up Everybody" 178

"Walk on By" 104
"Walking in the Rain with the One I Love" 309
"(We'll Be) United" 119
"What Am I Gonna Do with You" 314
"Whatcha See Is Whatcha Get" 59
"When Will I See You Again" 277
"Who'd She Coo" 201
"Wild Flower" 197
"Woman's Gotta Have It" 323
"Working My Way Back to You" 253
"World Is a Ghetto, The" 292
"You Are Everything" 265
"You Make Me Feel Brand New" 267
"You Ought to Be with Me" 94
"Your Sweetness Is My Weakness" 315
"You're a Big Girl Now" 263
"You're As Right As Rain" 266
"You're the First, the Last, My Everything" 313
"You've Been My Inspiration" 152

ALBUM INDEX

A Lonely Man 28
Afrodisiac 156
Al Green Explores Your Mind 97
Al Green Gets Next to You 92
Back Stabbers 218
Barry White Sings for Someone You Love 314
Bealtitude: Respect Yourself 258
Belle Album, The 98
Black Moses 112
Blue Magic 9
Can't Get Enough 313
Caught Up 126

Family Reunion 223
Feelin' Good at the Cadillac Club 232
Fire 204
(For God's Sake) Give More Power to the People 26
From Out of the Blue 13
He Is the Light 99
Honey 206
Hot Buttered Soul 107
Icon Is Love, The 317
Imagination 140
I'm Still in Love with You 93
I've Got So Much to Give 311
Isaac Hayes Movement, The 110
Joy 114
Just for You 145
Just Gets Better with Time 304
Let's Stay Together 93
Magic of the Blue, The 10-12
Man, The 314
Message in Our Music 223
Mighty Love 249
Neither One of Us 138
Pick of the Litter 252
Poet, The 328
Poet II, The 329
Ray, Goodman and Brown 103
Rejoice 73
Round 2 266
Shaft 104
Ship Ahoy 218
Skin Tight 204
So Full of Love 224
Stone Gon' 311
360 Degrees of Billy Paul 234
To Be True 175
Visions 143
Wake Up Everybody 178
War of the Gods 243
Why Can't We Be Friends 293
World Is a Ghetto, The 291